AN INTRODUCTION TO ANTHROPOLOGY

VOLUME ONE
Physical anthropology and archaeology

THE DORSEY SERIES IN ANTHROPOLOGY

VOLUME ONE

Physical anthropology and archaeology

Victor Barnouw

Professor of Anthropology
University of Wisconsin-Milwaukee

1982

THE DORSEY PRESS   Homewood, Illinois   60430
Irwin-Dorsey Limited   Georgetown, Ontario   L7G 4B3

FOURTH
EDITION

Cover: Temple II, circa 700 A.D., Tikal, Guatemala (Maya)
Photo: Dr. Danguole Variakojis

ISBN 0-256-02658-0
Library of Congress Catalog Card No. 81–82917

Printed in the United States of America

1 2 3 4 5 6 7 8 9 0 K 9 8 7 6 5 4 3 2

LEARNING SYSTEMS COMPANY—
a division of Richard D. Irwin, Inc.—has developed a
PROGRAMMED LEARNING AID
to accompany texts in this subject area.
Copies can be purchased through your bookstore
or by writing PLAIDS,
1818 Ridge Road, Homewood, Illinois 60430.

This book is dedicated to my wife
SACHIKO

Preface

This two-volume work is designed as a general introduction to the field of anthropology. Both volumes may be used together in a one-semester introductory course on that subject. Courses in Introduction to Anthropology are also often presented in two semesters, the first usually dealing with physical anthropology and archaeology, the second with ethnology. With this division in mind, Volume One of the present work was prepared to cover the first semester, Volume Two the second. A brief section on linguistics is included in Volume Two.

Anthropology today has to do with humans at all times and places; it is not limited to the study of early people and "primitive" non-Western cultures, as it was sometimes held to be. This two-volume work ranges from the distant past, before *Homo Sapiens* actually appeared on the scene, down to our troubled present and deals with both the physical and cultural evolution of human beings.

In general, my approach to this broad field has been eclectic. Where controversies occur I have presented the contending viewpoints, as, for example, in the different interpretations of the relationship between *Australopithecus africanus* and *Australopithecus robustus* in the evolution of the hominids.

Extensive revisions have been made of many chapters in this fourth edition of Volume One, but the main change has been the addition of a new chapter, Chapter Sixteen, "Two Centers of New World Civilization." There is also more emphasis on New World prehistory and archaeology in some of the other chapters than there was in previous editions.

I would like to thank the following critics who commented on the third

edition of this volume for the editors of The Dorsey Press: Jerald T. Mila-
nich, The Florida State Museum, University of Florida; Lynn Ceci, City
University of New York-Queens College; and Joseph B. Mountjoy, University of North Carolina. I acted on many of their suggestions and am grateful
for them.

Victor Barnouw

Contents

PART THREE   HOMINID EVOLUTION AND CULTURAL DEVELOPMENT
FROM THE PLIOCENE THROUGH THE PLEISTOCENE

CULTURAL EVOLUTION AFTER THE PLEISTOCENE   **PART FOUR**

PART ONE

Introduction

CHAPTER 1

Introduction: The field of anthropology

Anthropology is the study of human beings (from Greek *anthropos*, man, and *logia*, study). It is concerned mainly with a single species, *Homo sapiens*, rather than with many diverse organisms, as in the cases of botany and zoology, although physical anthropologists also study the various primate species related to ourselves. Our objective is to learn all we can about our species, how we have become what we are, what we have accomplished, and what our potentialities are.

Of course, anthropology is not the only field that focuses on human beings. There are many others, including sociology, psychology, history, law, economics, and political science. We do not need to draw clear-cut boundary lines between these various disciplines. While each field has its own distinctive characteristics and emphases, there are many areas in which they overlap.

Anthropology may be broadly divided into physical anthropology and cultural anthropology. Cultural anthropology may in turn be subdivided into three main branches: linguistics, archaeology, and ethnology. *Physical anthropology* is concerned with *Homo sapiens* (the zoological term for our species) as a physical organism and with the evolution of *Homo sapiens* from simpler forms of life.

Culture

The other main branches of anthropology—linguistics, archaeology, and ethnology—are concerned with aspects of human culture.

Culture is an important key word in the vocabulary of the social sciences. It refers to human learned behavior, acquired by experience, as opposed

3

to inborn, genetically determined behavior. This use of the term must be distinguished from older colloquial meanings expressed in phrases like "a man of culture." In the anthropological sense, all humans have culture.

Although anthropologists sometimes use the word *culture* in a broad generic sense, they also speak about *a culture*, like Eskimo culture or Hopi culture. Here is a definition of culture in this sense: *A culture is the way of life of a group of people, the complex of shared concepts and patterns of learned behavior handed down from one generation to the next through the means of language and imitation.*

Examples of patterns of learned behavior are: speaking English, Chinese, Bantu, or Hindi; wearing trousers in our society, kilts in Scotland, or togas in ancient Rome; sitting on chairs in the Western world or sitting cross-legged on the ground in many societies; eating at set mealtimes—breakfast, lunch, and dinner, or twice a day in some societies, or four times, as when the English add afternoon tea; using knife, fork, and spoon to eat with in the Western world, chopsticks in China and Japan, or the fingers of the right hand in India; believing in the tenets of Jesus Christ, Confucius, Mohammed, or Buddha; consulting the medicine man, the priest, the doctor, or the psychiatrist; making a Navaho sand painting, a Kwakiutl totem pole, or an abstract painting. A person is destined to learn the patterns of behavior prevalent in the society in which he or she grows up. A person does not necessarily learn them all, for there may be cultural differences appropriate to persons of different age, sex, status, and occupation, and there may also be genetically determined differences in learning ability. Moreover, the culture patterns of a society may change with the appearance of new inventions or through contact with other ways of life.

Linguistics is the study of languages. Although other animals besides human beings have communication systems, and although the cries of apes and monkeys seem to have communicative functions, no other organism is known to have as elaborate a system of symbolic communication as *Homo sapiens*. The transmission of culture from generation to generation is made possible by language, which enables humans to preserve the traditions of the past and to make provisions for the future.

Not all linguists are anthropologists, but some anthropologists specialize in the study of languages. Ethnologists (anthropologists who study contemporary cultures) often learn the language of the people whom they are studying in the field. It is possible to do ethnological fieldwork with bilingual interpreters, but it is much better if the anthropologist understands the local speech. All kinds of subtleties may be lost in translation, for example, in a discussion of religious concepts.

Ethnology is the study of contemporary cultures. Ethnologists go to a particular society, let us say an Eskimo group; they get to know the people, learn something of their language, and keep a record of observations and interviews. Ethnologists have varied interests and objectives, but all of them try to delineate some of the characteristic culture patterns of the group

they study. An ethnologist may, for example, be particularly interested in
how kinship is reckoned in an Eskimo community, what religious beliefs
the people have, or how the religion is related to other aspects of the
culture. He may study techniques of food getting, such as seal hunting,
and the material equipment used in the process: methods of making dog-
sleds, harpoons, warm clothing. He may be interested in how children
are brought up and what personality traits are fostered in the society under
study, how people get along with one another, how men acquire their
wives and how many they may have.

An ethnologist usually studies a particular society, or at least one at a
time. But it should be pointed out that ethnological works are not limited
to descriptions of particular cultures or to comparisons of two or three of
them. Efforts are also made to generalize on a broad scale about cultures
in general, for example about societies with a hunting-gathering basis of
subsistence, peasant societies, matrilineal societies, and so on.

There are various specialties within the field of ethnology. One is *social
anthropology*, which is concerned with the social structure of a society
and its patterns of social interaction, such as the workings of the kinship
system. Another specialty is *psychological anthropology* or *culture-and-per-
sonality*, which focuses on the mutual interplay of culture and personality,
the ways in which the culture of a society influences the individuals who
grow up within its milieu. *Medical anthropology* is concerned with concepts
of disease and methods of cure in different societies. Some ethnologists
make a particular study of religion or folklore, music, or art. Although
archaeology is classified as a branch of cultural anthropology, it will be
discussed after we have introduced the field of physical anthropology. The
two fields, physical anthropology and archaeology, are the main subjects
of this book.

**Physical
anthropology**

Physical anthropologists, as noted earlier, are interested in the evolution
of our species, *Homo sapiens*. (A *species* is an interbreeding population
of organisms, plants, or animals, that is reproductively isolated from other
such groups and that can produce fertile offspring.) *Homo sapiens* is zoologically classified as an animal, a vertebrate, a mammal, and a primate, the
order of mammals that also includes, among others, the apes and monkeys.
The animals to which we are most closely related are the chimpanzee
and gorilla, but we also have much in common with the gibbon and orangutan and, more distantly, with the Old World monkeys and other primates.
Physical anthropologists are concerned with tracing our relationships to
these related species, the fossil evidence for human evolution, and the
evolutionary branching and differentiation of the Primate order, particularly
with respect to humans and our closest relatives.

A *fossil* is the remains of an ancient form of life, often mineralized.
For example, the organic material in a primate skull of 10 million years

ago has been replaced by dissolved minerals, such as silica and lime, in ground water, so that gradually the skull has become mineralized. Sometimes, while the remains of an animal disintegrate, they form a mold into which minerals seep, filling up the emptied spaces to preserve the original form.

Physical anthropologists have pursued the following kinds of research with regard to primates: (1) the analysis of primate fossils, with an attempt to place them in a geological, temporal sequence; (2) comparative anatomical study of living primates, including such features as blood chemistry, tooth-cusp patterns, and many others; (3) observation of living primates in the field, with an emphasis on their patterns of social interaction; and (4) laboratory experimentation with apes, monkeys, and other animals.

In 1961 a chimpanzee named Ham was rocketed into suborbital flight before any human beings were sent aloft in space capsules. Ham was chosen for this important experiment because chimpanzees resemble human beings in so many ways. Chimpanzees have similar blood types and suffer from some of the same diseases that afflict humans, with similar symptoms. New types of surgical techniques are sometimes tried out on chimpanzees and other nonhuman primates before being attempted on humans. As will be discussed further in Chapter 4, the close resemblances between ourselves and the chimpanzee are not a matter of chance; they reflect relationship, a common ancestry. Chimpanzees, the other apes, and humans

Pioneer astronaut Ham reaches out for an apple, the first food he received after a 420-mile ride in a Mercury space capsule launched by rocket from Cape Canaveral on January 31, 1961.

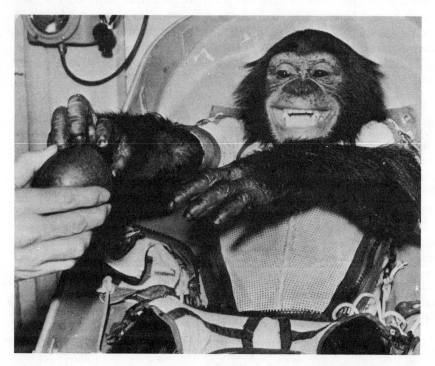

are zoologically classified together as *Hominoidea*. The earliest fossil forms of hominoids found so far date from about 28 million years ago. (Earlier forms of primates date back to more than 60 million years ago.) In later chapters we will trace the fossil record of our ancestry, as far as it can be determined at present. The main evidence lies in fossil skulls, jaws, and teeth recovered from strata of different ages. One focus of physical anthropology, then, is human evolution.

A second focus of physical anthropology is human variation. All human beings on earth today belong to a single species, *Homo sapiens*, and, therefore, are capable of breeding with members of other human groups and of producing fertile offspring. Within this single species, however, there is a good deal of variation. Some human populations are more dark skinned or light skinned than others. There are many varieties of hair form, some groups having straight hair, some curly, some wavy, while others have mixed forms. There are differences in nose height, nose breadth, hair color, eye color, and many other features.

On the basis of traits such as these, anthropologists in the past have tried to sort human beings into different races, such as Negroid, Caucasoid, Mongoloid, and others. Some physical anthropologists claim that such classifications are unreal and lack scientific validity. (The pros and cons of this issue are discussed in Chapter 18.) But no one denies the existence of human variations. Anthropologists are trying to determine how variations in pigmentation, hair form, and other features have come about in different populations.

Physical anthropologists not only study the distribution of such observable traits as hair form and skin color, but they are also interested in the distribution of blood types, such as A, B, AB, O, Rh, M, N, and other biochemical factors. They also study the incidence of ailments determined by heredity, such as sickle-cell anemia and hemophilia, and the relative susceptibility or immunity of different human populations to certain diseases. They have made studies of patterns of human growth and nutrition, climatic adaptation, and body composition.

Some studies of this sort concern human physical adaptations to particular environments, such as deserts, the Arctic, or high altitude. All animals that occupy varied environments have made such adaptations. But much of our own adaptation has been in the form of culture. Human beings adjusted to the Arctic, not by growing coats of fur, but by killing animals, skinning them, and making warm clothing, by building shelters and using fire. Our review of human development will deal with both human biological adaptations and cultural responses.

Some physical anthropologists engage in a form of applied anthropology. By making body measurements (anthropometry) of large samples of a population—for example, Air Force pilots—and also through studies of muscular strength and body structure (biomechanics), they have often contributed to the planning of design and arrangement of machines that must be worked by human beings—for example, in the arrangement of seats and equipment used in the cockpits of airplanes.

Another form of applied physical anthropology is the identification of skeletal remains in connection with forensic medicine and criminal cases. The biosocial aspects of drug use have also been studied by anthropologists. Sometimes the understanding of a particular disease requires knowledge of both biological and cultural factors. For example, the spread of a degenerative disease leading to paralysis, known as *kuru*, prevalent among the Fore of New Guinea, was shown to be borne by a latent virus which had probably been spread by cannibalism involving the consumption of human brains that had been infected by the *kuru* virus.

Within the United States anthropologists have often been involved in the field of public health; the relatively new specialty of medical anthropology is now well established.

The field of physical anthropology has expanded greatly in the past 30 years. Physical anthropologists were formerly concerned mainly with body measurements and the classification of human types. Their training is now more diversified and exhaustive, with an emphasis on genetics, blood chemistry, and the acquisition of specialized laboratory techniques. These emphases seem to have brought physical anthropology closer to the other biological sciences than to the cultural branches of anthropology. At the same time, the growing specialization of physical anthropology has made it difficult for cultural anthropologists to keep abreast of new developments in physical anthropology. Despite this specialization, physical and cultural anthropologists generally share a desire to see humans as a whole—as products of both physical and cultural evolution; for, ever since we first used tools, our physical evolution has been influenced by our culture; the cultures of *Homo sapiens* have always been affected by the nature of our physical structure.

Archaeology

Archaeology is the study of extinct cultures, as distinguished from ethnology, which is the study of living ones. Anthropological archaeologists are usually, although not always, concerned with what are called *prehistoric cultures*, those that existed before the development of written records. Archaeologists willingly make use of written records if they are available, as in Mesopotamia, Egypt, and Guatemala, but often they have nothing to work with but such relics and remains of bygone peoples as potsherds, arrowheads, clay figurines, and tools of bone, stone, or other durable materials.

An exception to the general focus on prehistory is the field of *historical archaeology*, which deals with the relatively recent past, such as the reconstruction of colonial American settlements. Some archaeologists even study contemporary American culture through the analysis of garbage, as has been done in both Phoenix, Arizona, and Milwaukee, Wisconsin. But most archaeologists are concerned with the period of prehistory.

Since systems of writing developed only about 5,000 years ago, while there were ancestors of ours who were able to make tools about 2.6 million years ago, it is evident that the period of prehistory is immensely long. We depend upon the archaeologist, working with the paleontologist, geologist, physical anthropologist, and other specialists, to reconstruct what happened during these hundreds of thousands of years. In many parts of the world—Australia, Melanesia, Polynesia, most of the New World, and Africa—writing had only a relatively recent introduction. Here, again, the archaeologist works to uncover the past.

The archaeologist seeks to reconstruct culture history and the lifeways of peoples of the past. An attempt is made to construct chronological sequences in cultural development. Moreover, the archaeologist tries to understand cultural processes insofar as they may be inferred from archaeological remains and other evidence. Merely to uncover the evidence of past culture change is not enough; if possible, archaeologists also try to understand why things happened as they did, what forces were at work.

Because much of human life is intangible and perishable, leaving no permanent imprint behind, the reconstruction of prehistory, past lifeways, and cultural processes will never be complete. There are many gaps in the archaeological record. There were many hunting-gathering peoples who left few durable artifacts behind them. Time, weather, and destruction by human beings and other animals have wiped out much of the evidence. Even so, archaeologists have been able to learn a great deal about the distribution and ways of life of the hunters of the Old Stone Age. They have also learned where horticultural settlements first appeared in the Old World and the New, where metal tools were first employed, and where writing and city life first developed. Through a combination of archaeology and ethnology, we can determine much about the evolution and spread of human cultures.

The different fields of anthropology may seem quite distinct, and there has been a great deal of specialization in each, but anthropologists tend to think of their field as a unified discipline. It is a relatively recent field, but one that has made rapid advances in the 20th century. Without the work of physical anthropologists and archaeologists we would have little understanding of the place of *Homo sapiens* in nature and of the long process of human evolution. This will be made clear by a consideration of the historical background of physical anthropology and archaeology.

During the Middle Ages, and even down to the 19th century, most Europeans believed that the creation of the world and of man had taken place only a few thousand years in the past. The orthodox view, as set forth by St. Augustine (A.D. 354–430), was that all human beings were descended from Adam and Eve, who had been created by God about

6,000 years before. In the 17th century a date of 4004 B.C. was widely accepted as the date of Adam and Eve's creation.

At that time little was known about *geology*, the study of the earth and its changes over time through the analysis of its different strata. Lacking knowledge of this field, people had no reason to doubt the date traditionally ascribed. However, a systematic comparative study of plants and animals began in the 18th century, which widened human knowledge about the varied organic forms on earth.

Linnaean classification

The voyages of exploration brought back to Europe many varieties of plants and animals, which led to an interest in the classification and comparison of organisms. The Swedish botanist Linnaeus (Carl von Linné, 1707–78) designed a binomial system whereby each plant and animal is assigned a genus name and a species name. In the 10th edition of his work *Systema naturae* ("System of Nature"), Linnaeus classified man with the apes under the term *Primates*.

This classificatory system has been much further developed since Linnaeus' time. The following chart shows how *Homo sapiens* is classified at present.

Classification of *Homo sapiens*

		Members
Kingdom	Animalia	All animals
Phylum	Chordata	Animals having a notochord at some stage of development, constituting an internal skeleton
Subphylum	Vertebrata	Animals having a vertebral column
Class	Mammalia	Warm-blooded animals that suckle their young
Infraclass	Eutheria	Placental mammals
Order	Primates	Lemurs, tarsiers, monkeys, apes, humans
Suborder	Anthropoidea	Monkeys, apes, humans
Superfamily . . .	Hominoidea	Apes and humans
Family	Hominidae	*Australopithecus, Homo erectus,* and modern humans
Genus	*Homo*	*Homo erectus,* Neanderthals, and modern humans
Species	*Sapiens*	Neanderthals and modern humans
Variety	*Sapiens*	All modern human beings, including all living races

The various classifications in this chart are discussed in Chapters 4 through 10.

By grouping humans with the apes, Linnaeus showed his awareness of the close physical similarity between them, but this did not lead him to speculate about their common ancestry or evolution. The very process of labeling species may have tended to freeze them into separate compartments, so to speak, so that the species currently known were assumed to be the same as those brought into being by the Creator at the beginning of time. But there were other 18th-century naturalists who did offer speculations about evolution, including the French naturalists Georges Buffon

Linnaeus or Carl von Linné.

(1707–88) and Jean Lamarck (1744–1829), and Erasmus Darwin (1731–1802), grandfather of Charles Darwin.

Meanwhile, another kind of investigation was under way that was ultimately to have great influence in the biological sciences: the use of the microscope. Magnifying instruments were known as far back as the 16th century. An Italian, Marcello Malpighi (1628–94), is considered to be the founder of microscopic anatomy, for he discovered that plants are made up of tiny units that we now call *cells*.

A Dutch contemporary of Malpighi's, Anton van Leeuwenhoek (1632–1723), made notes on animal blood cells and on the egg and sperm cells of different species, pointing out that even one-celled animals reproduce themselves. These early discoveries laid the basis for the 19th century *cell theory*, which stated that all living things are composed of cells and that all cells come from preexisting cells.

Development of geology

Physical anthropology and archaeology could not have come into being without the prior development of geology. Knowledge about geology greatly increased in the 18th century, as the Industrial Revolution led to the digging of mines and canals and the building of railways. An engineer who was involved in such work, William Smith (1769–1839), announced that geological strata could be identified by the fossils they contained and that lower strata generally were older than those above them. This principle is known as the law of *superposition*.

Another principle, the idea of *uniformitarianism*, is that the earth has been shaped, and still is being shaped, by natural forces operating over long periods of time, such as wind, water, heating, cooling, erosion, organic decay, and other forces. The classic expression of this view appeared in Charles Lyell's *Principles of Geology* (3 volumes, 1830–33), a work that greatly influenced Charles Darwin.

In the early 19th century the viewpoint of uniformitarianism was opposed by a rival doctrine known as *catastrophism*, which held that the earth had periodically undergone violent cataclysms or upheavals such as floods and volcanic eruptions. These disasters, which were sometimes held to have been worldwide, or nearly so, were believed to have extinguished previous organic forms so that new ones came to replace them. Catastrophism represented a compromise between the conservative biblical point of view and the growing knowledge of geology and *paleontology*, the study of ancient fossilized organisms. However, the notion of repeated creations was challenged by the cell theory mentioned earlier. The outstanding exponent of catastrophism was the great French zoologist, founder of comparative anatomy and vertebrate paleontology, Georges Cuvier (1769–1832). Cuvier rejected theories of continuous evolution and believed that the last great cataclysm was the biblical deluge; hence, human remains would not be apt to be found in the prediluvian (before the flood) strata of the earth. Despite his conservatism, Cuvier greatly advanced knowledge of the past; it was he who reconstructed and named the Pterodactyls, flying reptiles of the Mesozoic.

Questions raised by fossil discoveries

During the 18th century many fossil remains of strange extinct animals were found in Europe. In some cases they seemed to be associated with human remains. In 1715 the skeleton of an elephant-like creature was reported to have been recovered from gravel deposits near London, and next to it was a worked flint tool. In 1771 human bones were found in association with extinct cave-bear remains in a site in Germany. In 1797 hand axes were found along with the remains of extinct animals at Hoxne, England. How long ago did these people live?

A Frenchman, Boucher de Perthes (1788–1868), found hand axes in such deep geological strata that he declared them to be tools made by "antediluvian man," or man before the flood. This claim met with much skepticism but led others to search in similar deposits, where like finds sometimes were made.

In 1848 a primitive-looking human skull was found in Gibraltar. A similar one turned up in 1856 in the Neander valley in Germany, which gave us the name of Neandertal or Neanderthal man. But the significance of these finds was not realized at the time. A leading German scientist, Rudolf Virchow, dismissed the Neanderthal skull as pathological, a view that made it difficult for many scholars to consider Neanderthal man as a possible

Charles Darwin.

ancestor of ours. Neanderthal man is now classified as a form of *Homo sapiens* that lived between approximately 100,000 and 35,000 years ago.

In 1859 Charles Darwin published *On the Origin of Species by Means of Natural Selection*, in which he not only presented evidence that evolution had occurred among many organic forms but also a concept, that of natural selection, to help account for evolutionary change. This concept is discussed in Chapter 3. *Origin of Species* was about evolution in general, not human evolution, but Darwin turned to the latter topic in a later work, *The Descent of Man* (1871). Darwin's work represented a turning point in the history of science.

Advances in geology, the discovery of fossil finds, and the development of modern dating techniques have since contributed to documenting the age of the earth and the evolution of plant and animal forms. Traces of one-celled creatures, such as algae or bacteria, found in South Africa have been estimated to be at least 3.2 billion years old and may be 3.5 billion years old. Traces of bacteria resembling modern pond scum have been found in sediment that turned into rock in northwestern Australia; the bacteria have been dated at 3.5 billion years ago. The crust of the earth is judged to have been formed about 4.5 billion years ago. So it is no longer possible to talk about creation having occurred in 4004 B.C.

We know that many species of animals that formerly lived on earth have become extinct. Indeed, of an estimated 250 million species of plants and animals that have existed, only about 1 percent still survives, and many of these, too, are in danger of extinction. It is possible to trace in the fossil record how certain animals, such as the horse, have changed in appearance in their course of evolution. This also applies to humans. The most important discoveries of early human forms have been made since Darwin's time.

In 1891 Eugène Dubois, a Dutch doctor, found a primitive-looking skull-cap near the Solo River in Java. Later, he found a human left thighbone and two molar teeth nearby. Concluding that the skullcap and thighbone belonged to the same organism, Dubois gave it the name *Pithecanthropus erectus*, or erect ape-man, a creature whose cranial capacity was judged to be intermediate between that of African apes and modern man. In the late 1920s some very similar skeletal material was found near Peking, China. Like the Java find, these are now classified as *Homo erectus*, a stage of human evolution preceding Neanderthal man and living between approximately 1.5 million and 100,000 years ago.

A still earlier stage of evolution also was revealed in the 1920s in the find of *Australopithecus africanus* and related forms in South Africa and later in East Africa, known as australopithecines, which lived between 5.5 million and 1 million years ago.

The development of archaeology

At present, particularly in the excavation and analysis of fossil skeletal material, the work of physical anthropologists and archaeologists is closely interrelated. But archaeology has had a different origin and process of development from those of physical anthropology. We can trace the beginnings of archaeology to the time of the Renaissance in Italy, when there was a new interest in the past and in the recovery of information about ancient Greece and Rome. This interest quickly spread from Italy to other parts of Europe. By the end of the 16th century and during the 17th there were many antiquarians, and the collecting of classical statuary had become a hobby of the rich. Wealthy men built up private collections, some of which ultimately became museums. One example was the Ashmolean Museum of Oxford, built in 1683, which contained not only objects of classical art but also ethnological curiosities brought back from foreign lands: the mantle of the North American Indian chief Powhatan, made of deerskin and embroidered with shells; canoe paddles from Polynesia; and ivory spoons from the Congo. Europeans were thus gaining more knowledge about the past and the varieties of cultures and ways of life around the world.

Museums have always been associated with the work of ethnologists and archaeologists. Curators have to sort out and classify their objects in some way. It was a museum curator, Christian Thomsen (1788–1865), who, being obligated to systematize the artifacts in the Danish National Museum early in the 19th century, came up with the Three Ages classification of Stone, Bronze, and Iron. These were in chronological sequence: a long Stone Age preceded an age in which bronze was used, which in turn gave way to an Iron Age. This simple scheme proved to be a very useful framework, later elaborated upon and subdivided.

The term *prehistory*, first coined in 1857, was popularized by John Lubbock (1834–1913) in a book called *Prehistoric Times* (1865), in which a distinction was made between two subdivisions of the Stone Age: Paleolithic (Old Stone Age) and Neolithic (New Stone Age). Lubbock knew that during the Paleolithic there were animals living in Europe that later became extinct, such as the mammoth, cave bear, and wooly rhinoceros. He also knew that there were characteristic differences in the making of Paleolithic and Neolithic stone tools.

An interest in European prehistory was spurred by the discovery and excavation of well-preserved Swiss Lake Dwelling settlements during the 1850s and 1860s. Some of these were Neolithic, while others dated from the Bronze and Iron Ages. Stratification helped to establish culture sequences. Meanwhile, excavations were also being made in Paleolithic cave sites, particularly in the Dordogne region of France, where several sites became famous for their yields of skulls, skeletons, and artifacts, giving names to particular periods or types of early man: Le Moustier, La Madeleine, Aurignac, Cro-Magnon, and others.

In 1879 impressive Paleolithic cave paintings were discovered at Altamira, in Spain, although their authenticity was generally doubted for many years. In the following decades, much Upper Paleolithic art in bone, ivory, and clay was discovered, as well as more examples of cave painting.

Thomsen's distinction of three phases: a Stone Age, a Bronze Age, and an Iron Age, modified by Lubbock's subdivisions, proved to be useful in interpreting the new discoveries. Based upon the materials used for making cutting tools, the three phases not only represent progressive increases in human control over nature but also reflect an increasing specialization, division of labor, and growing complexity of social structure.

The Stone Age is now subdivided into Lower, Middle, and Upper Paleolithic (Old Stone Age); Mesolithic (Middle Stone Age); and Neolithic (New Stone Age). We know that cultural advance was more rapid in the Near East than elsewhere; so, while a Neolithic, or even Bronze Age, economy was in operation in the Near East, northern Europe had a Mesolithic way of life.

The fact that the foregoing scheme of cultural stages is tied to Europe and cannot be applied very well in other regions, such as the New World, has led to its rejection by some prehistorians. Nevertheless, it continues to be used by most archaeologists. Since the prehistory of Europe has been studied longer and is better known than that of most other regions, this conservatism is understandable. Until a new, generally accepted scheme for dividing the stages of prehistory comes along, we might as well go along with the old one. This text, therefore, will follow the traditional system.

With the foregoing qualifications kept in mind, the following approximate dates based partly on radiocarbon dating (see p. 33) may be given, with the focus on western Europe. The Lower Paleolithic dates from around 1 million to around 60,000 years ago, and the Middle Paleolithic between about 60,000 and 35,000 B.P. (before the present). We then have around 35,000–12,000 B.P. for the Upper Paleolithic and 12,000–5,000 B.P. for the European Mesolithic. The Neolithic starts earlier in the Near East than in Europe, from around 10,000 to 5500 B.P.

The terms Paleolithic and Neolithic are *cultural* terms, which should not be confused with *geological* terms such as Pliocene and Pleistocene. Both kinds of labels will be used frequently in the chapters on human evolution. The reader should remember which labels are cultural and which are geological.

Research in early civilizations

During the 19th century, work was done in the Bronze Age civilizations of the past: in Persia by Henry C. Rawlinson, in Assyria by Paul Émile Botta and Austen Henry Layard, at Troy and Mycenae by Heinrich Schliemann. This archaeological research was accompanied by linguistic achievements in the deciphering of inscriptions in Egypt, Persia, and elsewhere. A linguistic genius, Jean François Champollion (1788–1867), deciphered Egyptian hieroglyphs from the Rosetta Stone, while Rawlinson and others worked on Old Persian, Akkadian, and Elamite.

Through his archaeological work, Schliemann had shown that an earlier civilization lay behind that of classical Greece. Layard, Botta, and Schliemann had uncovered hitherto unknown centers of Bronze Age civilization. Beginning in 1899, Arthur Evans carried this search into the past a step further by excavating at Knossos in Crete and bringing to light the elegant civilization of the ancient Minoans. Another formerly unknown civilization was revealed by John Marshall in his archaeological work in the Indus Valley between 1922 and 1927. Still older than either the Cretan or Indus Valley civilizations was that of Sumer. Although excavations in Sumer began in the 19th century, the most revealing finds were made by Charles Leonard Woolley in the late 1920s.

Information about the ancient civilizations of the New World came primarily from the historical writings of William H. Prescott (1796–1859) and the vivid narratives of travel and discovery by John Lloyd Stephens, an American lawyer. Stephens, who did not know about Prescott's then current research, was excited by a vague report of the existence of some ancient buildings in Central America. He set out in 1839, accompanied by Frederick Catherwood, an English artist. The two men made their difficult way through the jungles of Honduras, Guatemala, and Yucatán,

Maya bas-relief.

coming upon one amazing Maya ruin after another, most of them overgrown with tropical vegetation. The Maya buildings, with their elaborate, baroque facades, were drawn with great exactness and skill by Catherwood. Another early American archaeologist was E. George Squier (1821–88), who carried out an extensive survey of early Indian mounds in the Mississippi Valley and later mapped and surveyed the ancient Peruvian city of Chan Chan. Thus, gradually, archaeologists opened up more and more forgotten centers of early civilization.

As time went on, moreover, the archaeologists refined their methods and techniques. A leader in this field was William Flinders Petrie, who established new standards in excavation procedures, note taking, and publication. He was interested in sequence dating, establishing a chronology based on stratification and typology of artifacts such as pottery. Petrie discovered that pottery like that found in one of his Egyptian sites also turned up in a Mycenaean Greek assemblage. When he visited Mycenae in 1891 he identified some Egyptian imports dated at around 1500 B.C., as well as the Aegean pottery (of Cretan origin) like that found in the Egyptian site. This not only showed that trade existed between these early civilizations, but the imported items also helped to establish a chronology for Egypt, Mycenae, and Crete. Establishing a date for one site helped date the others.

Toward the end of the 19th century, some writers such as Edward B. Tylor (1832–1917) and Lewis Henry Morgan (1818–81) began to synthesize the knowledge then available about human cultural development and to make generalizations about cultural evolution. They divided up the past into the stages of *savagery*, *barbarism*, and *civilization*, which would roughly correspond to Paleolithic, Neolithic, and Bronze Age. According to Tylor, the earliest religions were polytheistic, monotheism being a late development in the evolution of religion. Morgan held that the earliest family organization, following a stage of promiscuity, was based on matrilineal descent (reckoning descent through the mother), while patrilineal descent, reckoning through the father, came later.

A reaction against the speculations of 19th-century theorists developed among the first professional anthropologists under the leadership of Franz Boas (1858–1942) in the United States. Boas held that global reconstructions of human cultural evolution were premature. What was needed was intensive field work and the collection of detailed ethnographies in different parts of the world. Archaeologists have shared this emphasis on field work, but there is now a greater emphasis on hypothesis testing.

Current trends   The old aims of reconstructing culture history and past lifeways are still primary goals in archaeology, but some contemporary archaeologists now emphasize the need to study cultural processes. They are interested in such matters as ecological adaptation, demography, settlement patterns, and the analysis of cultural systems in connection with the sites they analyze. For the ultimate question is not where or when a particular cultural development took place, but why. Why, for example, did some peoples become increasingly dependent upon plant domestication in early Neolithic times? Some conflicting answers to this question are discussed in Chapter 13. One of the anthropologists who has dealt with this issue is Lewis R. Binford, who has hypothesized that demographic pressures in settled hunting-gathering societies must have impinged on marginal, less sedentary groups in their environs. Under these circumstances there would be selective pressures favoring the development of new means of food production in the marginal zones. Processual theorists like Binford try to formulate hypotheses, construct behavioral models, and make predictions about what sorts of patterns may be found in particular sites. This emphasis on the testing of hypotheses is clearly in the scientific tradition.

In the field of physical anthropology, as in archaeology, there has also been an increased interest in processes of change and human ecology, as in the studies concerning human adaptations to different environments, such as deserts, high altitudes, and the Arctic.

Both physical anthropology and archaeology are much more sophisticated fields of research than they were a generation ago. Both now draw upon a host of sister disciplines. Physical anthropology is concerned with physiology, biochemistry, and genetics. Archaeology draws upon geology, paleontology, botany, zoology, chemistry, and physics. Reconstruction of the past in both fields has been greatly advanced by dating techniques such as radiocarbon and other methods described in the following chapter.

Summary

Anthropology is the study of human beings. One way in which it differs from other fields that study humans (such as sociology, economics, political science, and history) is that it contains a main division, physical anthropology, which is concerned with *Homo sapiens* as a physical organism and with our evolution from simpler forms of life.

The other main division, cultural anthropology, is subdivided into the three branches of linguistics, archaeology, and ethnology, all of which deal with aspects of human culture, the shared behavior learned by members of a society. Linguistics deals with language, the principal medium through which culture patterns are transmitted. Archaeology is the study of past cultures; ethnology is the study of contemporary cultures. Although each field involves specialization, anthropologists tend to think of their field as a unified discipline. Advances in any one branch often depend upon contributions from one or more of the others.

Anthropology is a relatively recent organized discipline, coming into existence in the 19th century. The increased knowledge of botany, zoology, and geology in the 18th century made human beings aware of the great age of the world and of the human species, thus paving the way for wide acceptance of the notion of biological evolution and the concept of natural selection, when it was presented in Darwin's *Origin of Species* (1859). Subsequent fossil finds of early man (*Australopithecus*, *Homo erectus*, Neanderthal) indicated stages of hominid evolution.

The term *prehistory* was coined in 1857 and was subdivided into Paleolithic (Old Stone Age) and Neolithic (New Stone Age), which later were further subdivided, with the addition of Bronze and Iron Ages. The study of early civilizations was also pursued by pioneer archaeologists.

Suggestions for further reading

The history of evolutionary theory is well presented in Loren Eiseley, *Darwin's Century: Evolution and the Men Who Discovered It* (New York: Doubleday, 1958); John C. Greene, *The Death of Adam: Evolution and Its Impact on Western Thought* (Ames: Iowa State University Press, 1959).

A selection of texts on anthropological subjects dating from the 14th to the 18th century is available in J. S. Slotkin, ed., *Readings in Early Anthropology*, Viking Fund Publications in Anthropology no. 40 (Chicago: Aldine, 1965). See also Phyllis Dolhinow and Vincent M. Sarich, eds., *Background for Man: Readings in Physical Anthropology* (Boston: Little, Brown, 1971).

In the field of archaeology three successful works of popularization can be recommended: C. W. Ceram, *Gods, Graves and Scholars: The Story of Archaeology*, trans. from the German by E. B. Garside (New York: Alfred A. Knopf, 1951); Geoffrey Bibby, *The Testimony of the Spade* (New York: Alfred A. Knopf, 1956); Glyn Daniel, *The Idea of Prehistory* (Baltimore: Penguin Books, 1964).

A two-volume work that presents much of the history of archaeological research in the form of short selections by archaeologists describing their own excavations and contains an introduction by the editor offering a survey of the history of archaeology is Jacquetta Hawkes, ed., *The World of the Past* (New York: Alfred A. Knopf, 1963).

On more current approaches, see Sally R. Binford and Lewis R. Binford, eds., *New Perspectives in Archaeology* (Chicago: Aldine, 1968); Patty Jo Watson, Steven A. LeBlanc, and Charles L. Redman, *Explanation in Archaeology: An Explicitly Scientific Approach* (New York: Columbia University Press, 1971).

CHAPTER 2

Methods of archaeology and physical anthropology

In their efforts to reconstruct culture history and past lifeways and to find clues to the processes at work in culture change in the past, archaeologists face such problems as the selection of sites for excavation, excavation procedures, methods of dating their finds, and the interpretation of the evidence.

How do archaeologists decide upon a particular site? How do they know where to dig? Sometimes the site is obvious, as in the case of the imposing Maya ruins that John Lloyd Stephens encountered in the jungles of Mexico and Guatemala in 1840. The ancient cities of Mesopotamia were also not hard to find, being built upon several layers of preceding habitations and debris and rising up like mounds from the level plain.

Barrows, mounds, and megalithic structures, like those of England, are also obvious features, as are kitchen middens—huge piles of refuse containing shellfish—like those accumulated by Mesolithic peoples along the shores of northern Europe. Since early hunting-gathering peoples often lived in rock shelters or caves, their dirt floors have often been excavated in search of their remains. Sometimes archaeological material is revealed accidentally through erosion or through workers blasting or digging in construction sites, quarries, or mines, making highways, or laying pipes.

The presence of house sites may sometimes be inferred by the presence of vegetation. If buried walls of brick or stone lie beneath a field, the plants growing above them are apt to be shorter than the surrounding crops, and they may ripen sooner and be lighter in color because of the relative lack of nutrients available to the roots. The outlines of house founda-

Selection of a site

Tikal, Maya site in
Guatemala. Maya sites
such as these were
overgrown by jungle
when they were
explored by John Lloyd
Stephens in 1841–42.

tions may therefore be seen. If there are buried garbage dumps, pits, or
ditches, on the other hand, their greater moisture produces more flourishing
plants. In the survey of an area, an archaeologist looks for such telltale
contrasts in vegetation.

Chemical analysis of the soil may indicate the likelihood of former human
occupation, such as through the presence of phosphate, which is present
in human flesh, bones, feces, and urine, and remains in the soil long after
a site has been abandoned.

The outlines of banks and ditches may sometimes best be seen in early
morning or late afternoon, when the sun is low on the horizon, throwing
shadows that bring out contours not usually seen.

Similarly, sites are sometimes best detected from the air. Features that
are not noticed by a person walking through the field may be clearly evident
from an airplane. For this reason, air reconnaissance has been used in
some archaeological surveys. O. G. S. Crawford, a leader in this type of
site detection, illustrated the principle involved by publishing together two

photographs of a carpet. One was a cat's-eye view seen close to the carpet; the other was a man's-eye view from above. The pattern of the carpet is immediately apparent to the man, but since the cat is so close to the fibers of the carpet, it cannot see the overall design.

The streets and gardens of Eski Baghdad were first noticed from the air during World War I by a British colonel who was taking photographs for military purposes. He wrote that the city was well planned

> . . . with wide main streets or boulevards, from which wide roads branched off. . . . Had I not been in possession of these air-photographs the city would probably have been merely shown [on the map] by meaningless low mounds scattered here and there, for much of the detail was not recognizable on the ground, but was well shown up in the photographs, as the slight difference in the color of the soil came out with marked effect on the sensitive film, and the larger properties of the nobles and rich merchants could be plainly made out along the banks of the Tigris (Crawford 1928, quoted in Hawkes 1963:I, 131).

The colonel could also see the outline of a series of detached forts that would not have been noticed on the ground; also, the outline of an ancient irrigation system.

Pre-Columbian ridged fields covering large areas have been detected from the air in eastern Bolivia, western Ecuador, northern Colombia, and coastal Surinam. From the ground one might not suspect the existence of such extensive man-made earthworks, but they are clearly seen from the air.

Sites are sometimes detected by surface finds. Bits of pottery may be strewn over a field, and an archaeologist may decide to dig a test pit or trench there to see if the area deserves further exploration. Broad-scale surface surveys are sometimes carried out, one of which is described below.

One way of helping to determine the precise place for excavation is *electrical resistivity*. When an electric current is run through the earth between two electrodes, the amount of resistance is measured on a meter. Water is a good conductor of electricity; hence, if the soil is damp, there will be less resistance than in the case of dry soil or stone or brick foundations that have airspaces. Successive readings of resistance over a grid thus indicate the possible presence or absence of buried house foundations or other solid structures.

Another technique for the same purpose is *magnetic location*, in which a proton magnetometer is used like a wartime mine detector to discover the presence of underground iron objects.

Probes have sometimes been used in archaeological surveys, especially to locate walls and pits.

A method used in connection with unexplored Etruscan tombs has been to drill a hole in the top of the tomb and to lower a flashgun camera to take photographs of the inside. When the pictures are developed, archaeologists can decide whether they want to excavate the tomb.

Thus, there are various methods that help the archaeologist decide where to dig. Of course, there are different types of sites: *living sites*, where people lived; *butchering sites*, where animals were cut up; *workshop sites*, or "floors," where tools were made; *quarry sites*, where flint or minerals were extracted; *ceremonial sites;* and *burial sites*, such as graves and tombs.

Social and cultural inferences

Different kinds of information may be derived from these different kinds of sites. From a living site one may be able to make a rough assessment of the size of a settlement's population on the basis of the number and size of the dwellings and the general size of the settlement. If there is an adjacent cemetery, the number of burials may also provide clues, although one would have to determine how long the cemetery had been in use and estimate the characteristic life-span. Of course, one could not be sure that all the people who lived in that community were buried there, but at least a rough approximation of the population could be made.

Caves, or parts of them, were sometimes living sites, such as those of Neanderthals in Europe and the Near East. From a living site one may also determine the basis of subsistence, whether hunting-gathering or agriculture. Animal bones and plant remains may be examined. There may be storage rooms, silos, or storage pits for grain. The impressions of grain on clay bricks or pottery are sometimes as clear evidence as the grains themselves. But ancient plant remains are often preserved, both in very dry environments, as in Peru and the American Southwest, and in damp peat bogs, as in Scandinavia.

A living site may give some evidence of the nature of social organization. There may be evidence of planned settlement—large communal dwellings, a grid layout of streets, and walls enclosing the settlement—or else small, dispersed units may indicate a more atomistic social order. A living site may also provide evidence of class stratification, implied by striking differences in the size of dwellings or by the concentration of valued objects, such as jade, in limited areas. Implications of trade are suggested by objects such as sea shells or obsidian that must have come from considerable distances.

In living sites, tools used in food preparation, such as metates, manos, cooking pots, and butcher knives, give evidence of the kinds of foods eaten. Direct evidence of what people have eaten has come from the intestines of corpses preserved in peat bogs in northern Europe and also from *coprolites* (human feces fossils) found in dry caves. Analyses of coprolites may tell not only what was eaten but also how the food was prepared.

Butchering sites yield less information than living sites, but they may give evidence of communal hunting, as in a late prehistoric site in Montana where buffalo were stampeded over a cliff. Large numbers of the animals were killed at one time but were butchered in such a way as to get the maximum amount of meat, much of which was dried or made into pemmican at the site itself, for no parts of the carcasses were taken away (Kehoe and Kehoe 1960). The butchering site at Torralba also gave evidence of communal hunting (see p. 144).

Workshop sites and quarry sites yield information about technology, the making of tools. Ceremonial sites give an indication of the importance of religion in the life of the people. If there are representations of deities, some ideas may be gleaned about the kinds of gods worshiped. There may be archaeological evidence of sacrifice or of the existence of a priest-hood. Burial sites not only yield skeletal material but very often grave goods as well, and indications of relative status may be deduced from the kinds of such associated material. They may testify to the existence of class stratification. Collective burials, as in the Neolithic passage graves of Europe, may indicate the importance of lineages or clans. There are also sites where petroglyphs and pictographs are found.

Surface surveys

People think of archaeologists as diggers armed with shovels, but archaeologists also carry out surface collections. David H. Thomas and his colleagues carried out a broad surface-collecting sampling survey in the upper Reese Valley of central Nevada to reconstruct the lifeways, settlement patterns, and seasonal movements of the hunting-gathering Shoshone Indians of the past—from around 5000 B.C. to the historic period. An area about 15 miles wide by 20 miles long was divided into 140 tracts, in each of which all the artifacts found on the surface, finally totaling about 3,500, were collected, catalogued, and mapped. A series of measurements were made on each artifact and an IBM card prepared for each specimen. The data were then analyzed by a computer, with artifacts being classified according to functional types.

Two types of Reese Valley settlements were distinguished in this survey: *shoreline settlements*, which seem to have been summer camps, and *piñon settlements* found on low mountain ridges containing piñon and juniper trees, which were occupied after fall pine cone harvests. Butchering sites were also found. Thomas characterizes the subsistence pattern as a dual central-based wandering pattern, corresponding to one described by Julian Steward for the Shoshone of recent historic times (Thomas 1973).

Analyses of the range of movement of such groups sometimes make use of the concept of *catchment area:* ". . . the further the area is from the site, the less it is likely to be exploited, and the less rewarding is its exploitation (unless it is peculiarly productive) since the energy consumed in movement to and from the site will tend to cancel out that derived from the resource. Beyond a certain distance the area is unlikely to be exploited at all: in terms of the technology available at the time, its exploitation becomes uneconomic" (Vita-Finzi and Higgs 1970:7).

Excavation procedures

After a site has been chosen for excavation, the usual procedure is to stake it out in a grid plan, with the area divided into numbered squares.

Before excavation, a scale map is made of the area. A fixed point, known as the *datum point*, is established on or near the site, marked by an object of steel, cement, or other durable material. This is the reference point for the excavations. If work is done on the site in later years, it can be determined where the earlier excavations were made. A grid may be dispensed with if a structure such as a house with different rooms is being excavated. The rooms may then become convenient units, rather than grid squares.

Preliminary test pits or trenches may be dug first. As the excavation proceeds, photographs are taken from different vantage points. When an artifact is uncovered, its position is recorded in its particular square and also in depth; it is numbered, cataloged, and listed in a register. Objects are placed in strong paper or cloth bags, labeled with identifying numbers.

Sites are often stratified. Objects found in lower strata are generally older than those nearer the surface, although this stratification may be disturbed and sometimes reversed. For example, the former inhabitants may have dug a large hole and piled up the dirt from it nearby. Animal burrowings, frost heaving, and other natural forces may cause disturbances in strata. Another possible source of confusion is that members of a community may have started a new settlement next to the old one. The second site may not overlap the older one and may seem to be on the same level. Thus time sequences may be difficult to interpret.

Objects found together presumably come from the same time period, although there may be exceptions, as in the preservation of heirlooms. It is necessary to have records of the spatial location of all the material found if one is to make an adequate interpretation of the remains.

Excavation site at Tiahuanaco, Bolivia, showing grid layout.

The associated material found in a site, known as an archaeological *assemblage*, consists of *artifacts*, which are man-made objects; *features*, which are man-made but are usually not removed from the site, such as storage pits; and objects that are not made by man, such as animal bones, plant seeds, shells, and ashes.

Even then, various alternative interpretations may be made to account for an assemblage of artifacts. K. C. Chang gives an example of a site where three objects appear: a pottery beaker, a metal sword, and a skeleton. The beaker and the sword are separated by 2 feet horizontally and 6 inches vertically; the beaker is near the head and the sword at the waist of the skeleton. These seem to be grave goods, but Chang points out some alternative possibilities. The pottery might belong to one stratum and the sword to another and thus represent different time periods or settlements. Perhaps the sword caused the man's death and was left in his body. Chang (1967:19–22) explores still other possibilities.

Animal bones and remains of plants and pollen are preserved for analysis by specialists to determine the types of animals and plants collected or domesticated. These remains may also help to date the site. If the dig is in an area suitable for the application of tree-ring analysis, logs or beams are preserved. These may require special treatment to prevent decay and decomposition. Bits of charcoal are also collected for dating purposes, as will be explained later. Shells found in the site may give an indication of climatic conditions. It may be determined if they are of local origin or brought or traded from a distance. The sources of pieces of stone or metal may also be deduced, as well as techniques of manufacture of artifacts made from stone, bone, metal, or other materials. Casts and molds are sometimes made of valuable objects, particularly perishable ones, and tracings or rubbings may be made of rock carvings or of bas-reliefs if they are present, as has been done in the Camonica Valley in Italy and in Maya sites in Guatemala.

Field methods in archaeology have become progressively more painstaking and detailed. This is partly because of recent advances in dating methods, which have shown the value of preserving and analyzing organic materials, pollen, logs, and other objects that formerly received little attention. But the great care taken with excavations nowadays is also due to the realization that a site can properly be excavated only once, for to excavate a site is to destroy it.

Underwater archaeology

Archaeologists do not only dig; they also sometimes dive under water, or have professional divers do it for them. Ancient Roman wine jars and marble statues have been brought up from wrecked ships at the bottom of the Mediterranean. Maya incense burners have been recovered from the bottom of Lake Amatitlán, Guatemala. It is common human practice to throw garbage into a lake or stream, where refuse piles may accumulate, often containing objects in a good state of preservation. Sacrifices to the water have been made in different parts of the world. Reindeer hunters in northern Europe, around 17,000 years ago, used to throw a whole reindeer, weighted with a heavy stone, into a lake, perhaps as a thanks offering or bribe to the spirits. The Maya of Yucatán tossed human sacrificial victims into deep wells, and also bowls, vases, earrings, beads, and other valuable offerings.

There is an unusual underwater site in southwestern Florida called Little Salt Spring, where a shallow basin has formed above a deep underwater cave. Nearby is an Archaic cemetery with about 1,000 burials. (For a discussion of the Archaic Tradition, see p. 188.) According to radiocarbon dating (see p. 33), an extinct form of giant tortoise was killed by human beings about 12,030 years ago. The Little Salt Spring sinkwater was formerly a source of fresh water for hunting peoples from around 12,000 to 9,000 years and from 6,800 to 5,200 years ago. Ancient organic remains and artifacts have been preserved in the water. A notable item in this collection is a nonreturning form of oak boomerang, which may be the oldest specimen of this type of boomerang in the world. Similar forms have been found in Australia, Egypt, and western Europe (Clausen et al., 1979).

It is interesting to note that the grid system used in archaeological excavations on land has sometimes been employed in underwater archaeology. At Yassi Ada, off the southwestern coast of Turkey, a scaffolding of pipe and angle iron was set up over a submerged shipwreck. The position of objects within the grid could thus be accurately plotted. Underwater "vacuum cleaners" removed dirt, and underwater photographs were taken during the process of uncovering the wreck. This turned out to be an old Roman ship, dated from the cache of gold coins at between A.D. 610 and 641, during the reign of the emperor Heraclius (Bass 1963, 1966).

Laboratory analysis

The first step in laboratory work is to identify and classify artifacts and to determine what they were used for.

Stone tools

A Russian investigator, S. A. Semenov, was a pioneer in making microscopic analyses of wear patterns, striations on stone tools, in order to get a better idea of their possible functions. Some striations run parallel with the sides of a blade, for example, whereas others are at right angles. By analyzing the type of wear, one may deduce whether the tool was apt to have been used for cutting, scraping, or piercing. Such analyses have also been carried out by several American archaeologists.

Archaeologists have sometimes made use of computers to help analyze their material statistically. The range, mean, and standard deviation in size of certain classes of artifacts may be determined. The relative incidence of types of tools in different settlements of a population may give clues to seasonal variations in subsistence or else may indicate different kinds of activities associated with different kinds of sites, such as living sites, on the one hand, and butchering sites, on the other.

Differences in tool kits may reflect a division of labor. In some European Neanderthal sites, for example, it has been deduced that notched tools made from local flint were probably used by women in processing food at the base camp, while men ranged further afield while hunting and made use of more distant flint, worked in a somewhat different fashion (see p. 155).

When archaeologists are able to determine the original sources of stone such as flint, they can make some deductions about mobility and trade relations among human groups. For example, in the Turkish Neolithic site of Çatal Hüyük pieces of obsidian were found which came from distant volcanoes, while marble came from western Anatolia. Other materials were also imported, leading archaeologists to conclude that these people strongly depended on trade with other groups.

Plant remains

It is in the laboratory that investigations are made of the animal bones and plant remains recovered from a site. These may be turned over to specialists such as botanists and zoologists. Botanists can identify plant remains, including pollen, and can also distinguish between wild and domesticated plants. Even ancient carbonized seeds may be recovered. To locate such small plant remains at a site, archaeologists use the technique of *flotation*, in which soil samples are deposited in a watery medium. Robin W. Dennell (1978), who excavated Neolithic sites in Bulgaria, made use of a technique called *froth flotation*. Air is pumped into a water tank through small bubblers like those used in fish tanks, and then chemicals are added which make charcoal fragments more susceptible to flotation, so that they rise to the surface and then fall over the tank rim into a channel, from which they can be retrieved for analysis.

Pollen analysis

Although very small, the pollen released from flowering plants is quite durable under certain conditions. Pollen trapped in peat bogs is almost indestructable. Pollen grains are also well preserved for long periods of time in lake mud, alpine and desert soils, and glacial ice, where the action of bacteria is restricted. By analyzing the pollen found in a stratum of peat, one can find out what kinds of trees and other plants were growing at about the time of its deposition. By similarly analyzing earlier strata of peat at the site, one can see what changes took place in the local flora from one period to another. In this way, pollen analysts have reconstructed the stages of forestation in Europe after the retreat of the glaciers. It appears that birch forests appeared first, followed by pine, and later by mixed oak forests.

Pollen analysis is not only, or even primarily, useful as a dating technique. It also provides a picture of the ecological conditions to which humans had to adjust at different times in the past. The ratio of tree pollen to other kinds of pollen, for example, gives an indication of forest density. Pollen analysis can even find evidence for human agricultural activities and forest clearing, as in the case of some European Neolithic sites where slash-and-burn horticulture was practiced. James Deetz (1967:71) writes:

> Pollen "profiles" made up by identifying the pollen from layer to layer in sites in the area, show this sequence clearly. The lowermost levels have pollen of forest trees, followed at times by a thin layer of charcoal representing the burning of a plot in the vicinity. Atop this charcoal layer is found the pollen of domesticated plants, and finally the pollen of wild grasses, showing the abandonment of the plot and its reversion to grass cover.

Pollen analysis has also been useful in New World archaeology. For example, E. S. Deevey and associates (1979) showed, partly through pollen analysis, that in the Maya area of the Petén lake district in Guatemala the forests had been essentially cleared by the Early Classic period (A.D. 250–550). Between A.D. 250 and 850 the population of the lowland Maya area was at least 5 million, and Tikal and other urban centers were built, but after that period there was a rapid collapse of the Maya social system, and depopulation set in. Pollen analysis was one of a number of natural-science techniques that archaeologists used to determine what brought about the collapse of Maya civilization in this region. Another such technique was the analysis of phosphorus concentrations in lake soil deposits.

Animal remains

Zoologists can identify animal remains, which sometimes, like plants, give evidence of domestication. They may also suggest the extent to which people at a given site depended on hunting and what animals were hunted. Animal bones also provide clues to chronology, particularly in the case of extinct animals when the date of their disappearance is approximately known. Different kinds of animals flourish in warm and cold periods. During warmer periods there were animals like elephants and hippopotami in Europe; during cold periods of glacial advance there were reindeer and cave bears, although the "tropical" hippopotamus survived in Italy until near the end of the Mousterian period (Bordes 1968:18). Small animals may be particularly useful for clues to climatic conditions, for rodents, birds, and especially mollusks are very sensitive to changes in climate.

Pottery

Pottery is commonly found in the sites of agricultural communities, although sometimes in those of hunting-gathering peoples as well. Pots tend to be decorated, and since styles of decoration tend to change over the years, it sometimes is possible to reconstruct the stylistic sequences in a region where ceramics have been used for a long time. This technique, known as *seriation*, is a method of relative dating.

Pottery can be analyzed for the type of clay and temper used as well as according to shapes and designs. It is sometimes possible to show that the pots in a particular site were not made from local clay but come from a different region, thus suggesting the likelihood of trade relations.

American archaeologists have a special interest in the characteristics of North American ceramic ware. The oldest North American pottery is found along the coasts of the southeast, in Florida, Georgia, and South Carolina. One problem facing potmakers is that pottery may crack in the firing process. Around 2500 B.C. North American potters added plant fiber to the clay, which prevented cracking. Later, from around 1000 B.C., they used grit and sand for tempering. The earliest North American pottery was not decorated with designs; it began to be decorated around 1500 B.C. Thus, clay vessels give information about time periods, sources of clay, and craft methods. Pottery can often be dated, not only through seriation but also through the technique of thermoluminescence (see p. 36).

Dating techniques

The most valuable and widely used system of dating is *radioactive carbon dating*, but it is less precise than some other techniques that have a more restricted range, such as *dendrochronology* and *varve analysis*. These techniques are forms of *chronometric dating*, that is, they provide dates in terms of numbers of years. Radiocarbon and potassium-argon dating is also chronometric, although less specific, giving dates within a certain time range, plus or minus a certain number of years. Another form of dating is *relative dating*, of which stratigraphy, seriation, and fluorine dating are examples. Through these means it can be ascertained that some objects are older than others within a particular site or region; they can be placed in a relative time sequence but not given specific dates.

Dendrochronology

A tree adds a new growth ring each year. By counting the annual layers one can find out just how old the tree was when it was cut down. The oldest bristlecone pine tree in California has been alive for 4,900 years. The rings on a tree are sometimes thick and sometimes thin, depending upon the amount of rainfall during the year. When plenty of moisture is available, they are wide; in times of drought, they are narrow. In subarctic

Cross section of a tree, showing annual growth layers.

regions, warmth is the critical factor. Since all the trees within a particular area are affected by the same weather conditions, their tree-ring sequences show the same patterns. Let us say that we have three thin layers, then a fat one, then two thin ones, then three fat ones, and so on. By comparing the tree-ring sequences of many trees in a particular area, a master chart may be drawn up to show the characteristic tree-ring sequence for that area. This chart can be extended far back in time, as progressively older trees are found whose later tree-ring sequences overlap those of younger trees.

The technique of dendrochronology has been used in the southwestern United States, where a master chart of tree-ring sequences goes back almost to the time of Christ. As will be seen later, a still older sequence is available from tree-ring analyses of bristlecone pines in California. If a Pueblo ruin is excavated in Arizona, let us say, a cross section of a beam is analyzed to see how its tree-ring sequences fit into the master chart. In this way it is possible to say in which year the beam was cut, which may also give the year in which the Pueblo structure was built. There is a minor catch, however, for the beam might have been used in an earlier house and later transferred to the Pueblo structure; it might have been added to the house some time after it was built. Despite such ambiguities, tree-ring analysis has been very helpful in dating sites in the American Southwest. Thus, Pueblo Bonito was built between A.D. 919 and 1130, while Mesa Verde was built between A.D. 1073 and 1262.

Dendrochronology cannot be applied to all kinds of trees or in all kinds of environments. Apparently it will not work in New Zealand, and it cannot be used in areas where there is little annual variation in rainfall. However, tree-ring analysis has been practiced with some success in England, Germany, Norway, Turkey, Egypt, and various parts of the United States, including Alaska. Dendrochronology has been applied to some problems related to radiocarbon dating. This is discussed in the section on radiocarbon dating below.

Varve analysis

Varves are annual layers of sediment deposited by ice sheets in glacial lakes. During the summer thaw, melting glacial ice runs down into the lake, carrying sediments, the coarser of which sink to the bottom of the lake. When winter comes, the lake freezes over and the melting stops. During the winter, the finer sediment gradually sinks down and settles on top of the coarser silt at the bottom of the lake. When the melting process resumes in the following summer, another annual layer is deposited with first a band of coarse sediment, later followed by one of finer sediment.

Varves vary in thickness from less than half an inch to more than 15 inches, depending upon the warmth and length of the summer period. This is reminiscent of the annual layers of trees.

Counting varves gives a date in years for the period of the melting and retreat of the glaciers. In Sweden and Finland, dates have thus been determined going back to before 10,000 B.C. This is based on the assumption that each varve stands for a year, which may not always be true. Nevertheless, the method provides considerable accuracy for dating late Pleistocene and early Recent times in northern Europe.

Radiocarbon dating

The most widely used archaeological dating technique is radiocarbon dating. This method is based on the discovery that all living things, both plants and animals, contain a radioactive carbon (radiocarbon) known as carbon-14 (C^{14}). Plants absorb this carbon from the atmosphere. Animals acquire it by eating plants or by eating animals that have eaten plants. The amount of C^{14} normally present in a living plant or animal species is known. Although some disintegration of radiocarbon may take place during the life of an organism, it is balanced by the intake of C^{14}; so, in a living organism, the amount of radiocarbon remains fairly constant. After death, however, no more C^{14} is taken in, and disintegration of C^{14} proceeds at a steady rate. In 5,730 years, half of the C^{14} in the organism has decayed; this is known as the *half-life* of carbon.

Since the rate at which C^{14} disintegrates is known, it is possible to date the time of death of some organic material by determining how much radiocarbon remains in it. Charcoal is among the most suitable such material for analysis. Shells are less reliable. Carbon-14 dates derived from mollusks may have to be corrected by the addition of several hundred years, since some freshwater shellfish take in carbonates from seawater. Other shellfish do not and thus are amenable to C^{14} dating.

The date yielded by the radiocarbon method is not a definite, specific date but one plus or minus a certain number of years, giving a standard deviation. Thus, instead of 15,300 B.P., the date would be given as 15,300 B.P. $\pm$ 300, which means that there is a 67 percent chance that the correct figure will fall between 15,000 and 15,600 B.P. It does not mean that the correct figure *must* fall between these two extremes. Note that B.P. (before present) is used instead of B.C. (before Christ). In radiocarbon dating the B.P. date refers to the number of years before A.D. 1950.

This technique was tried out by testing it with various objects whose ages were known through historical records or other sources, such as linen from the Dead Sea Scrolls and wood from an Egyptian tomb known to be dated between 4,700 and 5,100 years ago. The radiocarbon dates met these tests very well. Since then the method has been applied to archaeological sites all over the world.

A relative dating system such as seriation can sometimes be tied in with absolute dating to give a more definite chronological order. Let us say that a particular Pueblo site in Arizona has been dated through tree-ring analysis or C^{14}. The pottery found at the site can thus be approximately dated, and subsequent finds of such pottery at other sites can then be cross-dated, falling into the same period.

Despite its many advantages, there have been some difficulties in using C^{14} for dating purposes. One of the assumptions underlying its original application was that the C^{14} content in the atmosphere has always been constant. This has now been shown to be untrue. There was much more radiocarbon in the atmosphere 6,000 years ago than there is today. Changes in the earth's magnetic field and solar radiation may account for such differences. The decrease in radiocarbon in the atmosphere was brought to light by a combination of radiocarbon dating and dendrochronology applied to the world's oldest living trees, the bristlecone pines of the White Mountains of California, which can reach an age of more than 4,000 years. Samples of wood from tree rings whose ages were known were given the usual C^{14} laboratory tests. The ages derived from dendrochronology and radiocarbon dating ought to be the same, but there turned out to be discrepancies, particularly in the older years. It was thus shown that the radiocarbon method seems to work well enough back to around 1200 B.C., but after that the dates have to be revised or calibrated and set back by several centuries. At 3000 B.C. it is necessary to add as much as 800 years. A continuous tree-ring sequence of bristlecone pines, based on both living and dead trees, now goes back nearly 8,200 years. On this basis, calibration charts for radiocarbon dates have been drawn up. The new calibrated dates still have standard errors given (Renfrew 1973:69–83). There seems to be confidence among archaeologists that the calibration dates between approximately 2000 B.C. and 5000 B.C. are pretty reliable, but there is uncertainty about dates older than 5000 B.C. Except when otherwise specified, the early radiocarbon dates given in this text have not been corrected by the bristlecone process; so the reader should keep in mind that such dates are probably too recent.

Even with the new calibrations, the radiocarbon method is not foolproof. Sometimes objects have been contaminated by recent radioactivity. Sometimes different laboratories have given quite different dates for materials taken from the same site. The reason for such apparent failures to give consistent dates is not always understood. Nevertheless, radiocarbon dating seems to be the most useful dating technique for the archaeologist. Unlike dendrochronology and varve analysis, it is applicable in all parts of the world. When first developed, C^{14} dating could be tried only with objects dating back about 30,000 years, but now, through new methods, its range has been extended to about 60,000 years. However, since there is greater magnitude of error at this time period, archaeologists place less emphasis on C^{14} dates older than 40,000 years ago.

Potassium-argon dating and other methods

Another dating technique, which follows principles similar to C^{14}, was used to date the hominid remains at Olduvai Gorge in Tanzania, East Africa, an important archaeological site which will be discussed in Chapter 7. It produced a date of 1.75 million years ago for the bones in question. This method is *potassium-argon dating*. In this case, a radioactive form of potassium decays at a known rate to form argon, having a half-life of 1.3 billion years. The ages of some rocks can be dated by measuring the potassium-argon ratios. One advantage of this technique is that it can be used to date older sites than those within the range of C^{14} dating. But most archaeological sites cannot be dated by the potassium-argon method. It is mainly useful for sites dating to 500,000 years or more ago, and it is applicable only to rocks or sediments rich in potassium, such as volcanic ash. Intense heat is needed to drive off excess argon. Potassium-argon dating has not been possible in nonvolcanic areas such as South Africa.

Another chronometric method is *fission-track dating*, involving Uranium-238, which has a fission half-life of 10^{16} years. This method has been used to date pieces of volcanic glass and associated hominid remains at

Olduvai Gorge. In combination with potassium-argon dating and other techniques, it has also been used to date the hominid fossils found at Koobi Fora, arriving at an age of about 1.87 million years (Hay 1980). Fission-track dating is limited to mineral or glass material that contains some uranium, in which "substantial damage to the lattice is caused by recoiling fragments from the spontaneous fission of uranium-238 nuclei. These damage tracks can be made visible under the microscope by etching with hydrofluoric acid, the damaged regions being less resistant to attack. . . . The tracks are sufficiently stable . . . for the number present to be used as a measure of age . . ." (Aitken 1974:12).

Paleomagnetism (or archaeomagnetism) is a technique related to shifts in the earth's magnetic poles. It works best with fireplaces and pottery kilns. "When baked clay cools down from firing it acquires a weak permanent magnetization in the same direction as the field and of a strength proportional to the intensity of the field. To be a useful record of *direction* the clay must be part of a kiln, hearth, or oven so that it has exactly the same orientation today as when it cooled down." (Aitken 1974:6)

Paleomagnetic dating has been applied to sites in Mexico and Arizona dating back to 3,000 years and has also been used in the dating of some Paleolithic and Mesolithic sites of the Old World.

A technique known as *racemization* has been used for material dating between 40,000 and 100,000 years ago, the period of the Neanderthals. This involves an analysis of the arrangement of amino acids in organic material. The 20 amino acids found in all living things usually have the same configuration, but they undergo a change after the death of the organism, with the "left-handed" molecules gradually becoming "right-handed." This process forms the basis for the "protein clock." One difficulty is that the rate at which amino acids change their configuration varies with temperature conditions. However, many fossils have undergone no changes in temperature sufficient to throw off the calculations. This technique was devised by Jeffrey Bada of the Scripps Institution of Oceanography. To test it, Bada dated a hominid bone from Olduvai Gorge and came up with a reading of 135,000 years ago, which agreed closely with a date reached by Louis B. Leakey from geological evidence.

The technique of *obsidian hydration* depends upon the fact that obsidian usually contains only about 0.2 percent water, but when a piece of obsidian is broken, it absorbs water at a fairly uniform rate until it reaches a saturation point of about 3.5 percent water. However, the rate of hydration is affected by different climatic conditions, and there may be different kinds of obsidian. Obsidian artifacts are exposed to hydration when human beings work on them by flaking techniques, so that the date of a working may be roughly gauged by measuring the extent of hydration.

Still another chronometric dating technique is *thermoluminescence*. If some ancient ground-up pottery is quickly heated to 500°C, some measurable light is emitted, which is known as thermoluminescence (TL). This comes from the radioactive influence of metallic elements in the clay and surrounding soil, such as uranium and potassium. In the original firing of the pottery, any geological TL was driven off; but since the firing the pottery has been exposed to a steady radiation dosage from the natural radioactivity in the pottery and soil. "The natural TL measured in the laboratory now is directly related to the total radiation the ceramic has experienced since a 'time zero' was set up by the original firing." (Fleming 1976:111)

An ingenious combination of techniques, involving pollen analysis, radiocarbon dating, and other methods, to reconstruct past climatic conditions in North America has been involved in the analysis of wood-rat middens in Nevada and Texas. Twigs and seeds of juniper were found in nine wood-rat middens in a desert region in Nevada, whose contents give them radiocarbon dates between 7,800 and more than 40,000 years ago. There are no junipers in the region today. Since the foraging range of the wood rat is limited, the plant contents of the middens represent local vegetation of the past more accurately than wind-blown pollen might do. Partly on the basis of such evidence, Philip V. Wells has shown that during the late Pleistocene there were forests rather than only grasslands and deserts in the Great Plains of North America (Wells and Jorgensen 1964; Wells 1966, 1970).

Relative dating

Fluorine analysis provides relative dates for bone materials, indicating whether a particular bone in a deposit is the same age, more recent, or older than another. Bones lying in the earth accumulate fluorine from the surrounding soil; the longer they have lain there, the higher their fluorine content will be. This does not provide an absolute chronological age, since different soils contain different amounts of fluorine. However, fluorine analysis can establish an index for the relative dating of bones found within a particular site. Bones at the same level should contain about the same amounts of fluorine if they are of equal age. Discrepancies in fluorine percentage indicate that the bones are of different age.

Seriation is the typological classification of artifacts for purposes of relative dating. William Flinders Petrie, the great Egyptologist, made a relative dating sequence of Egyptian tombs on the basis of changes in the form of the pots found in them. Early pots, he concluded, had handles that gradually became smaller over the years, until finally there was nothing but a painted line in the place where the handle had formerly been. Tombs with pottery of the latter type were judged to be later than those that contained pots with handles.

Since Petrie's day seriation has been used in many studies. A way of illustrating changes in types over time is to construct a graph in which a bar represents the frequency of a particular form during a certain time

Typical stylistic
sequence from a New
England cemetery
(Stoneham, Mass.). The
three styles produce
nearly perfect curves
through time.

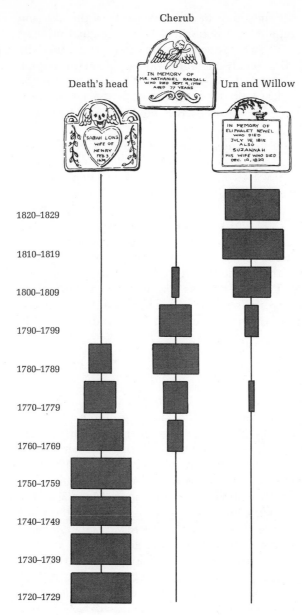

period. The succeeding period is represented in a bar directly over the
first, and so on, up to the top of the page. The width of the bar shows
the relative frequency of the form in question. It bulges out during a
period of maximum popularity and then diminishes, while an alternative
form or forms appear on the scene. James Deetz (1967:31) examined grave-

stones in an 18th-century New England cemetery and found a change over time in the popularity of certain designs. A long-established death's head design finally gave way to a cherub head, which in turn was replaced by an urn-and-willow design. This sequence, illustrated here, is marked by characteristic "battleship-shaped" curves of expansion and diminution.

In the analysis of early primate and human remains, archaeologists and physical anthropologists have to work closely together. For much of the earlier fossil record of human evolution, physical anthropologists have to depend on the analysis of tooth and jaw fragments.

Methods used by physical anthropologists

Osteology

Osteology is the study of bones, but that includes the study of teeth. Teeth, which are so subject to decay in the living human mouth, tenaciously outlast all other parts of the body after death and, compared to other body parts, are relatively well preserved in the fossil record. For the earlier primates particularly, teeth are about all physical anthropologists have to work with. It is fortunate if they know the geological stratum in which these teeth were found and the climatic and environmental conditions it suggests.

The teeth give some indication of the size of the animal, and they may suggest the type of diet to which it was accustomed. Physical anthropologists study living primates as well as fossil forms. A knowledge of the anatomy and physiology of different apes and monkeys helps the physical anthropologist to interpret the skeletal material of extinct species. Where there is much similarity between a living form and a fossil find, some relationship may be inferred.

If limb bones and parts of the vertebral column are present, the animal's form of locomotion may be deduced, whether it went on all fours or with upright posture, or whether it used to swing from branch to branch through the trees by brachiation. Some inferences may also be made about the animal's musculature:

> We can make deductions about the size and form of the nerves and muscles with which they formed a single functional unit. Muscles leave marks where they are attached to bones, and from such marks we can assess the size of the muscles. At the same time, such parts of the skeleton as the cranium give us considerable evidence of the size and form of the brain and spinal cord (Campbell 1974:2).

Evolution of the brain

One of the determinations made by physical anthropologists is the cranial capacity of skulls, which has a clear relation to brain size, although it is larger, since the braincase also contains membranes, a layer known as dura mater, and cerebrospinal fluid. Cranial capacity is determined by first plugging up the holes in a cranium to prevent leakage and then filling the inverted skull with seeds, water, or small shot, which are then poured into a graduated container.

Hominid evolution has been marked by an increase in brain size and cranial capacity. African apes have a cranial capacity of about 500 cubic centimeters. Australopithecine cranial capacity was about the same. *Homo erectus* skulls ranged between 900 and 1,225 cubic centimeters, while modern skulls have a capacity of about 1,400 cubic centimeters. But the evolution of the brain has involved not only increases in size but also changes in shape and organization, with an enlargement of parietal and temporal cortex. An idea of such morphological features may be obtained by making endocasts of fossil skulls, another method used by some physical anthropologists (Holloway 1974). Laboratory studies of living primates also contribute to our knowledge of brain anatomy and neural organization.

Determination of sex and age

It is sometimes useful to know the sex and approximate age of persons whose skeletal material is analyzed. For example, the first australopithecine skull to be found, labeled *Australopithecus africanus*, was judged to be that of a five- or six-year-old juvenile. How do physical anthropologists arrive at such conclusions? Although the estimates are usually rough and mistakes are always possible, they do have a number of ways of determining sex and approximate age from teeth and bones.

Top of skull, showing sutures between the different bones of the skull vault.

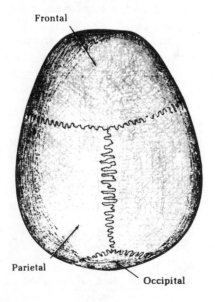

Frontal

Parietal

Occipital

Age may be determined partly from the appearance of the teeth, the presence of milk teeth (as in the original find of *Australopithecus africanus*) or permanent dentition, the degree of tooth wear and decay, and loss of teeth and the consequent absorption of bone in the jaws of older persons.

In the skull, one indication of age is the degree of closure of the sutures. The skull is not made of continuous bone but of different bones that remain separate in the newly born child, allowing the brain to grow and expand. These skull bones gradually meet, forming irregular, serrated edges called *sutures*. In the mature adult the sutures may become obliterated, especially in older persons.

In the 11th prenatal week in humans, there are some 806 centers of bone growth; at birth, about 450. These centers "disappear" through union with adjacent centers. Approximate age in the prenatal months and early years may be gauged from the appearance of centers, their union, and the degree of ossification. The right and left hipbones meet in front to form the pubic symphysis, the appearance of which provides an indication of age in more mature skeletons. Women have a broader and lower pelvic structure, suitable for giving birth to large-brained babies, while men have a high, narrow pelvis.

In "sexing" a skull, size and degree of ruggedness are determining factors. Generally, larger skulls are male; smaller ones, female. Female skulls are rounder and lighter boned; they have smoother, more "gracile" foreheads. In males the cheekbones and supraorbital ridges are more fully developed. Males have thicker jaws, broader palates, squarer chins, and larger mastoid processes. The long bones of males are longer and more massive than those of females (Krogman 1962).

The methods used by physical anthropologists, briefly reviewed here, bear on the reconstruction of primate and human evolution, which will be our main concern in the next few chapters. But physical anthropologists also study variation in modern humans. Methods used in that respect involve demographic and epidemiological studies, investigations of growth and maturation, and studies of genetically based traits such as blood group types. These topics are dealt with in Chapters 18 and 19.

Summary

Archaeologists seek to reconstruct culture history and lifeways of the past and to understand the processes at work in cultural change in past times. Broad-scale surface surveys are sometimes carried out before the digging of test pits and excavation of a site.

Different types of sites have been distinguished, including living sites, butchering sites, workshop sites, ceremonial sites, and burial sites.

Not only artifacts, objects made by humans, but all objects found at a site are collected and analyzed, including pollen, seeds, and animal bones. The analysis of pollen helps to reconstruct ecological conditions at the time the site was occupied. Pottery and stonework are analyzed in the laboratory with regard to manufacturing techniques and also to determine the sources of clay and stone. Pottery is useful in dating, either through seriation or thermoluminescence.

In the past 50 years an impressive array of dating techniques has been made available to archaeologists. Some of these, like dendrochronology (tree-ring analysis) and varve analysis, provide specific dates in terms of years. Less specific but still providing chronometric dates, plus or minus a certain number of years, are various techniques provided by the natural sciences: radiocarbon, potassium-argon, fission-track dating, paleomagnetism, racemization, obsidian hydration, and thermoluminescence. In contrast to chronometric methods, relative dating does not provide dates in terms of numbers of years but it does indicate that certain items are older than others within a particular site or region. Examples are stratigraphy, seriation, and fluorine dating.

Physical anthropologists concerned with the evolutionary record give much attention to the analysis of bones and also of teeth, which outlast all other parts of the body after death. The teeth give some indication of the size of the organism and the characteristic type of diet. The analysis of skulls includes assessment of cranial capacity and determination of sex and age.

Suggestions for further reading

For methods in archaeological research, see Frank Hole and Robert F. Heizer, *Prehistoric Archaeology, A Brief Introduction* (New York: Holt, Rinehart & Winston, 1977). A more exhaustive survey, useful mainly for professional archaeologists, is Don Brothwell and Eric Higgs, eds., *Science in Archaeology: A Comprehensive Survey of Progress and Research* (New York: Basic Books, 1963).

For dating methods, see Kenneth P. Oakley, *Frameworks for Dating Fossil Man* (Chicago: Aldine, 1969); Martin J. Aitken, *Physics and Archaeology* (Oxford: Clarendon Press, 1974); and Stuart Fleming, *Dating in Archaeology. A Guide to Scientific Techniques* (London: J. M. Dent & Sons, 1976). For some aspects of the analysis of prehistoric sites, see Creighton Gabel, *Analysis of Prehistoric Economic Patterns* (New York: Holt, Rinehart & Winston, 1967). See also Bruce C. Trigger, *Beyond History: The Methods of Prehistory* (New York: Holt, Rinehart & Winston, 1968).

For microscopic analysis of stone tools, see S. A. Semenov, *Prehistoric Technology*, trans. from the Russian by M. W. Thompson (New York: Barnes & Noble, 1964).

On methods in physical anthropology, see Gabriel Ward Lasker, *Physical Anthropology* (New York: Holt, Rinehart & Winston, 1973), chap. 1; and a good collection of readings: Solomon H. Katz, ed., *Biological Anthropology* (San Francisco: W. H. Freeman, 1975).

PART TWO

Primate evolution

CHAPTER 3

Mechanisms of evolutionary change

Evolutionary changes are such remarkable developments that they are hard to believe. That a single-celled animal should give rise to a multicelled one, that an invertebrate should evolve into a creature with a backbone, that fishes should start to live on land—all these seem like miraculous transformations. And how can we explain the formation of such a wonderful organ as the human eye or the human brain? These and many other aspects of evolution seem almost incredible.

Some writers, who may be characterized as vitalists, finalists, or telefinalists, have argued that evolution is directed by a mystical life force or by God, perhaps leading, as Tennyson put it in the last two lines of *In Memoriam*, to "one far-off divine event/To which the whole creation moves."

These views may be right, but they have not, so far, shed much light on evolutionary processes. As George Gaylord Simpson, the eminent paleontologist, has written, "The most successful scientific investigation has generally involved treating phenomena *as if* they were purely materialistic, rejecting any metaphysical or transcendental hypothesis as long as a natural hypothesis seems possible" (Simpson 1967:128). To follow such an approach does not necessarily mean to commit oneself to a mechanistic or materialistic view of life. It is through such an approach that scientists have discovered much about the mechanisms that operate in evolutionary change. These discoveries do not lessen the mystery inherent in evolution, for as we learn more, more mysteries appear.

An early naturalistic theory about evolutionary change, which is not generally accepted today, developed from the suggestion of Lamarck that organs are strengthened through use and come to atrophy through disuse.

He interpreted the long neck and long forelegs of giraffes as due to their stretching up to browse in the upper leaves of trees over long periods of time. Blind cave fishes have been found in both Europe and America; Lamarck would explain their blindness as being caused by the atrophy of organs that have ceased to be used in the dark.

The difficulty with these views is that they assume the inheritance of characteristics acquired in the lifetime of an organism. Most scientists today do not accept the notion that such acquired characteristics are inherited, although that was, until not long ago, a dogma in Soviet biological science.

Another evolutionary theory, that of *orthogenesis,* holds that there is a constant direction in the evolution of organisms, leading seals, for example, to become increasingly streamlined or giraffes to develop progressively longer necks. No special mechanism has been posited for such tendencies, merely a vague directive influence. The idea of orthogenesis is therefore similar to vitalistic and finalistic interpretations of evolution. Such views have not helped to clarify the processes of evolutionary change.

Our present understanding of the mechanisms involved in evolution has been derived largely from the work of two men: Charles Darwin (1809–82) and Gregor Mendel (1822–84). Darwin provided the concept of natural selection and synthesized data bearing on the theories of evolution; Mendel founded the science of genetics.

Natural selection

Darwin's *Origin of Species* (1859) opens with a discussion of variation among cultivated plants and animals. Darwin drew attention to the great changes that breeders have been able to develop in domesticated species through artificial selection by isolating and breeding strains of organisms characterized by a variation in a particular desired direction, such as length of legs and speed in racehorses or increased weight and early maturity in cattle. But changes also take place in nature through the operation of natural selection. Everywhere in nature there is a struggle for survival— for resources of food and sunlight and the other needs of life. Plants and animals reproduce many more of their kind than can survive, and most of them perish.

The principle of natural selection is stated as follows:

> Owing to this struggle, variations, however slight and from whatever cause proceeding, if they be in any degree profitable to the individuals of a species, in their infinitely complex relations to other organic beings and to the physical conditions of life, will tend to the preservation of such individuals, and will generally be inherited by the offspring (Darwin 1859:51–52).

Darwin pointed out that organisms, if unchecked, tend to increase in geometrical ratio. The elephant is the slowest-breeding animal known; but Darwin calculated that if an elephant pair were to give birth to six young in a lifetime of 100 years and if this rate continued, in a period of 740–

750 years there would be almost 19 million elephants alive, descended from the first pair. Darwin cited some actual instances of "population explosion" among species under favorable environmental conditions, when natural enemies or other checks had been removed.

However, in spite of the tendency to multiply, species generally have fairly constant populations. Their numbers are, in fact, held in check by the universal struggle for life and by the fact that, while a species may multiply, its available food supply is apt to remain constant. Since many individuals in every species perish, favorable variations of any sort must greatly enhance an organism's chances of survival and reproduction. Thus, Darwin would explain the long necks and forelegs of giraffes, not in terms of their straining up to nibble lofty leaves for many generations, but in a quite different manner, reasoning that if some members of the species were born with longer necks and forelegs than others, this might be a favorable selective difference, which would give them a greater chance to survive and propagate than their shorter-necked contemporaries. Over a period of time, the long-necked variety would therefore increase at the expense of the short necks, culminating, as an evolutionary end product, in the giraffe we know today.

Darwin was struck by the fact that most beetles on the island of Madeira are unable to fly. He saw this as a selective advantage, since beetles that could take to flight would often be blown out to sea and destroyed. Darwin also considered a Lamarckian explanation for the wingless beetles; perhaps disuse of wings led to their atrophy. In any case, he argued, wingless beetles would be more apt to survive in Madeira than those with fully developed wings. This, then, would be an example of natural selection.

To take another example, consider the advantages of protective coloration. There are both brown and green mantises. Scientists have performed some experiments with them, tethering both types of mantis in both brown and green grass. In an environment of green grass, the brown insects were soon destroyed by natural enemies, while the green mantises survived. In brown grass, it was the other way around; there the brown mantises were favored and continued to live, while the green ones perished. Thus the protective coloring became an instrument of natural selection.

Adaptations of this sort are complicated by the fact that organisms may move to new environments or there may be seasonal changes, as in the turning of leaves in autumn. Hence, what was formerly protective may become highly unfavorable under changed conditions and what was unfavorable may become beneficial. Both dark- and light-colored moths are found in the English countryside, but the light moths predominate because they have more protection from their enemies. But during the last 100 years, dark, almost black, moths have become much more numerous than light ones in the sooty industrial cities of England. The dark moths are hardier, but they had formerly been exposed to their enemies when seen against light-colored tree bark covered by lichens. Now, in a new environment of gray towns and factories, as well as in rural areas with soot-covered tree bark, they have flourished. The pigment-producing substance in moth wings is called *melanin*, and the process involving the change in incidence of dark-colored moths is known as *industrial melanism*.

Darwin did not know how new variations arise in an organism; that was later to be shown by geneticists. But he argued that, once a new feature, such as a change in color or size appears, it may either help or hinder the organism in its adaptation to the environment. If it hinders that adaptation, the organism will be less apt to survive and reproduce, and the new feature will not be perpetuated. But if it enhances the organism's chances of survival and reproduction, the new feature will be maintained, and organisms possessing the trait will flourish at the expense of those not having it. In this way, changes gradually take place in the appearance and structure of an organism. Since organic forms have been living for many millions of years, there has been plenty of opportunity for plants and animals to adapt to many different environments, progressively deviating from parental forms as they establish more appropriate adjustments to their surroundings.

The crucial factor in natural selection is the net reproductive success of a group of organisms, the number of offspring that have survived to the point where they can successfully reproduce themselves. At the same time, if too many offspring are born, it may be difficult to raise them all effectively, and overpopulation may destroy the resources on which the organisms depend.

After the publication of *Origin of Species*, the work was criticized on various grounds. Darwin and his supporters were able to answer most of his critics. But there was one criticism that shook Darwin's faith in his own theories. The question was raised: If an organism appears with a new trait that has survival value, how can it be maintained? If it is to reproduce, the organism must mate with other members of its species which are apt to lack the new variation. Within a few generations the new trait will be swamped and should disappear. It could only be maintained if several organisms were to simultaneously vary in the same direction. But acceptance of this possibility would involve an orthogenetic view of evolution lacking the fortuitous character of natural selection.

To cope with this objection Darwin developed a complex theory of inheritance, which has since been shown to be inadequate. Darwin might have solved the problem if he had known about the work of his contemporary, Gregor Mendel. But, although Mendel gave two reports dealing with his findings before the Brünn Society for the Study of Natural Science in 1865 and he published his paper the following year in the *Proceedings* of that society, Mendel's work was, for all practical purposes, unknown in the Europe of his day. The few people who heard or read his report in 1865 and 1866 evidently did not understand it or grasp its significance. It was not until 1900, 16 years after Mendel's death, that his forgotten treatise was simultaneously discovered by three scholars in three different European countries. And then the science of genetics was born.

Gregor Mendel's experiments

Gregor Mendel was an Austrian monk who, over a period of eight years, performed some careful experiments with plants in a patch of garden beside his monastery. His most important work was done with garden peas. One reason for his success in these experiments was that he crossed strains of peas that differed from each other in one definite character. Some had round seeds; others had wrinkled ones. Some were yellow; others, green. Some of the plants were tall; others, short. Mendel took pollen from a plant that regularly produced round seeds and placed it on the stigma of a plant that produced wrinkled ones. In the same way he crossed the yellow with the green plants and the tall with the short. He did this with seven pairs of contrasting characters.

Another reason for Mendel's success in these experiments is that he kept quantitative records of the appearance of his plants in each generation. Moreover, he kept records of large numbers of plants so that accidental variations present in groups of small numbers did not significantly influence his findings. After crossing the peas with the round and wrinkled seeds, Mendel found that the peas of the offspring were all round; none were wrinkled. In the yellow-green cross, the peas of the offspring were all yellow. In the tall-short cross, the offspring were all tall. These results were surprising, for one might have expected to find some blending of the contrasting traits. Instead, in each case, one factor appeared to be dominant over the other. However, the submerged (recessive) factor did not disappear. This was shown when Mendel next cross-pollinated his hybrid plants. This time the round-wrinkled hybrids produced about three round peas to every wrinkled one; apparently the wrinkled factor of one of the grandparents had not been lost. The same 3-to-1 ratio was found for the other factors as well. The recessive traits for greenness of the pea, for shortness of the plant, and the other recessive traits were all preserved.

Mendel found that when the peas were allowed to reproduce by self-fertilization, the wrinkled-seed plants always had wrinkled peas and pure strains of the round-seed type always produced round peas. But the hybrids produced three round seeds to one wrinkled one. We shall return later to the question of why this 3-to-1 ratio appeared.

The term *genotype* has come to be used for the genetic constitution of an organism, while *phenotype* denotes its observable appearance. Phenotypically, members of the first generation of Mendel's round-wrinkled hybrids were all alike; all their peas were round. But the underlying genetic makeup of the hybrids was different, as was shown by the reappearance of the recessive factor in the following generation.

Mendel concluded that heredity is determined by discrete units that retain their original character for generation after generation. Nowadays

Diagram of a "typical"
animal cell.

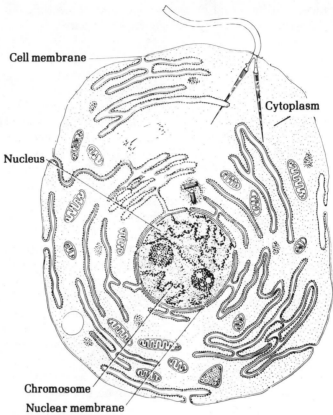

Cell membrane

Cytoplasm

Nucleus

Chromosome

Nuclear membrane

Illustration is reproduced from *Biological Science* by William T. Keeton. Illustrated
by Paula Di Santo Bensadoun, with the permission of W. W. Norton and Co., Inc.
Copyright © 1967 by W. W. Norton and Co., Inc.

we call these units *genes*. A gene may be defined as a unit of heredity in
a particular position on a chromosome or as part of a large DNA molecule.

**Genes and
chromosomes**

Since Mendel did not work with a microscope, he could not observe
the inner structure of cells. His conclusions were drawn from observation
and mathematics. Later, microscopes with great power and efficiency became available, and today we know a great deal about the composition
of cells that was unknown in Mendel's day. In the nucleus of a cell, there
are some rod-shaped bodies that can be seen much more clearly through
the microscope if they are stained. Hence, they have been called *chromosomes*, or colored bodies. These structures cannot be the genes themselves,
because there are too few of them. There is an intestinal worm that has
only two chromosomes. The fruit fly, *Drosophila melanogaster*, has eight,
but it has been roughly estimated that *Drosophila* has 10,000 genes. So

there are thousands of times as many genes as chromosomes. It was concluded that perhaps the genes are located on the chromosomes.

Drosophila melanogaster has very large chromosomes in its salivary glands during the larval stage. Through observation on the effects of radiation, the scientists who have worked with the fruit fly have been able to make detailed chromosome maps showing at exactly which part of a chromosome a particular gene is to be found. The genes themselves, however, are too small to be seen through a microscope. It is perhaps best to think of them as positions on a chromosome.

The genes on the chromosome are formed in pairs, which may be either of the same or of contrasting type. These partner genes are called *alleles*. When the alleles are of the same type, the organism is said to be *homozygous* for that trait. For example, if both alleles cause roundness in peas or if both cause wrinkledness, they are homozygous. But, if one allele causes roundness and its partner causes wrinkledness, they are *heterozygous*.

All cells undergo the process of cell division, or *mitosis*, which creates new cells. In this process the chromosome divides so that each cell has the same number of chromosomes with the same genes. The new cells are exactly like the parent cells. A somewhat different process takes place in the reproductive cells that develop into the egg and sperm. In their cell division, called *meiosis*, the daughter cells have only half the traditional species number of chromosomes. There is one member present from each chromosome pair, not just any half. The alleles, or gene pairs, separate, with one going to each daughter cell. The maternally and paternally derived chromosomes assort randomly, making a great number of combinations possible. Thus, when the egg and sperm unite in fertilization, each brings half the normal number of chromosomes, and in their fusion the full number of chromosomes characteristic of the species is provided for the embryo.

The combination of genes that takes place at fertilization is a matter of chance. This can be shown if we return to Mendel's experiment with the round and wrinkled peas. We are now in a better position to understand the 3-to-1 ratio that Mendel discovered in his third generation of plants. The following paragraphs may be clarified by reference to the accompanying chart. Mendel began with a pure round strain, containing two alleles for roundness, and a pure wrinkled strain, with two alleles for wrinkledness. Every offspring of this cross must contain both a round and a wrinkled gene; they are all heterozygous. Phenotypically, their peas are all round, since roundness is the dominant trait.

Consider now what happens when two of these heterozygotes are crossed. At fertilization the dominant round gene of the first pair of alleles could join either with the dominant round gene or with the recessive wrinkled one of the other pair. The recessive wrinkled allele of the first pair could join either with the dominant round gene or with the recessive wrinkled one of the other pair. We thus have four possibilities: round-round, round-wrinkled, wrinkled-round, and wrinkled-wrinkled. Since the first three com-

Mendel's 3-to-1 ratio.

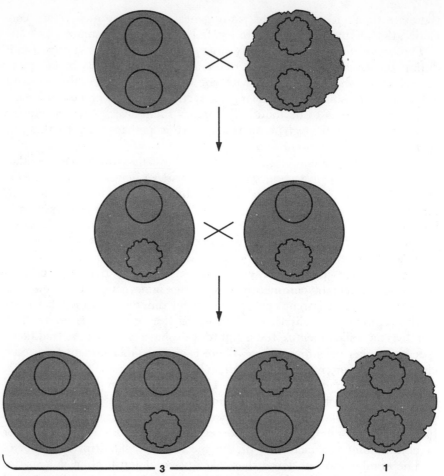

This chart shows three generations of peas, with the first generation on the top row. On the top left there is a pure round pea having two genes for roundness, represented by the two smaller circles inside. On the top right there is a pure wrinkled pea having two genes for wrinkledness. When these two peas are crossed, each member of the next generation (second row) is heterozygous, having received one of the two genes for roundness-wrinkledness from each parent. Although they each have a gene for wrinkledness, they all look round, since roundness is a dominant trait. When members of this second generation are crossed, there are four possible combinations in the third generation (third row). Since the first three peas all have a gene for roundness, they all look round. The fourth, being pure wrinkled, looks wrinkled.

binations all contain a round allele, these will all appear round. Phenotypically, then, we have a 3-to-1 ratio.

It should be noted that a 3-to-1 ratio is not always obtained in the crossing of heterozygotes, for traits are not always clearly dominant or recessive, and genes that are dominant under some conditions may be recessive in others. There are cases where a kind of blending takes place, as in the skin color of mulattos.

Another qualification that needs to be made about Mendel's findings has to do with the implication that a single gene always affects a single trait, such as the roundness or yellowness of peas. We now know that a particular trait may be influenced by several genes and that linkages may occur among genes, as among those found on the same chromosome. For example, hemophilia and color blindness are called sex-linked traits, because the genes responsible for them are located on the X chromosome, one of the two chromosomes that determine sex.

In the preceding paragraphs, we have been considering processes involved in sexual reproduction, which is characteristic of the majority of plants and animals. But not all plants and animals have sexual reproduction; many reproduce asexually by mitotic cell division. The more common and more complex processes of sexual reproduction must have been favored by natural selection. Their advantage evidently lies in the variety made possible by the genetic recombination in sexual reproduction. In mitosis each new cell gets a set of chromosomes just like the parental set; thus asexual reproduction provides little opportunity for variation and for evolutionary change. Genetic recombination, however, does provide variety in the raw material upon which natural selection acts.

Genes seem to be remarkably stable. They are always making faithful copies of themselves and so continue for generation after generation. But sometimes an inheritable change takes place in the structure or the chemistry of a gene or chromosome. This is called a *mutation*. A new gene or chromosome has, in effect, appeared, which may result in a difference in coloring, size, or other attributes of the organism. Three types of mutations have been distinguished: gene mutations, chromosome mutations, and genome mutations. Gene mutations cannot be seen under a light microscope, but chromosome mutations can. They involve changes in the structure of a chromosome due to breaks, translocations, duplication or loss of chromosome material. Genome mutations bring about changes in chromosome number, either loss or increase. Some human ailments, such as Turner's syndrome and Klinefelter's syndrome, are brought about by genome mutations. Turner's syndrome leads to abnormal ovarian development in females, while Klinefelter's syndrome is a glandular disturbance in males that results in testicular atrophy (Eckhardt 1979:131–36). Most mutations are harmful to the organism and may lessen its adaptability. This is because every organism has established a *modus vivendi;* it has acquired successful means of coping with the world. An innovation is more apt to be harmful to it than helpful. Harmful genes tend to disappear before long, since the carriers may either die out or fail to reproduce.

Sometimes mutations occur that have no apparent effect for generations. New recessive traits may be masked for decades and only become manifest if mating takes place between two carriers of the trait. To give an example of a recessive trait resulting from mutation, in 1931 a Wisconsin mink

Mutation

rancher found a light-furred female in a batch of otherwise normally dark-furred offspring. The light color was a recessive characteristic due to mutation. The rancher crossed the female with one of her offspring. In this way, a homozygous strain was developed which bred true—a kind of homogenized mink. In the wild state such a mutation might not have had much survival value. Under domestication it was profitable, at least to the mink rancher, who introduced platinum mink to the world. Naturally, it was preserved and perpetuated.

Not all types of mutations are possible, and there are some that no doubt recur again and again. Very likely, light-furred mink have often been born in the past, but they were not favored by natural selection. Mutations leading to blindness are, of course, harmful to the organisms affected and tend to be weeded out, but in cave fish living in the dark, such mutations make no difference and may therefore accumulate—an interpretation to be contrasted with Lamarck's notion of atrophy through disuse.

Mutations occur with some regularity, although with relative rarity, in all species. The rates of mutation may be increased by exposure to X-ray or cosmic radiation and by exposure to some chemicals or to heat. Although most mutations are harmful, it sometimes does happen that a favorable mutation occurs—one that enhances the survival and breeding potentialities of the organism. An example was given earlier of the dark-colored moths in the industrial areas of England. Mutations toward dark pigmentation must often have occurred among these moths in the past, but they did not prove to be useful until parts of England became sooty enough to favor their selection.

DNA

The field of molecular biology has provided much information about the structure and chemistry of genetic material. As a result, we are hearing a bit less about genes and a good deal more about "coding." Chromosomes consist partly of chains of DNA (deoxyribonucleic acid) molecules and partly of protein. A DNA molecule is believed to consist of two intertwined sugar-phosphate strands, shaped like a spiral staircase. The nitrogenous bases—adenine, guanine, cytosine, and thymine—form internal links like steps in the staircase. The DNA of all plants and animals seems to have this structure and chemical composition, but variety is made possible by variations in the four kinds of "steps." A thread of DNA has been compared with a recording tape that codes instructions. These instructions are issued in the form of chemicals. A gene may be considered as a position on the tape that issues a particular kind of message.

In addition to DNA, all plant and animal cells contain a similar substance called RNA (ribonucleic acid), which contains a sugar called *ribose*. (The ribose of DNA has one less oxygen atom; hence the "deoxy" in its name.) DNA is always found in the nuclei of cells; RNA is usually found in the

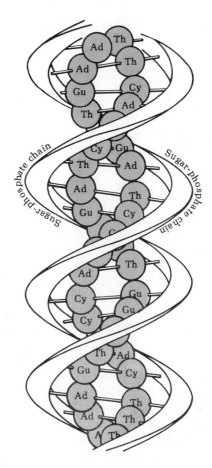

The double helix, or Watson-Crick, model of a DNA molecule.

cytoplasm. Within the nucleus, DNA transmits messages concerning protein manufacture to various forms of RNA called "messenger RNA." The essential business of life, the determination of heredity and the manufacture of proteins necessary for life, is therefore carried out by these minute molecules.

A failure in the coding process may result in a mutation. An example is sickle-cell anemia, which results from the failure of the organism to produce a particular amino acid. This ailment will be discussed in Chapter 19.

Split genes

Much of our current knowledge about molecular biology has come from the study of the bacterium *E. coli*. It was assumed that what was true of this bacterium was also true of higher organisms in relation to genetic transmission. But some research begun in 1977 has called this assumption into question.

In the un-nucleated bacterium, the gene coding for a protein exists as one continuous length on a strand of DNA—the master molecule of heredity. In higher organisms the gene may be split into several discontinuous segments, separated by intervening sequences or gene inserts. These inserts are also DNA. . . . It is a process involving cutting and splicing of genetic information in a way that requires the instructions encoded in widely separated parts of a DNA molecule to be snipped out and reassembled as a cohesive genetic message. (Patrusky 1979:39)

This discovery has raised many problems that require further investigation.

Isolation and species formation

Evolutionary change is fostered by geographic and reproductive isolation, resulting in the formation of new species. A species may be defined as an interbreeding population of organisms reproductively isolated from other such groups. Within a species, fertile offspring are produced. While mating may take place across species lines, the offspring that may result usually are infertile or sterile.

Let us consider an imaginary animal species that has spread out across an island. In this process some groups of the species have become geographically isolated from others due to the formation of barriers, such as streams. Each group then begins to adapt to somewhat different environmental conditions and, in time, assumes some different physical traits, such as contrasts in pigmentation. We may call these groups *subspecies*, groups that are potentially capable of becoming separate species. If the ecological barriers now are withdrawn or surmounted and if the groups are allowed to mingle with one another and produce fertile offspring, it is evident that they still belong to the same species, even though the subspecies have developed contrasting traits in color, size, or other attributes.

Let us now allow more time for our imaginary animal species, so that each group within it continues to adapt to its own environmental setting, with the development of still more variation. Such variation may reach the point where the former subspecies can no longer interbreed, or they may have sterile offspring, or else their hybrid offspring may be at a disadvantage of some kind. In the latter case, those animals that mate with members of their own kind are apt to leave more offspring than those that interbreed with the other subspecies. Hence, even if interbreeding is possible, the separation between the two subspecies will widen.

The subspecies that have been isolated from one another may develop incompatible features. For example, differences in size prevent interbreeding between the small oak toad and the much larger Gulf Coast toad. A feature such as this, which prevents an exchange of genes, is known as an *isolating mechanism*. There are various kinds of isolating mechanisms. Mating or flowering periods may come at different seasons; there may be noncorrespondence of genitalia or floral parts; there may be contrasting courtship movements or other patterns leading to copulation. If two former subspecies reach the point of reproductive isolation through some such mechanism, *speciation* has taken place. There are now two separate species where formerly there was one. Even if these groups are allowed to intermingle, they will not interbreed; or if they should succeed in doing so, their offspring will be sterile. If a male donkey copulates with a female horse, the mare may give birth to a mule, but mules are sterile and cannot reproduce. Obviously, the two species of horse and donkey are related; they belong to the same genus, *Equus*. Technically, the horse is called *Equus caballus* and the donkey, *Equus asinus*. A lion and tiger may also mate but have infertile offspring. These two species belong to the genus *Felis;* the lion is called *Felis leo* and the tiger, *Felis tigris*. Thus, genus, species, and subspecies represent progressive differentiations. The species is a reproductively isolated group in which fertile offspring are produced.

An example of the effects of isolation is provided by the finches that Darwin found on the islands of Galapagos, which he visited during the voyage of the Beagle in 1835. Lying on the Equator, the Galapagos islands are 600 miles from Ecuador in South America, the nearest land mass. Despite the great distance, it is probable that all the flora and fauna on the islands came from South America, including the finches. The Galapagos finches show great diversity. Some have developed into woodpecker-like forms; others resemble warblers. This radiation was made possible by the absence of competing birds, for the finches must have colonized the islands before other land birds arrived. If woodpeckers had already been there, it is unlikely that woodpecker-like finches would have developed; and if warblers had been present, no warbler-like finches would have evolved. In the absence of predators, the finches of Galapagos were checked only by limitations of food supply; hence they specialized in different kinds of diet for which different kinds of beaks developed. Some searched the ground for food, others searched in the trees. There were seed eaters, fruit eaters, and insect eaters, ecologically isolated from one another. This occupation of different niches reduced the competition for food resources (Lack 1947:107–62).

Darwin's finches

Evolution does not concern an individual alone but a whole population of organisms. An individual changes in appearance from birth to death but does not evolve. Evolution takes place within an interbreeding population. Natural selection affects differential fertility within a species and brings about changes in gene frequencies. Evolution takes place through changes in the *gene pool* of a population, a gene pool being the total collection of genes of the members of the breeding population. Despite changes, there is a tendency for the proportions of genotypes to remain constant from one generation to the next. If random mating occurs in a population, there should be genetic equilibrium without evolutionary change. Random

The study of populations

The 14 species of Galapagos and Cocos Island finches. **A** is a woodpecker-like finch; **C, D,** and **E** are insect eaters; **F** and **G** are vegetarians; **H** is the Cocos Island finch. The birds on the ground **I, J, K, L, M,** and **N,** eat mostly seeds. **I** which has a powerful beak, lives on hard seeds.

mating means that mating occurs without bias and that every member of the population has an equal chance of mating with any mature member of the opposite sex. A bias would occur, for example, if people of the same height or skin color were preferred partners. In practice, preferential mating patterns are common in human societies. In some societies, for example, it is the accepted practice for cousins to marry one another. In random mating, on the other hand, there is no such tendency in mate selection. Although the assumption of random mating in a population is somewhat artificial, the assumption has been useful in the development of calculations of gene frequencies in populations. The field of research concerned with such matters is known as *population genetics.*

One of the mechanisms involved in changes in the gene frequencies of a population is *genetic drift.* This is the result of a chance sampling "error" such as might result from the migration of a small subgroup from a larger population. For example, a large human population contains both blue-eyed and brown-eyed persons, with a somewhat larger percentage of the latter. A small migrant group from this stock contains only blue-eyed persons, as the result of chance, just as one might draw a handful of blue marbles from a sack containing equal numbers of blues and browns. If the migrants land on an island and start to interbreed, their descendants will deviate genetically from the parent stock in having only blue eyes. A similar effect could be brought about by drastic population reduction resulting from a war, famine, or epidemic. Either through migration or through population reduction, then, there is a *founder population,* a new breeding population in which the genetic frequencies differ from those of their parent stock, a condition known as the *founder effect.*

Genetic isolation like that of our hypothetical blue-eyed islanders may also come about through sociocultural mechanisms, such as rules of *endogamy* requiring members of a particular caste or religion to marry only members of that group. For example, the Jews of Rome, confined to a ghetto area for many generations, now have a higher frequency of blood group B than do other Jewish groups and a much higher frequency of B than that of the general Italian population.

Luigi Cavalli-Sforza and his colleagues have studied the operation of genetic drift in the Parma Valley of north-central Italy, where there have been no major immigrations since the seventh century B.C. They hypothesized that drift would be more pronounced in the small, isolated populations of mountain villages than in the less isolated communities of the hills and plain. Blood group samples (ABO, Rh, and MN) were taken and a computer simulation was made of the populations of 22 villages, which tended to support the hypothesis (Cavalli-Sforza 1975).

Opposed to isolation is *gene flow* or *hybridization,* which involves an exchange of genes between populations. The resultant genetic diversity may lead to an improved strain. Animal and plant breeders, when crossing distinct varieties, have sometimes produced a population superior to either parental strain. This phenomenon is known as *heterosis* or *hybrid vigor.* Some examples of studies of population genetics relating to humans, including a discussion of blood groups, will be found in Chapter 18.

Summary

This chapter has dealt with the problem of how evolutionary changes are brought about in plants and animals.

Darwin's concept of natural selection, when combined with modern knowledge of genetics, gives an understanding of how evolutionary changes have come about. Genetic variability is provided by genetic recombination, hybridization, changes in chromosome structure and number, and gene mutation. Geographic or reproductive isolation allows for the operation of natural selection upon a particular species in different environmental settings, leading to species differentiation.

Knowledge of genetics has helped to solve some problems Darwin could not answer and to explain why a new variant form need not be "swamped" through matings with organisms that do not have the trait in question. In the following chapters we shall trace sequences of evolutionary development that led to our species. At each stage, at every moment in this evolutionary process, the mechanisms discussed in this chapter must have been in operation.

Suggestions for further reading

Charles Darwin's *Origin of Species* (1859) still makes interesting reading. It is available in a Modern Library edition, along with Darwin's *The Descent of Man* (1871). For a history of evolutionary theory, see Loren Eiseley, *Darwin's Century: Evolution and the Men Who Discovered It* (New York: Doubleday, 1958); and John C. Greene, *The Death of Adam: Evolution and Its Impact on Western Thought* (Ames: Iowa State University Press, 1959). For a critical discussion of vitalism, finalism, and orthogenetic theories, see George Gaylord Simpson, *The Meaning of Evolution* (New Haven, Conn.: Yale University Press, 1967); and *This View of Life: The World of an Evolutionist* (New York: Harcourt Brace Jovanovich, 1964).

A recent work on human evolution that includes information about modern genetics is Robert B. Eckhardt, *The Study of Human Evolution* (New York: McGraw-Hill, 1979). For a classic but difficult work, see Theodosius Dobzhansky, *Genetics and the Origin of Species* (New York: Columbia University Press, 1951). See also G. Ledyard Stebbins, *Processes of Organic Evolution* (Englewood Cliffs, N.J.: Prentice-Hall, 1966). See also J. B. Birdsell, *Human Evolution: An Introduction to the New Physical Anthropology* (Chicago: Rand McNally, 1972). For a recent introduction to human genetics, see Daniel L. Hartl, *Our Uncertain Heritage. Genetics and Human Diversity* (Philadelphia: J. B. Lippincott, 1977).

CHAPTER 4

How human beings are classified among the vertebrates

Early in the first chapter, it was stated that *Homo sapiens* is a vertebrate, a mammal, and a Primate. These categories represent progressive refinements of classification. Let us consider each category in turn and, in doing so, trace our evolution from simpler forms of life.

Vertebrates are bilaterally symmetrical animals that have segmented backbones. Running through the backbone is a spinal cord connecting with the brain, which is usually enclosed in a skull. Thus the brain and central nervous system are well protected. The backbone is flexible, since it is made up of a series of bony rings.

Characteristics of vertebrates

The head of the animal contains sense organs, such as nose, eyes, and ears, and a mouth, sometimes equipped with teeth. A heart pumps blood containing food, oxygen, and other substances to all parts of the body. A liver stores food, and a urinary system eliminates wastes. These characteristics, as you must recognize, are true of humans. They are also true of fishes, amphibians, reptiles, birds, and all the mammals.

The features just mentioned have some advantages over the body plans of the invertebrates—such literally spineless creatures as worms, mollusks, insects, starfishes, and octopuses. Some invertebrates are held together by external armor, but this is not so efficient and mobile a system as an internal skeleton. Vertebrates are generally able to move about quickly. They can readily mobilize energy and have well-developed nervous systems. Because of these advantages some vertebrates have attained huge size, like the whales and elephants of the present day. Although *Homo sapiens* is much smaller than they, we are much larger than the vast majority of animals. Relatively speaking, we are giants. Large size may sometimes be disadvantageous, but it also has some advantages. Bulk may be useful in defense or attack. And, since larger animals tend to have slower rates of metabolism, they tend to live longer than small animals, whose internal organs wear out more quickly.

The first vertebrates, which appeared about 480 million years ago, were water dwelling, for life originated in the waters of the earth, and it was only gradually that first plants, and later animals, appeared on land and made their ways inland.

The amphibian stage

Amphibians, such as frogs and salamanders, are vertebrates that have half climbed out of the water, so to speak. In their adult forms they move about readily on land, but they first pass through a fishlike tadpole stage in the water. Their method of reproduction is also like that of most fishes, for their eggs must be laid in water. As tadpoles, frogs have gills through which they breathe, but in the adult stage they develop lungs and breathe air much as the higher land-dwelling vertebrates do. They also develop two sets of limbs, so that the skeleton of an adult frog has many resemblances to that of a human being. Early ancestral amphibians probably had limbs that did not raise the animal off the ground; they helped to drag him along in water, mud, and on dry land. The limbs have three segments each. First, there is a single bone (like the humerus, upper arm, or femur, thighbone); then, there are two parallel bones (like the radius and ulna or the tibia and fibula); then, there are the bones that make up the "hands" and "feet" with their separate digits. Our limbs are based on the same plan as that of the early amphibian limbs. In this respect, man has remained very conservative, while animals such as horses and cows have limbs that deviate a great deal from the early amphibian type of limb.   .

The earliest fossil amphibians that have been found had relatively small limbs, as one might expect. These replaced the lateral fins that help to propel and balance fishes. Some early amphibian remains have been recovered from Devonian strata dating from about 360 million years ago.

Some new problems faced the first amphibian land dwellers. One was to avoid drying up. This could be partly solved by keeping close to the water, but there is evidence that some of the early amphibians also developed tough skins. Another problem was the effect of gravity, which was experienced with much more force on land than in the water. In this case, adaptations were made in strengthening the limbs and spinal column.

The reptile stage

The amphibians were pioneers, but they were neither fish nor fowl, so to speak, having made only a partial adaptation to life on land. A new set of developments took place among some creatures which gave rise to

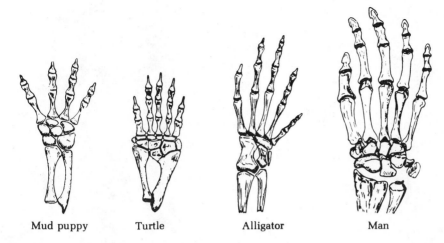

Right hand of mud puppy, turtle, alligator, and man, from dorsal view.

Mud puppy   Turtle   Alligator   Man

the class of reptiles. The most dramatic innovation was a change in the method of reproduction. Amphibians and most fishes, as we have seen, lay their eggs in water, where they are fertilized. The new development, associated with copulation as the means of fertilization, was the laying of eggs encased in a hard shell. Such eggs could be laid on land, for the watery medium required by the embryo had now been transferred from the outside world to the inside of the shell. The shell was strong enough to protect the embryo from at least some of its enemies. It was porous enough to permit respiration. Food was available in a yolk sac, which enabled the embryo to take nourishment and to grow in a protected environment. When the young animal was strong enough to break the shell, it could step out onto dry land. Thus, for the first time, a purely terrestrial way of life was made possible.

Reptiles also became equipped for life on land by the development of stronger limbs, which in some cases raised the body off the ground. Several extinct forms of reptiles, including some of giant size, ran about on their hind legs. Although the snakes eventually lost their limbs, primitive reptiles generally had limbs containing the same number of fingers and toes as we have. Reptiles had more efficient lungs and circulatory systems than amphibians.

The transition from amphibian to reptile took place about 260 million years ago. Since they were better adapted to life on land than the amphibians were, the reptiles increased and radiated, or diversified, at a great rate, particularly during the Mesozoic period, which has been called the Age of Reptiles. Despite their improved adaptations, reptiles have some weaknesses. Since they are not warm-blooded animals, they can be active only in warm weather. They slow down and may have to assume a state of suspended animation when it gets cold. Overexposure to the sun also may be fatal. The reptiles' range of movement is therefore restricted, and the

Chart showing
appearance of different
forms of life on earth at
different periods.

ERA	SYSTEM AND PERIOD	SERIES AND EPOCH	YEARS BEFORE PRESENT
CENOZOIC	Quaternary	Recent	From 10,000
		Pleistocene	From 1.8 million
	Tertiary	Pliocene	From 5 million
		Miocene	From 23.5 million
		Oligocene	From 35 million
		Eocene	From 58 million
		Paleocene	From 65 million
MESOZOIC	Cretaceous		
			135±5 million
	Jurassic		
			180±5 million
	Triassic		
			230±10 million
PALEOZOIC	Permian		
			280±10 million
	Carbon-iferous	Pennsylvanian	
			310±10 million
		Mississippian	
			345±10 million
	Devonian		
			405±10 million
	Silurian		425±10 million
	Ordovician		
			500±10 million
	Cambrian		
			600±50 million
	Precambrian		

giant forms of the Mesozoic may have been particularly vulnerable to changes in climate.[1]

As the giant reptiles left the scene, some less impressive but ultimately more successful creatures began to increase in number. These were the birds and mammals, both of which evolved from reptilian ancestors and developed warm-bloodedness. The birds retained the reptilian method of reproduction of laying eggs, and they developed feathers, their most distinctive feature.

We now come to the mammals, the class of vertebrates to which we belong. Archaic mammals appeared in the Mesozoic about 160 million years ago. Eutherian, or placental, mammals, a higher form of mammals, date from the end of the Mesozoic era about 65 million years ago. The first of these to appear were insectivores, believed to be ancestral to the other orders of eutherian mammals. The Primate order, to which we belong, is closely related to the insectivores; it is thus a relatively old and conservative mammalian order.

We are mammals

Mammals are warm-blooded creatures that are able to maintain a constant high body temperature. They are thus less at the mercy of the environment than are the cold-blooded amphibians and reptiles. Mammals live in diverse parts of the world, even in the Arctic, where one finds representatives of different mammalian orders, including seals, polar bears, whales, and *Homo sapiens*. Mammals radiated like the reptiles before them, some becoming aquatic, like the whales; some flying, like the bats. But most became either terrestrial or tree dwelling.

Mammals have an efficient circulatory system powered by a four-chambered heart. They generally have a covering of hair or fur and a skin equipped with sweat glands. All of these features have to do with regulating the temperature of the body. They also have a diaphragm that separates the thoracic from the abdominal parts of the body and helps to draw air into the lungs. The lower jaws of reptiles consist of several bones, but in mammals there is only one bone on either side; it articulates directly with the skull.

Mammalian dentition is said to be *heterodont*, having different kinds of teeth with different shapes and functions, as opposed to the *homodont* dentition of reptiles. Reptile teeth, which are often incurved, serve to grasp or trap food and all have the same general appearance and function. The mammalian jaw became stronger in the course of evolution, and teeth became specialized for different functions, with incisors for cutting, canines for grasping and piercing, premolars and molars for crushing and grinding.

---

[1] However, Robert T. Bakker, of Harvard's Museum of Comparative Zoology, believes that, unlike other reptiles, dinosaurs probably were warm-blooded.

Different kinds of tooth specialization developed as animals came to special-ize as carnivores or herbivores. Some mammals underwent a loss of teeth; cows lost their upper front teeth and baleen whales lost them all, but for most mammals the heterodont dentition remained an important adaptation:

> . . . the heterodont dentition released to mammals the full food value locked up within the hard outer skeleton of insects and in plant-food storage organs (such as nuts and other seeds). The densely packed carbohydrates and fats of seeds, the sugars and starches of underground tubers and roots, and all the plant proteins locked up in tough vegetation were released to mammals by the chewing and grinding action of their teeth, thus making possible the maintenance of constant body temperature and more or less continuous activity (Campbell 1974:45).

The eutherian mammals have two sets of teeth. In the young animal there is a temporary milk set of teeth. When the jaw is more fully formed, the permanent teeth appear. The ancestral mammals are believed to have had 44 teeth, but present-day species have lost some of them in the course of evolution. Human beings usually have 32 teeth, which is more than most mammals have. (Many people, however, have only 28 teeth, and many have impacted third molars.)

The mammalian system of reproduction is quite different from those of fishes, amphibians, reptiles, and birds. Mammals do not lay eggs, except for the duckbill platypus and the spiny anteater, or echidna. In all the other mammals the embryo remains within the mother's body for a time and is born in a more-or-less helpless condition. It then receives nourishment from the mother's breasts *(mammae)*, from which the class gets its name.

Among the marsupials, or pouched mammals, like the kangaroo and the opossum, the embryo does not remain long in the mother's body;

Reptile homodont teeth.

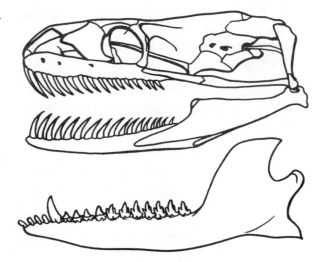

Mammalian heterodont teeth.

after birth it is shifted to a sort of incubator in the mother's pouch, located near the nipples.

The eutherian mammals have evolved a better system. There is an organ in the maternal uterus known as the placenta from which the fetus gets nourishment and oxygen. This is missing or weakly developed among the marsupials. The placenta makes it possible for the embryo to stay and grow for a long time in the mother's body.

Most adult male mammals have scrotal testes. This feature represents an adaptation to high body temperature. If the testes were to remain within the body, where they are first formed, the internal body heat would be too high for the production of sperm.

Mammalian reproductive processes are controlled by a complex endocrine system operating through hormones, chemical substances that are carried in the bloodstream to different parts of the body.

Some other general characteristics of mammals include: much larger brains than those of lower vertebrates; eardrums set deeper in the skull than in reptiles, with an outer earflap for concentrating sound waves; separation of nasal and oral passages; and the presence of seven cervical (neck) vertebrae. Human beings have all the features mentioned above.

Within the grouping of eutherian mammals, humans belong to the mammalian order of Primates. The order includes the lemurs, tarsiers, monkeys, apes, and *Homo sapiens*. Some authorities include the tree shrews within the order, while others classify them as Insectivora.

The outstanding characteristic of primates is their *prehensile* (grasping), five-digited hands and feet. In discussing the amphibian stage of evolution, attention was drawn to the conservatism shown in the structure of human limbs. Both arms and legs are characterized by having, first, a single upper bone, then, two parallel bones, then, wrist or ankle bones, and, then, five digits. This limb structure is a very ancient one. Very ancient also is the structure of the human hand, which remarkably resembles that of some tortoises. Terrestrial quadrupedal animals have limbs that differ greatly from the early amphibian limb. In the horse the parallel bones have become fused, and only one functional digit remains. The horse depends upon limbs for locomotion and nothing else. Such limbs cannot grasp anything, and they lack the mobility and flexibility of early amphibian limbs. Primates have retained this mobility and further developed it. Their forearms, for example, possess the power of pronation and supination, that is, the ability of the forearm to turn over and back again without moving the upper limb.

The hands and feet of many primates also have opposable digits in the thumb and big toe. The thumb can touch the other digits. When you grasp a branch, the thumb goes around one side, while the other four fingers wrap around the other. We cannot do this with our toes because

Primate traits

our feet have become specialized for support and locomotion. Our big toes are in line with the other toes and not set apart from them as the thumb is set apart in the hand. The other primates, however, can generally grasp as well with their feet as with their hands, and their big toes are opposable.

Another feature of primate hands and feet is the presence of flat or slightly curved nails on the digits. Some of the lower primates have claws on some of their digits, but not the higher primates.

How have the primates been able to retain the early amphibian-reptilian type of hand? The answer must be that our early mammalian ancestors did not take to quadrupedal terrestrial life as did the ancestors of the ungulates, or hoofed mammals. It is believed that the first mammals were arboreal, or tree dwelling. Most of the primates of the present day still live in trees. Only a few, such as the baboon, gorilla, and humans, move about on the ground. The grasping hands and feet of the primates are admirably suited to life in the trees, and it must have been their adaptation to such an environment that preserved the mobility and flexibility of the limbs and maintained their original structure with so little change.

Another important function of the grasping hand and foot is seen in the clinging of a monkey infant to its mother. All monkeys are born with a clinging reflex; the infant hangs onto its mother's fur. The mother must often be very active, moving about through the trees, with hands and feet occupied in locomotion and exploration. If the infant could not hang onto its mother, it would die. The grasping primate hand is therefore essential to survival in such species.

Another feature of the primate skeleton, useful in an arboreal habitat, is the clavicle, or collarbone. This, again, is an early structure found in some amphibians but missing in many terrestrial mammals. It serves as a strut to keep each forelimb at the side of the body, thus allowing more space in which a primate can move.

Most primates, then, became adapted to life in the trees, and this adaptation enabled these mammals to maintain some features of the early amphibian-reptilian skeleton that have been lost by mammals that became adapted to other environments.

The teeth of primates are less specialized than those of most other mammals. Their jaws are generally rather short, and they have short faces, in contrast to the long-snouted terrestrial quadrupeds.

Vision, brain, and body size

Life in the trees demands good eyesight, but a sharp sense of smell is not so important. For ground-dwelling nocturnal animals, on the other hand, a keen sense of smell may be more important than good vision. It is not surprising to find the sense of smell deficient in primates, especially among the higher ones, in contrast to most terrestrial animals. Many terrestrial animals have eyes set on either side of a snout so that they do not have overlapping stereoscopic vision. But most of the primates, whose eyes are set close together on the frontal plane, do have this feature. It may have developed originally as a response to the insect-catching diet of the simpler primates. At any rate, stereoscopic vision gives the primates a better conception of depth, so important for life in the trees. Moreover, the higher primates also have color vision.

An arboreal habitat is demanding. Leaping from branch to branch requires agility and good timing. The primates, therefore, are generally rather intelligent, high-strung creatures, and their brains are relatively large in proportion to body size. Most of the primates are quite small. Bulk is not suitable for life in the trees. *Homo sapiens* seems to have acquired large size after adjusting to life on the ground. The gorilla, a large and heavy primate, also spends much of the time on the ground.

An arboreal habitat had many advantages for the primates: **Advantages of**
arboreal life

> An enormous proportion of the energy received from the sun is converted
> into trees, as distinct from herbs, and the primates were able to consume
> not only the foliage but also the fruit and seeds of the forest. Fruit and
> seeds have high food value, and arboreal animals obtained access to food
> resources of quite a different order of richness from those available to the
> grazing animals of the plains (Campbell 1974:206).

Color vision helped the primates identify fruits and seeds.

By taking to the trees, the primates were able to escape from the competition of terrestrial rodents, carnivores, and other rival species. The trees provided a refuge area rich in stimulating challenges for the inquisitive, exploratory primates.

Although most primates are quadrupedal, they are capable of sitting or standing in an upright position. When climbing, their bodies are vertical. Their forelimbs and hindlimbs have become differentiated, with the forelimbs being used for exploration and the lower limbs for support. Monkeys pick up objects with their hands and examine them. They also feed themselves with their hands, unlike long-snouted terrestrial animals that have to close in on food with their large jaws. Primates have flatter faces than such animals.

Primates usually bear only one offspring at a time, and the females usually have only one pair of breasts, although there are some exceptions among the lower primates.

The order of Primates is subdivided into two suborders: the Prosimii, or prosimians, and the Anthropoidea. The Prosimii include the lower primates, such as the lemurs and the tarsiers. The tree shrews, which are sometimes included in this group, represent a form transitional with the Insectivora.

**The lower
primates**

The tree shrews, or *Tupaia*, are classified by some authorities as Primates and grouped by others with the Insectivora. In either case they deserve some discussion, since they seem to be close to the ancestral form of the Primate order. Tree shrews are not really shrews and do not spend much of their time in trees. They are small, omnivorous animals with long, moist muzzles, found in India, Malaya, Indonesia, and the Philippines. They have claws, rather than nails, on their digits, which are not truly opposable. Another feature that characterizes tree shrews is the presence of a sort of second tongue, consisting of cartilage, underneath the main tongue. Tree shrews may give birth to litters of from two to five young at a time, although sometimes only one offspring is born. They may have two or three pairs of mammary glands. Since the *Tupaia* have eyes set on either side of the snout, they do not have the stereoscopic vision characteristic of most primates, whose eyes are both on the frontal plane.

If the *Tupaia* are not considered to be in the Primate order, then the lemurs must be regarded as the most primitive primates. They have rather

White lemur or sifaka of
Madagascar.

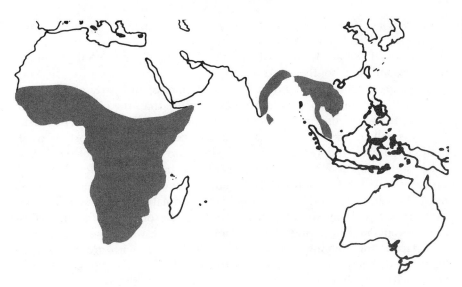

Distribution of modern lorises.

long snouts, heavy coats of fur, and bushy tails. Like the tree shrews, lemurs may give birth to two or three offspring at a time and have an extra pair of breasts to accommodate them. They have a second cartilaginous tongue, like that of the *Tupaia*, which is used along with their lower front teeth as a comb in currying fur.

Tarsier.

Lemurs are found only on the island of Madagascar. Lorises, which are nocturnal and have large eyes, have many features in common with the lemurs. They are found in tropical Africa south of the Sahara and in parts of south and southeast Asia.

The tarsier, which is found in Borneo, Sumatra, and parts of Indonesia and the Philippines, is a more advanced creature than the other prosimians and has many features in common with the higher primates. The tarsier is very small in size. It has a large head and brain in proportion to its body, large ears, and very large eyes, which are set close together so that it has stereoscopic vision. In that respect, the tarsier resembles the higher primates but does not have color vision as they do. Nor does the tarsier need it, being nocturnal. Like the higher primates, the tarsier has eyes that are set in bony sockets, in contrast to the other prosimians whose eyes are enclosed by a ring of bone lacking a back wall. The tarsier's feet are adapted for hopping and leaping, which it does with great speed. Its legs are extremely long in proportion to its body. It is the elongated tarsial bone, with which it leaps so well, that has given the tarsier its name. Insects form the tarsier's main diet, but it also eats tree frogs, snails, and other small animals.

Early Prosimii and Anthropoidea

The earliest primates we know anything about were small prosimians resembling modern tree shrews or lemurs, dating back to the Paleocene epoch, about 60 million years ago. Lemurs and tarsiers of various kinds had become abundant by the Eocene epoch, about 57 million years ago, when they spread across North America and parts of Eurasia. Then their numbers declined. They continued to exist in parts of the Old World, but by the end of the Eocene they appear to have become extinct in Europe and North America, where their once-abundant fossil record comes to an end. This debacle may have been due to the development of competing mammals, such as rodents and carnivores, and in the Old World to the appearance of higher primates that had evolved from prosimian forms. Increasingly colder weather conditions may also have played a role. Whatever the reasons, the range of prosimians contracted. Although more than 20 different fossil types of Eocene tarsioids have been identified, there is now only one living genus, *Tarsius*, with three living species.

From an analysis of fossil prosimian skeletal material, it has been deduced that these animals engaged in the same sort of vertical clinging and leaping as do present-day prosimians. They are judged to have been largely insectivorous. All of these prosimians were small.

It is often characteristic of successfully adapting animal forms to increase in size in the course of evolution, and this is what happened to the primates. The Anthropoidea, or higher primates that evolved from prosimian forms, tended to be larger. Increased body size brings various benefits. One is greater longevity, with an extension of various life periods, including gestation and juvenile dependency. Other benefits involve larger brains and greater body strength. But increased size also may become a problem in an arboreal habitat, particularly in the small outer branches bearing fruits and leaves. A successful adjustment in the Anthropoidea was an increased prehensile ability in the hands and a replacement of claws by nails. In present-day tree shrews all the digits have claws, but that is not true for most of the Anthropoidea.

The higher primates

The Primate suborder to which we belong is the Anthropoidea, which also includes the Old World and New World monkeys and the apes. Members of this suborder have eyes set in the frontal plane, so they have stereoscopic vision. Both eyes can focus on the same object in front of the face, and since each eye sees it from a slightly different angle, there is a heightened sense of depth. Moreover, members of the Anthropoidea have color vision. In this respect, they differ from some of the lower primates. Stereoscopic and color vision used to be considered traits that distinguished the Anthropoidea as a group from the prosimians, but it is now recognized that many prosimians have these features. John Buettner-Janusch has written, "The prosimians are usually listed as not possessing either color or stereoscopic vision. The latter is very obviously present in most of the diurnal genera, and the former probably is also. There is no conclusive evidence that color vision is not present" (Buettner-Janusch 1966:330).

Color vision has been found in some fishes, insects, and birds but not in most mammals. The higher primates have the best-developed color vision in this class of vertebrates. Among the Anthropoidea, there is a back wall to the eye socket. Brains are larger and more highly developed than those of the Prosimii, with the occipital lobes overhanging the cerebellum. There is only one pair of breasts, set high up on the chest.

The Anthropoidea may be divided into three superfamilies: Ceboidea (New World monkeys), Cercopithecoidea (Old World monkeys), and Hominoidea (apes and humans).

The New World monkeys

The Ceboidea, or New World monkeys, which are found in Central and South America, evolved from a prosimian base in the New World. They have nostrils separated by a broad nasal septum. Some of these primates, including the howler and spider monkeys, have prehensile tails. They can wrap the tail around a branch and hang from it. None of the Old World monkeys have developed this feature, which is found, however, among some other orders of mammals. Spider monkeys *brachiate*, swing from limb to limb with their arms, a technique that also was developed

Spider monkey, showing use of prehensile tail.

by some of the apes in the Old World. The spider monkey has many resemblances to the gibbon, the expert brachiator of the Old World. These similarities are due to parallel evolution, or the development of similar traits by different species, another example of which is the appearance of stereoscopic and color vision in both the New World and Old World primates.

The New World primates have a different dental formula from that of the Old World monkeys, apes, and humans. Among the latter, the characteristic dental formula is

$$I\frac{2}{2}\,C\frac{1}{1}\,P\frac{2}{2}\,M\frac{3}{3}\times 2 = 32.$$

This means that, in the jaws of either side, above and below, one will find two incisor teeth, one canine, two premolars, and three molars. Among lemurs and New World monkeys there are three premolars instead of two.

The Old World monkeys

The Cercopithecoidea, or Old World monkeys, have a two-disk placenta, in contrast to the apes and humans, who have a single disk. A notable feature of the Old World monkeys is the presence of *ischial callosities*—bare patches of calloused skin on the buttocks. These are thought to provide some protection for the monkeys when they spend the night sleeping in a sitting position in the fork of a tree. Old World monkeys may also have a sexual skin that sometimes becomes brilliantly colored. Some of these monkeys, like the baboons, have cheek pouches that can be stuffed with food to be subsequently digested.

The Old World monkeys are divided into two subfamilies having different types of digestive systems: the Colobinae (langur and colobus monkeys), who eat huge quantities of leaves and little else and can go for months without drinking water; and the Cercopithecinae, including all other Old World monkeys, such as baboons, macaques, and rhesus monkeys, who have a more varied diet. Since they are leaf eaters, the langur and colobus monkeys are more strictly arboreal than the baboons and macaques, who spend much of their time on the ground.

There are interesting differences in temperament between langur and rhesus monkeys and baboons. Phyllis Jay, an anthropologist who has made field studies of langurs in India, has described them as peaceful and relaxed. There is little fighting among them, and dominance hierarchies (see p. 96) are not so noticeable as among baboons. Rhesus monkeys engage in more fighting and squabbling and bear more scars than do langurs. Dominance-submission is more fully developed among baboons, but despite the aggressive character of male baboons, there is relatively little ingroup aggression. Their aggressive character, together with the males' long, sharp canines, serves to defend the group from the attacks of predators. The more arboreal langurs save themselves by individual escape to the treetops.

In contrast to the leaf-eating langurs, ground-dwelling baboons have a varied diet consisting of many kinds of vegetable foods, seeds, flowers, grasses, leaves, roots, and bulbs; but they also eat insects, scorpions, and lizards. Baboons that live along the seacoast consume mussels, crabs, and limpets. Inland baboons in Kenya have been known to sometimes catch and eat hares, birds, small gazelles, and vervet monkeys. Such carnivorous behavior is rare, however. It is always an individual activity, not a group enterprise, and it seems to be more common in some baboon groups than in others. Predation of this sort appears to be more common in the rainy season, when many animal species drop their young.

Most monkeys, both Old and New World, have an essentially quadrupedal manner of locomotion, making their ways along the tops of branches or on the ground. They have long, narrow trunks like those of dogs and cats.

There are about 150 species of monkeys in the world, as compared with only one species of *Homo sapiens*. And monkeys are very numerous, outnumbering human beings in many parts of the world. Some monkeys, such as vervets, have a population density that man came to equal only after he had acquired a knowledge of agriculture. The apes, who are more

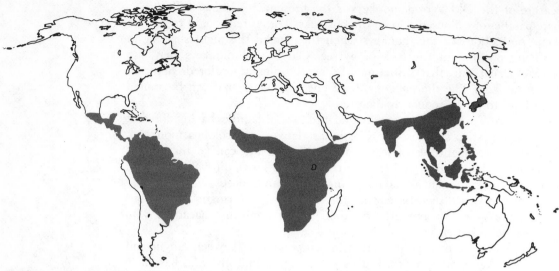

Distribution of modern Old and New World monkeys.

closely related to us, have not been so successful, and their numbers are dwindling.

The great variation among monkey species is best explained by their adaptations to different environments. Arboreal monkeys tend to be divided into more species than terrestrial ones. Ground-dwelling baboons and macaques show less variation. These monkeys are found in large numbers over enormous tracts of territory in Africa and Asia.

The Hominoidea

The superfamily within the Anthropoidea to which we belong is that of the Hominoidea. Its other members are the apes, who differ from the monkeys in lacking external tails and cheek pouches. They usually do not have ischial callosites, although gibbons have them, and they are sometimes found in orangutans, chimpanzees, and gorillas. The last three apes all build nests to sleep in at night, and there may be a connection between this pattern of behavior and the disappearance of the horny seat pads. The apes all have long arms and relatively short legs. The apes do not have erect posture as we do, except for brief periods. When they stand supported by arms and legs, the spine is not parallel to the ground as in regularly quadrupedal animals, since their arms are longer than their legs. This gives them a semi-erect posture. When a chimpanzee or gorilla is in motion, its long arms serve to bear its weight, a method of locomotion known as "knuckle-walking." In keeping with this semi-erect posture, the

Lowland gorilla in knuckle-walking position.

pelvis of apes is broader and more basin shaped than those of monkeys and more like that of humans.

The apes are divided into two subfamilies: the Hylobatinae, or lesser apes, which includes the gibbons, and siamangs; and the Ponginae, or great apes, which includes the orangutan, the chimpanzee, and the gorilla.

Gibbon

The gibbons range from the eastern Himalayas to Hainan, Borneo, and Java. They are the smallest, lightest, and most acrobatic of the apes, with very long arms adapted to brachiation. The Hylobatinae all have long narrow hands and fingers, to hook onto branches; and their thumbs are rather stunted. Gibbons have relatively longer legs than the other apes and can walk and run with agility on the ground while holding up their long arms for balance. Gibbons are very vocal and make a lot of noise. In this respect and in their walking ability, the gibbons seem quite human, but in other ways they are less like us than the other apes. What has been said about the gibbons applies as well to the concolors and siamangs. All have heavy coats of fur, unlike the coarse hair of the other apes.

Gibbon.

Orangutan

The orangutan is also a Southeast Asiatic ape, now found only in Borneo and Sumatra. He weighs as much as a man but is only about 4 feet tall. (Males are twice as big as females). The orangutan's arms are very long and his legs short. He has a barrel chest and a large abdomen. With a body built like this, it is not surprising that orangutans are rather sluggish, slow-moving creatures, lacking the grace and elan of the gibbons. The orangutan has a rather high, domed forehead with less of a brow ridge than any other ape. Adult males have cheek pads, not found in other apes, and they have air sacs in the throat that are more prominent than those of the other Ponginae. Orangutans hang by their feet a good deal. They lack a ligament, found in other Hominoidea, that holds the thighbone in its hip socket. This gives the leg more mobility. Orangutans are not built to walk with an upright posture.

More humanlike than the Southeast Asiatic apes are the African apes—the chimpanzee and the gorilla. Both spend a good deal of time on the ground, especially the gorilla, and both can walk erect for short distances.

Chimpanzee

In contrast to the quiet, sluggish orangutan, chimpanzees are noisy, sociable, and boisterous. Psychologists have worked more with chimps than

Orangutan.

with the other apes, not because the chimps are more intelligent (which remains to be determined) but because they can be friendly and cooperative. Chimpanzees have been taught to do a variety of things—riding bicycles, opening beer cans, getting water from the tap or food from the refrigerator. Some have learned to work for rewards, earning slugs that must be taken to a slot machine and inserted to get raisins. Some can use keys to open locks. At least one chimp has been taught to hammer nails and use a screwdriver both to insert and extract screws.

This ability with tools has its foreshadowings in the wild state. Jane van Lawick-Goodall, who studied free-ranging chimpanzees in Tanzania, East Africa, over a period of four years, has observed chimpanzees poking sticks into ant and termite nests. When they pull them out, the sticks are covered with termites, which the chimps lick off and eat. The stick

A chimpanzee eating a
monkey.

has to be the right length and shape. If it is too long, the chimpanzee
breaks off part of it. If there are leaves on the stick, he strips them off.
One chimp was seen to carry a stick for half a mile to where some termite
nests were located. Chimpanzees also use leaves as a sponge to soak up
water for drinking and show their young how to do it. Gorillas have not
been seen to use tools in this way. Nor is there any evidence that gorillas
eat meat in the wild state. Chimpanzees, however, sometimes eat meat,
although fruit constitutes their main diet. They have been known to eat
colobus monkeys, juvenile baboons, bush pigs, small antelopes, and infant
chimpanzees.

   Their most common prey seems to be baboons, probably because these
two species are so often together in the same environment. Chimpanzee
hunting behavior is mainly an adult activity and almost exclusively male.
This hunting is sometimes coordinated. Geza Teleki once saw five males
working together to surround three baboons which had taken shelter in
trees (Teleki 1975:92–93). When a chimpanzee has made a kill, other
chimps may move in to eat the carcass, and there seems to be little squabbling over the meat, although Teleki states that he never saw an ape yield
the brain or any part of it to another. Both Teleki and Adriaan Kortlandt
have described the "requesting" behavior of chimpanzees who hold out

hands as if begging for a handout. Of 395 requests observed by Teleki, 114 were rewarded. "In the total of 43 hours of meat-sharing that I observed not once did two chimpanzees fight over possession of meat" (Teleki 1975:100).

Gorilla

The gorillas are the largest and strongest of the apes. In the wild state, adult males weigh between 300 and 450 pounds, while adult females weigh between 150 and 250 pounds. They weigh much more in zoos, where they have nothing to do but sit around and eat and therefore sometimes attain weights of 500 or 600 pounds. Gorillas have powerful, long arms and barrel chests, which they beat with their hands to frighten intruders. Their hands and feet are quite humanlike, although the fingers and toes are webbed nearly to the first joint. The foot has something of a heel bone. Another humanlike feature is the presence of mastoid processes at the base of the skull. The adult male gorilla has massive brow ridges and crests on the top and sides of his skull; these sagittal crests serve to anchor his heavy chewing muscles. Gorillas have large interlocking canine teeth. They live on vegetable food, and eat for six to eight hours a day. Although gorillas do not eat meat in the wild, they have sometimes become accustomed to eating it in captivity.

Let us now consider how human beings differ from the apes and other primates. The most important distinguishing features of *Homo sapiens* are upright posture, highly developed central nervous system, and large brain. The human brain is more than twice as large as that of the gorilla, who has the next largest brain among the primates. Compared with the brains of most primates, which have a small size, the human brain is enormous. But this is a relatively recent development in evolution, preceded by the assumption of upright posture. We infer this because the brains of the australopithecines, who had bipedal locomotion, were little larger than those of apes.

As mentioned in Chapter 2, the evolution of the human brain has involved not only an increase in size but also an enlargement of parietal and temporal cortex. Moreover, humans seem to differ from other primates, indeed from other mammals in general, in that learned behavior is considerably controlled by one half of the brain. The primary language areas of the brain are thought to be located in the left hemisphere (Geschwind 1972).

Several of the distinctions between man and other primates have to do with the assumption of upright posture. For example, in the lumbar region in *Homo sapiens*, there is a curvature of the spine that is not found among other primates. A human being has an S-shaped spinal column

Distinctive traits of *Homo sapiens*

Side and front views of human skull.

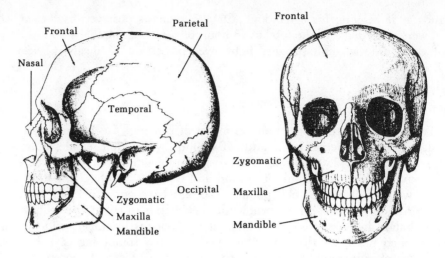

adapted to upright posture, while other primates have a more bow-shaped spine. The human pelvis has *ilia* (blades), which are much shorter than those of the larger apes and have been bent backward in the course of time. The pelvis is broad and basin shaped, particularly in females. The *gluteus maximus* muscles of the hip are well developed. Like apes, but unlike the monkeys, we lack external tails and have no ischial callosities. In contrast to the apes, our straight and heavily muscled legs are much longer than our arms. Humans are walkers, not brachiators.

Human feet show a number of specializations resulting from their functions of support and bipedal locomotion. The foot is arched from front to back and from side to side and is equipped with a heel. The big toe is not set apart from the other toes, like a thumb, but is lined up with the others, and it is not opposable.

The human face also shows some modifications from an earlier form. *Homo sapiens* does not have heavy brow ridges and crests on the skull as some of the apes do. Humans have a bony nose bridge with an extension of cartilage, which gives a more prominent nose than other primates (except for the proboscis monkey). Beneath the nose there is a groove in the upper lip called the *philtrum*, which is peculiar to humans. On either side of the nose, below the eye sockets, is a depression known as the *canine fossa*. The human face is relatively lacking in *prognathism*, or facial protrusion.

The mouth and jaws of humans have various distinctive characteristics. Our lips are outrolled, with the membranous red portion showing, in contrast to the thin lips of other primates in which the membranous portion is not easily seen. Modern humans have a chin that juts forward, in contrast to the sloping jaw of the ape. There is no simian shelf (a bar of bone that binds together the lower jawbones of apes). The canine teeth do not interlock, so there is no *diastema*, or gap in the upper row of teeth

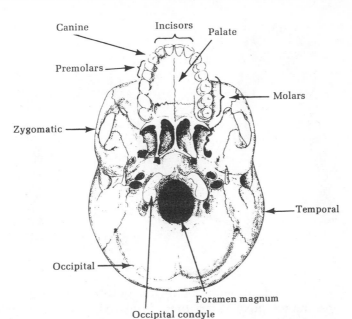

Canine

Incisors

Palate

Premolars

Molars

Zygomatic

Temporal

Occipital

Foramen magnum

Occipital condyle

Base of human skull.

to receive the lower canine. The jaws flare out and are parabolic, in contrast to the long, narrow, U-shaped jaws of the apes.

At the bottom of the skull there is a large hole called the *foramen magnum*, through which the spinal cord connects with the brain. This is located at the rear of the skull in quadrupedal animals. At birth it is in the center of the base of the skull in all primates, but ends up being further back in the course of growth. In humans, however, the *foramen magnum* remains in the center of the base of the skull, for the skull is balanced on the spinal column. Since it is balanced in this way, we do not need a lot of neck muscles, like those of the gorilla. Our necks are longer than those of the apes.

The human body is relatively hairless, in comparison with the bodies of other primates, although there are some hairy individuals. But we usually have a lot of hair on our heads. (Again, there are exceptions.) These human patterns are particularly manifest in women, whose head hair is particularly abundant while their body hair is scanty. The form of human hair shows some specializations; kinky or tightly curled hair is not found among the other primates.

Humans differ from other primates in the appearance of the genitalia and in sexual behavior. The human male has no penis bone. Prosimians, most monkeys and apes, and most carnivorous mammals have a cartilaginous or bony element in the penis. The human male has the largest penis in length and thickness of any primate.

Sexual receptivity in female monkeys and apes is often restricted to a

Chimpanzee and human
lower jaws seen from
above.

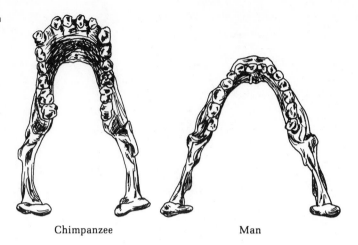

Chimpanzee   Man

week, or a little more, of their monthly cycle, while the human female
may be receptive at any time. Moreover, coitus lasts much longer among
humans than among other primates. Among most nonhuman primates,
the sexual act is over in about 15 seconds. Human females are unique
among primates in their ability to experience orgasm.

The assumption of upright posture and the forward shift of the female
genital organs has made it possible for human beings to copulate ventrally,
unlike most other animals. A survey in our society has shown that 70
percent of the people follow only this frontal approach in sexual relations,
and a cross-cultural survey of nearly 200 societies in different parts of the
world has shown that the dorsal approach is not the usual one in any of
these societies. There has been some speculation to the effect that the
development of the frontal approach has led to a more personal relationship
between the sex partners, involving more courtship and sex play than among
other primates.[2] Also, uniquely among mammals, human females may experience intense pain during childbirth, another consequence of the assumption of upright posture.

One final point of difference between humans and the other primates:
We mature more slowly than do the other primates, making necessary a
longer period of dependency in childhood. This also makes possible a much
longer period of learning, which is important in the transmission of culture
from one generation to the next. The acquisition of culture is the crucial
distinction between humans and the other primates, more important than
the morphological differences between ourselves and the apes. But morphological features such as the greater size and complexity of the human brain

---

[2] On these matters, see Morris 1967; chap. 2; Harrison and Montagna 1969; chap. 10. See also
Hockett and Ascher 1964:142; La Barre, *Comments*, ibid.:149. For a comparative study of sexual
behavior, see Ford and Beach 1951.

and the development of upright posture made possible the acquisition of culture. Through culture human beings came to occupy a new ecological niche and a partially artificial environment of their own making. Through their acquisition of language, human beings became "time-binding" creatures; speech made it possible for them to talk about things that happened in the past and to make plans for the future. Human beings use tools. Chimpanzees also use tools to some extent; but humans reached a point in their development when culture and tool-use became necessary for the continuation of life, which is not the case with any other primate (Mann 1972).

In reviewing the distinctive traits of *Homo sapiens*, the ways in which we differ physically from other primates, it will be seen that many of these features, such as the lumbar curve, the characteristics of the pelvis, the long legs, and the specialization of the feet, represent adaptations to upright posture and bipedalism. Some of the differences are matters of degree—larger brains, less body hair. Some of the features mentioned have been acquired rather recently by *Homo sapiens* and were not characteristic of early hominids such as the australopithecines, Java man, and Peking man, who did not have chins or high nose bridges.

The differences that separate us from the pongids are not numerous. The striking thing, perhaps, is the extent of the resemblance between the apes and ourselves. This resemblance extends to matters of body chemistry. A number of biochemical studies show that *Homo sapiens* has more in common with the apes than *Homo sapiens* has with other primates. This is true of such features of the blood as purine metabolism, MN blood groups, and gamma globulin. The ABO blood groups are found in the Old World monkeys and the apes, as well as in *Homo sapiens*. The albumins of chimpanzee, gorilla, and humans are closely similar. Apes and human beings suffer from some of the same diseases, with similar symptoms, and they harbor some of the same parasites.

The extent of the similarities between apes and ourselves suggests that we share a common ancestry with them. This is what most anthropologists and zoologists believe, but William L. Straus, Jr. (1962) has argued that the human race stems from a generalized catarrhine primate, not an ape. Straus is struck by the fact that *Homo sapiens* is in many ways more "primitive" and unspecialized than the apes. But if we are descended from a generalized catarrhine, how can we explain the numerous similarities between the apes and humans mentioned above? Straus attributes these similarities to parallel evolution rather than to common descent, but in the majority view this solution is unacceptable. One reason is that there are so many similarities between human beings and apes in biochemical features and molecular biology, particularly between humans and the African apes. Strands of chimpanzee DNA may be fitted to human DNA strands in the laboratory with only a 2.5 percent difference in fit, but monkey DNA shows a difference of 10 percent. Comparisons of hemoglobin chains in humans and other primates demonstrate that humans and chimpanzees have no differences at all, whereas gorillas have 2 differences and monkeys 12 differences from humans. There is similar evidence of the close relationship between humans and apes, particularly the chimpanzee, in the formation of antibodies and in aspects of albumin and transferrin (Washburn and Moore 1974:3–29).

Although chimpanzees have one more pair of chromosomes than humans, their chromosomes are very similar to ours except for one pair. The chromosomes of the Asian apes are not as similar to the human ones as are those of the African apes. A suggestion has been made that our closest anthropoid relative is the pygmy chimpanzee. Adrienne L. Zihlman et al. (1978) argue that the pygmy chimpanzee *(Pan paniscus)* represents the best prototype among living species for the common ancestor of humans, chimpanzees, and gorillas. Gorillas are much larger and have a more specialized diet and restricted habitat. Pygmy chimps are more generalized in body size, build, and sexual dimorphism than the common species of chimpanzee; they have smaller facial and canine dimensions, and their upper and lower limbs are of about equal length in contrast to the longer arms of the common chimpanzee. In captivity pygmy chimps walk bipedally more than do the common chimpanzees. Moreover, pygmy chimpanzees are similar in body size and in cranial features to *Australopithecus*, the first well-represented and widely distributed hominids.[3] On the other hand, studies on ape chromosomes by Dorothy A. Miller (1977) suggest that the gorilla may be more closely related to human beings than the chimpanzees.

Similarities and differences in DNA, proteins, and other factors have provided the basis for a "molecular clock" devised by Vincent Sarich and his colleagues to estimate the time when the divergence between apes and hominids took place. This is discussed on page 114.

Summary

Proceeding from broader to narrower classifications, human beings are vertebrates, eutherian mammals, and primates; we belong to the suborder Anthropoidea, the superfamily Hominoidea (along with the apes), and the family Hominidae, genus *Homo*, and species *sapiens*. As vertebrates we are bilaterally symmetrical animals with segmented backbones and brains enclosed in a skull. By virtue of being eutherian mammals we are warm blooded, maintain a constant high body temperature, and spend considerable time in the mother's body before birth, receiving nourishment from a placenta. Along with the other primates we have prehensile five-digited hands with opposable thumbs, and like other members of the Anthropoidea we have eyes on the frontal plane, with stereoscopic and color vision.

Human beings differ from the other primates mainly in having upright posture, a larger brain, and a more highly developed central nervous system.

---

[3] For a debate on these issues, see Johnson 1981.

Various anatomical features are related to the assumption of upright posture, such as a lumbar curve in the spine, a broad basin-shaped pelvis, and feet which have arches and a heel.

Human beings mature more slowly than do other primates, which results in a longer period of dependency in childhood. This also facilitates learning and the acquisition of culture, the crucial distinction between human beings and the apes, our closest relatives, who otherwise resemble us in many details of biochemistry and molecular biology.

Suggestions for further reading

One well-illustrated general discussion of the primates is Sarel Eimerl and Irven De Vore, *The Primates* (New York: Life Nature Library, 1965). See also George Schaller, *The Mountain Gorilla: Ecology and Behavior* (Chicago: University of Chicago Press, 1963); Adriaan Kortlandt, "Chimpanzees in the Wild," *Scientific American* 206 (1962): 128–38. For Jane van Lawick-Goodall's data on chimpanzee tool-using in the wild, see Jane Goodall, "Chimpanzees of the Gombe Stream Reserve," in *Primate Behavior: Field Studies of Monkeys and Apes*, ed. Irven De Vore (New York: Holt, Rinehart & Winston, 1965), pp. 425–73. See also Jane van Lawick-Goodall, *In the Shadow of Man* (Boston: Houghton Mifflin, 1971). For the food habits of chimpanzees and baboons, see Geza Teleki, "The Omnivorous Chimpanzee," in *Biological Anthropology*, ed. Solomon H. Katz (San Francisco: W. H. Freeman, 1975), pp. 91–102.

On human anatomy and physiology, see Richard J. Harrison and William Montagna, *Man* (New York: Appleton-Century-Crofts, 1969).

For a well-executed blend of lyricism and science concerning evolution, see Loren Eiseley, *The Immense Journey* (New York: Random House, Modern Library, 1957).

CHAPTER 5

The social life of primates

It is important to note that, with the exception of some prosimian species, the primates are social animals that live in groups the year round. This is not true of all animals. Among the lower vertebrates, which lay eggs, there may be no continuing tie between mother and offspring. This is not the case among birds, which nest and feed their young, but reptiles, after laying their eggs, usually go off and forget about them. The baby reptile that survives steps out of the shell into a world that has no family structure. A baby primate, however, whether a lemur, a baboon, or a human being, is born into a social world.

It must be kept in mind that primates are mammals. The mammalian pattern of suckling provides for a continuing tie between mother and offspring. While this is true of all mammals, the mother-child relationship is stronger and longer lasting among primates than it is among most of the others. This is because the complex nervous system and brain development of primates requires a longer time to become coordinated. Although the gestation period is longer among more advanced mammals, the young are born in a relatively helpless condition, which increases their dependence upon the mother. There is a great contrast in this respect between primates and ungulates. On the day of birth a baby deer or antelope can walk about; within a week it can run with great speed. It thus becomes self-sufficient much more quickly than a baby primate. Rodents and carnivores are more helpless at birth than ungulates, but rats and rabbits reach maturity at five or six months and can shift for themselves after a month or so.

Mother-child relations

Hamadryas baboon
group.

Baby primates, on the other hand, cling to the mother's body for the
first weeks or months of life. Gibbon babies do so for about seven months.

The interaction between mother and child is not only determined by
the helplessness of the child but also, apparently, by the maternal attitude
of the mother.

When a baby langur is born, it is soon surrounded by subadult and
adult females who make efforts to hold and inspect the newcomer. One
of them may take the infant and move away with it.

> When the newborn starts to whine another adult female reaches out and
> takes the young one. In this manner it may pass from female to female,
> until as many as four females have held it, before the real mother comes
> and takes it back. During the time the infant is being carried and inspected
> the mother keeps constant and close watch on it, although she may remain
> at a distance of from 30 to 40 feet. Should the newborn whine loudly, the
> mother will quickly retrieve it (Jay 1963:117–18).

Primate females are not always so "maternal" in their behavior. There
are differences in maternal behavior in different species. Howler monkey
mothers are said to be relatively indifferent to their offspring. Baboon and
macaque mothers will not allow other females to take their offspring away
from them during the first month after birth, as the langurs do. Chimpanzee

mothers seem to be guilty of maternal overprotection, carrying their children about until they are around four years old and seldom leaving them out of sight.

Male-female relations

Primate social groups contain adult males who remain with the females and offspring the year round. Again, this is not true of all mammals. Among many mammals, the males remain with the females only during a rutting or mating season. Among most of the higher primates, there is no special mating season; females are sexually receptive throughout the year, and pregnancies may occur at any time. But some monkeys do have restricted mating seasons. Among some Japanese macaques, for example, mating is limited to the winter months, particularly January and February, and over 90 percent of the births occur from May to September. Rhesus monkeys, isolated on the Caribbean island of Cayo Santiago, do not copulate from February to June. During this period, the males undergo testis regression and a cessation of spermatogenesis.

Among monkey groups that have special breeding seasons, the males continue to remain with the females throughout the year. It cannot be sexual attraction that keeps the primate males together with the females in this way. Another function of the continuing social bond is the protection afforded by the social group. There is safety in numbers. Monkeys that stay within a group are more likely to survive. Loners may be picked off by predators. Thus, natural selection must have favored a genetic capacity for group life.

Adult male-young relations

Adult males in most primate groups are either tolerant or helpful in their attitudes toward the young. In many species, especially the more terrestrial ones, protective behavior has been reported, and there have been many observations of adult males rescuing or carrying away young animals from danger. Adult male baboons sometimes seem to supervise juvenile play groups and to intervene if the fighting gets too rough. The arboreal langurs are somewhat different in these respects; the males are more aloof and disinterested in the young. Their protective function is not so vital as it is for the ground-dwelling baboons.

Young peer relations

Among the Japanese macaques and similar monkeys whose offspring tend to be born within a particular season of the year, there are "age sets"; that is to say, there will be many infants of the same age. As they become older, the juveniles form play groups, chase each other, wrestle, and engage in vigorous play. This is also done among primates that have no breeding seasons. Some juveniles of similar age range are generally available to form play groups of this sort. As the young primate gradually lessens its dependence upon the mother, he spends more and more time with his peers. This shift may be accelerated by the weaning process and maternal rebuffs, particularly after the birth of a younger sibling. But the shift to the play group seems to be a natural transition. In play groups among macaques and baboons there are usually more males than females, and the juvenile females often remain with the adult females. Through active play with others, the juvenile not only acquires physical skills but also learns to interact with others. In groups where dominant-submissive relations are important, the relative status of individuals may be worked out in the course of rough-and-tumble play.

Variations in composition of primate social groups

We find, then, that most primates live in social groups containing males, females, and offspring. The size and composition of such groups, however, vary a great deal. In a general way, there has been an increase in group size from prosimian to more advanced forms. Insectivorous, nocturnal forest primates are sometimes solitary or have small family units consisting of a male, female, and offspring. Leaf-eating diurnal arboreal species tend to have slightly larger groups consisting of an adult male, often more than one female, and some immature males. In such groups there are apt to be small home ranges or defended territories, with spacing being effected by the practice of chorusing. A basically uni-male system of this sort may be transformed into an age-graded male system, which is found in both fruit-eating and leaf-eating arboreal primates. In such a system there is still a leading adult male with no other fully adult males of equivalent age. Terrestrial primates that occupy forest fringes and savannas tend to have fairly large multi-male groups which contain several adult males. The age-graded male troop may be seen as intermediate between the uni-male and multi-male structures. It is apt to have proportionately fewer males than the multi-male troop (Eisenberg, Muckenhirn, and Rudran 1972; Crook and Gartlan 1966).

The males in terrestrial species may be much larger and stronger than the females and often assume protective functions against predators. Savanna baboon troops commonly number between 30 and 50 individuals, with 5 to 10 adult males and 10 to 20 adult females.

There are often exceptions to such generalizations about relationships between group size and particular environments. For example, terrestrial patas monkeys have small social units, while drills inhabiting forests have been seen in groups numbering more than 100 (Kummer 1971:55).

There is much variation in social organization among the apes. Gibbons live in small, monogamous family groups consisting of a male, female, and offspring. The monogamous nature of the gibbon family is perpetuated by the aggressive behavior of the male when another male approaches the group, or by that of the female when another female approaches. Moreover, as offspring mature, they leave the family unit.

Orangutans are relatively asocial. They rarely form groups of more than three or four. Sometimes lone adult males are encountered in the jungle; they often leave the female and offspring and wander off by themselves. As among the gibbons, then, the social units are small. In this respect the Asiatic apes contrast with those of Africa.

Gorilla groups vary from 2 to 30 members, with an average of 6 to 17. Their social groups are more compact and consistent than those of chimpanzees. A dominant male usually determines the movements of the group, leading the way. According to George Schaller (1963), who made a two-year study of mountain gorillas in eastern Congo and western Uganda, gorillas are normally quiet and make few vocalizations, in contrast to the noisy gibbons and chimpanzees. In temperament these large apes are described as calm, independent, and aloof.

The social life of chimpanzees is complex and variable. The composition of groups frequently changes. Some bands consist of mothers and young, some have adults of both sexes with some adolescents, and others consist of adult males only. Such groups may merge, split, or regroup. Subgroups number between 2 and 30. Adult males seem to do more traveling than mothers with offspring, whose ranges are more restricted. Chimpanzee mothers are extremely solicitous of their young. According to Adriaan Kortlandt (1962), who studied chimpanzees in the Congo, they carry them around for the first four years of life. The young do not learn to be independent, although they show great curiosity about the environment. Indeed, Kortlandt considered them to be retarded in comparison to chimpanzees raised in captivity. Chimpanzees seem to respect the aged as well as showing solicitude for the young. Kortlandt describes an old chimp, which he judged to be over 40. Despite his infirmities, he was deferred to by stronger and healthier chimpanzees. Chimpanzees that inhabit the forest sometimes make a great deal of noise, hooting, screaming, and drumming on trees. This hullabaloo does not seem to function as a spacing mechanism, like the calls of howler monkeys. Instead, it may be a means of summoning other chimpanzees to an area where there are ripe fruit trees. This fluid kind of "open" society has not been found among monkeys.

Chimpanzees not only eat meat on occasion but have been seen to kill and eat young chimpanzees in their natural habitat. Jane Goodall and her colleagues in the Gombe Reserve saw five gang attacks by the males of one chimpanzee group on the males of another group that had splintered off. All seven of the males of the splinter group were eventually killed. Cannibalism was also seen. One female chimp and her daughter ate as many as 10 newborn (Goodall 1978, 1979).

The sex ratio varies in different primate species. In howler groups there are more than twice as many females as males. A predominance of females is quite common among primates, as is the case among humans, partly because the death rate is generally higher for males. The disparity is more striking in the older age brackets. There are other factors that help to account for the higher incidence of females in such species as the howler monkeys, macaques, and baboons. In these groups the males have a much slower rate of maturation, and some males may live for awhile outside the social group. Among Indian macaques, which have a large proportion of females, some males are expelled from the group and form "bachelor" bands on the fringes of the heterosexual group. Such bands include both adolescent young monkeys and old males which have lost their dominant status. Spider monkeys in South America also have small "bachelor" bands, numbering from 3 to 10 individuals. Multi-male groups are found among vervets, macaques, and most langurs, baboons, and South American monkeys. One-male groups with several females are found among patas, geladas, and guenons.

It is significant that there are not only contrasts in group size and composition in different species of primates but there may also be differences within a species among groups that have adapted to different environments. It was mentioned above that savanna baboon troops containing both adult males and females and offspring number between 30 and 50 individuals. In these groups the adult males have access to all the females. Such multi-male groups are stable social units. Forest groups of baboons are smaller; they are also more fluid, often changing in composition. Females and their offspring form the core of a group; males come and go. In dry areas of Somalia and Ethiopia, on the other hand, hamadryas baboons form groups in which one male dominates a small harem of females and their offspring, making sure that they all keep together. These one-male groups join large congregations of hamadryas baboons at night, when they sleep on the walls of cliffs. Each group goes off by itself the next day, and there is little interaction between the one-male bands.

Learned primate behavior

The occurrence of variation of social organization within a species shows that such organization is determined not only by genetic factors but also by the animals' responses to particular ecological conditions. Primates are animals that learn from one another and that may change their patterns of behavior in different settings. The long period of childhood dependence facilitates social learning among primates.

Reference was made earlier to the chimpanzee practice of poking sticks into termite nests and then licking them off. This is something young chimpanzees learn by watching and imitating older ones. The practice is not found in all chimpanzee groups.

Another example of learned behavior is the custom of washing sweet potatoes, which developed in a group of macaques living on an island off the coast of Kyushu, Japan. This began when a 16-month-old female washed a sweet potato in a brook to get rid of adhering sand. Other monkeys imitated her practice, and it caught on. After four years about half the macaques were doing it, and after nine years, 71 percent. Some monkeys began to carry their sweet potatoes to wash in the sea, rather than in the nearby brook, perhaps because of the salty taste. Wading into the sea and carrying their sweet potatoes, the monkeys assumed an erect posture, which they continued to carry on land more frequently than before. Here is a whole complex of learned behavior traits not shared by other monkeys of the same species.

It is interesting that new patterns of learned behavior like these often are initiated by the more plastic and playful youngsters and later taken up by older members of the group. It was adult females rather than males who imitated the innovative youngsters. Since the young ones feed together, they imitate one another. Females interact with the young and hence may pick up the new pattern, but the males feed separately from the females and young and do not learn the innovation.

If primates can learn so much, why don't they learn still more? For example, why have primates never learned to store food, which is done by many lower animals? Chimpanzees and gorillas build nests to sleep in, but not shelters. Despite the presence of learning ability, there are evidently limitations to it. For example, Jane van Lawick-Goodall observed baboons watching chimpanzees eat termites by poking sticks into termite nests and licking the sticks. Baboons also like to eat termites, but although they could see what the chimps were doing, they did not pick up the practice from them.

Habitat, food, and the social order

Now that we have seen that there may be variability of social organization within a primate species and that primates exhibit learned behavior and flexibility in adjusting to different environments, we can go on to inquire why one-male groups should be found among Ethiopian hamadryas baboons and multi-male groups on savannas. A British scientist, John H. Crook, found similar contrasts in different environments on the part of weaverbirds and antelopes, and he assumed that there must be some common ecological factors to account for similar adaptations made in different classes of animals. Crook concluded that when food is abundant in large patches, sociable feeding is possible—witness the herds of various grazing mammals in East Africa or the buffalo on the western plains of North America. But, when food is found in small scattered clumps, there is more likely to be individual or solitary feeding, as among many insectivorous birds and primates. In an arid environment like Ethiopia, food items would be dispersed. If there were large multi-male baboon troops in such a setting, the more dominant males would tend to appropriate food resources at the expense of the females. An advantage of a one-male group is that procreation is still assured, while male food exploitation is limited, thus allowing the females to survive, reproduce, and rear their offspring. This seems to be a reasonable solution to the problem, although other interpretations probably will be offered.

Dominance-submission

Different species of primates vary with regard to the degree of dominance and submission manifest within the group. Something like the pecking order of birds is found in many animal species. Dominant animals are those that display more aggression, win most of the fights, appropriate most of the food if there is a limited amount, and have priority in sexual relations. Dominant animals are the focus of attention of other members of the group. Where dominant-submissive polarities are found among primates, males are generally dominant over females, and some males are dominant over others.

The dominance of males over females is associated with sexual dimorphism, or the appearance of striking differences in size and strength between males and females. Sexual dimorphism is more marked among terrestrial primates like baboons and gorillas than among arboreal ones like the gibbon. In general, dominant-submissive patterns seem to be associated with terrestrial activity and the defensive functions of the males who, as among baboons and macaques, have developed an aggressive sort of temperament, which helps them to face predators in defense of the group.

The existence of dominant-submissive patterns does not mean that a lot of fighting is always going on among the adult males. On the contrary, fighting tends to be inhibited in such groups, since everyone's position in the hierarchy is relatively fixed and recognized. A threatened individual in a baboon troop may run toward a dominant male for help as a frightened baboon infant runs to its mother. Dominant male baboons will not let others fight and may dash to the scene of a quarrel to prevent it. There is not much fighting over food resources among baboons in the wild, since the troop is usually spread out over a fairly wide area with each individual seeking its own food.

Order of march in savanna baboons, with the dominant males, females, and infants occupying the center of the band and the young males the periphery.

Among monkey troops that move about, foraging as they go, there may be some structure to the group. At least this is the case among baboons and Japanese macaques. Dominant males and mothers and infants are usually found in the center of the band and young males on the peripheries. Dominance-submission patterns may therefore contribute to order and stability in the group.

Incidentally, the dominant females in a troop may confer their privileged status on their offspring, who stay with their mothers in the center of the group along with its other dominant members. The offspring of less-dominant females are more apt to be extruded to the periphery. To be sure, the privileged insiders have to maintain their status on their own merits, but they do have an initial advantage. At the same time, it has been noted in some baboon troops that peripheral young males are more demanding for attention from their less-dominant mothers and seem to be less "secure."

Baboon mothers give their infants a lot of attention during the first year but start to reject them during the second year, when they are no longer nursing. Although rejected by the mother, the young baboon is accepted by the older males, toward whom he now runs for protection when in danger.

We tend to think of monkey behavior as being largely instinctual. But it is important to remember that monkeys behave differently in different situational contexts. Indian rhesus monkeys who live in temple compounds display more aggression than those who live in the forest. Baboons studied in the London Zoo showed more aggression than those observed in the wild state. When C. R. Carpenter transported more than 100 rhesus mothers and infants from India to Puerto Rico, he found that the mothers, cramped in small cages and sparingly fed, fought their own offspring away from the food, and about nine mothers killed their infants. This sort of behavior would not be apt to occur under normal conditions.

What is still more striking is that a rhesus monkey who has been brought up in caged isolation from birth and later, after about a year and a half, introduced to the company of other members of its species, does not know how to interact with them. Mature male rhesus monkeys who have been socially deprived in this way cannot even perform the sexual act. Mature female rhesus monkeys who have been raised in isolation from birth and later impregnated by normal males do not behave in a maternal manner toward their offspring. Indeed, they are quite indifferent toward them, reject them, and often treat them with unfeeling cruelty.

These experiments suggest the enormous importance of adequate maternal care for the normal development of primates. Other such experiments, performed by Harry Harlow and his colleagues at the University of Wisconsin, suggest the equally great importance of peer relations. Infant monkeys

Significance of the social matrix

who have been deprived of their mothers but allowed to play with other young members of their species for 20 minutes a day seem to develop normally with regard to social and sexual interaction. These experiments show that sexual behavior, which we might have assumed to be instinctive among monkeys, depends upon the development of adequate patterns of social interaction with other members of the species.

Even when they are part of a social group, ape and monkey infants who have lost their mothers often fail to develop normally. The plight of such an infant is mitigated by the attentions of other adults. The passage about langur monkeys by Phyllis Jay quoted above shows how much interest other females take in a new baby. Primatologists refer to this as "aunt behavior" (without implying any blood relationship). Aunt behavior is most often exhibited by adolescent females who have not yet borne children. In handling an infant, an "aunt" learns maternal roles that prepare her for later motherhood, while the infant learns to adjust to other adults besides the mother.

An older female is thus likely to "adopt" a primate orphan. Jane van Lawick-Goodall (1971:226) gives an account of how one chimpanzee orphan, Merlin, was adopted by his older sister. "She waited for him when she went from place to place; she allowed him to share her nest at night; she groomed him as frequently as his mother would have done." But, despite his sister's care, Merlin became listless and emaciated and played less frequently with other youngsters. Jane van Lawick-Goodall watched him develop over a period of years and noted that he often showed disturbed behavior, becoming more abnormal in his sixth year, when he would sit hunched up with his arms around his knees, rocking from side to side. Jane van Lawick-Goodall watched the progress of a few other chimpanzee orphans and noted frequent signs of depression and other indications of disturbance among them, despite the fact that they were all looked after by one or more adults.

Temperament, instinct, and behavior

Some observers have commented on differences in the characteristic temperaments found in different primate species: the phlegmatic gorilla, the lively chimpanzee, the aggressive male savanna baboon. John O. Ellefson (1968:137) has suggested that: "The modal or normative personalities of species have adaptive significance; that is, norms of personality are the result of an adaptive process, an interplay between natural selection and the genetic variation intrinsic to sexual reproduction and mutation through time in populations." Thus, the aggressive temperament of male savanna baboons may have developed as an adaptive response to a terrestrial environment in which there are many predators.

This raises the question of what sort of temperamental traits were fostered in the course of *human* evolution. A number of writers have claimed that human beings are particularly aggressive animals and that this aggressiveness is related to the adoption of hunting and a carnivorous diet on the part of our ancestors and also due to a human territorial instinct—the urge to defend a particular range of territory against intruders. The writings of Konrad Lorenz, Robert Ardrey, Desmond Morris, Robin Fox, and Lionel Tiger, as well as other writers along these lines, have become popular during the past decade. In rebuttal against this school of thought there have also appeared some books and articles, by writers such as Ashley Montagu, Alexander Alland, and others, attacking these assumptions. (See Suggestions for Further Reading at the end of this chapter.)

The idea that man is basically a nasty, aggressive creature is at least as old as the doctrine of Original Sin. It was expressed by the 17th century philosopher Thomas Hobbes and more recently by Sigmund Freud, among others. It is, therefore, a view of man that many people have been ready to accept. It is admittedly one way of making sense out of today's headlines and the long, bloody history of the human species. But the reader who has come this far in this chapter should be able to see some of the weaknesses in this view of humans. The animals most often cited by Ardrey, Tiger, and Fox for insights into the behavior of our protohominid ancestors are the baboons. This may be partly because baboons have been studied more than other nonhuman primates. It also may be because savanna baboons occupy territory similar to that presumably inhabited by our ancestors. But human beings are not as closely related to the baboons as they are to the gorillas and chimpanzees, whose social organization, temperament, and behavior patterns differ in various ways from those of baboons. We have noted, moreover, that differences in social organization and troop size may appear *within* a species such as baboons, among groups that have adapted to different environments, and that this plasticity is related to the learning abilities of primates, which are thus not totally at the mercy of instinctual drives.

Our ancestors of 4 million or 5 million years ago must have been more adaptable than baboons, since they developed a culture, a way of life dependent upon learning and the use of language. Moreover, human beings have adapted to a great range of environments. To derive present-day human behavior from instincts fostered during man's early hunting stage seems at least oversimplified. The importance of aggression also may have been exaggerated by Lorenz, Ardrey et al., not only as far as human behavior is concerned but also in relation to other animal species. "When Lorenz says that 'fighting is an ever-present process' in nature, he must be forgetting all the moles, hedgehogs, raccoons, opossums, woodchucks, otters, chipmunks, squirrels of several kinds, rabbits, lemmings, moles, muskrats and beavers . . ." (Carrighar 1968:48). Among these animal species there is little show of aggression. In relation to territoriality also, there may have been an overemphasis on the part of Lorenz, Ardrey, and others.

Territoriality

In all classes of vertebrates there are species characterized by *territoriality*, that is, the pattern of defending a particular range of territory, principally against other members of the same species. This concern may be confined to a particular period, especially the breeding season, or it may be a more permanent preoccupation. Generally, small animals have small territories and large animals have big ones, although carnivorous animals tend to have larger territories than herbivores. A kind of territoriality has been found among many, but not all, primate species. Among some prosimians, urination and defecation help to demarcate the territory, providing boundary stakes, so to speak. Among some of the higher primates, such as the howler monkey and the gibbon, vocalization helps to indicate which group belongs in which part of the forest. Gibbons and howlers both make a lot of noise. Aggressive gestures and cries greet invaders of the territory, who usually retreat. But according to Paul E. Simonds (1974:75), most wild primates that have been studied do not defend territories.

Terrestrial primates are apt to wander over a wider range of territory than arboreal ones. Gelada herds cover less than 4.5 miles a day, but hamadryas and savanna baboons can cover about 12 miles (Simonds 1974:76). According to Kummer (1971:62), hamadryas cover an average of 8 miles a day. Baboons seem to stay within a particular range of land, but they do not fight other baboon groups to defend their territory. Similarly, gorillas do not try to defend particular areas. While the gibbons do exhibit territorial behavior, this is not true of the gorilla and chimpanzee, the animals most closely related to humans. The clearest cases of primate territoriality occur among leaf-eating forest dwellers, who are much more distantly related to us.

Teaching of chimpanzees by humans

Since chimpanzees show so much intelligence and learning ability, some efforts have been made by humans to teach them to talk. Two extensive efforts were made to bring up a young chimpanzee in an American home, exposing it to socialization practices from an early age, including the attempt to learn speech (Kellogg and Kellogg 1933; Hayes 1951). Neither of these attempts was successful, although the chimp in the second experiment did learn to say four words: "mama," "papa," "cup," and "up."

R. Allen Gardner and Beatrice Gardner, psychologists at the University of Nevada, have tried a different approach in making use of the American Sign Language for the deaf. This has been a much more successful enterprise, since their chimpanzee pupil, Washoe, has been able to imitate and learn standardized gestures and to acquire a "vocabulary" of 160 items. This success is understandable, since chimpanzees use gestures in communicating with one another in their natural habitat, and they evidently find much less difficulty in comprehending and imitating human gestures than vocal sounds. The first gesture word learned by Washoe was not "mama" or "papa" but "more" a functionally useful term for a young chimp. This simian Oliver Twist often wanted to get into various closets and cupboards which were normally locked. Washoe learned to ask "open key food" to get into the refrigerator or "open key blanket" to get a blanket. Her teachers noted that she used a consistent word order when trying to get access to these places.

By using sign language with Washoe, the Gardners can compare the development of her communication with that of deaf children using sign language and with the language development of normal children. Washoe started her sign language training when she was 11 months old. The Gardners are now experimenting with younger chimpanzees who were exposed to sign language within one or two days after birth. Among those teaching these young chimps are persons who were born deaf and who can therefore use the sign language more fluently than could the Gardners at the outset of their work. Although she was a late starter, considering the rapid maturation of apes, Washoe showed linguistic productivity in combining signs in a creative fashion. Once, on seeing some swans, she named them "water birds." A similar feat by a seven-year-old female chimpanzee was to call a watermelon "drink fruit." These parallels to our own language are rather remarkable.[1]

Washoe has now been moved to the Institute for Primate Studies in Oklahoma, where there are about a dozen chimps learning sign language. But before describing the work done there, let us consider another attempt to communicate with chimpanzees. David and Ann James Premack of the University of California at Santa Barbara have taught a young female chimpanzee, Sarah, to "read" and "write," using variously shaped and colored pieces of plastic, each of which stands for a particular word. These include not only nouns like "apple" but also verbs like "give" and abstract concepts such as "same," "different," and "name of." Incidentally, the symbol for apple is neither round nor colored red; it is represented by a blue triangle. This corresponds to the arbitrary nature of language, in which the sound of a word bears no direct relation to the named object. Although Sarah could not speak, she was able to symbolize if she accepted the convention that a blue triangle can stand for an apple. An interrogative symbol was included, so that Sarah could answer questions about whether two objects were the same or different. Sarah has a "vocabulary" of about 130 terms and uses them with a reliability of between 75 and 80 percent (Premack and Premack 1972). Although this experiment is a tribute to Sarah's intelligence, it does not permit much spontaneity or initiative on the part of the subject. Sarah could not communicate with other chimpanzees as readily as those who have learned sign language. She cannot lug around her language board and assorted plastic symbols from one chimp to another in the hope of striking up a conversation.

It is the potential spread of sign language among chimpanzees that

---

[1] See Gardner and Gardner 1969, 1975; Fouts 1974; Linden 1974.

Roger Fouts communicating with a chimpanzee at the Institute for Primate Studies in Oklahoma.

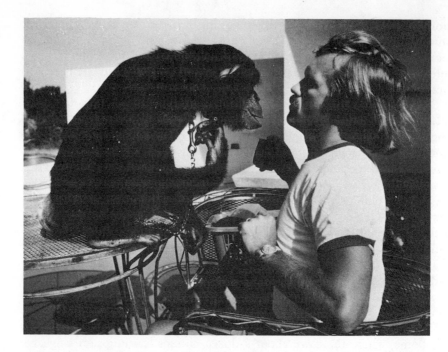

gives significance to experiments now under way at the Institute for Primate Studies in Oklahoma. Some of the young chimpanzees who were born there have been "adopted" by human families who communicate with them through sign language. They are later introduced to others of their species on an island at the institute. The question now is how much use they will make of sign language in their mutual relations with one another.

Some interesting experiments are being planned. Some objects will be introduced to the island for which only Washoe knows the sign. The aim is to see if she teaches it to the others. Also, a mysterious new object will be brought in for which not even Washoe knows the sign. Will the chimps coin a name for it? If so, how will the new sign spread from one to another? These are among the intriguing questions for the future (Linden 1974:130–34, 151–52, 168–69).

However, in the midst of all this lively interest in ape-human communication, a pailful of cold water has been dumped on these investigations by the complaints of three skeptics: Herbert S. Terrace, Thomas A. Sebeok, and Donna Jean Umiker-Sebeok. Terrace, a psychologist at Columbia University, was one of the researchers trying to establish a dialogue with a chimpanzee. His subject, whom he christened Nim Chimpsky, in honor of the linguist Noam Chomsky, was born at the Oklahoma Institute for Primate Studies. Nim was flown to New York in 1973 when he was only one week old. He first lived in Terrace's home but was later moved to a mansion in the Bronx, which he shared with three of his teachers who treated him, as much as possible, like a human child. During his four years in New York, Nim was taught by more than 60 volunteers. American Sign Language was used as the medium of communication.

Terrace was particularly interested in seeing if Nim could develop a grammar, but after five years of research he decided that Nim showed no evidence of grammatical competence. He did learn 125 signs but could not really use them in sentences. What Nim did was to mimic his teachers, an ability that does not constitute language, any more than does a dog's responsiveness to commands. Nim's speech did not become more complex as time went on, and his utterances showed no spontaneity. Eighty percent of them were preceded by a teacher's utterance. Terrace examined the videotapes and records of other students of ape communication and found the same patterns there too.

Sebeok and Umiker-Sebeok have drawn attention to what they call the Clever Hans effect. This refers to a famous stallion that was supposed to be able to read, spell, and solve mathematical problems. Clever Hans, who was exhibited by his owner around the turn of the century, communicated by tapping a front hoof on a wooden board. Numbers were assigned to the letters of the alphabet, and in that way Clever Hans "spelled out" answers to questions put to him. Oskar Pfungst, a psychologist, discovered how this was done. The horse evidently responded to the unconscious body movements and postures of his questioners, for when nobody knew the answer to a problem, Clever Hans was unable to give it. It is claimed that the same awareness of nonverbal clues affects human-chimp communication and that there is also a tendency among the researchers to interpret chimpanzee actions as constituting successful communications, so that more meaning is often read into them than is warranted. For example, Washoe's "water bird" signing may be simply two separate responses to water and bird respectively and not a brilliant combination, as was assumed.

One way to get around the Clever Hans effect is to construct double-blind experiments in which neither the experimenter nor the subject knows which responses are correct or appropriate. The Gardners did carry out such experiments with Washoe, but Sebeok and Umiker-Sebeok are critical of the way in which these experiments were done. On the other hand, chimpanzee-to-chimpanzee symbolic communication was successfully carried out in a laboratory setting, where it is hard to see how the Clever Hans effect could account for the results (Savage-Rumbough, Rumbough, and Boysen 1978).[2] No doubt, the various researchers in ape-human communication whose work has been criticized by Terrace, Sebeok, and Umiker-Sebeok will respond to their charges, as some have already done. No final verdict can be given as yet, but there is probably wider skepticism about chimpanzee linguistic ability at present than there was a few years ago.

---

[2] The well known behaviorist psychologist, B. F. Skinner, got two pigeons to communicate in much the same way by depressing keys in adjoining cubicles. Skinner attributes their success to behavioral conditioning (*Time*, Feb. 11, 1980:53).

Methods of studying primate behavior

The teaching program of the Premacks described earlier is an example of a laboratory experiment in which chimpanzees live under artificial circumstances far from their original setting. The same is true of those cases in which chimps have been brought up in an American home. In the laboratory, information can be acquired about primate learning abilities, physiological reactions, and responses to isolation. Although the laboratory, with its cages and testing apparatus, is far from a normal setting, it does at least allow for standardized testing procedures with controlled variables. Observation of primates in the wild is less controllable. The animals may be out of sight much of the time and hard to get close to; yet much may be learned in this way. Some outstanding field studies have been referred to in this chapter, such as those of Hans Kummer, George Schaller, and Jane van Lawick-Goodall, studies that have given us valuable new insights into primate behavior.

Another technique is also available, which falls between the laboratory and the field situation. A group of primates may be released into an enclosed area that facilitates observation, as in the chimp island in the Oklahoma Institute for Primate Studies. This is less artificial than the laboratory but does not really approximate the wild state.

Sometimes field observations may be converted into a more controlled situation by provisioning. Food is set out near the camp; the animals get

A chimpanzee at the language board in the experiment at the University of California at Santa Barbara. The sentence on the board reads: "Elizabeth give apple Amy." Elizabeth is the chimpanzee's name; Amy is the experimenter.

used to feeding there and become accustomed to the presence of human beings. But this may change the behavior patterns of the group. When she made bananas available to chimpanzees in this way, Jane van Lawick-Goodall found that their groups were getting larger and more aggressive. "They were sleeping near camp and arriving in noisy hordes early in the morning" (1971:141). As in fieldwork among human beings, the fieldworker may learn that his presence alters the behavior of those whom he studies.

Summary

An examination of primate social life is helpful for insights into primate and human evolution. Except for some prosimian species, the primates are social animals that live in groups the year round. Suckling provides for a continuing bond between mother and dependent offspring. Males and females also tend to remain together throughout the year. Adult males in most primate groups are either tolerant or helpful in their attitudes toward the young and may play a protective role, especially in terrestrial species.

The size and composition of primate groups varies widely. In general there has been an increase in group size from prosimian to more advanced forms. Terrestrial primates tend to have fairly large multi-male groups, but there may be differences in group size and composition within a species among groups that have adapted to different environments. This suggests that social organization is not determined by genetic factors alone but also by learning and adaptation to changing conditions.

Some writers have argued that human beings have inherited aggressive tendencies related to hunting and territorial defense. But territoriality is not characteristic of all primate species; the gorilla and chimpanzee, our closest relatives, do not show territorial behavior.

Some efforts have been made to teach the American Sign Language to chimpanzees, apparently with some success. However, there have been criticisms that such work involves the Clever Hans effect and that more meaning is often read into ape communications than is warranted.

Suggestions for further reading

For the social life of primates, see Irven De Vore, ed., *Primate Behavior: Field Studies of Monkeys and Apes* (New York: Holt, Rinehart and Winston, 1965); C. R. Carpenter, *Naturalistic Behavior of Nonhuman Primates* (University Park: Pennsylvania State University Press, 1964); Phyllis C. Jay, ed., *Primates: Studies in Adaptation and Variability* (New York: Holt, Rinehart and Winston, 1968): Michael R. A. Chance and Clifford J. Jolly, *Social Groups of Monkeys, Apes and Men* (London: Jonathan Cape, 1970); John H. Crook, "The Socio-ecology of Primates," in *Social Behavior in Birds and Mammals: Essays on the Social Ethology of Animals and Man*, ed. John H. Crook (London: Academic Press, 1970), pp. 103–66; Alison Jolly, *The Evolution of Primate Behavior* (New York: Macmillan, 1972); Phyllis Dolhinow, ed., *Primate Patterns* (New York: Holt, Rinehart and Winston, 1972); Charles H. Southwick, ed., *Primate Social Behavior:*

An Enduring Problem: Selected Readings (Princeton, N.J.: Van Nostrand Reinhold, 1963): Desmond Morris, ed., *Primate Ethology* (Chicago: Aldine, 1967); Jane van Lawick-Goodall, *In the Shadow of Man* (Boston: Houghton Mifflin, 1971).

For Harlow's experiments on social deprivation, see Harry F. Harlow, "The Heterosexual Affectional System in Monkeys," *American Psychologist* 17 (1962):1–9; and Harry F. Harlow and Margaret K. Harlow, "Social Deprivation in Monkeys," *Scientific American* 207 (1962):137–46. See also Hans Kummer, *Primate Societies: Group Techniques of Ecological Adaptation* (Chicago: Aldine and Atherton, 1971); John MacKinnon, "The Behavior and Ecology of Wild Orangutans *(Pongo pygmaeus),"* *Animal Behavior* 22 (1974):3–74.

For the aggression-carnivore-territoriality group of writers, see Konrad Lorenz, *On Aggression,* trans. Marjorie K. Wilson (New York: Harcourt Brace Jovanovich, 1966); Robert Ardrey, *African Genesis: A Personal Investigation into the Animal Origins and Nature of Man* (New York: Atheneum, 1961), *The Territorial Imperative* (New York: Atheneum, 1966), and *The Social Contract* (New York: Atheneum, 1970); Desmond Morris, *The Naked Ape* (New York: McGraw-Hill, 1967); Lionel Tiger, *Men in Groups* (New York: Random House, 1966); Lionel Tiger and Robin Fox, *The Imperial Animal* (New York: Holt, Rinehart and Winston, 1971): Antony Jay, *Corporation Man* (New York: Random House, 1971).

For views opposing the foregoing, see M. F. Ashley Montagu, ed., *Man and Aggression* (London: Oxford University Press, 1968); Alexander Alland Jr., *The Human Imperative* (New York: Columbia University Press, 1972); David Pilbeam, "The Fashionable View of Man," *New York Times Magazine,* September 3, 1972, pp. 10–11, 28–30.

For the work by the Gardners and the Premacks in communicating with chimpanzees, see R. Allen Gardner and Beatrice T. Gardner, "Teaching Sign Language to a Chimpanzee," *Science* 165 (1969):644–72; Ann James Premack and David Premack, "Teaching Language to an Ape," *Scientific American* 227 (October 1972):92–99.

See also Eugene Linden, *Apes, Men, and Language* (New York: Saturday Review Press/E. P. Dutton & Co., 1974).

For the criticisms by Terrace, Sebeok, and Umiker-Sebeok, see Herbert S. Terrace, *Nim: A Chimpanzee who Learned Sign Language* (New York: Alfred A. Knopf, 1979); and Thomas A. Sebeok and Donna Jean Umiker-Sebeok (eds.), *Speaking of Apes: A Critical Anthology of Two-Way Communication with Man* (New York: Plenum, 1980).

CHAPTER 6

The earliest hominoid fossils

Let us begin by clarifying some terms. *Hominid* refers to members of the family Hominidae, to which we belong. *Hominoid* refers to members of the superfamily Hominoidea, which includes both apes and human beings. So the latter term, Hominoidea, is the broader classification. Hominid, human being, and *Homo sapiens* are not interchangeable terms in a strict sense. The human beings of the present day are all of one species, *Homo sapiens*. We are the only living hominids. But there were formerly other types of hominid in existence, like the australopithecines, which, although not human beings, had more in common with us than with the apes.

The australopithecines will be discussed at length in the next chapter. For the present, it will be enough to say that they lived in the late Pliocene and early Pleistocene epochs, from around 4 million to 1 million years ago, and that they had upright posture but much smaller brains than modern human beings have. In the present chapter we will be concerned with their possible precursors of the Oligocene and Miocene epochs, in an effort to reconstruct the human family tree.

The best candidates for the earliest hominoid fossil finds come from Oligocene deposits in the Fayum, Egypt, dating from about 35 million years ago. The Fayum was then a wet tropical region containing land tortoises, turtles, and crocodiles. In those days the Mediterranean reached about 100 miles inland in this area, which was then a border region between sea and jungle. More than 100 specimens of primate finds have been recovered in the Fayum, including the remains of *Oligopithecus savagei*, a foot-

Oligocene primates in the Fayum

high creature on or near the ancestral line of the Old World monkeys. *Oligopithecus* is the oldest known primate having 32 teeth of the catarrhine type. It has been dated at about 32 million years ago. Also found in the Fayum were the jaw and tooth remains of *Propliopithecus*, a possible early ape or perhaps a generalized form in the line of evolution leading to the present-day apes and humans. *Propliopithecus* had rather human-looking teeth; the canines were not large like those of modern apes.

Dated at around 28 million years ago, later than *Propliopithecus*, was *Aegyptopithecus zeuxis*, another Fayum primate, which is represented by an almost complete skull and other skeletal material. This early hominoid, which is sometimes called the first true ape, is believed to have lived an arboreal life and to have been about the size of a modern gibbon, almost twice as large as the other Oligocene primates from the Fayum. *Aegyptopithecus* may have developed from the earlier *Propliopithecus* and may have been in the line of descent of the later East African apes of Miocene times. Unlike the apes of the present day, *Aegyptopithecus* had a tail. *Pithecus*, which appears in these names, means ape.[1]

More hominoid fossils have been recovered from deposits of the Miocene epoch, dating between approximately 5 million and 23.5 million years ago. During this time, Africa formed a single continent with Eurasia. It was a time of volcanic upheavals, during which the African Rift Valley was formed.

Time scale for the evolution of the primates

Epoch	Approximate years B.P. (before the present)	Some important representative primate species
Pleistocene	10,000–1,800,000	*Homo sapiens, Homo erectus, Australopithecus*
Pliocene	1,800,000–5,000,000	*Australopithecus*
Miocene	5,000,000–23,500,000	*Ramapithecus, Oreopithecus, Dryopithecus*
Oligocene	23,500,000–35,000,000	*Aegyptopithecus, Propliopithecus, Oligopithecus*
Eocene	35,000,000–58,000,000	Tarsiers, lemurs
Paleocene	58,000,000–65,000,000	Prosimians like tree shrews or lemurs

Various kinds of Miocene apes, generally classified as *Dryopithecus* ("forest ape") have been found in Europe, Africa, the USSR, India, and China.

---

[1] According to a report in *Time*, May 21, 1979, some fossil rivals to *Aegyptopithecus* for an ancestral position have been found in the Pondaung Hills west of Mandalay in Burma, dated at more than 40 million years ago. Christened *Pondaungia* and *Amphipithecus*, these primates have been described by Donald Savage of the University of California as "a sort of monkey with apelike teeth" that weighed about 30 pounds and resembled the modern rhesus monkey.

Map showing distribution of Miocene hominoid fossils.

Source: Harry Nelson and Robert Jurmain, *Introduction to Physical Anthropology* (St. Paul: West Publishing, 1979), p. 223.

The lower molar teeth have what has been called the *Y-5,* or *dryopithecus pattern*—a pattern found also in man, but not among Old World monkeys. The crowns of monkey molars have a cusp at each corner, while the crowns of chimpanzee, gorilla, and human lower molars usually have five cusps. In between the cusps there is a groove that looks like the letter *Y.* This tooth pattern is found only in the lower molars of chimpanzees, gorillas, and humans and in some of their precursors.

More complete than the remains of other early hominoid fossils are those of *Dryopithecus africanus,* sometimes called "Proconsul," a dryopithecine ape dating from the early Miocene in East Africa. Here we have not only jaws and teeth, but also skull and limb bones. At least three species have been identified, one of which is as small as a gibbon, another as large as a gorilla. *Dryopithecus africanus* did not have heavy brow ridges like those of present-day apes, nor did the lower jaw have a simian shelf. The teeth had the Y-5 pattern, and the canines were large. The arms and legs were rather humanlike in appearance, and *Dryopithecus* does not seem to have been a brachiator like the gibbon. It is thought that the advanced kind of brachiation of modern apes was a late development in their evolution, perhaps occurring in later Pliocene times. The fossil record seems to show that the apes of the present day are less humanlike than some of their ancestors, and we are less apelike than our ancestors. Apes and humans have adapted to different environments and have evolved in

Molars of a monkey *(top),* ape *(center),* and man *(bottom),* showing the Y-5 or dryopithecus pattern in ape and man.

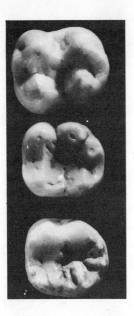

different directions. The ancestral apes had more humanlike limb proportions, lighter brow ridges and less-pronounced canine teeth than their descendants. Like our assumption of upright posture, the long arms of the apes may have been a relatively recent development in primate evolution.

The ramapithecines

From some widely separated Miocene sites in northwestern India, East Africa, Europe, and China come the fossil remains of jaws and teeth that are different from those of *Dryopithecus* and have been thought to be

Dryopithecus africanus (20–10 million years ago).

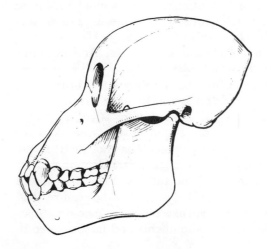

humanlike in some respects. These finds have been dated between 8 million and 14 million years ago. A lower jaw from Greece, identified as *Ramapithecus*, is dated at about 8 million years ago. While the Indian find is associated mainly with forest conditions, the Greek mandible is associated with grassland mammals such as gazelles and three-toed horses, giving a suggestion of adaptation to a savanna environment. There is also an indication of this in the African *Ramapithecus* finds (Andrews and Walker 1976:302). However, Pilbeam (1972:99) states that *Ramapithecus* was "a predominantly forest-living, arboreal animal, capable of arm-swinging and suspension in the trees, yet coming to the ground for food."

The teeth and jaws of *Ramapithecus* lack some apelike features. Apes have large, interlocking canine teeth that require the presence of a *diastema*, a gap in the tooth series for reception of the canine tooth from the other jaw. Large, interlocking canine teeth are not found in *Ramapithecus*, and the incisors are also small. It is assumed that a foreshortened face went with such a jaw. The cheek teeth are large, and the teeth have thick enamel, features that may be associated with ground-dwelling and foraging. Thickness of enamel is a late development, not known in Africa before the appearance of *Ramapithecus* about 14 million years B.P. Early descriptions of the *Ramapithecus* jaws gave them a parabolic appearance, like those of modern humans, instead of the long, narrow, U-shaped jaws of apes. A more recent reconstruction of *Ramapithecus wickeri*, however, presents a more primitive picture. The palate is described as being long and narrow and not rounded or parabolic (Andrews and Walker 1976:289).

No tools have been found in association with *Ramapithecus* jaws and teeth. *Ramapithecus* finds have sometimes been recovered in the same sites as *Dryopithecus* remains, and Grover S. Krantz has even suggested that ramapithecines were female dryopithecines—a matter of sexual dimorphism. With regard to their alleged hominid status, Krantz points out that two Indian specimens of *Ramapithecus* have a precanine diastema (Krantz 1975:147). Nevertheless, it has been speculated that *Ramapithecus* may have had upright posture and some think he may have been a true hominid, although there are no limb bones or other skeletal material to demonstrate upright posture.

Bipedalism

It does seem likely that a differentiation took place at around this time with regard to habitat and locomotion, with the apes adjusting to a more arboreal habitat with an emphasis on brachiation, while our ancestors, perhaps the ramapithecines, became more terrestrial and developed bipedalism. In bipedalism the burden of locomotion is on the feet, thus freeing the hands for carrying things and using tools. Upright locomotion, then, would be a valuable preadaptation to the regular use and manufacture of tools. It also would enable the females to carry their dependent young. Moreover, the assumption of upright posture results in an increased range of vision.

We cannot be sure when bipedalism originated, but there is evidence of it in footprints left in volcanic ash deposits dated at around 3.6 million years ago at Laetolil, in northern Tanzania, 25 miles south of Olduvai Gorge. These are footprints of some humanlike creatures, one of which was about four feet, eight inches tall, while another was only four feet tall. Perhaps the first of these was a male and the second female. Mary D. Leakey, who announced this discovery in February 1978, said that she was 75 percent certain that these were hominid prints, although they were broader than any hominid prints she had seen. The big toes pointed forward and not to the sides, as among apes. Leakey estimated that the creatures walked with a slow, rolling gait and had upright posture. (For photographs, see Mary D. Leakey 1979). Remains of two dozen teeth and jaws extracted from the Laetolil tuff (petrified volcanic ash) since 1974 and dated between 3.6 and 3.8 million years, are very similar to those of hominid fossils found at Hadar, Ethiopia, that date from between 2.6 and 3.3 million years ago. Pelvic and limb bones included in the assemblage suggest that these creatures also had upright posture. These Ethiopian finds are discussed in the following chapter.

Although there are some dissenting minority views about this matter (also to be discussed below), it seems likely that bipedalism was well established among the australopithecines by the beginning of the Pleistocene, about 1.8 million years ago. The fact that the hipbones of the australopithecines were already similar to modern hipbones suggests hundreds of thousands of years of prior adaptation to erect posture. Moreover, australopithecine foot bones found at Olduvai Gorge in Tanzania differ in only minor details from those of modern feet.

At Koobi Fora, near Lake Turkana in northwestern Kenya, more footprints were found in 1979. These are more recent than those at Laetolil and have been dated at around 1.5 million years ago. In this case the prints—about the size of modern feet—were made by a single individual, who is judged to have been about 5 feet tall and weighed about 120 pounds. He might have been either *Australopithecus* or *Homo erectus*, but more likely the latter, judging from the width of the stride.

We saw earlier (p. 81 ff.) that various aspects of the human skeleton reflect the adjustment to upright posture and bipedalism: the lumbar curve, basin-shaped pelvis, long legs, and arches of the feet. Animals that adapt successfully tend to gain in size; since hominids did so, their legs became longer and they could become increasingly swift and effective as hunters.

Many human beings today know the price mankind has paid for the adjustment to upright posture and bipedalism: such troubles as varicose veins, hernias, back pains, sacroiliac twinges, and slipped discs. Although the female pelvis has become broader, human fetuses have large heads; so the process of birth is often difficult and dangerous.

One of the explanations offered for the reduction in canine size among the ramapithecines is that perhaps they not only walked erect but also

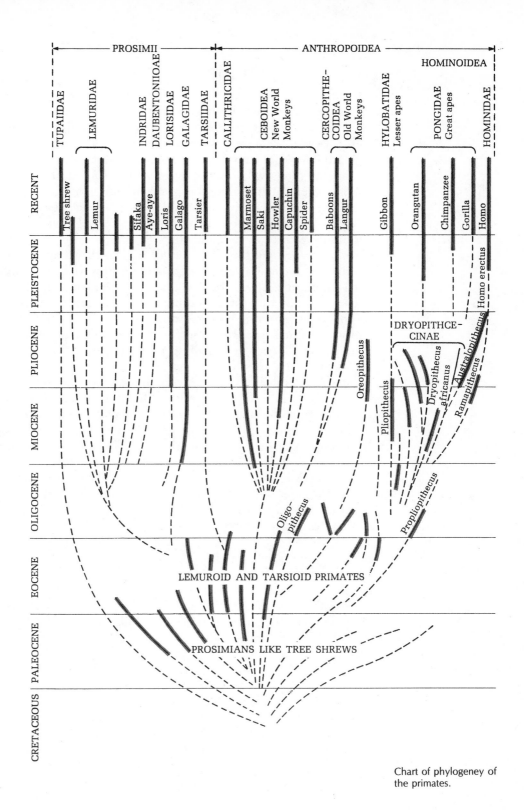

Chart of phylogeney of the primates.

had the use of tools, as did the later australopithecines. In ground-dwelling baboons the long, sharp canine teeth form weapons of defense and attack. The argument runs that the ramapithecines must have also had to defend themselves against predators; so perhaps they used tools as weapons, which would make large canines unnecessary. Primates also use their canines for breaking the husks of fruits, but tools could do this job as well. A difficulty with this interpretation, however, is that the earliest stone tools known so far have been dated at around 2.6 million years ago, while the humanlike teeth of the ramapithecines are many millions of years older. Perhaps the hominids were derived from some early form like *Propliopithecus*, which never did develop large canine teeth.

Another theory, put forth by Clifford Jolly, is that reduction in anterior tooth size was brought about by a change in diet, involving a specialization in seed eating in relatively treeless grasslands. A change in tooth patterns parallel to man's, with smaller canines and broader molars, is found in open-country, seed-eating baboons when their jaws and teeth are compared with those of their woodland and forest relatives (Jolly 1970). Reduction in canine size did not necessarily expose the ramapithecines to savanna predators; the large cats had not yet evolved.

In northern India and East Africa the ramapithecines coexisted with dryopithecine apes in the same areas. This would likewise be true of the finds in Europe and China, where dryopithecines also lived. The competitive exclusion principle holds that two closely related species with similar food habits cannot coexist for long in the same area. As will be seen in the next chapter, there seem to have been exceptions to this rule in the hominid line, and there is also the possibility, as Krantz has suggested, that they were not two species but simply males and females of the same species. At any rate, a differentiation of food habits between apes and protohominids may then have taken place, with the ancestors of the chimpanzees eating mainly fruits and our own ancestors becoming more omnivorous, also eating seeds, roots, and small animals.

**The pongid–
hominid
divergence**

When, then, did the pongid and hominid lines differentiate? The answers to this question have ranged remarkably. One estimate is that this split occurred less than 8 million years ago, perhaps about 4 million or 5 million years ago. This estimate, based on a molecular analysis of similarities and differences in DNA, protein, and immunological factors in chimpanzees, gorilla, and man has been put forward by Vincent Sarich (1971). (The biochemical and immunological factors are briefly summarized at the end of Chapter 4.) A very recent estimate for the ape-hominid split also has been offered by Sherwood L. Washburn and David A. Hamburg (1965), who place the divergence at about 2 million to 4 million years ago. Washburn's belief is that the practice of tool-use speeded up the course of evolution, so that the separation of hominids and pongids may have occurred

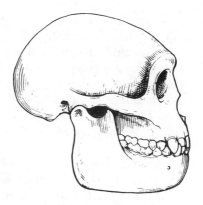

Oreopithecus bambolii
(14–8 million years ago).

within the Pleistocene epoch (Washburn 1971) and that "distinctively human mental abilities (speech, skill, degree of intelligence) evolved only in the last 4 to 6 hundred thousand years" (Washburn and Hamburg 1965:11).

This is far from the usual view. A more generally accepted date for the ape-hominid divergence than 400,000–600,000 years ago is between approximately 20 million and 25 million years ago.

Oreopithecus

Oreopithecus bambolii is another early primate that some authorities have classified as hominid, although most have not. *Oreopithecus* dates from Miocene times, about 13 million years ago. Remains of this fossil form, including a complete skeleton, have been found in some coal mines in north central Italy. *Oreopithecus* was about 4 feet tall and weighed about 80 pounds. He had a rather flat face, small canine teeth, and no diastema. There was no simian shelf. These are all hominid features. However, the brain case was small and the brow ridges heavy. *Oreopithecus* seems to have brachiated; he did not have upright posture. Moreover, the teeth of *Oreopithecus* differ in many ways from those of humans. For these and other reasons most authorities declare that *Oreopithecus* was not a hominid. He is generally classified as a member of the Hominoidea.

Gigantopithecus

There were once huge apes, larger than gorillas, that lived in India and southern China. They have been called *Gigantopithecus* ("giant ape"). The first *Gigantopithecus* teeth were discovered by G. H. R. von Koenigswald, who found them not *in situ* but in a Chinese drugstore. While on his travels, von Koenigswald had the custom of visiting Chinese drugstores and asking to see the local collection of "dragons' teeth." These are fossilized teeth of various sorts that Chinese customers buy for magical, medicinal purposes. Since fossil primate teeth sometimes appear in these collections, von Koenigswald was always on the lookout for something relevant to hominoid evolution. It was thus that in Hong Kong he acquired three huge molars, which he christened *Gigantopithecus blacki*. *Blacki* does not refer to the presumed color but was meant as a tribute to Davidson Black, known for his work with the Peking man fossils. The *Gigantopithecus* teeth have a volume five times that of modern human molars. At first it was considered possible that they were hominid molars, perhaps of some giant human ancestor, but the name given to the teeth indicates they were finally judged to be those of an early ape, a view that has since prevailed.

Since the first appearance of these *Gigantopithecus* teeth, many more have been discovered on the Chinese mainland by Chinese paleontologists. Over 1,000 teeth and three mandibles have been found, one of which came from a cave high up on the face of a steep cliff accessible only by climbing or flying. The cave was full of bones of Middle Pleistocene animals such as boar, deer, tapir, and elephant, none of which could either climb or fly. No tools or signs of human occupation were found in the cave. It was first thought that the remains of the large animals were hauled up the hillside by the giant ape, but it is now thought more likely that the ape was among the hunted rather than being the hunter.

The Chinese finds have a relatively late date, which would place *Gigantopithecus* outside the line of human descent. But a much earlier *Gigantopithecus* discovery has been made in India, a jaw dating from about 5 million years ago, which might conceivably represent a stock ancestral to later hominids. It is thought likely that *Gigantopithecus* first evolved in India and spread out from there to the north and east.

At the time of the discovery of the giant eastern Asiatic fossil finds, there was some speculation to the effect that perhaps humans went through a giant phase in the course of evolution. These notions were expressed by Franz Weidenreich (1873–1948), one of the leading physical anthropologists of his day. Weidenreich believed that *Gigantopithecus* was not a giant ape but a giant man. Another find he believed to be that of a giant hominid was called *Meganthropus palaeojavanicus* (large man of old Java), which had one of the largest and thickest primate jaws known. *Meganthropus* is now considered by many authorities to have been an australopithecine and thus a hominid. Weidenreich held that, although primates were originally small, they became larger in the course of evolution, until man's ancestors reached a giant size before the time of *Pithecanthropus erectus* and then began to get smaller again. It was in this way that Weidenreich explained the thickness of the human skull. It may seem surprising, but the human skull is thicker than those of the anthropoid apes. Even the bones that make up the gorilla's braincase are thinner than those of modern man. But the bones that make up the skull of *Pithecanthropus* are about twice as thick as modern man's. Weidenreich argued that the thickness of the *Pithecanthropus* skull and of later human skulls can be seen as a heritage of the giant stage of human development. The *Meganthropus* and *Gigantopithecus* teeth were held to be relics of that earlier stage. Weidenreich was not sure that the whole human species had passed through a giant phase, but he thought that at least part of it had done so. When we speak of "giant stage," this should not be interpreted too literally or sensationally. If the molar teeth of *Gigantopithecus* have five times the volume of modern man's molars, it does not mean that this hominoid was five times, or even twice, as large as man, although a Chinese scholar, Pei, estimated that it was about 12 feet tall. Limb and pelvic bones among similarly large-toothed remains in South Africa, on the other hand, are of relatively modest size.

Most modern paleontologists do not agree that *Gigantopithecus* was human; they consider the creature to have been an ape. (The jaws of *Gigantopithecus* had a simian shelf and a diastema). However, some physical anthropologists (Eckhardt 1975, Frayer 1973, Robinson 1972) have revived the argument that *Gigantopithecus* may have been a hominid. Eckhardt points out that the Middle Pleistocene age ascribed to the Chinese specimens is not well supported and that ". . . the evidence as it now stands no longer allows us to rule *Gigantopithecus* out of a position ancestral to the australopithecines with any degree of assurance. Moreover, there is much better evidence than for any other known Miocene or Pliocene hominoid that *Gigantopithecus* was a hominid" (Eckhardt 1975:125). Robinson (1972) believes that the Pliocene specimen, *Gigantopithecus bilaspurensis*, is more hominidlike in mandibular morphology than the later *Gigantopithecus blacki*. He sees *G. bilaspurensis* as a possible ancestor of the robust australopithecines and as constituting a more likely ancestor for hominids than *Ramapithecus*, which he considers to be more pongid than hominid.

Summary

The earliest primates in the fossil record were small prosimians dating back to about 60 million years ago. They were abundant in North America and Eurasia during the Eocene epoch, but then their numbers declined. The earliest hominoid fossils that have been recovered from Oligocene deposits in the Fayum, Egypt, dating from about 35 million years ago, include one that has been called the first true ape. There are more widespread apelike forms in the Miocene epoch, dating between around 23.5 million and 5 million years ago. Some of these finds have humanlike features in some respects, suggesting that apes and humans evolved in different directions. The ancestral apes had more humanlike limb proportions, lighter brow ridges, and smaller canine teeth than their descendants.

Between 8 and 14 million years ago there were creatures termed ramapithecines which some authorities consider to have had hominidlike features, including perhaps upright posture and bipedalism. They may have given rise to the australopithecines which flourished between 5 million and 1 million years ago. On the other hand, some physical anthropologists have suggested *Gigantopithecus bilaspurensis* as a possible hominid ancestor.

Suggestions for further reading

See John Napier, *The Roots of Mankind* (Washington, D.C.: Smithsonian Institution Press, 1970); David Pilbeam, *The Ascent of Man* (New York: Macmillan, 1972); Elwyn L. Simons, *Primate Evolution. An Introduction to Man's Place in Nature* (New York: Macmillan, 1972); Maitland A. Edey and the Editors of Time-Life Books, *The Missing Link* (New York: Time-Life Books, 1972). Also recommended is Alison Jolly, *The Evolution of Primate Behavior* (New York: Macmillan Co., 1972). See also Charles F. Hockett and Robert A. Ascher, "The Human Revolution", *Current Anthropology* 5 (1964): 135–47.

For an interesting collection of papers, see Russell H. Tuttle, ed., *Palaeoanthropology: Morphology and Paleoecology* (The Hague: Mouton, 1975).

Franz Weidenreich's views about the presumed giant phase of human evolution are set forth in his book *Apes, Giants, and Man* (Chicago: University of Chicago Press, 1946).

PART THREE

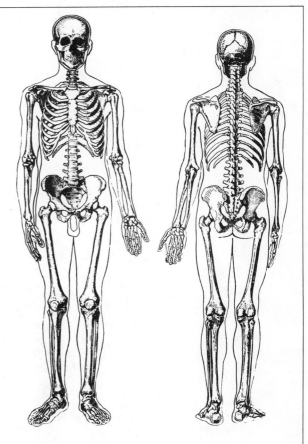

Hominid evolution and
cultural development
from the Pliocene
through the Pleistocene

CHAPTER 7

The australopithecines

The four chapters that follow deal with hominid evolution and cultural development from the early Pliocene to the late Pleistocene epoch. The Pliocene is dated between approximately 5 million and 1.8 million years ago, while the Pleistocene epoch is dated between 1.8 million and 10,000 years ago. The Pleistocene was a period of geological upheavals—volcanic activity, the upthrusting of mountain chains, great drops in temperature, and the periodic spreading of ice sheets across the northern continents. "Although permanent ice covers only about 10 percent of the world's land surface today, it extended over 32 percent at the time of maximum Pleistocene glaciation" (Butzer 1964:96). Glaciers covered most of Europe; in the New World they reached down to where Chicago and New York City are today. Geologists James Kennett and Robert Thunell believe that the great dip in temperature during the Pleistocene was related to the volcanic activity of that epoch. So much dust is added to the atmosphere during volcanic eruptions that sunlight has difficulty reaching the earth. The eruption of Krakatoa in 1883 was followed by very cool weather in many parts of the world for a few years. But that was only one eruption, whereas the Pleistocene seems to have been marked by repeated eruptions in different parts of the world, judging from widely distributed layers of volcanic ash recovered from cylindrical core samples of ocean sediment dug up in deep-sea drilling operations. Another explanation for the onset of the ice age has been given by a team of British and American geologists headed by James D. Hays of Columbia University. They attribute it to cyclical changes in the earth's orbit around the sun.

The beginning stage of the Pleistocene is sometimes called the *Villafran-*

Geological and archaeological divisions of time, with subdivisions of the Pleistocene epoch and the Paleolithic correlated with periods of glaciation.

YEARS AGO (X 1000)	GLACIATIONS (ALPS)	GEOLOGICAL DIVISIONS	ARCHAEOLOGICAL DIVISIONS
	Postglacial	Holocene	Neolithic Mesolithic
10			
	Würm	Upper Pleistocene	Upper Paleolithic
35			
			Middle Paleolithic
75			
100			
	Riss	Middle Pleistocene	
200			
275			
	Mindel	Lower Pleistocene	
500			
	Günz		Lower Paleolithic
		Basal Pleistocene	
	Donau and Earlier Stages		
2000			

chian, a term originally applied to a group of mammals widespread during that period, particularly elephants, horses, and cattle. Bones of Villafranchian fauna have been found in association with the bones of *Australopithecus,* which so far have been found mainly in southern and East Africa.

The above chart shows subdivisions of the Pleistocene. Note that the divisions of the Pleistocene in the central column are *geological* divisions, while the terms for Lower, Middle, and Upper Paleolithic in the right-hand column are *cultural, archaeological* divisions. The column on the left shows the timing of the four great glaciations—Günz, Mindel, Riss, and Würm—that spread over Europe. In between these glaciations were warmer interglacial periods.

In 1924, Raymond Dart, an anatomist at the University of the Witwaters-rand, acquired a well-preserved fossil skull that seemed to be that of an immature ape. It came from some limestone bluffs at Taung, South Africa. The skull was evidently that of a five- or six-year-old juvenile, since its milk teeth were intact. The first four permanent molar teeth were also present. Although somewhat apelike in appearance, the juvenile's braincase was as large as that of an adult chimpanzee. Dart gave this find the name of *Australopithecus africanus*, or South African ape, but he drew attention to many humanlike features in the skull. There were no heavy brow ridges or projecting canine teeth. The appearance of the teeth was more human than apelike. The face was quite flat and the skull a bit rounded on top. There were implications of upright posture in the central position of the *foramen magnum*. As critics pointed out after Dart published his findings, most of these features are not unusual in immature apes, which have flatter faces, smaller brow ridges, less projecting canines, and higher foreheads than adult apes. But what was unusual, in any case, was the location of this find. The present-day African apes, the gorilla and chimpanzee, live in tropical forests 2,000 miles farther north. Taung is in a dry, savannalike environment, and Dart estimated that climatic conditions were not very much different a million years ago, when the Taung child was thought to have lived. His diet must have been quite different from those of chimpanzees and gorillas. Perhaps, like the baboons who now live in such terrain, he ate berries, grubs, lizards, and birds' eggs. He was probably more of a meat eater than most primates, but such shifts of diet are not uncommon

Australopithecus africanus

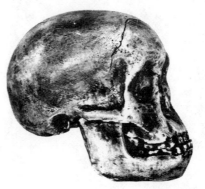

Reconstructed plaster cast of the Taung child fossil, labeled *Australopithecus africanus* by Raymond Dart.

in the different orders of mammals. The panda, for example, although classed among the carnivores, has become a strict vegetarian.

About 10 years after Dart's discovery, a number of fossils of similar type were found in South Africa; they have come to be known as australopithecines. Their skeletal material, now abundant, consists not only of skulls, jaws, and teeth but also of limbs and pelvic bones. A nearly complete australopithecine foot was found at Olduvai Gorge in Tanzania. Most of a vertebral column and pelvis come from Sterkfontein in South Africa. Many hundreds of fossil finds have been made. A total of 1,022 bones have come from the South African sites alone. In recent years 182 hominid specimens have come from the Omo area in Ethiopia, consisting of 162 isolated teeth, 7 postcranial bones, and 13 skull and jaw bones; and 125 hominid fossils have been recovered from the Lake Turkana (or Lake Rudolf) area in East Africa, consisting of 50 postcranial bones, 16 isolated teeth,

An outline map of Africa, showing location of australopithecine sites.

and 59 skull and jaw bones. Perhaps not all this material can be identified as australopithecine. However, on the material so classified thus far, it has been judged that the australopithecines had upright posture and either partial or complete bipedal locomotion. At the same time, they had small brains, which suggests that hominids assumed upright posture before developing a large brain. The cranial capacity was about 600 cubic centimeters, not much larger than that of African apes. But their brains were larger in proportion to body size than those of the great apes.

The australopithecines had large, chinless jaws, with canine teeth that were relatively small. There was no diastema. Mastoid processes like those of modern humans appear on the skulls. Some had a good deal of facial protrusion, with heavy brow ridges and crests on top of the skull. These are apelike features, but there is general agreement that the australopithecines should be classed as hominids; they had more in common with us than with the apes.

Progressively older forms keep being discovered. The oldest is a mandible (lower jaw) from Lothagam Hill east of Lake Turkana in Kenya, East Africa, found in 1967 and dated by potassium-argon at around 5.5 million years ago. According to Elwyn L. Simons (1978:559) there is no doubt that it is hominid; it has been tentatively identified as *Australopithecus africanus*. The Lothagam mandible is the oldest hominid find about which there is general consensus. There are still older fossils which have been labeled hominid, but there is disagreement about their status, as there has been about *Ramapithecus* and *Gigantopithecus*. McHenry and Corrucini (1980) report that the Lothagam mandible is morphologically intermediate between modern pongids and *Australopithecus afarensis* (see below).

Reference was made earlier (p. 112) to the remains of teeth and jaws found at Laetolil near the footprints, dated between 3.6 and 3.8 million years. These closely resemble fossils found at Hadar, Ethiopia. At Hadar, Donald C. Johanson and Maurice Taieb found remains of more than 20 hominids, dated at about 3 million years. The most valuable find consisted of 40 bones of a single individual, making up 40 percent of the skeleton, including not only parts of the spinal column, lower jaw, and teeth but also parts of the pelvis, the sacrum, and parts of the hand and foot. This is one of the most complete, as well as oldest, hominid skeletons found to date. The bones suggest, among other things, the presence of bipedalism and upright posture. Another hominid feature is the nonprojecting canine teeth. At first Johanson and Taieb provisionally assigned some of the hominid finds to genus *Homo* and others to *Australopithecus africanus*, but they now believe that both the Laetolil and Hadar specimens belong to a more primitive species of *Australopithecus* than was previously know, for which they propose the name *Australopithecus afarensis* (Johanson, White, and Coppens 1978).

Despite the hominid impression given by the upright posture and nonprojecting canines, the Afar hominids also present some apelike features. The length of the arms is relatively long in comparison to the length of the legs. C. Loring Brace (1979:267) remarks: ". . . if we were to judge on the basis of the jaws and teeth alone, we might reasonably conclude that the material was pongid." But he judges the pelvis to be completely hominid in form.

No tools were found at either Laetolil or Hadar with the hominid remains. There has been speculation that these early hominids might have used wooden digging sticks which would have helped them to compete with baboons for the food resources of the savannas. Pointed sticks could also have been used in defense against predators (Brace 1979:269). Since these hominids present such a primitive appearance, it is perhaps possible that the pongid-hominid split occurred not long before this time, in keeping with the views of Sarich, Washburn, and Hamburg, although the hominid status of the Lothagam mandible would not support that position.

Evidence of hunting

The presence of animal bones at australopithecine sites suggests that the australopithecines ate meat. Mary Leakey, the wife of Louis S. B. Leakey, mapped a 3,400-square-foot "living floor" at Olduvai Gorge, a site that has been dated by the potassium-argon method at about 1.75 million years ago. Within the Olduvai site there is an area with a 15-foot diameter littered with smashed animal bones, which were evidently broken to get at the marrow. Stone tools were also found. The evidence suggests that the Olduvai hominids were both tool users and meat eaters.

Some of the animals whose meat was eaten were very large, including an elephant and an extinct *Deinotherium*. Their remains were found at butchering sites, not on the living floor. These animals may have died of natural causes or else been trapped and butchered in a swampy area. In any case, as many as 123 stone cutting tools were found with the elephant remains; there were 39 associated artifacts with the *Deinotherium* remains.

If they were hunters, the australopithecines risked encounters with dangerous predators, such as lions and hyenas. But the two latter species are mainly nocturnal, and the australopithecines could have avoided them by hunting in open savannas during the day, thus entering a new ecological niche.

Home base

The Leakeys uncovered a semicircular wall at Olduvai, which may have served as a windbreak and has been dated at around 2 million years old ± 280,000 years—the oldest man-made structure known (Pfeiffer 1969:79).

The windbreak and the living floor with its bone collection suggest the presence of a home base. A home base is a pattern associated with carnivores rather than with primates, but the smashed animal bones at Oldowan sites show that at least some of the australopithecines were meat eaters and thus qualified as both primates and carnivores, if not in zoological classification. Something like a home base is foreshadowed in some other primate species. Baboons require nesting places for sleeping that keep them out of reach of predators. These are usually trees, but in arid regions in Ethiopia hamadryas baboons occupy cliffs at night. Reliance on a particular refuge area is not so different from a home base. Simonds (1974:74) notes: "Females with newborn infants tend to remain closest to the core areas since they are the safest part of the home range." A home base serves the same functions among human hunters; it provides a refuge for the old and sick as well as for females with young.

A study of the eruption rates of australopithecine teeth suggests that their young were as dependent upon adults as children are today. A long period of maturation facilitates learning, and this may have made possible a reliance upon culture among the hominids of that time.

It seems likely that the inhabitants of such a site shared their meat. After all, chimpanzees do so (see p. 80–81). The more advanced australopithecines had only to carry the practice a step further by bringing meat back to the home base. Being bipedal or partially bipedal walkers, with hands freed, they could have carried both weapons and meat in their hands.

The Olduvai home base seems to have been close to water, either a stream or lake shore, judging from the remains of fish, aquatic birds, and crocodile. Early sites in the Omo Valley region also seem to have been close to water. Presumably trees grew in such an oasis area and provided shade.

The use of tools

The stone tools at Olduvai consist mostly of pieces of lava and quartz, which must have been brought to the site from about three miles or more away; they do not occur naturally at the site itself. Crude, rounded pebble tools called choppers are among the artifacts. But surprisingly advanced-looking tools also were found. John Pfeiffer (1969:79) has noted: ". . . a site at the bottom of the gorge contains eleven different kinds of stone implements, such as engraving-gouging tools, quadrilateral 'chisels,' large and small scrapers, and other special-purpose tools generally made of difficult-to-work lavas and quartz."

Some stone tools from the Omo River region in Ethiopia are dated at about 2 million years; and tools found near East Lake Turkana in northern Kenya are about 850,000 years older than the oldest tools from Olduvai. So, the evidence for toolmaking in East Africa goes back to nearly 3 million years ago.

But the use of tools may be much earlier than that. Early hominids probably used perishable materials like wood for tools, since even chimpanzees use sticks for getting termites. But there would be no archaeological record of that after 3 million years.

Early stone tools

Because of the relative absence of tools of other materials, we must learn what we can from the imperishable remains of stone tools dating from the australopithecine period. It is not always easy to determine whether a particular piece of stone was deliberately fashioned by man. Early man made much use of flint, which fractures easily when given a blow. But stone can be flaked by natural agencies—by rapid changes in temperature, frost, glacial action, and other causes. However, a close examination of the stone may reveal whether man-made blows dislodged a flake. As a leading authority on the subject has written: ". . . the surface of a fracture due to a sharp external blow appears clean-cut, and shows a definite bulb of percussion with faint radial fissures and ripples originating at a point on the edge of the flake or flake-scar" (Oakley 1964a:17).

The earliest stone tools showing deliberate flaking were choppers, pebble tools with a jagged cutting edge formed by striking off a few flakes. Choppers were the most common tools found in Bed I in Olduvai Gorge; they have come to be known as *Oldowan tools*. Such tools, sometimes flaked on both sides or in two directions, have been found from the Cape in South Africa to the Transvaal, Kenya, Morocco, Algeria, and Ethiopia. There were hominids early in the Pleistocene using Oldowan choppers in most parts of Africa before stone tools first appeared in Europe. Later, simple choppers were used by the Peking hominids and have been found in many parts of eastern Asia, including China, Burma, Indonesia, and India. Some early European sites also have yielded tools similar to the Oldowan and Peking choppers, notably Clacton-on-Sea and Swanscombe in southeastern England, Vértesszöllös in Hungary, near Menton in southern France, and a couple of sites in Romania. In Africa the Oldowan chopper gradually gave rise to a more advanced tool, the hand axe, which is discussed in the following chapter.

Plaster casts of choppers used by the Peking hominids. These are similar to African Oldowan tools.

Although the chopper is the most common and most characteristic tool in the lower strata at Olduvai Gorge, it is not the only type of stone tool. There were also stone balls and scrapers. The round stone balls may have been used as *bolas*, such as were used on the pampas of South America. Two or three stones tied with thongs are thrown to entangle an animal's legs.

Tools of bone and horn

Raymond Dart has argued that the earliest tools used by the australopithecines were not likely to have been made of stone but rather of bone and horn. This contention is still being discussed, and there are some arguments in its favor. In the carcasses of animals, either killed by themselves or by other predators such as lions, the australopithecines would have found sharp, pointed bones and horns useful for piercing and stabbing and heavy limb bones useful as clubs. Such naturally shaped tools of bone, horn, and antler may have been the hominids' first weapons. Dart has published photographs of many pieces of bone, horn, and antler taken from australopithecine sites, which he thinks were used as tools. Since they show little evidence of having been worked, this testimony is not convincing by itself.

Dart drew attention to 42 baboon skulls collected from three different cave sites associated with australopithecine remains. All of the skulls had been bashed in, with seemingly intentional violence; 27 had been struck from the front. In several cases the blows appear to have been inflicted by a double-headed weapon, which Dart believes to have been an antelope humerus bone, the distal end of which fits into the baboon skull depressions rather well. Dart's conclusions about the probable use of bone and horn for tool use by australopithecines seem justified, especially in view of the fact that stone tools were used in Africa 2.6 million years ago. It seems likely that at least some of the australopithecines used tools of bone and horn as well as stone—and probably wood also.

If australopithecines used tools, does that mean that they also had a language? Could they have given instruction in toolmaking without it? And could they have engaged in cooperative hunting? These questions are not easily answered. The brain size of australopithecines was no greater than that of chimpanzees. Chimpanzees learn to use the termite-fishing stick without verbal instruction. Stone tools are more complex but their manufacture could conceivably be taught without words.

Did australopithecines talk?

Chimpanzees have been known to engage in communal hunting; so, of course, do wolves, lions, and other carnivores. Some of the latter have home bases too, so that does not require a language either. On the other hand, human beings did learn to speak at some point in their evolution, and it might have begun at this time. All animals communicate in some way, but the human communication system seems to be unique. Chimpanzees communicate by touching, by facial expressions such as baring the teeth, and through gestures such as the cupped hand used in begging for meat. On special occasions they engage in tree drumming. Gorillas sometimes thump their chests. Warning barks and grunts may be made. The primate vocal repertoire is usually limited to between 10 and 15 sound-signal types, although chimpanzees are said to have 25 distinct calls. This sound production may have provided a basis for human speech, but human beings have developed something much more elaborate and complicated in their use of language. The apes share most of our "organs of speech," as they might be called—palate, tongue, larynx, pharynx, vocal cords, and so on—and they make sounds with them, but they do not have a language. Although the production of voiced sounds is essential in verbal communication, the significant factor is the coding that takes place in the brain, with associations being made between particular concepts and certain arbitrary sounds. This is not only a matter of having names for things; word order is important too. Every human language has a system of grammar and syntax, knowledge of which is shared by speakers of the language, though at a largely unconscious level.

All present-day languages are complex. There are no "primitive" languages that could provide us with earlier stages of linguistic development; so it is hard to figure out how this remarkable system first got started. Perhaps, as Gordon Hewes (1973) has argued, the early hominids had a gestural language. Both tool use and gestures involve manipulation of the hands. The Gardners' success in communicating with Washoe gives some support to Hewes' hypothesis. But even if gestures preceded speech, the latter finally replaced gestural language. We do not know when that may have been, but it seems likely that verbal language was established by the time of *Homo erectus*, discussed in the following chapter.

Suggested subdivisions of the australopithecines

John T. Robinson, one of the leading students of the South African finds, suggested that the australopithecines should be divided into two groups. He first proposed that one genus was *Australopithecus;* the second was *Paranthropus*. More recently Robinson has promoted *Australopithecus* to the genus *Homo* and christened him *Homo africanus*. This terminology has not been adopted by most anthropologists. Species terms more generally used for the two subdivisions are *Australopithecus africanus* for the first type and *Australopithecus robustus* for the second, which was first called *Paranthropus*. To simplify matters, let us call them, as is commonly done, *A. africanus* and *A. robustus*.

According to Robinson, these types were found in different sites and differed markedly in size and weight. *A. robustus* had about the height of present-day human beings and weighed between 100 and 200 pounds. *A. africanus* was much shorter and weighed less than 100 pounds. *A. robustus* had a round, low skull, while *A. africanus* had a narrow, slightly domed one and his brow ridges were less prominent. In contrast to *A. africanus*, *A. robustus* had crests on the top of his skull, like those of an adult male gorilla, although less pronounced. *A. robustus* had heavy cheekbones that protruded further forward than his flat nose, but *A. africanus* had more facial protrusion. *A. robustus* had much larger molar teeth but smaller canines and incisors than *A. africanus*. The contrasts in dentition and in the framework of the skull suggest to Robinson that *A. robustus* depended more on a vegetarian diet, which required a great deal of chewing and grinding of food, whereas *A. africanus* is presumed to have been more carnivorous or omnivorous. *A. robustus* sites were believed to be later than those of *A. africanus*. Robinson said there was good evidence that the climate of the region was much wetter in the time of *A. robustus* than in that of *A. africanus* (Robinson 1962; for his more recent views see Robinson 1972). But now there is doubt about this. It seems likely that both forms occupied a similar environment.

Kelton R. McKinley (1971) states that the average age at death for *A. africanus* was 22.9 (114 samples) and 18.0 for *A. robustus* (188 samples.) The assumed age for sexual maturation in both species was 11 years, the median between that for chimpanzees and humans.

Some authorities deny that there were different hominid species at this time. Milford Wolpoff (1971b) claims that the differences between *A. africanus* and *A. robustus* were no greater than those found in present-day human groups or among gorillas and chimpanzees. In Africa today there are very tall people like the Watussi and very short ones like the Pygmies of the Congo, just as there are both large and pygmy forms of chimpanzee. Variation in size need not prevent gene flow. If the early hominids had adapted through the means of culture, they would all have occupied the same general niche. This *single-species hypothesis* is based on the competitive exclusion principle (see p. 114). In keeping with the single-species hypothesis is the notion that the larger types classified as *A. robustus* were the males of the species, while the more gracile *A. africanus* types were the females. C. L. Brace, who favors this view, classifies all australopithecines as *A. africanus*. He does not recognize a separate species of *A. robustus* (Brace, Nelson, and Korn 1971:20). Brace (1972) points out that terrestrial primates like baboons and gorillas have marked sexual dimorphism, with males having twice the bulk of females. This is not true of human beings today but may have been true of our early terrestrial forebears. Although culture subsequently weakened this dimorphism, it seems likely to have been a characteristic of early hominids. Indeed, there are still marked contrasts between male and female Neanderthals at a much later stage.

A second view, that of John T. Robinson, is that *A. robustus* is closer to the original form from which the australopithecine genus was derived. The early ground-dwelling protohominids were probably vegetarian. *A. ro-*

bustus may have remained a plant eater, while *A. africanus* began to specialize as a hunter and carnivore. Robinson believes that is was *A. africanus* that evolved into *Homo erectus,* while *A. robustus* was only an aberrant form that finally became extinct (Robinson 1963). The dental evidence cited by Robinson to show that *A. robustus* was a vegetarian has been viewed with skepticism by some authorities. Robinson has drawn attention to scratches on *A. robustus* teeth that he attributes to grit eaten along with vegetable food. But scratches appear on the teeth of *A. africanus* as well, and they might have resulted from chewing on bone.

It has been shown that the Taung site, from which Dart's original *A. africanus* skull came, is much more recent than was formerly believed. The Taung cave, which was thought to have been one of the oldest South African australopithecine sites, is now held to be one of the youngest, dating to around 900,000 years ago. Phillip V. Tobias (1973) believes that the Taung child was an immature *A. robustus* rather than *A. africanus.*

As we have seen (p. 125), Donald C. Johanson and his colleagues have suggested the differentiation of a particularly primitive species, *Australopi-*

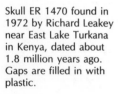

Skull ER 1470 found in 1972 by Richard Leakey near East Lake Turkana in Kenya, dated about 1.8 million years ago. Gaps are filled in with plastic.

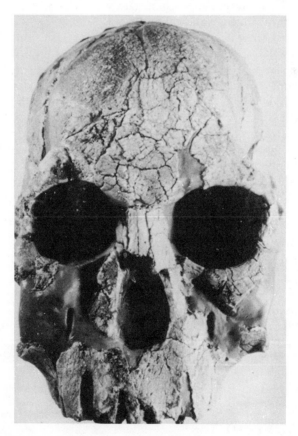

thecus afarensis. At a more advanced level, Tobias and Napier have proposed the establishment of a new genus, *Homo habilis,* to represent a hominid stage of evolution between *Australopithecus* and *Homo erectus.* Most authorities seem to regard *Homo habilis* as a relatively progressive *A. africanus.* Again, Louis S. B. Leakey and some of his colleagues have assigned a separate genus (while some have assigned a separate species label) to the most primitive form found at Olduvai Gorge, which Leakey named *Zinjanthropus boisei* and others call *Australopithecus boisei.* Many physical anthropologists consider the latter to be simply a form of *A. robustus.* Others, however, consider the distinction between *A. boisei* and *A. robustus* to be significant, since the North African *A. boisei* is described as being a "super-robust" type, even more rugged than the South African *A. robustus.*

Richard Leakey has found three skulls, together with more than two dozen mandibles and other skeletal material at Lake Turkana. Much of the material has been assigned to the *A. boisei* type, dating back to more than 2 million years ago. That would make *A. boisei* a very stable form. Moreover *A. boisei* coexisted in East Africa during this long stretch of time with the more gracile type.

To add to the confusion of this picture, Richard Leakey (1973) has found some skulls of more advanced forms which he classifies in the genus *Homo.* A skull found near Lake Turkana in 1972 has a cranial capacity of about 800 cubic centimeters. Working in the same area, Glynn Isaac unearthed 300 simple stone tools of about the same date.[1]

In 1976 Leakey reported the discovery of a complete skull in northern Kenya which he dates at 1.5 million years ago, and which closely resembles the skull of the Peking forms of *Homo erectus.* It is the best preserved single *Homo erectus* cranium yet found in Africa. But this hominid was contemporary with australopithecines in the same region. This discovery led Leakey and Walker (1976) to challenge the single species hypothesis. If it is true that two closely related species with similar food habits cannot long inhabit the same environment (the competitive exclusion principle), one would expect to find only one hominid species at a time in a given region. But in this part of northeast Africa pithecanthropines (representatives of *Homo erectus*) coexisted with australopithecines; hence the single species hypothesis is not supported here. It may be noted that *Homo erectus* also seems to have been contemporaneous with australopithecines in South Africa. (The following chapter includes a review of *Homo erectus* fossil finds). The usual view has been that *Homo erectus* evolved from *Australopithecus,* but this seems to be challenged by their contemporaneity. However, C. Loring Brace and Ashley Montagu (1977:292) consider this argument

---

[1] At first Isaac doubted that these tools could have been made by *Australopithecus,* but he later decided that *Australopithecus* was capable of making hand axes, some of which were found near Olduvai Gorge at a site dated between 1 million and 1.5 million years ago. See "Science and the Citizen," *Scientific American,* vol. 231 (1974), pp. 49–50.

to be dubious ". . . for it is quite possible for the unmodified descendants of ancestral forms to live into the same period as other descendants that have undergone more or less considerable evolutionary change. . . . Finally, an important fact that needs to be underscored is that the brains of the large-brained australopithecines virtually fall within the range of those of the small-brained pithecanthropines. We therefore see no difficulty in viewing the australopithecines as ancestral to the pithecanthropines."

Summary

The australopithecines have been classified as hominids; they had upright posture combined with a small cranial capacity like that of present-day African apes. There is evidence that these hominids were hunters, used tools, and had home bases. Some authorities divide the australopithecines into different species such as *A. africanus*, *A. robustus*, and *A. boisei*, although other authorities prefer a single species hypothesis, one version of which holds that the more gracile forms were females and the more rugged ones were males. The australopithecines apparently coexisted with more advanced forms of *Homo erectus* in both South and East Africa, which has led some authorities to challenge the single species hypothesis, while others still support it.

Suggestions for further reading

The discoveries of the *Australopithecus afarensis* finds are described in the recent book *Lucy: The Beginnings of Humankind* by Donald C. Johanson and Maitland A. Edey (New York: Simon & Schuster, 1981).

A lively presentation of Raymond Dart's views is set forth in the book he wrote with Dennis Craig, *Adventures with the Missing Link* (New York: Harper & Row, 1959). A stimulating, but overly sensational work is Robert Ardrey's *African Genesis: A Personal Investigation into the Animal Origins and Nature of Man* (New York: Atheneum, 1961).

Excellent drawings of an artist's reconstructions of *Australopithecus africanus*, *A. robustus*, and other early hominids may be found in F. Clark Howell and the Editors of Life, *Early Man* (New York: Life Nature Books, 1965).

Two papers by J. T. Robinson are recommended: "The Australopithecines and Their Bearing on the Origin of Man and of Stone Tool-Making," in *Ideas on Human Evolution: Selected Essays, 1949–1961*, ed. William Howells (Cambridge, Mass.: Harvard University Press, 1962), pp. 279–94; and "Adaptive Radiation in the Australopithecines and the Origin of Man," in *African Ecology and Human Evolution*, ed. F. Clark Howell and François Bourlière, Viking Fund Publications in Anthropology no. 36 (Chicago: Aldine, 1963), pp. 385–416.

A stimulating article showing the relevance of carnivore behavior to an understanding of the australopithecines is George B. Schaller and Gordon R. Lowther, "The Relevance of Carnivore Behavior to the Study of Early Hominids," *Southwestern Journal of Anthropology* 25 (1969): 307–41.

For a well-illustrated account of some of Leakey's finds concerning *Zinjanthropus*, see L. S. B. Leakey and Des Bartlett, "Finding the World's Earliest Man," *National Geographic*, September 1960, pp. 420–35.

See also Maitland A. Edey and the Editors of Time-Life Books, *The Missing Link* (New York: Time-Life Books, 1972).

For a roundup of data about the australopithecines, much of it very technical, see Glynn Ll. Isaac and Elizabeth R. McCown, eds., *Human Origins: Louis Leakey and the East African Evidence* (Menlo Park, California: W. A. Benjamin, 1977).

See also Clifford J. Jolly, ed., *Early Hominids of Africa* (London: Gerald Duckworth & Co., 1978).

CHAPTER 8

From *Homo erectus* to *Homo sapiens*

Homo erectus was a form of hominid, more advanced than *Australopithecus*, dating back to between 1.5 million and about 100,000 years ago. Fossil discoveries that fall under the heading of *Homo erectus* have been made in Europe, Africa, China, and Indonesia. The principal advance at this level of hominid development was an increase in cranial capacity. *Homo erectus*, of course, used tools and probably had a language. The remains of fire have been found in association with skeletal remains in China. From the neck down, *Homo erectus* seems to have been much like ourselves, but the skull was low browed, keel domed and thick walled, with a cranial capacity ranging between 780 and 1,300 cubic centimeters. *Homo erectus* had heavy brow ridges and lacked a chin. Behind the brow ridges there was a postorbital constriction. The proportion of arms to legs was greater than for present-day humans.

Since *Homo erectus* looked so much like us, it seems snobbish not to assign him/her the status of *Homo sapiens*, but this has not been the custom until recently. John Buettner-Janusch (1966:172, 178) however, would so classify *Homo erectus*. It is only recently that the Neanderthals have been admitted to the *Homo sapiens* club. We are gradually extending membership in our species further back in time to our more primitive ancestors.

Hunting-gathering peoples tend to have larger ranges than nonhuman primates, whose ranges are generally small, with the exception of some, such as baboons, chimpanzees, and gorillas. Man's effectiveness as a hunter must have increased greatly during this period and led to wider dispersal. Aided by the use of fire, some representatives of the *Homo erectus* group

1. Java
2. Peking
3. Lan-t'ien
4. Heidelberg
5. Vertesszollos
6. Petralona
7. Torralba/Ambrona
8. Terra Amata
9. Ternifine
10. Olduvai
11. Swartkrans

An outline map of the
Old World showing
where sites of *Homo
erectus* have been
found.

were now able to make their way up into cold northerly areas, such as
northern China, while others continued to inhabit warmer regions in Africa,
southern Asia, and Indonesia.

The migrations of *Homo erectus* may have been facilitated by the upheavals and climatic conditions of the Pleistocene epoch. Thus, heavier rainfall
in Africa may have led to occupation of and movement through the Sahara
Desert. The locking up of water farther north, with the advent of cold
arctic weather, lowered water levels in the Mediterranean and may have
provided land bridges, for example, at the Dardanelles, permitting the migration of peoples—in the latter case from Turkey into Europe. At any rate,
there were hominids in Europe between approximately 750,000 and 1 million years ago, as evidenced by finds at the caves of Vallonet and Escale
in France and Vértesszöllös in Hungary, discussed in a later section.

The first *Homo erectus* fossil to be found was Eugène Dubois' discovery of what he called *Pithecanthropus erectus,* or erect apeman. Dubois was a Dutchman with a French name, an anatomist and paleontologist with an interest in evolution. Having acquired a medical post in what was then the Dutch East Indies, Dubois used some of his time to search for the "missing link," a hypothetical ancestral form common to both human and ape. He even managed to get some government support to carry out his paleontological research. It seemed to Dubois that Indonesia would be a likely area to yield a missing link, for the somewhat humanlike gibbon and orangutan lived there, and Borneo and Sumatra were once attached to the mainland of Asia. Dubois did uncover a good deal of valuable fossil material in Java, including some early hominid skulls, but his principal discovery was a thick-boned fossil skullcap, the part of the skull above the ears. This find was made near the Solo River in 1891. In the following year, Dubois resumed digging near the same spot and this time uncovered a left human thighbone about 40 or 50 feet from where he had found the skullcap. Nearby, Dubois also found two molar teeth.

At first he thought the thighbone and skullcap belonged to two different individuals, but later he concluded they belonged to the same organism. Dubois may have been right the second time, but this was one point on which he was criticized after he announced his discovery. The thighbone was a straight femur of modern human type with a ridge *(linea aspera)* to which were once attached muscles used in upright locomotion. This, then, was a creature with upright posture, about five feet, eight inches in height. The skullcap was very primitive in comparison. It was low, had heavy brow ridges, and a cranial capacity of about 900 cubic centimeters. The brain was therefore intermediate in size between those of the African apes (having about 500 cubic centimeters) and modern man (with about 1,400 cubic centimeters). Because of the combination of human and apelike features in these fossil remains, Dubois gave his creature the name of *Pithecanthropus erectus* and stated that it was a transitional form of early human.

Publication of Dubois' findings set off a lot of controversy. This was the first discovery of so early a hominid. *Australopithecus africanus* was not known until 1925; the Peking discoveries were announced in the late 1920s. Since this was the first reported find of a type more primitive than Neanderthal, it is understandable that there was much skepticism. How, it was asked, could so small a brain go with such a modern femur? Why not assume that the femur was that of a modern human and the skullcap that of a large ape? Perhaps they even came from different time periods.

These were sensible enough objections at the time, but there are now so many australopithecine and *Homo erectus* fossils available for study that we know Dubois was right. It is true that we cannot prove that thighbone and skullcap belonged to the same individual, and doubts about this association have recently been revived. However, there is no longer any incongruity in finding upright posture associated with a small brain. The australopithe-

The first *Homo erectus* discovery

cines, who lived long before *Pithecanthropus,* combined these features and had even smaller brains. Besides, eight more skulls of the same type as Dubois' find have since been found in Java; and near Peking in China the remains of a closely related hominid have been found which show essentially the same characteristics. This was a widespread type of early human.

The more recently discovered skulls from Java were found by G. H. R. von Koenigswald and his Indonesian students and colleagues. The skulls show the same traits: thick walls, heavy brow ridges, and low elevation. These finds come from two geological strata, the earlier Djetis beds and the later Trinil beds. A date of perhaps around 800,000 years ago has been assigned to the fossils from the Trinil beds, where Dubois' *Pithecanthropus* was found. The Djetis beds are much earlier, perhaps as old as 1.9 million years. A very thick-boned adult skull from the Djetis beds has an estimated capacity of 750 cubic centimeters. Five Trinil skulls have an estimated brain volume of 860 centimeters. The molar teeth are longer than those of modern humans but reduced compared to those of the australopithecines. No tools or evidence of fire have been found in association with *Pithecanthropus erectus,* but it is likely that these hominids used tools and had a culture, for tools have been found in association with several other forms of *Homo erectus.*

The Lan-t'ien skull

The oldest hominid skull discovered in China is that of Lan-t'ien man, found in 1963 in Shensi Province and dated between 1.5 million and 600,000 years old. The skull has low elevation, thick walls, heavy brow ridges, and a cranial capacity of about 780 cubic centimeters. It looks much like the Javanese skulls. The skull was found in association with stegodont elephant, an ancient small bear, saber-toothed cat, Sanmen horse, tapir, giant deer, and bison.

The Peking fossils

In the late 1920s, the contents of some limestone caves were excavated at Choukoutien near Peking. This rich site yielded the remains of about 40 *Homo erectus* individuals. Their bones were splintered and fragmented but some fairly complete skulls could be assembled, and limb bones and other skeletal parts were recovered. The individuals were of both sexes and different ages. The cave seems to have been occupied off and on over a period of thousands of years, so the 40 or so persons were not necessarily members of the same family or band.

The physical type represented in this collection was very similar to that of the Java find, though with a higher cranial capacity, ranging from about 925 cubic centimeters (in the immature skull of an eight- or nine-year-old boy) to 1,225 cubic centimeters. The larger skulls are within the modern human range. The Peking skulls are low and thick walled, with a slight

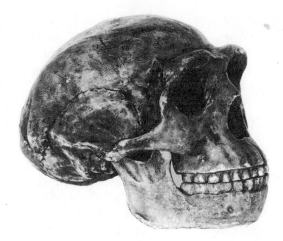

Plaster cast of reconstructed skull of Peking *Homo erectus*.

ridge along the top and heavy brow ridges over the eyes. The jaws and teeth are large. When seen from above, the dental arch is more parabolic, or V-shaped, than that of apes. The Peking molars have enlarged pulp cavities, a condition known as *taurodontism,* found later in Neanderthals and some modern populations. The upper incisors are "shovel shaped," with the sides seeming to curl inward, a characteristic of modern Mongoloid incisors, sometimes also found in non-Mongoloid people. There is no diastema. The jaw has no chin. The nose is broad and low bridged. The men of Choukoutien are judged to have been a little over 5 feet tall and the women a little under. However, it is not always possible to determine the sex of the bones, especially since they are so fragmented.

The Peking hominids were definitely toolmakers and users of tools. Stone choppers were found in the cave at Choukoutien. Although their workmanship was rough, they were deliberately flaked. There were also thousands of quartz flakes that show no sign of retouching but must have been used as tools. These pieces of quartz must have been brought to the cave from elsewhere, for no quartz is found within two miles of the site. Worked bits of bone and horn were also found. Charred hearths in the cave provide the earliest evidence in Asia of the human use of fire—perhaps around 500,000 or more years ago. The discovery of the uses of fire may have made it possible for people to live so far north. It seems likely that the Peking hominids cooked the animals they hunted, although the animal bones in the cave show no evidence of charring. Charred ostrich egg shells have been found, however. Fire was later used for cooking plant foods, but probably not at this stage. Humans cannot digest most plant foods of any caloric value without cooking. Analyses of human coprolites, desiccated feces, from much later Neanderthal sites dating between 50,000

The culture of the Peking hominids

and 100,000 years ago have so far shown no evidence of plant remains (Bryant and Williams-Dean 1975). *Homo erectus* may have gathered nuts, fruits, and some seeds, roots, and shoots. Many hackberry seeds were found in the Choukoutien cave, but the plant diet must have been limited. In any case, fire would have provided protection against predators at night, as well as warmth and visibility. Without fire, cave habitation would be dangerous.

The use of fire must have had some important psychological consequences for early humans. A fire provides a rallying point, a center, a circle of warmth in the dark night. Fire must have given early humans a greater sense of security and perhaps heightened the feeling of solidarity of those grouped around it. It may also have had aesthetic and religious connotations; for fire, with its warmth and mysterious beauty and its potentialities for both destruction and protection, has always been a source of awe for human beings.

Fire also made possible an extension of working hours. People could now sit up late, staring into the embers as we now stare into a television set, perhaps continuing to chip away at some piece of stonework in the artificial light. Animals tend to have built-in time clocks that regulate their sleeping hours. Humans have moved away from strict biological controls of this sort. Perhaps this break was encouraged by the regular use of fire with its artificial extension of daytime.

Another use of fire was in the making of tools: splitting stones by heating, and sudden cooling and hardening of the tips of wooden shafts.

A more negative note must now be added, insofar as the Peking hominids are concerned; many authorities believe that they were cannibals, as is suggested by the appearance of the bones, which, as already mentioned, were splintered. They were probably broken and split to get to the marrow. Brains seem to have been extracted from the skulls, which were broken in at the base. Cannibalism also seems to have been practiced by other Paleolithic groups; evidences of cannibalism are also found in Neanderthal sites in Europe. This does not mean that all humans were cannibals in Paleolithic times, but evidently many of them were.

Although this view is widely held, Harry L. Shapiro does not consider the evidence for cannibalism at Choukoutien to be sufficient. Shapiro (1974:84) doubts that any ritual cannibalism was practiced. The fact that the skulls and bones are broken and fragmented may best be explained by rock falls which crushed the bones in the caves. There is no need to assume human agency.

At any rate, even if they did engage in some cannibalism, that could only have constituted a small part of the diet of Peking hominids. Three fourths of the animal bones found at Choukoutien were of deer; so the favorite food of these hunters was venison. Other animal bones found in the cave deposits included boar, sheep, mammoth, water buffalo, bison, camel, ostrich, and otter.

A detailed analysis of the Peking skeletal material was made by Franz Weidenreich. Casts were made of the bones and also drawings and photographs. That was fortunate because all these bones later disappeared, and their present whereabouts is a mystery. At the time of the Japanese invasion of northern China, an attempt was made to move the Choukoutien material away from possible capture by the Japanese. An American Marine colonel, who was given the valuable fossils, packed them in some footlockers, and on December 5, 1941 they were sent off on a train to the Chinese coast, where they were to be transferred to the American liner *President Harrison*. Two days later came the attack on Pearl Harbor; the train on which the bones were sent was captured, and the *President Harrison* was grounded by her crew. Nobody knows what happened to the bones. The Chinese Communist regime has alleged that they have been hidden in the vaults of the American Museum of Natural History; museum officials deny it.

Christopher Janus, an American businessman, was a member of one of the first groups to visit China after President Nixon's surprise visit to Peking in 1972. Janus made a public offer of $5,000 for information leading to the recovery of the Choukoutien bones, a sum later raised to $150,000. He received some tantalizing leads and mysterious communications with cloak-and-dagger overtones described in his book (Janus 1975). (See also Shapiro 1974.) Although Janus followed trails to Hong Kong, Taiwan, and Thailand, he never succeeded in finding the bones.

Disappearance of the bones

Contemporaneously with the Java and Peking representatives there were hominids living in Europe. Remains of a pebble-tool culture in a cave on the French Riviera, dated at about 1 million years ago, were reported in April 1974 by Henry de Lumley. There was no evidence of fire in the cave. However, the earliest evidence of fire from Europe is even older than that from Peking, dating from as far back as 750,000 years ago at the Escale Cave in the Durance Valley, not far from Marseilles in southern France; hearths of charcoal and ash have been found in the cave, along with the remains of primitive wolves and saber-toothed cats. Another site of about the same age is the Vallonet Cave in southeastern France on the Mediterranean, which contains tools dating from between 750,000 and 1 million years ago. Two choppers like those of Olduvai Gorge were found, along with a few other worked stone tools and the fossil bones of such animals as rhinoceros, elephant, horse, and whale.

A Middle Pleistocene skull found at Petralona in Greece is considered by William Howells (1973:78) to be a rather advanced form of *Homo erectus*. It has a possible date of 700,000 years ago. This would make the Petralona skull the oldest human remains in Europe, probably *Homo erectus*. The famous Heidelberg jaw is roughly contemporary with the Petralona skull and the Vértesszöllös site, discussed below. The appearance of this heavy, chinless jaw is similar to those of the eastern Asiatic pithecanthro-

Early hominids in Europe

pines. However, although the jaw is large and thick, the teeth are relatively small, within the range of variation of modern human teeth. No artifacts or other skeletal parts were found.

A very robust partial cranium with heavy brow ridges has been recovered from a cave at Arago in the Pyrenees in the south of France and dated at more than 300,000 years ago. It is judged to be that of a man about 20 years of age. Two mandibles (which do not belong with the cranium) have also been found—one judged to be male, the other female. They are thick and massive, like the Heidelberg jaw, but different from the *Homo erectus* mandibles found in Asia and Africa. Brace et al. consider Arago to be "unquestionably" *Homo erectus*.

At Vértesszöllös in western Hungary an occupation site has been found that shows many parallels with Choukoutien. First of all, the Oldowan-like chopping tools are similar; second, there is evidence of the use of fire. In this case it is clear that the animals eaten were cooked; many bones show traces of charring, although there were also many unburned bones. Finally, there is some skeletal material, of which the three teeth of an immature child show similarities to immature teeth found at Choukoutien. On the other hand, there is also an occipital bone (rear part of the skull) that seems more advanced than that of Peking man, although the ridge for muscle attachment is a primitive feature of the skull. One estimate of the cranial capacity of the Vértesszöllös skull is about 1,300 cubic centimeters, which is higher than that of either Java or Peking man or any other representative of *Homo erectus*. J. B. Birdsell considers it to be an early *Homo sapiens* skull. Milford H. Wolpoff (1971a), however, considers the Vértesszöllös skull to be more like *Homo erectus* than like any other fossil hominid group.

Some interesting archaeological finds relating to the activities of early humans have been made at two sites in north central Spain, Torralba and Ambrona. Here there is evidence that elephants were deliberately trapped in bogs by setting fire to surrounding grass and driving the animals into the marsh where they could be attacked when they floundered and sank. There are indications that elephant bones were hacked off and removed. Many artifacts have been recovered from these Spanish sites, which have been dated at about 300,000 years ago. There are no human skeletal remains. Work here has been done by F. Clark Howell (1964:85–99). There is evidence that animals were driven into swamps in parts of sub-Saharan Africa during Middle Pleistocéne times (Clark 1960:314).

Another site dated at about 300,000 or 400,000 years ago is at Terra Amata, part of Nice on the Riviera in France, where remains have been found of some apparently oval-shaped dwellings about 50 feet long and 12–18 feet wide, containing fireplaces. Holes about 1 foot in diameter are believed to have held upright beams. The site was near a stream running into the sea. Remains of rhinoceros, *Elephas antiquus*, rabbit, deer, and wild boar have been found.

Although the sites of Escale, Torralba, Ambrona, and Nice are roughly contemporaneous with the eastern Asiatic *Homo erectus*, it cannot be asserted that the people at these places had the same physical characteristics, although it would not be at all surprising if they had.

In 1954 and 1955 the French paleontologist Camille Arambourg excavated three hominid mandibles, together with many teeth and a right parietal bone, at Ternifine in Algeria, North Africa. The appearance of these bones is like those of the eastern pithecanthropines: thick parietals, no chin, broad ascending ramus of the jaw, and big molars with enlarged pulp cavities. Associated with the bones were some roughly made hand axes, a tool type discussed in the following section.

Homo erectus in Africa

A complete *Homo erectus* skull found in North Africa, the Salé skull from Morocco, is dated perhaps as late as 100,000 years ago, with a cranial capacity of around 940 cubic centimeters, which is small for so late a skull. An incomplete cranium in Bed II at Olduvai Gorge also has been classified by some authorities as *Homo erectus*. Hand axes were found in association with the skeletal remains. Two other skulls found at Olduvai may also be *Homo erectus*. As was noted in the preceding chapter, a skull found by Richard Leakey at Lake Turkana in northern Kenya seems to be *Homo erectus*. It has a cranial capacity of more than 800 cubic centimeters.

A *hand axe* is a pear-shaped core tool of some stone, like flint, that can be fractured. Here we must distinguish between *core* and *flake* tools. Suppose you grasp a rough piece of flint and give it a blow on the top or side with another stone. If you keep banging away at it effectively enough, you will knock off some flakes or slivers of stone. If you can dislodge these flakes so as to shape the original piece of stone into the kind of tool you want, you end up with a *core* tool, so called because it consists of the core of the stone that has been trimmed.

The hand axe

It might happen that one of the flakes struck off from the core has a sharp cutting edge. It might make a good knife or scraper. If you use it as a tool, you have a *flake* tool. Both core and flake tools were used in the Lower Paleolithic. The hand axe, also known as a *core-biface* (because trimmed on both sides) and as a *coup de poing* (from the French "blow of the fist"), was the characteristic tool of the Acheulean period of the Lower Paleolithic dating back more than 1 million years ago. The Paleolithic is marked by a gradual increase in the number and kinds of flake tools, which became particularly prominent in the Upper Paleolithic.

Hand axes were fashioned so as to have a continuous cutting edge all around the bottom part. They were not hafted to handles but held in the hand. They may have been all-purpose tools, used for cutting, banging,

Some Lower Paleolithic
hand axes.

scraping, and digging. The hand axe had a wide distribution throughout Africa, western Europe, and India. The appearance of hand axes was very stable throughout this vast area, so that one found in Madras looks just like one that comes from South Africa or France.

In Africa, hand axes have been found in association with skeletal remains of *Homo erectus*. It seems likely that the use of this tool spread northward into Europe during the Lower Pleistocene and eastward to India. But the hand axe did not extend into China and other parts of eastern Asia, where the chopper remained the characteristic stone tool of the Lower Paleolithic.[1]

The distribution of the hand axe in Europe is rather puzzling. It is found in Spain, Italy, England, and France, but not east of the Rhine.

While earlier hand axes are rough in appearance, later hand axes often have straighter, less-irregular cutting edges. Kenneth P. Oakley (1964b:179) writes: ". . . in the Acheulean stages man had acquired such good mastery over stone that the form of the biface is indistinguishable whether it be made in lava, dolerite, ironstone, or quartzite. Even the fineness of craftsmanship was scarcely affected by the type of rock."

A technique used in the Upper Acheulean period to dislodge flakes was to strike the core with a relatively soft hammer of bone or antler rather than with another stone.

During the Acheulean period a new technique, called *Levallois*, was developed for making flake tools. This involved trimming and preparing a core before dislodging flakes. Flakes detached from such specially prepared "striking platforms" were larger and more symmetrical than flakes knocked off in the hit-and-miss fashion of earlier times. With this invention flake

---

[1] Hand axes did, however, appear in Java, perhaps as an independent invention, according to François Bordes (1968:81, 136, 139).

tools became more important and there was more control over their production.

The Levallois technique was widely used in Africa, western Europe, the Near East, and India, but, like the hand axe, it did not spread as far east as China in Middle Pleistocene times. The invention, however, may have been independently arrived at in several different areas where people habitually worked flint. For example, it may have been developed independently in Africa and Europe. Flakes made in the Levallois manner also appear in Hopewell sites in ancient North America, again probably due to independent invention.

The various finds that have been reviewed seem to indicate that there was a widespread type of hominid whom we call *Homo erectus* living between 1.5 million and 100,000 years ago, a hunter and gatherer with a variable stone technology, sometimes using crude choppers and sometimes hand axes. In at least some cases this type of early hominid had the use of fire. Choukoutien and other sites suggest that home bases were in use. These seem to have been used earlier by australopithecines (see p. 126), but at the time of *Homo erectus*, the advantages of the home base were strengthened by the use of fire.

The culture of
Homo erectus

The fireplace would be the symbolic center of the group, a beacon by day and by night for the men who had left camp to hunt. At the stage of *Homo erectus*, there must have been some division of labor, with men specializing as hunters and women as collectors and perhaps preparers of food. No doubt the women looked after the children, fetched wood and water, and kept the fire going. Such groups would be apt to split up during the day but have some agreed-upon place to return to in the late afternoon or evening.

Planning of this sort requires a language. Primitive though they may have appeared, with their heavy brow ridges, low skulls, and large chinless jaws, these men had relatively large brains, which were often within the range of modern humans. It seems likely that their brains had become sufficiently developed for language to be possible.

Instruction in toolmaking and the use of fire would certainly be facilitated by the use of language, although perhaps conceivable without it. The tools used by *Homo erectus* had become more elaborate than those of the australopithecines, and *Homo erectus* hunted large mammals, which probably demanded planning and collective action.

Some articles by Philip Lieberman and his associates to be discussed later in this chapter have suggested that Neanderthal communication was deficient. *Homo erectus* was lower on the evolutionary ladder than Neanderthals; so perhaps, if Lieberman et al. are right, use of language by *Homo erectus* was even more rudimentary. The view taken here, however, is that some sort of language was probably spoken by *Homo erectus*.

From around 100,000 years ago there were hominids whom we call Neanderthal living in Europe, North Africa, the Near East, and parts of Asia. "Neanderthal man" was long considered to be a species distinct from the modern one and was labeled *Homo neanderthalensis*. Now, however, the Neanderthals are classified as a subspecies, *Homo sapiens neanderthalensis*. Fossil remains of this type have been found in Spain, France, Belgium, Germany, Italy, Czechoslovakia, Hungary, Yugoslavia, the Crimea, Uzbekistan, Iraq, Israel, Lebanon, Libya, and Morocco.

In between clearly defined *Homo erectus* and more advanced *Homo sapiens* fossils there is a range of intermediate forms that are hard to classify.

Between *Homo erectus* and the Neanderthals

For example, at Steinheim in Germany an almost complete skull, thought to be female, was found, dated from the second interglacial period about 250,000 years ago. Some authorities, notably Carleton Coon, see modern features in the appearance of the skull, although it has thick brow ridges, little elevation, and a cranial capacity of around 1,150 cubic centimeters. Coon says that, except for some taurodontism, the teeth are like those of a modern European woman (Coon 1962:495).

The back part of a young adult skull at Swanscombe, England, along with some Acheulean stone tools (see p. 145), was also dated through associated animal bones at around 250,000 years ago. The bones of the skull are thick and the vault is rather low, but some physical anthropologists consider the skull to tend in the modern direction. It cannot be known whether thick brow ridges were present or what the facial region looked like, since these parts are missing. Skeletal material has also been recovered from Montmaurin and Fontéchevade in France which seem to represent a population intermediate between *Homo erectus* and *Homo sapiens*. Intermediate types have also appeared in Africa, best known of which are the Rhodesian finds.

Remains of two individuals were found in a quarry at what was then Broken Hill, Northern Rhodesia (now Kabwe, Zambia). The skull of the first and more complete find has a very primitive appearance in its low elevation, huge brow ridges, large eye sockets, wide mouth, and long face. The cranial capacity is about 1,300 cubic centimeters. A skullcap similar to that of Rhodesian man was found at Saldanha Bay, about 90 miles north of Capetown; it also resembles a skull from Olduvai Gorge. Apparently this was a widespread type of early human found in southern and eastern Africa. Rhodesian man was formerly assigned a relatively late Upper Pleistocene date, but recent dating techniques have now given an earlier date of more than 125,000 years ago in the later part of the Middle Pleistocene (Klein 1973:311–12).

Twelve skulls and two tibia were found together near the Solo River in Java, dated at perhaps around 100,000 years ago. The skulls were resting

A plaster cast of the Rhodesian skull dating from the late Middle Pleistocene in Rhodesia, South Africa, with a cranial capacity of about 1,300 cubic centimeters, huge brow ridges, large eye sockets, and long face.

on their tops, bases facing upward. Since only skulls were found, without other skeletal material besides the tibia, and since all of the bases, except two, were broken or partly removed, it looks as though cannibalism was practiced. These skulls are thick walled and seem more primitive than Neanderthal skulls. Carleton Coon classifies them as *Homo erectus*, but the more common practice has been to characterize them as "Neanderthaloid," or transitional between *Homo erectus* and the Neanderthal form of *Homo sapiens*. Perhaps the same can be said of the Rhodesian and Saldanha skulls.

An important evolutionary change between *Homo erectus* and the Neanderthals was an increase in brain size. The Peking hominids had a cranial capacity of about 1,100 cubic centimeters. European hominids of the second interglacial period also seem to have had relatively small skulls. The Steinheim skull had a capacity of 1,150 cubic centimeters. Two skulls from Saccopastore near Rome had 1,200 to 1,300 cubic centimeters. But the Monte Circeo (Italy) Neanderthal skull had 1,550 cubic centimeters; the man of La Chapelle aux Saints in France had 1,620 cubic centimeters; a man from Shanidar, Iraq, had over 1,700 cubic centimeters; and a skull from Amud, Israel, had 1,740 cubic centimeters.

Neanderthals generally retained various characteristics of *Homo erectus*—thick skull walls and brow ridges, heavy chinless jaws and teeth, and some prognathism, or facial protrusion, but the Neanderthal facial region was larger. The skull often had low elevation. This may seem paradoxical, since a large cranial capacity has just been cited as a characteristic Neanderthal

Neanderthal physical traits

Reconstructed plaster
cast of skull of a
"Classic" Neanderthal
(La Chapelle aux Saints).

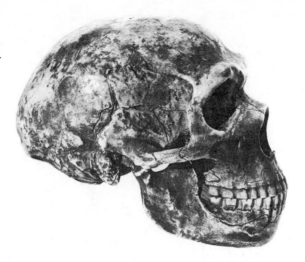

feature. The explanation is that Neanderthal skulls were often very long, compared to those of modern humans, which are rounder and more highly domed, and the Neanderthal skull broadened out behind the ears. The frontal part of the skull was not so fully developed as in modern humans. Neanderthals often had a broad nose, large eye sockets, and a forwardly projecting upper jaw. Frequently there was no *canine fossa* on either side of the nose, as in modern humans; instead there was a slight puffing out of bone in this region. The mouth was very broad, and the neck was thick and heavily muscled.

It used to be thought that Neanderthals did not stand quite erect and walked with a shambling, shuffling gait with their heads thrust forward. Our cartoon conceptions of Stone Age humans are based on this stereotype. One reason for this reconstruction is that some Neanderthal leg bones are very bowed. Our impression of what Neanderthals looked like was based largely on a detailed reconstruction made by Marcellin Boule in 1911–13 of the skeleton of the man from La Chapelle aux Saints. Boule emphasized this man's brutish appearance, his slumped-forward posture and bent-knee gait. It was not until 1957 that two anatomists, William Straus and A. J. E. Cave, made a careful reexamination of the skeleton. They found that the man of La Chapelle aux Saints had suffered from arthritis, which affected his jaw and spinal column. Straus and Cave claimed that the man of La Chapelle aux Saints was not essentially different anatomically from modern humans.

Another aspect of our cartoon conception of Stone Age men is that they were very hairy, but this cannot be known from the fossil evidence. There is one aspect of the stereotyped picture that does have justification: Neanderthal men were barrel-chested and had powerfully muscled arms and legs. They were about 5 feet tall, or a little taller.

Although some of the earlier stereotyped notions about Neanderthals now seem to be passé, a controversial idea has been introduced that may revive them; it has been claimed that Neanderthals could not speak very well. Philip Lieberman, Edmund S. Crelin, and Dennis H. Klatt (1972) have made measurements of the neck vertebrae and the base of the skull of the man of La Chapelle aux Saints and have concluded that Neanderthals did not have a pharynx like that of modern humans and consequently were unable to pronounce a number of vowels and consonants that we can pronounce today. This does not mean that Neanderthals had no language, but Lieberman et al. believe that linguistic communication among Neanderthals was considerably slower and less efficient than among ourselves.

Criticism of the findings of Lieberman and his associates has come from two articles in the *American Journal of Physical Anthropology*, in which the following points are made: (1) the brains of Neanderthals were at least as large as those of modern humans; (2) the Sylvian fissures of the brain, as seen in the endocranial cast of the skull of La Chapelle aux Saints, resemble those of modern humans, implying that speech was present; (3) modern adults who have features like those described by Lieberman et al., such as prognathism and flattening of the base of the skull, are quite able to speak complex modern languages; and (4) Lieberman and his associates have reconstructed the hyoid bone of the La Chapelle aux Saints individual in a position too high to permit swallowing, not taking into account the influence of upright posture and bipedalism on the position of the larynx (Le May 1975; Falk 1975).

Neanderthal language capability

There has been much argument among anthropologists about the relationship between *Homo sapiens sapiens* and the Neanderthals. Fossil remains of the latter seem to disappear from Europe after the retreat of the last glaciation. In place of Neanderthals we now find humans of modern physical type, equipped with a high-domed skull, a chin, and other characteristics of present-day *Homo sapiens*. What became of the Neanderthals, then? There are at least three possible answers: (1) Modern humans evolved from Neanderthals. (2) Neanderthals became extinct in Europe as humans of modern physical type moved in after the retreat of the glaciers. Perhaps the modern types wiped out the Neanderthals or displaced them by being more efficient hunters. (3) Humans of modern physical type interbred with Neanderthals. At least some modern Europeans would then be descendants of the resultant hybrid stock.

Many writers on the subject of our evolution seem to have been reluctant to think that we could have evolved from such brutish characters as Neanderthals. They have argued that humans of modern physical type already existed at the time of Neanderthals; hence, we need not be descended from the latter. Moreover, the disappearance of Neanderthals and the associated

Our relation to the Neanderthals

Mousterian culture was rather sudden. There would not have been enough time, it has been argued, for modern humans to have evolved from the European Neanderthals. Modern types of humans must have been living elsewhere, developing the Upper Paleolithic culture they brought into Europe.

The variability of Neanderthals

There are many problems involved in the issues just raised. One problem is what constitutes the Neanderthal type. What do we mean when we speak of "Neanderthal man"? In the general description of physical traits given earlier, the terms "often" and "frequently" were used when referring to particular traits, such as heavy brow ridges. That is because such traits are not invariable; there seems to have been much variation in the Neanderthal population and also in their predecessors. Most of the traits listed are common in what have been called the "Classic" Neanderthal skeletons found in western Europe: Spain, France, Belgium, Germany, and Italy. The complex of traits is less evident in many of the Near Eastern Neanderthals found in Israel and Lebanon, which have been called "Progressive." The latter often had rounder, more highly domed skulls with less continuous brow ridges, and they often differed in other respects from the Classical type. For example, the skull of a seven-year-old boy found near Beirut, Lebanon, with one radiocarbon date of about 43,750 years ago, lacked brow ridges, although such ridges have been found in the skulls of other Neanderthal children of about the same age. The boy's forehead was vertical, the profile straight, and his jaw had a chin.

Some authorities consider the Classic Neanderthals to have been a specialized stock adapted to the cold weather conditions of glacial times. Neanderthals occupied southern Europe at a time when most of Europe was covered by ice. They lived in caves and used fire. There were also warmer times during the last interglacial period. During the cold period, there were many mammals with heavy coats of fur, such as the mammoth, wooly rhinoceros, and cave bear. Neanderthals were able to kill these large animals, whose bones have been found in their caves. During the last, or Würm, glaciation, the European Neanderthals became confined to the southern parts of Europe. Escape was blocked by the Mediterranean to the south and by glaciers to the north and east, although there was a narrow corridor through central Europe. One interpretation, then, is that Classic Neanderthals represented a physical type that developed in response to the prolonged cold weather in Europe. The thickset body build, like that of the Eskimo, should have helped to conserve body heat. The puffed-out bone in the region where modern humans' *canine fossa* is found may have helped to warm the air breathed in. But it is hard to account for the wide nasal aperture in such Darwinian terms; Eskimos have a narrow one. It has been argued, however, that a large projecting nose may have adaptive advantages in a cold climate (Howells 1973:107–9). If the Classic Neanderthals were specially adapted to particular climatic conditions, they may have been a "dead-end" stock which became extinct when the weather got warmer and more advanced humans with Upper Paleolithic cultural traditions moved into the area. Those who hold this view derive the modern type of *Homo sapiens* from Progressive Neanderthals who originally lived farther east.

One difficulty with this interpretation is that Classic Neanderthals were not limited to western Europe and must often have lived beyond the confines of the glaciers, as shown by a skull found at Casablanca in 1962 and by the skeletal material at Shanidar. Between 1953 and 1960, archaeologist Ralph Solecki found seven Neanderthal skeletons with Classic features in a large cave at Shanidar, Iraq. The deposits have been dated between approximately 60,000 and 45,000 years ago. One male of about 40 years of age was taller than the European Neanderthals, being about 5 feet, 8 inches; he also had an enormous cranial capacity—over 1,700 cubic centimeters. His face resembles that of the man of La Chapelle aux Saints in its length and thick brow ridges. There is no *canine fossa* but some appearance of a chin.

Problems are also presented by the apparent coexistence of Neanderthaloid and more modern types of humans at Mount Carmel in Israel, where a great range of variation appears in the skeletal material. Remains of about a dozen individuals have been recovered from two caves at Mount Carmel, showing a combination of Neanderthal and modern human traits. Although all have heavy brow ridges, some individuals have fairly high-domed skulls and some have chins. The caves date from around 40,000 to 35,000 years ago. There seem to be three ways of accounting for the variability of the Mount Carmel population: (1) This was an area where Neanderthal types were evolving into the modern form of *Homo sapiens*. (2) This was an area where two types of humans, Neanderthal and *Homo sapiens sapiens*, came together and interbred. (3) The population was simply characterized by a great deal of variability.

Geneticists are said to disfavor the first view. The second view has the advantage of a certain dramatic appeal and is supported by some authorities. But the third view seems to present a sufficient explanation. Moreover, the only other Neanderthal population that has remains of more than ten individuals (at Krapina in Yugoslavia) shows the same kind of variability as that found in Israel. It may be that anthropologists have been led to expect too much uniformity in the fossil record and to expect all Neanderthals to look like the man of La Chapelle aux Saints. Evolution in the direction of modern humans did, after all, take place. It should not be surprising, then, to find a variable Neanderthal population in which some persons had chins, high-domed skulls, and other modern features. The division of Neanderthals into Classic and Progressive types may be a premature ordering of the fossil material, for there must have been a good deal of variation in western Europe, even in areas where the Classic type was prominent (Brace 1962a).

Human facial structure underwent an evolution from the large facial region with prominent teeth and heavy brow ridges of the Classic Neanderthals to a reduction of these features. C. L. Brace has argued that early humans up to the time of Neanderthals must have used their front teeth as tools for cutting meat or for softening leather as Eskimos do. Such teeth always show considerable wear. Brace believes that with the invention and diffusion of more effective cutting tools in the Upper Paleolithic, it was no longer necessary for people to have such large teeth and powerful jaws. Their reduction could therefore take place without selective disadvantage; mutations in that direction could occur without detriment. The development of cooking and the use of fire to soften meat would also make massive jaws and teeth less necessary. This seems to be a convincing explanation for the modifications in Neanderthal facial structure in the course of evolution leading to modern humans (Brace 1962b; Brose and Wolpoff 1971).

Mousterian tools

Mousterian tools, associated with Neanderthals, have been found north of the Sahara, from Europe to China, in the Middle Paleolithic period, dating from about 80,000 to 32,000 B.C. During this period the Levallois flaking tradition continued. Although hand axes were still in use, their numbers declined, and the main emphasis was on flake tools. The first known projectile points, evidently used on hand-thrown spears, appear at a site at Ehringdorf, Germany, near the edge of the northern Eurasiatic plains, which humans were beginning to occupy.

Some use was made in Mousterian times of bone, but only in a rudimentary way, in contrast to the Upper Paleolithic, when bone tools become prominent.

Mousterian tools are characterized by great variety, marking a considerable advance over the period of *Homo erectus*. French archaeologist François Bordes distinguished about 60 different types of stone tools. He also found that there seem to be different kits of tools at different sites. One European kit is known as denticulate (toothed) Mousterian, because it contains flakes with toothed edges, usually found in association with the bones of wild horses. Bordes thinks the variation in different kits occurred because there were different traditions of toolmaking in different bands or tribes of Neanderthals. Each band probably kept pretty much to itself and did not often encounter strange bands. If such bands did meet, they were not likely to exchange much information about toolmaking processes.

A different interpretation of Mousterian tool variability has been advanced by Lewis and Sally Binford, who have a functional approach to the problem. In excavating a Neanderthal site in Israel near the Sea of Galilee, a collection of stone implements was found, which was then compared with those from other Neanderthal sites. A factor analysis of tool types was made by the Binfords, which resulted in the discrimination of

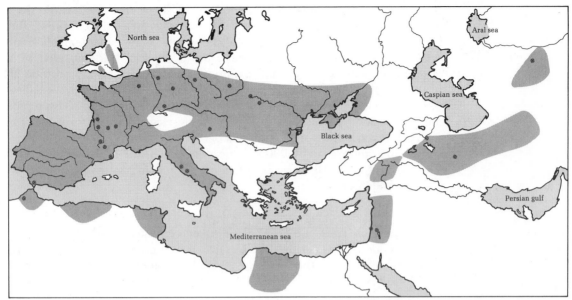

Map showing the known distribution of the Mousterian stone tool tradition.

five tool kits (groups of artifacts having a high order of mutual covariance) that seem to have been used for different purposes. One kit was primarily used for killing and butchering, another for shredding and cutting wood or other plant materials, and so on. The predominant tool kit at the Israeli site dealt with maintenance activities, repairing old tools and preparing new ones. The other two kits primarily in evidence had to do with food preparation, killing and butchering, suggesting use of the site as a base camp. Not all Neanderthal sites show these particular patterns. Another site, in Syria, seems to have been mainly a temporary butchering site and work camp.

In a later investigation of European Neanderthal sites, the Binfords examined the possibilities of sexual division of labor. They reasoned that men probably ranged away from camp to hunt animals, while the women stayed at the base camp. Women would then be apt to make tools from locally available flint, while the men's flint tools might come from more distant places. It turned out that the hunting tools used by male Neanderthals were worked by the Levallois technique and often were made of flint from distant sources, while the tools probably associated with women's work tended to be denticulate, or notched, tools that were used in the processing of food and were made from local flint (Bordes 1961; Binford and Binford 1966; Pfeiffer 1969:173–95).

Although the stone tools were well made, the culture of Neanderthals was still primitive, when compared with that of the Upper Paleolithic. There is not much evidence of art, ornament, and decorative design. However, there is at least some such material, which shows that the Neanderthals did have potentialities that are more dramatically in evidence during the Upper Paleolithic. From Neanderthal sites have come pendants made from a reindeer phalanx and a fox canine; a bovid shoulder blade covered with fine parallel lines; and a carved mammoth molar, dated by radiocarbon at around 50,000 B.C. The latter piece, which is quite beautiful, shows skilled workmanship. It is reproduced in color in Marshack 1976:143. Also reproduced in color by Marshack is a remarkably elegant statuette of a horse carved in mammoth ivory found at Vogelherd in South Germany in 1931 and dated at more than 30,000 B.C., near the end of the Mousterian period. This work of art is 10,000 years or more older than the cave paintings of Lascaux and Altamira.

Evidence of religious beliefs

Neanderthals were the first people known to bury the dead. They did not always do so—sometimes their bones, mixed up with those of animals, appear in disorder in the backs of caves. But sometimes graves were dug in the dirt floors of their caves. The limbs were often flexed, perhaps to save space, although there may have been other reasons for this practice. In these burials we see the beginnings of a practice that became more elaborate in later periods—the placing of grave goods with the dead. At Le Moustier in the Dordogne region of France, a youth was buried with his head resting on a pile of flint fragments, with the charred and split bones of wild cattle around him and a fist axe near his hand. In a burial at La Chapelle aux Saints, also in the Dordogne, were a number of shells, some Mousterian flints, and various animal bones. At Mount Carmel, some large animal jawbones were included in the burial. At Teshik-Tash in Uzbekistan, a child's corpse was surrounded by six pairs of goats' horns, whose points were pushed into the ground.

Where grave goods are buried with the dead among present-day peoples, the practice is usually associated with the idea of an afterlife and with the notion that the spirit of the dead person will use the object in the other world. Neanderthals may have had such ideas, which are certainly very old, to judge by their universality among primitive peoples. To be sure, there may be other explanations for these burial practices.

A remarkable discovery was made in the excavation of the Shanidar cave. Ralph Solecki collected samples of pollen from a grave for botanical analysis. It turned out that they came from flowers of a bright-colored species that had apparently been heaped on the dead body, the earliest record of honoring the dead in such a fashion.

There are other implications of religious beliefs held by Neanderthals in the collections of bear skulls found in their caves. The mere preservation of skulls need not suggest anything religious, but in some cases special attention was given to their placement. In one cave, five bear skulls were found in niches in the cave wall. The skulls of several cave bears in a

A drawing made by a Japanese artist around 1890 of the bear cult of the bearded Ainu in northern Japan, one manifestation of circumpolar bear ceremonialism.

group have been found surrounded by built-up stone walls, with some skulls having little stones placed around them, while others were set out on slabs.

All this suggests some kind of bear cult, like that practiced until quite recently by the Chippewa and other North American Indians. After a Chippewa hunter had killed a bear, he would cut off the head, which was then decorated with beads and ribbons (in the period after contact with Europeans). Some tobacco was placed before its nose. The hunter would then make a little speech, apologizing to the bear for having had to kill it. Bear skulls were preserved and hung up on trees so that dogs and wolves could not get at them. Bear ceremonialism of this and related kinds had a wide circumpolar distribution—from the Great Lakes to the northwestern coast of North America in the New World and from the Ainu of northern Japan through various Siberian tribes, such as the Ostyaks and the Orochi, to the Finns and Lapps of Scandinavia. So wide a distribution of this trait, associated as it was with other apparently very early circumpolar traits, suggests great age. It is possible, therefore, that some aspects of this bear ceremonialism go back to Middle Paleolithic times.

Summary

Homo erectus flourished in Europe, Africa, China, and Indonesia between 1.5 million to about 100,000 years ago. These hominids were thick skulled, had heavy brow ridges, and lacked a chin, but they were taller and had larger brains than did the australopithecines. At least some bands of *Homo erectus* had the use of fire, and they employed a variable technology, some groups using crude choppers and others hand axes. It seems likely that they had a language.

In between *Homo erectus* and modern types of *Homo sapiens* there is a range of intermediate forms, such as Swanscombe in England and Steinheim in Germany, both dated at about 250,000 years ago, the Rhodesian type dated at more than 125,000 years ago, and the Solo skulls from Java, about 100,000 years ago.

The Neanderthals were a later, more advanced form, now classified within our species as *Homo sapiens neanderthalensis*. They lived in Europe, North Africa, the Near East, and parts of Asia between around 100,000 to 35,000 years ago. The principal evolutionary change between *Homo erectus* and the Neanderthals was an increase in brain size, although the skull still had low elevation. Like *Homo erectus*, the Neanderthals had thick skull walls and brow ridges and heavy chinless jaws, although these traits were variable.

The Mousterian tools associated with the Neanderthals are well made and marked by great variety, but there is not much evidence of art, when compared with the later culture of the Upper Paleolithic. The Neanderthals, however, were the first people known to bury the dead and to include grave goods with the corpse, which suggests possible belief in an afterlife. Their preserved collections of bear skulls also give evidence of bear ceremonialism. Thus the Neanderthals showed the first indications of religious beliefs and practices.

Suggestions for further reading

For a brief survey, see William Howells, *Evolution of the Genus Homo* (Reading, Mass.: Addison-Wesley Publishing, 1973). For illustrations of the principal early hominid skulls, with commentary, see C. Loring Brace, Harry Nelson, Noel Korn, and Mary L. Brace, *Atlas of Fossil Man* (New York: Holt, Rinehart & Winston, 1979).

On the role of culture in human evolution, see M. F. Ashley Montagu, ed., *Culture and the Evolution of Man* (New York: Oxford University Press, 1962); Charles F. Hockett and Robert Ascher, "The Human Revolution," *Current Anthropology* 5, no. 3 (June 1964): 135–68.

Some good works that deal with the stone technology of early man are Kenneth P. Oakley, *Man the Tool-Maker* (Chicago: University of Chicago Press, Phoenix Books, 1964): S. A. Semenov, *Prehistoric Technology*, trans. from the Russian by M. W. Thompson (New York: Barnes & Noble, 1964); Robert J. Braidwood, *Prehistoric Men*, 8th ed. (Glenview, Ill.: Scott, Foresman, 1975); François Bordes, *The Old Stone Age*, trans. from the French by J. E. Anderson (New York: McGraw-Hill, 1968). See also Jacques Bordaz, *Tools of the Old and New Stone Age* (New York: Natural History Press, 1970). See also Grahame Clark and Stuart Piggott, *Prehistoric Societies* (New York: Alfred A. Knopf, 1965).

For a survey of Paleolithic cultures, see J. M. Coles and E. S. Higgs, *The Archaeology of Early Man* (New York: Praeger Publishers, 1969).

For the development of language, see Eric H. Lenneberg, *Biological Foundations of Language* (New York: John Wiley & Sons, 1967).

For a brief review about the Neanderthals, see Kenneth A. R. Kennedy, *Neanderthal Man* (Minneapolis: Burgess Publishing Co., 1975). A well-illustrated survey is George Constable and the Editors of Time-Life Books, *The Neanderthals* (New York: Time-Life Books, 1973). See also C. Loring Brace, "The Fate of the 'Classic' Neanderthals: A Consideration of Hominid Catastrophism," *Current Anthropology* 5, no. 1 (February, 1964): 3–46.

For a statement of the traditional view about the "dead end" "Classic" Neanderthals, see F. Clark Howell, "The Evolutionary Significance of Variation and Varieties of Neanderthal Man," *Quarterly Review of Biology* 32, no. 4 (1957): 330–47.

For a description of the Shanidar excavation, see Ralph S. Solecki, *Shanidar: The First Flower People* (New York: Alfred A. Knopf, 1971).

For a recent statement on human evolution, see Gail Kennedy, "The Emergence of Modern Man," *Nature* 284 (March 6, 1980): 11–12.

CHAPTER 9

Homo sapiens sapiens in the Upper Paleolithic

Approximately 40,000 years ago, *Homo sapiens sapiens* appeared—humans of modern physical type, represented by such early examples as Cro-Magnon man found in the Dordogne region of France. Other such finds in France were made at the sites of Combe-Capelle, Chancelade, and Grotte des Enfants on the Riviera. Apparently earlier than these was the Předmosti skull from Czechoslovakia.

But *Homo sapiens sapiens* was not limited to the European scene at this time, for a contemporary skull of modern type was found in Niah cave in Malaysian Borneo. Also modern in appearance is the Florisbad skull from the Transvaal of South Africa, dated at around 33,000 B.P. or earlier. There are skulls of an older date (45,000–55,000 years ago) in the caves of Skhul, Israel, which some authorities have labeled *Homo sapiens sapiens.* A still earlier skull from Omo, Ethiopia, has been compared with those from Skhul and seems to be essentially modern in general form (Pilbeam 1972:182–88). These people were like ourselves but more ruggedly built. The Europeans of the Upper Paleolithic had relatively narrow heads, rather short from front to back, with higher foreheads and smaller, more divided brow ridges, in contrast to the more continuous ridges of earlier forms. Their skulls were more domed or vaulted than those of *Homo erectus* and the Classic Neanderthals. The cranial capacity was that of present-day humans. The facial region was less protrusive than in earlier forms. Their jaws had prominent chins.

When the glaciers began to retreat in Europe during the last interglacial period, 50,000 years ago, they left behind a relatively treeless tundra, across which blew loess, the yellowish brown dust deposited by the glaciers. In warmer, moister weather, loess was gradually converted into loam. During the warm summer months, grasses and other vegetation sprang from this soil, providing admirable grazing grounds for the four-footed, herbivorous ungulates that flourished in Europe at that time. Wild horses, reindeer, mammoth, bison, rhinoceroses, and other animals moved across the open plains, providing splendid opportunities for human hunters.

The human skeletal remains of this period in Europe are much more common than those of their predecessors, suggesting that a steady population increase was taking place at this time, due partly to the abundance of game. But we must also credit human ingenuity in devising new hunting tools, for this was a period that saw many cultural innovations, despite the fact that the Upper Paleolithic covered only a fraction of the whole Paleolithic period.

Upper Paleolithic inventions

One of the new inventions was the spear-thrower, or throwing-board. Spears had been in use for a long time before this, but the new device gave them greater impetus. Instead of being thrown directly by hand, the spear was now propelled from a grooved board, gripped near the front end. The butt of the shaft was held by a projection at the back of the board. With a twist of the wrist, a spearsman could send a shaft through the air with much greater force than with the unaided arm. This invention is probably earlier than that of the bow and arrow. The throwing-board was used by early American Indians, the Eskimos, and the Australian aborigines. The widespread use by hunting peoples of different continents suggests great age. The Aztec name for spear-thrower, *atlatl*, is sometimes used for this device in anthropological literature.

In Europe the bow and arrow is known to have been in use in the later Mesolithic period but was possibly also used in the Upper Paleolithic. One bit of early evidence is a collection of about 100 wooden arrows found near Hamburg, which may be dated at about 10,500 years ago. What look like representations of feathered arrows (although they may have been darts) appear in the cave paintings of Lascaux.

Harpoons with detachable heads were used by Upper Paleolithic hunters, as they have been used by Eskimos. Eskimos harpoon seals and other sea mammals, and we think of harpooning as a technique for killing whales and seals. Bibby (1956:166–67) believes that the earliest use of harpoons was against land animals such as reindeer, although they also may have been used for spearing fish. Some former reindeer hunters who settled along the fjords of central Norway around 7000 B.C. are believed to have been the first to transfer the harpooning technique to the killing of sea mammals. Leroi-Gourhan, on the other hand, thinks that Upper Paleolithic harpoons were used for spearing fish, and he believes that the weapon was not thrown but held in the hand (Leroi-Gourhan 1967:59).

It may be noted that these hunting devices—spear-thrower and har-

Upper Paleolithic tools *(left to right):* blade with sharp cutting edge; blade core from which blades are struck off; borer, or drill; blade; burin, or graver.

poon—are not only ingenious, far from obvious inventions, but they also required a good deal of training and practice to be effective. Moreover, they are composite tools consisting of different parts, often of different materials. Instead of having fire-hardened tips, spears and harpoons now had separate heads made of antler, bone, ivory, and flint. The harpoon consisted of three parts: head, shaft, and line.

Another hunting device was the *leister,* a trident-shaped spear with a point flanked by two prongs of bone that could hold a speared fish.

The characteristic stone tools of the Upper Paleolithic were blade tools. A blade is a sharp-edged flake with long parallel sides at least twice as long as they are wide. It is made from a carefully prepared core of flint or obsidian from which the flakes are knocked off. Blades were used as knives and scrapers. Burins are also found in Upper Paleolithic assemblages. A *burin* is a chisel-like stone tool that may be made from a blade and is used as a graver. Burins were used for working bone, antler, ivory, and wood.

More use was made of materials other than stone. Bone was used for chisels, gouges, and arrow-straighteners. The presence of bone needles and ivory pins suggests that skin clothing was worn. Various materials were used for decoration. In Upper Paleolithic burials necklaces have been found made of shells, fish vertebrae, deer teeth, and pieces of bone and ivory.

Decorative art

Decorations and animal figures were often engraved on the shafts of spear-throwers, shaft-straighteners, and other objects. Some of this artwork is quite beautiful.

An implement of bone or horn, looking somewhat like a monkey wrench, is called a *pierced staff.* Such "staffs" are often decorated, particularly with

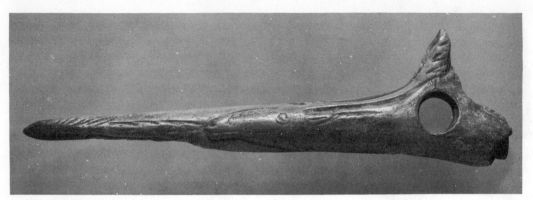

Upper Paleolithic *bâton
de commandement.*

the figures of horses. Since much artistic elaboration had been devoted
to these objects, it was formerly thought that they were scepters, or *bâtons
de commandement,* as they were called. More recently it has been decided
that they were thong-stroppers or else shaft-straighteners, similar to objects
used by Eskimos and Indians for straightening arrows and spears.

Other decorated tools included bone spatulas, half-rounded horn rods,
and objects (perhaps pendants) evidently meant to be suspended since
they had holes for the insertion of cords.

With the exceptions noted previously, the people of the Upper Paleolithic
are the first artists whose work has been preserved. One might expect
that the first known artwork of early humans would be rather crude, but
the art of the Upper Paleolithic is not at all crude; it is vigorous and
well executed. This art was produced in various media: clay sculpture, engraving in antler and ivory, and paintings on the walls of caves. The major
subject matter of the representational art consisted of the animals hunted
by Upper Paleolithic men, such as reindeer and deer, mammoths, wild
horses and cows, bison, and rhinoceroses.

Cave paintings   The most impressive Upper Paleolithic artworks are the cave paintings
of Spain and southern France, where walls were covered with the forms
of animals, some small, some as large as 20 feet in length. These were
painted with mineral oxide pigments, the main colors being black, red,
and yellow. At Lascaux Cave, dated between 35,000 and 17,000 years
ago, large bulls were painted, outlined in black, but there were also filled-
in, shaded figures with more subtle colors, such as lavender and mauve.
Blue and green do not appear, although it is possible that the artists used
such colors of organic origin that have since disintegrated. The colors that
remain are still fresh and clear.

The pigments sometimes seem to have been used solid as pastels, sometimes mixed with water or grease. They were applied directly with the

fingers, smeared on with pads of moss or lichen or applied with some kind of brush. In some cases it looks as though the paint may have been blown through a bone tube, for some of the animals have vague, fuzzy outlines, reminiscent of Chinese wash drawings. Hollow bones filled with ocher have been found in the caves. Shoulder blades of large animals, stained with color, have also been found, as well as naturally hollowed stones containing pigments. These were probably mortars in which mineral oxides were crushed and ground.

The animals are not depicted in settings or landscape. Earlier observers were struck by the seeming absence of composition. For example, a later animal figure is sometimes superimposed over an earlier one. But there is some degree of composition, as in some of the groupings at Lascaux.

The animals are drawn with skill, showing good anatomical observation. There is no doubt about which animals were meant to be shown. However, the drawings are not always complete. Legs and belly lines were sometimes left out. Sometimes natural features of the rock were utilized in the painting, so that an outward bulge of rock, for example, was turned into a horse's flank.

Human figures are seldom shown in the cave art. When they appear, they are sometimes stick figures, lacking the close observation and accuracy of the animal drawings. When men are depicted, they often wear animal masks or have animal heads.

Some of the large animal figures, such as the bulls of Lascaux, 13 and 16 feet long, must have involved a lot of work and perhaps the cooperation of several men. Some figures on the ceilings of caves suggest that scaffolding was erected. So these must have been serious projects involving some group planning and cooperation.

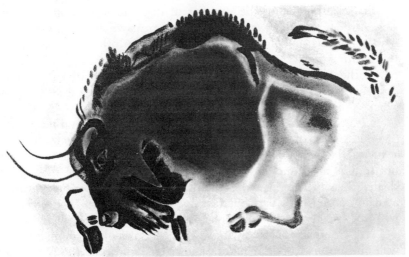

Cave painting of bison, Altamira, Spain.

Why did Upper Paleolithic people make the numerous animal paintings? We do not know for certain. A commonly accepted explanation has been that the paintings had magico-religious functions and were designed to increase the number of game animals or to win control over them. It was pointed out that the main motive cannot have been aesthetic; it was not a question of art for art's sake. This is suggested by the fact that many of the paintings are found in deep recesses, in pitch darkness, a long way from the entrance. Some cave art at Niaux in the Dordogne is over two thirds of a mile from the mouth of the cave. Sometimes, in order to reach the paintings, one has to crawl through narrow tunnels. The difficulty of access, remoteness, and darkness are testimony to the serious, religious nature of cave art.

We can only speculate about why people explored these dark caves, so far from daylight, and why they painted on the rocky walls. It seems likely that humans first made paintings and engravings near the mouths of caves and later moved into more remote recesses. The earlier paintings might conceivably have been a kind of decoration to brighten up the home, if people lived at the cave entrances; but the later paintings cannot have had such a function.

Figures of bison, horses, and mammoths sometimes show darts or arrows sticking in them. Some animals painted on rather soft rock are pitted with holes. It has been inferred that spears were violently thrown at these paintings. A cave at Montespan has 20 clay animals that seem to have been similarly speared. This is reminiscent of the old and widespread magical practice of sticking pins into a doll that represents an enemy. By making a representation of something, one gets control over it; by damaging it, one wounds the object or person it represents. Thus, by painting animals, the Paleolithic hunters might have thought they were getting control over them; by spearing them, they ensured their later slaughter.

On the other hand, the number of depictions of wounded animals is small, amounting to fewer than 10 percent. As we shall see, Leroi-Gourhan, who made this statistical assessment, has given other reasons for doubting the hunting-magic interpretation.

Another proposition of the hunting-magic view is that the hunters not only magically killed their game but also magically increased it by depicting female animals as pregnant.

The human female figurines of the Upper Paleolithic, rather oddly named "Venuses," also often have a pregnant appearance; at any rate, the secondary sexual characteristics are exaggerated: broad hips, large breasts and abdomen, but spindly arms and stunted legs. No facial features are shown, although the hairdo may be indicated. It seems unlikely that Upper Paleolithic women actually looked like that, but perhaps it was an ideal type or expressed a wish for fertility, as in the "pregnant" animals painted in the caves.

Leroi-Gourhan is not convinced that the fat-looking animals on the cave walls are meant to be pregnant; it is often impossible to say whether they are male or female animals. Maybe they are simply fat.

The hunting-magic hypothesis seems reasonable, but there are other possible ways of interpreting Upper Paleolithic cave art. A recent line of inquiry has been pursued by Annette Laming-Emperaire and Leroi-Gourhan. They have made statistical analyses of the different kinds of animals painted and the locations of the paintings on the cave walls. Their findings suggest that certain animals had a symbolic significance for the artists.

Not all animals known to the Paleolithic hunters were painted on the cave walls. The number of species depicted is smaller than that known to have existed at the time. In Leroi-Gourhan's analysis of 2,188 animal figures from 66 caves and rock shelters, the following species are the most common: 610 horses, 510 bison, 205 mammoths, 176 ibexes, 137 "oxen," 135 hinds, 112 stags, 84 reindeer, 36 bears, 29 lions, and 16 rhinoceroses.

These animals tend to appear in particular parts of caves; they are not distributed at random. Some species tend to be found in the central portions of caves: 91 percent of bison, 92 percent of "oxen," 86 percent of horses, and 58 percent of mammoths. Remaining species have a percentage of less than 10.

Stags and ibexes are found at the entrances and backs of caves. Twelve percent of the horses are found with the stags and ibexes. Stags, ibexes, and horses seem to have been associated symbolically, for these form the overwhelming majority of animals depicted on spears, harpoons, spear-throwers, and handles of pierced staffs. Partly because of their association with men's weapons, Leroi-Gourhan classifies stags, ibexes, and horses as male animals, while the bison, "oxen," and hinds are classified as female. Human female figures are often found in the center along with the large herbivores, while male figures are found at the backs of caves or on the peripheries of a central composition.

One difficulty with this male-female classification is that the horse is called a male "framing" animal, like the stag and ibex, and yet 86 percent of the horses are found in the center. On the other hand, they are usually smaller than the wild cattle, which are sometimes huge in comparison. While peripheral animals may appear in the center, bison and "oxen" are not found in peripheral zones.

Various signs or symbols commonly appear in the caves, such as dots, strokes, ovals, and triangles. Although a dubious Freudian projection may be involved here, Leroi-Gourhan has divided these into male and female signs. Dots, strokes, and barbed signs are held to be male, while enclosed signs, such as ovals, triangles, and rectangles, are considered female. It is consistent with Leroi-Gourhan's analysis that male signs usually occur at entrances and backs of caves, although sometimes also in the center, while female signs, like bison and "oxen," do not occur at entrances and backs of caves but are concentrated in the center, where they are matched with male signs.

While some of this analysis may be doubtful, the work of Laming-Emperaire and Leroi-Gourhan has brought to light a hitherto unsuspected order and pattern that applies to many caves and rock shelters. There is evidently more sophistication and symbolism in Upper Paleolithic art than was formerly believed. Leroi-Gourhan (1967:144) writes:

> What constituted for Paleolithic men the special heart and core of the caves is clearly the panels in the central part, dominated by animals from the female category and female signs, supplemented by animals from the male category and male signs. The entrance to the sanctuary, usually a narrow part of the cave, is decorated with male symbols, either animals or signs; the back of the cave, often a narrow tunnel, is decorated with the same

signs, reinforced by horned men and the rarer animals (cave lion or rhinoceros).[1]

Even if this symbolism be granted, we still do not know the exact purpose of Upper Paleolithic cave art. Some effort to control or increase the supply of game is still a possibility. On the other hand, the caves may have been settings for initiation ceremonies, rites of passage for boys entering manhood. Most of the footprints found in the caves seem to be those of youths or boys. The dark caves would, of course, have been an awesome setting for an initiation, and we can imagine the effect it may have had when lighted torches suddenly revealed the procession of animal figures on the cave walls.

When we focus on the possible religious and magical functions of Upper Paleolithic art, we should not forget its aesthetic aspects. If one draws an animal to spear, control, or increase it, one need not draw it well. But the Upper Paleolithic artists often drew with great skill. This suggests that aesthetic satisfaction accompanied the magico-religious motivation, whatever that may have been. The engraved antler rods, for example, seem to be purely decorative and beautifully done. Art had evidently become an important value for human beings by Upper Paleolithic times.

Possible lunar notations

A persuasive case has been made that Upper Paleolithic humans kept records of the changing phases of the moon, lunar notations, and calendric tallies. Many pieces of bone have been found with numerous sets of engraved marks. What was their purpose? This is not certain, but Alexander Marshack, who has carefully analyzed many such tallies, believes they were notational rather than decorative in intent, and he thinks they were probably lunar notations. Marshack also believes that the art and religion of the Upper Paleolithic were related to the changing seasons, with their varying flora and fauna. If he is right about the lunar calculations, humans of the Upper Paleolithic were much more intellectual and sophisticated than they were formerly believed to have been. But, perhaps, that should not be surprising in view of the many new breakthroughs in inventions: the spear-thrower, harpoon, and perhaps the bow and arrow, and the remarkable development of the arts in Upper Paleolithic times (Marshack 1972).

Expansion during the Upper Paleolithic

Following the herds of wild game and aided by their new inventions, *Homo sapiens sapiens* explored new territories during the Upper Paleolithic period. One of the Upper Paleolithic cultures known as the *Gravettian* ranged from southern Russia to Spain but centered mainly in central and eastern Europe. Gravettian tools included flint points and knife blades.

---

[1] For some criticisms of the Leroi-Gourhan study, see Ucko and Rosenfeld 1967.

The Gravettians in central and eastern Europe and in southern Russia were mammoth hunters, and they made use of mammoth ivory for weapons; implements such as spoons, necklaces, and pins; and artwork. Shovels or scoops were made of mammoth ribs. Mammoth bones seem also to have been used as fuel.

The Gravettians were skilled artists. In Czechoslovakia they made figurines of animals in clay, which were fired like pottery: mammoths, cave bears, bison, horses, rhinoceroses, and other animals. Figurines were also carved from bone, ivory, limestone, and steatite. It was the Gravettians who made the Venus figurines, found in Upper Paleolithic sites from Russia to France. They also made elaborate decorative carvings in ivory and antler with meanders, chevrons, and other patterns. Cave paintings of mammoths, cave bears, and horses in Russia resemble those of southern France.

In parts of Europe where caves were available, the Gravettians occupied them, but in the Russian plains they seem to have built dwellings. It is hard to reconstruct such shelters, but they may have been skin tents with poles, the corners being held down by stones and mammoth bones. Burials were more elaborate than they had been in the Middle Paleolithic period. Corpses, with knees flexed, were sprinkled with red ocher and sometimes sheltered by large stones or bones. Radiocarbon dates for the Gravettian culture in Europe range from $26,000 \pm 225$ to $20,830 \pm 140$ years ago (Clark 1969:66; Klein 1974).

Some bands in Upper Paleolithic times also pushed their way across Siberia. A Soviet archaeologist claims that men hunted mammoth, musk-ox, bison, and woolly rhinoceros along the Aldan River in eastern Siberia about 35,000 years ago. A more recent site is Mal'ta, in the middle of Siberia. It contains bones of more than 200 killed reindeer, 7 mammoths, and many tools, such as scrapers, burins, and needles, and figurines. The site has been given a radiocarbon date of $14,750 \pm 120$ B.P. By this time, there were already people in the New World whose ancestors must have crossed the land bridge that connected eastern Siberia with Alaska.

The population increase and the dispersal of human beings in Upper Paleolithic times show that human adaptations at this time were very successful. Humans had not yet reached the Pacific islands of Micronesia and Polynesia, but otherwise they were spreading rapidly across the world. By about 40,000 years ago, human beings had arrived in Australia; some entered Japan around 24,000 years ago, while the continent of North America was being inhabited.

Capacities of man the hunter

There is no doubt that by now language was spoken. The anatomical problems raised by Lieberman and his associates concerning Neanderthal speech do not apply to *Homo sapiens sapiens*. As we have seen, Upper Paleolithic tool kits were more elaborate than Neanderthal assemblages,

Australian aboriginal hunters.

and there is more evidence of symbolic thinking related to art and religious practices. William S. Laughlin (1968:316) has argued that the dispersal of mankind during this period favored evolutionary developments in human biology: "Small, isolated populations, with many subdivisions, frequently strained through genetic bottlenecks, and with migrant sampling ('founder's principle') as a major form of moving into new territories and new continents constitute the ideal conditions for rapid evolution. . . ." Moreover, according to Laughlin, hunting is an activity which stimulates intellectual faculties. With such implements as bows and arrows, harpoons, and spears, an animal is usually shot at closer than 30 feet. Thus the hunter must get as close as he can to his quarry and must often engage in long hours of stalking and waiting for changes in the wind. Most animals are not killed outright by the first shot but must be pursued, sometimes for several days. A large animal like an elephant or giraffe can keep on moving, although shot with a poisoned arrow. By the nature of their livelihood, hunters are forced to learn a lot about the anatomy and behavior of the animals they hunt, and they must develop faculties of endurance, alertness, and skill. However, despite the apparently successful adaptation of human beings to their environment in the Upper Paleolithic, they eventually had to make new adjustments when the climate, flora, and fauna underwent changes in the post-Pleistocene period.

Summary

By around 40,000 years ago there were humans of modern physical type in Europe, Israel, Borneo, and no doubt many other regions. These people had relatively narrow heads with high foreheads, domed skulls, divided brow ridges, and prominent chins.

In Upper Paleolithic times the grassy plains of Europe provided fine grazing grounds for many species of animals, such as wild horses, reindeer, mammoths, and bison, all of which were hunted by the people of the time. New hunting inventions were devised: spear-thrower, harpoon, and leister. Antler, bone, and ivory were used in Upper Paleolithic technology. The characteristic stone tools included blades, burins, and gravers. There was a new development of decorative art and cave paintings.

New regions of the earth were explored as population increased. By around 40,000 years ago there were human beings in Australia. There were hunters in eastern Siberia about 35,000 years ago and in Japan about 24,000 years ago.

Suggestions for further reading

Grahame Clark and Stuart Piggott, *Prehistoric Societies* (New York: Alfred A. Knopf, 1965) is again recommended. Chester S. Chard's *Man in Prehistory* (New York: McGraw-Hill, 1969) presents a good world survey.

For its analysis of Upper Paleolithic cave art, see the beautifully produced book by André Leroi-Gourhan, *Treasures of Prehistoric Art* (New York: Harry N. Abrams, 1967). Another handsome book with a stimulating thesis is Alexander Marshack, *The Roots of Civilization* (New York: McGraw-Hill, 1972). Also beautifully illustrated is Tom Prideaux and the Editors of Time Life Books, *Cro-Magnon Man* (New York: Time-Life Books, 1973).

Also recommended are: Jacquetta Hawkes, *Prehistory: History of Mankind, Cultural and Scientific Development* (New York: Mentor, in cooperation with UNESCO, 1963), vol. I, pt. 1; François Bordes, *The Old Stone Age*, trans. from the French by J. E. Anderson (New York: McGraw-Hill, 1968); and J. M. Coles and E. S. Higgs, *The Archaeology of Early Man* (New York: Praeger Publishers, 1969).

CHAPTER 10

The first Americans

Siberia and Alaska are not far apart. On a clear day one can see the Siberian shore from the heights of Cape Prince of Wales, Alaska. St. Lawrence Island, Big Diomede Island (USSR), and Little Diomede Island (U.S.) form stepping stones in between. During a large part of the Pleistocene, this area was dry land. With water being locked up in glaciers, there came a lowering of sea levels. When the Wisconsin glacier reached its maximum, the sea level is estimated to have dropped more than 300 feet, leaving a corridor about 1,000 miles wide. This corridor is believed to have existed from before about 35,000 years ago, between 20,000 and 14,000 years ago, and for a period between 14,000 and 10,000 years ago (Hopkins 1979).

With some interruptions, then, this corridor was available for thousands of years, during which many animals and plants moved from Siberia to Alaska, while others passed in the reverse direction. Among the animals to move from Asia to America were moose, caribou, yak, bison, antelope, bighorn sheep, and musk-ox. The human beings who unwittingly entered a new continent must have been hunting these animals. It seems likely that the movements of the new migrants into the interior of the continent were sometimes held up by ice sheets; if so, they still had about 200,000 square miles of hunting land in Alaska in which to roam about. Some ice-free corridors to the south appeared during the latter part of the last period of glaciation. Thus, the newcomers were able to make their way southward, some probably following the eastern flanks of the Rocky Mountains, while others traveled between the Rocky and Cascade Mountains to the Pacific Coast, to California and Mexico. Some groups moved eastward, fanning out across North America. Others continued to head south through Mexico, the Isthmus of Panama, and into South America.

Some early skeletal material comes from the northern Yukon. A child's jawbone found at Old Crow Basin has been dated at 27,000 years B.P., and a carved caribou bone from Old Crow has been given the same age. The oldest evidence for the domesticated dog comes from the Yukon— at least 30,000 years B.P. More evidence for early human presence in the New World comes from further south, in California. There is a cranium, dated through the analysis of amino acids in bone protein (see p. 36) at about 48,000 years ago, although there has been skepticism at so early a date. Skeletal material at Laguna Beach has been given a radiocarbon date of 17,150 ± 1,470 years ago. There are also human bones from the La Brea tar pit dated at more than 23,600 years old.

Still further south, an engraved mastodon bone from Valsequillo, Mexico, has been dated at 22,000 years B.P., and spear points found in mastodon skeletons in Taima-Taima, Venezuela, have been given a date of 13,000 years B.P.

The first migrants to the New World

The first migrants from Asia must have brought with them a rather simple Paleolithic material culture, perhaps including scrapers and chopping tools like those used in eastern Asia. They probably knew how to make fire and may have woven mats and made baskets.

One possible clue to the content of the early American cultures lies in the fact that there are many *biperipheral* traits found to be largely restricted to the most northerly groups of North America, on the one hand, and to the more southerly tribes of South America, on the other. They are missing in the central areas from Mesoamerica to Peru, where the higher civilizations developed and where the early biperipheral traits were apparently displaced by later patterns. Among these traits are folklore motifs, such as tales of a rolling-head monster, and various games, including lacrosse, hoop and pole, ring and pin, and multiple two-sided dice. Other items include fire-making with pyrites and flint, use of fish glue, sewed bark vessels, smoke signaling, and the taking of scalps. There are also various similarities in puberty rites, religious concepts, and musical styles. Some of these parallels in extreme northern North America and far southern South America may be due to later independent inventions, but it seems likely that many of them are survivals from very early times (Kroeber 1948:781; Meggers 1964:514).

We gather, then, that the early migrants in the New World were hunting-gathering peoples with simple technologies but having many nonmaterial culture patterns which have left no permanent traces in the archaeological record. These early Americans spoke many different languages, or else their languages eventually became very differentiated through isolation, for it has been estimated that by 1492 there were about 2,000 mutually unintelligible languages spoken in the Americas. There seem to be no clear-cut relationships between any of these languages and the languages spoken in the Old World. This linguistic differentiation suggests a very long time span for the occupation of the New World.

Richard S. MacNeish (1976) has reviewed data from about 50 sites in the New World yielding radiocarbon dates earlier than 12,000 B.P. He suggests dividing Paleoindian prehistory into four stages and has tried to fit particular sites into this framework. MacNeish would date Stage I as far back as 70,000 ± 30,000 B.P. in North America but later, of course, in South America. Artifacts associated with this stage include bifacial chopper tools, cleavers, and hammers. At Pikimachay Cave, Ayacucho, in highland Peru, about 80 artifacts were found in association with extinct giant sloth, horse, deer, and giant cat. MacNeish speculates that hunters probably attacked the sloths (over 10 feet tall!) in their den and then stayed to butcher and eat the kill. Choppers, cleavers, hammers, and flake tools were among the artifacts found. This site provides the best evidence for the existence of MacNeish's Stage I. The radiocarbon dates are between 14,700 ± 1,400 and 20,200 ± 1,000 years ago.

Another site assigned to Stage I is at Lewisville, Texas, where a chopper, hammer, flakes, and burned bone were found along with hearths and remains of extinct animals. Charcoal from the hearths has been radiocarbon dated at more than 37,000 years ago.

Stage II is dated between 40,000 and around 25,000 B.P. in North America. The dates in Central America range between 25,000 and 15,000 B.P., and in South America from 16,000 to 12,000 B.P. The stone tools in this stage include projectile points, scrapers, and burins. Bone tools are also found. Pikimachay Cave provides evidence for Stage II at higher strata than the Stage I remains, with a radiocarbon date of 14,150 ± 180 years ago. Tools of the types just cited were found in association with bones of extinct sloth, horse, camel, and other animals. Similar artifacts have been found at Los Toldos cave in Argentinian Patagonia, dated at 12,600 years ago. Other Stage II sites are located in Mexico, Nicaragua, Colombia, Chile, Argentina, Pennsylvania, Texas, California, and Canada, but most of these sites have not yet been well described.

Stage III dates between approximately 25,000 and 13,000 B.P. in North America, and between 15,000 and 11,000 B.P. in Mesoamerica and South America. At this time men were specialized hunters of big-game animals, using an advanced stone technology with large well-made bifacial projectile points, blades, and burins. As in the case of Stages I and II, the best evidence for this stage comes from South America. At three sites in Venezuela, Stage III artifacts have been found along with various extinct animals, including mastodon and horse, dated between approximately 15,000 and 12,000 years ago.

MacNeish's stages of Paleoindian prehistory

Early sites of man in the New World

Stage I

1. Pikimachay Cave, Ayacucho, Peru
2. Lewisville, Texas
3. Alice Boer, Rio Claro, Brazil
4. Fort Liard, N.W.T., Canada
5. Richmond Hill, British Honduras
6. Frazer Canyon, Yale, B.C., Canada
7. San Isidro, Nuevo Leon, Mexico
8. Tequixquiac, central Mexico
9. Calico Hills, California

Stage II

10. Pikimachay Cave, Ayacucho, Peru
11. Los Toldos, Cave, Patagonia, Argentina
12. Valsequillo, Puebla, Mexico
13. El Bosque, Nicaragua
14. Tlapacoya, Valley of Mexico
15. Tagua-Tagua, Chile
16. Cueva de la Indies, San Raphael, Argentina
17. Guitarerro Cave, Peru
18. El Abra Cave, Bogota, Colombia
19. Meadowcroft Rockshelter, Pennsylvania
20. Old Crow, Yukon Territory, Canada
21. Dawson City, Yukon Territory
22. Santa Rosa Island, California
23. Levi Rockshelter, Texas
24. Fort Liard, N.W.T., Canada

Stage III

25. Taima-Taima, Venezuela
26. Muaco, Venezuela
27. Cucuruchu, Venezuela
28. Huanta, Peru
29. Hueyatlaco (Valsequillo), Puebla, Mexico
30. Coxcatlan Cave, Puebla, Mexico
31. Wilson's Butte Cave, Idaho
32. McGee's Point, Utah
33. Fort Liard, N.W.T., Canada
34. Flint Creek-Bedwell complexes, Yukon Territory and Alaska
35. Chivateros I, Lima, Peru

Stage IV

36. El Inga, Ecuador
37. Los Toldos, Cave, Patagonia, Argentina
38. Fell's Cave, Patagonia, Chile
39. Pali Aike Cave, Patagonia, Chile
40. Arica, Chile
41. Tequendama Cave, Bogota, Colombia
42. Alice Boer, Rio Claro, Brazil
43. Lagoa Santa Cave, Brazil
44. Las Casitas, Venezuela
45. Tres Ventanas, Peru
46. Guitarerro Cave, Peru
47. Pikimachay Cave, Ayacucho, Peru
48. Inca Cave, Mendoza, Argentina
49. Cueva Negra, Cuenca, Ecuador
50. Chivateros II, Lima, Peru
51. Anafagosta, Chile
52. Sambaqui, Brazil
53. Ajuereado, Tehuacan Valley, Mexico
54. Valsequillo, Pueblo, Mexico
55. San Juan del Rio, Queretaro, Mexico
56. Lerma, Tamaulipas, Mexico
57. La Calzada, Nuevo Leon, Mexico
58. Devil's Mouth, Texas
59. Los Tapiales, Guatemala
60. Ventana Cave, Arizona
61. Duchess Quarry, New York
62. Folsom, New Mexico
63. Debert, Nova Scotia, Canada
64. Clovis, New Mexico
65. Hell Gap, Colorado
66. Plainview, Texas
67. Brohm, Ontario, Canada
68. Great Bear Lake, N.W.T., Canada
69. Modoc Rockshelter, Illinois
70. Hardaway, North Carolina
71. San Dieguito, California
72. Danger Cave, Utah
73. Lind Coulee, Washington
74. Healy Lake, Alaska
75. Onion Portage, Alaska

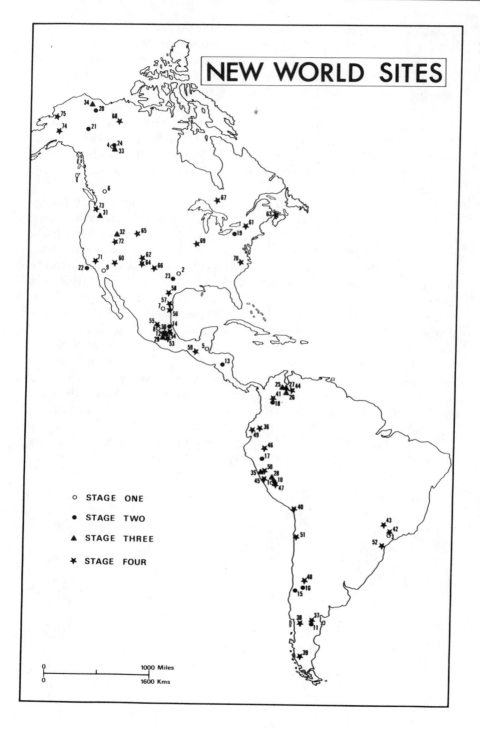

Map showing sites of early man in the New World, representing MacNeish's four stages.

The big-game hunters

Stage IV dates between approximately 13,000 and 8,500 years ago and includes the first clearly distinguishable culture in North America: that of the big-game hunters, which was organized around the hunting of herding animals, particularly in the western plains. The characteristic tools were projectile points of the Clovis, Sandia, Folsom, and Plano types. Clovis, Sandia, and Folsom are sites in New Mexico where the characteristic projectile points were discovered. These points usually have been found at kill sites, sometimes imbedded in the bones of extinct animals. Most radiocarbon tests for such sites give a date of around 10,000 or 9000 B.C. The tradition seems to have declined after 8000 B.C. with the advent of warmer, drier weather.

Clovis points were used to tip spears, not arrows. Extinct animals hunted by the big-game hunters included mastodon, mammoth, an extinct form of bison, camel, and horse. Although most of the sites have been found in the Great Plains and Southwest areas, fluted points have also turned up in many parts of eastern North America. Fluted points are characteristic New World artifacts; they are not found in Eurasia and must have been developed here.

A site in Colorado, dated at about 10,000 years ago, gives an indication of how some of the early hunters went about their work. There was organized group hunting in this case, with men driving long-horned bison into a stampede into a ravine, where the animals piled up, trampling one another. Some of the bison were speared, and their huge carcasses were then hauled out of the ravine, butchered, and skinned. Archaeologists found the skulls of 190 bison at this site (Wheat 1972). Similar techniques of killing buffalos were used by Plains Indians in historic times.

The long-horned bison found in the Colorado site are an extinct species. Many other animals hunted by the big-game hunters also became extinct

Projectile points.
A.   Sandia point.
B.   Clovis fluted point.
C.   Folsom fluted point.

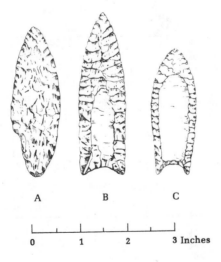

A   B   C

0   1   2   3 Inches

in the New World between 6,000 and 12,000 years ago, including the mammoth, mastodon, horse, camel, and ground sloth. Did the wholesale killing techniques of the big-game hunters bring about this extinction? Some authorities think so, although there were species of animals, like the modern bison, that managed to survive down to the present. Perhaps a change in climatic conditions was responsible, or a combination of factors.

We hear a lot nowadays about how modern humans endanger the environment in which they live. It is arresting to consider that man may have had a damaging effect upon his environment as much as 10,000 years ago. If so, it probably was the first time that human beings were strong enough or numerous enough to bring about such effects. Before Upper Paleolithic times, humans were few in numbers and probably no more damaging to other species than other predators were. But, by Upper Paleolithic times, humans had developed good hunting tools and cooperative hunting techniques, which made them more of a threat to other species of animals. Besides, there were more human beings around, although they made up only a very small fraction of our present huge world population.

Summary

The probable route of entry by human beings into the New World was via the Bering Straits land bridge. The date of their entry is less certain, but a child's jawbone from the Yukon has been dated at 27,000 years B.P., and some skeletal material from California has been dated at 48,000 years ago.

If Richard MacNeish is right, humans may have entered the New World as far back as 70,000 years ago. He has reviewed data from about 50 New World sites yielding radiocarbon dates earlier than 12,000 B.P. MacNeish divides Paleoindian prehistory into four stages, but it is only in the last of these stages that a clearly distinguishable culture is in evidence, that of the big-game hunters. These paleoindians hunted many animals that became extinct between around 6,000 and 12,000 years ago, perhaps wiped out by the hunters themselves, although this view has been greeted with skepticism by some zoologists.

Suggestions for further reading

The best general treatment of New World archaeology is Gordon R. Willey, *An Introduction to American Archaeology*, 2 vols. (Englewood Cliffs, N.J.: Prentice Hall, 1966 and 1971). See also Jesse D. Jennings, ed., *Ancient Native Americans* (San Francisco: W. H. Freeman, 1978).

For the theory that human hunters were responsible for wiping out many species of large animals in the New World in Pleistocene times, see Paul S. Martin, "Prehistoric Overkill" in Paul S. Martin and H. E. Wright, Jr., eds., *Pleistocene Extinction. The Search for a Cause* (New Haven: Yale University Press, 1967), pp. 75–150. For a criticism of that view, see Donald K. Grayson, "Pleistocene Avifaunas and the Overkill Hypothesis," *Science* 195 (February 18, 1977): 691–92.

For other reviews of New World archaeology, see William T. Sanders and Joseph Marino, *New World Prehistory: Archaeology of the American Indian* (Englewood Cliffs, N.J.: Prentice-Hall, 1970); Thomas C. Patterson, *America's Past: A New World Archaeology* (Glenview, Ill.: Scott, Foresman, 1973).

Two books deal with the early phases of man in the New World: Robert Claiborne and the Editors of Time-Life Books, *The First Americans* (New York: Time-Life Books, 1973); and Richard S. MacNeish, ed., *Early Man in America* (San Francisco: W. H. Freeman, 1973). This chapter has drawn heavily upon Richard S. MacNeish, "Early Man in the New World," *American Scientist* 64 (1976): pp. 316–27.

Not all archaeologists would agree with MacNeish's reconstructions or accept his early dates. Some distrust the older radiocarbon dates, which may have been affected by contamination in one way or another. For a conservative view, see Thomas F. Lynch, "The Antiquity of Man in South America," *Quaternary Research* 4 (1974): 356–77, and an article by the same author, "The South American Paleo-Indians," in the 1978 Jennings volume, pp. 455–89.

A well-illustrated article on early man in the Americas which could serve as a supplement to the MacNeish reconstruction is Thomas Y. Canby's "The Search for the First Americans," *National Geographic* 156, no. 3 (1979): 330–63. Canby distinguishes three main theories about the settling of the Americas: (1) "late arrival," assuming an entrance to the New World at around 12,000 years B.P.; (2) "middle entry" dating it at about 30,000 years ago; and (3) "early arrival," placing it at least 40,000 years ago and maybe much earlier.

See also *The First Americans*, ed. William S. Laughlin and Albert B. Harper (Stuttgart: Fischer, 1979).

PART FOUR

Cultural evolution
after the Pleistocene

CHAPTER 11

Post-Pleistocene transitions

About 12,000 years ago, with the withdrawal of the ice sheets from Europe, changes in climate and vegetation began to take place, which brought about some modifications in human culture. The weather became warmer. Forests began to appear—first birch, then pine, and later mixed oak forests. As the open plains of Upper Paleolithic times were gradually replaced by woods, the fauna necessarily changed. The herds of grazing animals, such as buffaloes, wild horses, and cattle, began to disappear; the mammoths were gone and reindeer made their way to the north. At the same time, animal figures vanished from the walls of caves. The Azilians, a European Mesolithic people who occupied some of the same caves, had a more abstract kind of art, painting pebbles with mysterious symbols, the significance of which is still unknown.

Climatic changes also took place in the Near East, which later became a center of plant and animal domestication. During the late Pleistocene much of the area consisted of steppes having a cool, dry climate, but around 11,000 B.C. the region became warmer, and there were savannas having scattered oak and pistachios.

In northern China, after the glaciers receded, forests of long-leafed trees spread out over the former plains, and animals like the woolly rhinoceros and mammoth died out, to be replaced by mammals adapted to warmer environments.

In North America similar changes took place. Forests spread out into the plains, and the large grazing herd animals of the Pleistocene began to disappear. In these different areas, then, people had to find new sources of food and new ways of life to come to terms with changed ecological conditions.

The Mesolithic in Europe

One important new development in the Mesolithic period, from around 12,000 to 5000 B.P. in Europe,[1] was the increased attention given to fish and seafood. Mesolithic settlements in northern Europe were found along the coast from England to Russia. (The coasts in those days did not follow the same outlines as the seacoast today, for the North Sea area was mostly dry and the Baltic was a lake.) The northerly coastal culture has been called *Maglemosian*, from a Danish phrase meaning "big bog," for remains of this culture have been found in swampy areas near lakes and streams. The Maglemosians had various devices for catching fish: hook, line, and sinker; spears or harpoons; and seine nets. People of the Upper Paleolithic ate fish, too, but this source of food seems to have become much more important in Mesolithic times, as the fishhooks and other implements suggest. Dugout canoes were invented at this time; animal skins were also used for boats, stretched over a framework, like the watercraft of the Eskimos.

Particularly toward the end of the Mesolithic period, the northern Europeans ate shellfish and left discarded shells in large heaps known as *kitchen middens*. Seals, which then were found in coastal waters, were also killed.

Inland, Mesolithic men hunted forest animals, which had replaced the fauna of Upper Paleolithic times—aurochs, moose, deer and elk, beavers, wild pigs, and other animals. They used bows and arrows, remains of which have been found preserved in bogs. Their bows were notched at both ends for the bowstrings. Spears were used, with heads of bone or antler.

A characteristic stone tool of the Mesolithic period was the *microlith*, a small stone tool made from a blade that had been split up into fragments. One kind of microlith was an arrowhead held in place by resin. Microliths were also set in handles of bone or antler as cutting or scraping tools.

One consequence of the growth of forests was an increased use of wood. For the first time, axes of stone, bone, or antler were hafted to handles. Crude but apparently effective axes and adzes were used for chopping down trees, making dugout canoes, paddles, and, perhaps, house construction. Wooden runners found in peat bogs show that sleds were used in wintertime. Wood could also be used in the construction of shelters. The large heaps of shellfish show that some settlements were long lasting.

In contrast to major dependence on a single source of food, such as big game, the Mesolithic peoples developed what Kent Flannery has called a *broad-spectrum* pattern of subsistence, which involves exploiting many aspects of a given region, both plant and animal resources (Flannery 1969).

---

[1] In parts of England and Scandinavia, Mesolithic cultures persisted until around 2500 B.C. or later.

If such a program is successfully carried out, sedentism, more permanent settlement, is made possible.

Sedentary village life has several advantages over a nomadic way of life. Nomadism imposes a hardship on the old and sick. Young children have to be carried, along with the worldly goods of the hunters. The Eskimos solved the problem by inventing the dogsled. Nevertheless, old Eskimo men and women often asked their relatives to kill them when they felt unable to keep up on the march. Or they might be left behind with some provisions, perhaps to survive, perhaps not. The Sirionó of eastern Bolivia, who are mainly hunting-gathering people, although they also practice some slash-and-burn horticulture, similarly abandon old, infirm persons when they break camp. This is not done by all nomadic peoples, but such practices demonstrate the difficulties involved. Newborn babies were often killed by the Eskimos, some Australian aboriginal tribes, and other nomadic hunters, not because they were hard-hearted people—quite the contrary—but because they already had too many children or because conditions were such that they could not adequately feed them and bring them up. Sedentary life thus provides for better care for the old, the very young, and the sick.

One example of a European Mesolithic settlement is Star Carr in Yorkshire, England, dated by both geological means and radiocarbon at around 7500 B.C. This was a small settlement occupied by about three or four families. Since it was located in a swampy area, the camp was built on a platform of birch brushwood. Animal bones and tools of flint, amber, and bone were found mixed up in the brushwood. Unlike many Mesolithic sites, there were no remains of fish. It was evidently a hunting camp, with red deer being the main animal hunted, to judge by the large number of red deer bones at the site; but the hunters also killed elk, wild ox, and other game. Star Carr was judged to be a winter camp occupied before January, based on the presence of full-grown deer and elk antlers which are normally shed after January. Star Carr seems to have been reoccupied several times; there were differences in the types of spearhead found at successive levels. No remains of huts or shelters were found, but there was evidence of felled trees, the oldest specimen of a felled tree found anywhere, and there were also remains of a wooden paddle (G. Clark 1963; J. G. D. Clark 1971).

The Near East

Similar adjustments took place in the Near East. Around 8500 B.C. there were some people, now called Natufian, living in various parts of Israel. They usually inhabited the mouths of caves, but there are also some open sites. Their stone technology included blades, burins, microliths, grinding and polishing stones, net stones, net weights, and hammer stones; they used bone for making skewers, needles, awls, harpoons, and fishhooks. Microliths constituted about 80 percent of their chipped flint work. There is evidence of hunting, principally of gazelle, which outnumber remains of deer, implying a dry climate like that of today. There are also remains of hyena, bear, wild boar, and leopard. The dog was present, but there is no other evidence of domestication. There is some evidence of harvesting of grain from the flint blades mounted on bone handles. Surviving examples of these implements have a sheen that seems to have been acquired by reaping, and well-made stone pestles and mortars attest to the preparation of plant food, although the plants that were harvested do not seem to have been domesticated.

It was evidently possible at that time for hunting-gathering peoples to live very well on stands of wild grain. In 1966 Jack R. Harlan, an agronomist from the University of Oklahoma, found a field of wild wheat on a mountain slope in eastern Turkey. Harlan stripped the grain from the stalks until his hands got sore. Later he experimented with using a 9,000-year-old flint sickle blade to reap the grain. After removal of the chaff, Harlan found that he had reaped more than two pounds of grain per hour, and he calculated that in three weeks a family of reapers with flint sickles could harvest more grain than they could consume in a year. The Natufians, then, might have lived very well on grain without domesticating it, and might have lived in such a region for a considerable time.

Ten major Natufian sites have been found so far. Some of them give evidence not only of extended occupation but also of population growth. One Natufian cemetery had 87 burials; another, more than 700. Walls and paved platforms were sometimes built, and at one site circular stone houses were constructed with plastered bell-shaped pits.

Contemporaneous with the Natufian culture is the Karim Shahir assemblage, which has been found in both caves and open-air sites in Iraq and Iran, dated by radiocarbon at around 8500 B.C. Like the Natufian, the Karim Shahir assemblage contains a great deal of chipped flint, particularly microliths, but there are not many sickle blades. There is, again, evidence of grinding and milling, mortars and querns. Stone beads and bracelets and bone needles were found. But there is also something different: indications of incipient animal domestication. There are more bones of animals capable of domestication such as sheep, goat, cattle, and horse, in contrast with earlier cave sites in the area, which have a high proportion of gazelle and deer bones (Braidwood 1975:109–15).

Nubia and Upper Egypt

A similar broad-spectrum subsistence pattern developed in Nubia and Upper Egypt between approximately 15,000 and 9000 B.C. The people along the Nile were then collecting wild grains and seeds and killing birds and fish, as well as larger animals. Around 12,000 B.C. there is evidence of population increase and also of warfare. A solution in such situations, at least for the weaker contestants, is escape through migration. But the

Nile Valley is a relatively enclosed zone, and escape to the desert is not a favorable outcome. This situation would give further impetus to intensive exploitation of resources within a limited area on the part of each local group along the Nile. Like the Natufians, the Nubians had much equipment that could be used for grinding seeds and grain. They made use of local grains, which were superseded when more suitable domesticated grains from Asia were introduced in the fifth millennium B.C. But, even after that, the local grains continued to be grown as minor crops (J. D. Clark 1971).

What Jerome Jacobson (1979:481) describes as a "full-fledged Mesolithic village" has been found on a lake bank in the state of southern Uttar Pradesh in India. It has been given a radiocarbon date of around 10,300 years B.P., the oldest date so far for an Indian Mesolithic settlement. Indian Mesolithic sites are characterized by numerous microliths, especially backed bladelets. They differ from Mesolithic sites elsewhere in not emphasizing the use of aquatic resources. The above-mentioned village, which represents an exception to this pattern, contains the largest number of human burials from a prehistoric South Asian site prior to the Harappa civilization (see p. 255 ff.).

Mesolithic sites in India

Developments comparable to those in the Nile Valley and the Near East also occurred in southern China in the lake region of Yunnan Province, where there were small settlements of people subsisting on shellfish before the introduction or full adoption of wheat cultivation. It has been suggested that people who engaged in this form of subsistence must have practiced some form of animal and plant conservation (Treistman 1972:39–40).

Hoabinhian and Jomon cultures in Eastern Asia

The term "Hoabinhian" has been applied to widespread Mesolithic assemblages in Southeast Asia, which include adzes and ground-stone knives. Reference will be made in the following chapter to early evidence of plant domestication in a Hoabinhian site in northern Thailand dated at about 7000 B.C.

Kwang-chih Chang has pointed to similarities between the Hoabinhian culture of Thailand and contemporaneous traditions in both northern China and Japan. The Japanese culture known as *Jomon* has been dated at about 9,000 to 500 years ago. It lacked agriculture but did have cord-marked pottery, which is also found in northern China in the valleys of the Weishu and Yellow Rivers. The Jomon culture stretched from Hokkaido, Japan's northernmost main island, to Kyushu, its most southerly. In the north, trout, salmon, and shellfish were collected, along with roots, nuts, and berries. Mounds of shellfish characterize Jomon sites, as in the coastal settlements of Mesolithic Europe.

The North American Archaic Tradition and other New World parallels

In North America, around 8000 B.C., the Big-Game Hunting Tradition gave way to the Archaic, which has many interesting parallels with the European Mesolithic. In both cases, because of the climatic changes, man-made decimation of fauna, or both, broad-spectrum food exploitation replaced an earlier dependence on big-game hunting. Subsistence became based on small-game hunting, fishing, and the collection of wild plants. Polished stone tools such as grooved axes and adzes were used for working wood. There were also tools for grinding wild seeds, including manos and metates, mortars and pestles. Carved and polished bone ornaments were made and stone vessels used. The Archaic cultures show a greater variety of tools and more sophistication than those of the earlier big-game hunters. Around 5000 B.C., people who lived along the rivers of Alabama, Tennessee, and Kentucky were subsisting on freshwater mussels, wild plants, and small game. In some cases there were permanent or semipermanent residences indicated by large shell middens. The earliest southeastern pottery which dates from around 2500 B.C. is most often found on such shell heaps. Some local plants such as sunflowers may have been cultivated in Archaic settlements, later to be replaced by maize, when it was introduced.

The Eva site in Tennessee, near a river bank, is characteristic of Archaic settlements in the area, dated by radiocarbon at around 5200 B.C. Freshwater clams were abundant, as testified by clam shell heaps which also contained other garbage, such as the bones of animals hunted: deer, elk, bear, wolf, and other forest animals. The Eva people also ate nuts, fruits, and roots. They had tools of chipped flint, but also fashioned stone tools by pecking and grinding. Mortars and hammerstones were used to grind seeds and nuts. Fishhooks were found and also bone awls and needles. Dogs were domesticated and buried, either along with human skeletons or in separate graves of their own (Lewis and Kneberg 1958).

Contemporary with the Archaic Tradition and having some parallel features was the Desert Tradition, dating from around 8000 B.C. and persisting in some groups down to historic times. This tradition was adapted to arid regions in the Great Basin, the Southwest, and Mesoamerica. Social units in these areas were small, consisting of extended families including men, their wives, and children. A pattern of cyclic wandering was common, depending on the ripening of plants or the availability of animals in different valleys and uplands. Material possessions were scanty, the most important being the basket and the flat milling stone. It was from variants of the Desert Tradition in Mexico that horticulture emerged. This development has been best studied in the Tehuacán Valley of southern Puebla. Archaeologists have estimated that the population of the valley amounted to only 6 to 12 persons in about 7000 B.C., but as many as 200 or 300 by 3000 B.C. Efforts were evidently made to increase the carrying capacity of the region at that time. Avocados, zapotes, and other wild fruits were planted along the banks of streams; amaranth and other seed plants were sown. These were probably plants native to the valley, but, later, the inhabitants

Excavation of Coxatlan cave, Tehuacán Valley, Mexico. Twenty-eight occupation levels were unearthed, of which the three lowest were of hunting-gathering groups.

began to import plants from other regions (Patterson 1973:52–54). The process of plant domestication in the Tehuacán Valley is discussed in the following chapter.

Similar developments took place along the coast of Peru, where there were hunting-gathering peoples who lived on seed and root plants, snails, fish, and shellfish, and hunted animals. Wild seeds were ground on milling stones. This was around the fourth millennium B.C., before the development of agriculture (Lanning 1967).

On different continents, then, small groups of hunting-gathering peoples made remarkably similar adjustments in the process of staying alive. They were discovering the nutritive properties of similar foods, such as seeds, grains, fish, and shellfish, and often fashioning similar tools, such as milling stones for grinding seeds. In all of these areas these hunting-gathering peoples were laying the groundwork for the domestication of plants, a turning point in the evolution of human culture.

Summary

Climatic changes in both the Old World and the New World ushered in new adaptations to altered environments in the post-Pleistocene period, beginning about 12,000 years ago. With warmer weather and increased forestation, the herding animals of the former grassy plains of Europe began to disappear. Human settlements proliferated along the coasts of northern Europe, and increased attention was given to fish and seafood. In technology an increased use was made of wood. Axes and adzes were hafted to handles. The bow and arrow was in use, and dugout canoes were made in Mesolithic Europe.

A widespread response to the changed ecological conditions was development of a broad-spectrum pattern of subsistence which involved exploiting the varied plant and animal resources of a region. Often included in this pattern was the harvesting of wild grain, such as was done by the Natufians of Israel around 8500 B.C. Mortars and pestles were used to prepare such plant foods. This dependence on wild grain helped to prepare the way for the ultimate domestication of plants.

Suggestions for further reading

Lewis R. Binford, "Post-Pleistocene Adaptations," in *New Perspectives in Archaeology*, ed. Sally R. Binford and Lewis R. Binford (Chicago: Aldine, 1968), pp. 313–41. This article is recommended for its analytic approach. For a more popular style of writing, see Book Two, "The Retreat of the Ice," in Geoffrey Bibby, *The Testimony of the Spade* (New York: Alfred A. Knopf, 1956), pp. 113–97.

For some findings on the Mesolithic period in South Asia, see Jerome Jacobson, "Recent Developments in South Asian Prehistory and Protohistory," in Bernard J. Siegel, Alan R. Beals, and Stephen A. Tyler, eds., *Annual Review of Anthropology*, vol. 8 (Palo Alto, Calif.: Annual Reviews, Inc., 1979), pp. 467–502.

For a description of the Archaic culture of eastern North America, see Joseph R. Caldwell, "Eastern North America," in *Courses Toward Urban Life: Archaeological Considerations of Some Cultural Alternates*, ed. Robert J. Braidwood and Gordon R. Willey (Chicago: Aldine, 1962), pp. 288–308.

A general picture of the emergence of food production in the New World is available in Thomas C. Patterson, *America's Past: A New World Archaeology* (Glenview, Ill.: Scott, Foresman, 1973), pp. 41–64.

CHAPTER 12

The domestication of
plants and animals

Plants may be said to be domesticated when their seeds, roots, or shoots are planted by human beings who keep them from one season to the next for this purpose. Plant domestication may facilitate certain kinds of mutations, for example, in the direction of the retention of seeds. In the wild state such mutations would not be favored by natural selection. Some cultivated plants are characterized by gigantism in certain organs. Human beings sometimes have found such alterations useful and, either consciously or unconsciously, have preserved and encouraged their development. Domestication is promoted, then, when people take organisms to niches for which they are not adapted, protect them from the hazards of natural selection, and select for traits that normally are not advantageous under natural conditions.

The domestication of plants seems to have developed in more than one center: in the Near East, in Southeast Asia or China, in Mesoamerica, and perhaps also in North Africa. Perhaps "center" is not the right word. We must conceive of plant domestication as a very gradual process engaged in to a greater or lesser extent by many hunting-gathering peoples in these different regions, as was suggested in the previous chapter.

The term *Neolithic* has been applied to the period of plant and animal domestication in the Near East[1] between approximately 8000 and 3500 B.C. *Neolithic* means new stone, for this period in the Old World was

Plant domestication in the Near East

[1] There is sometimes some confusion about the term "Near East" because of the competing term "Middle East." As used here, the Near East is equivalent to southwestern Asia and includes the present states of Iran, Iraq, Turkey, Syria, Jordan, and Israel.

characterized by the use of ground-stone tools, which are discussed in the following chapter, along with weaving, pottery, and other aspects of Neolithic culture. But the most significant feature of Neolithic life was the domestication of plants and animals. Such domestication must have occurred in or near regions where wild forms of these plants and animals were found. The wild ancestors of wheat and barley grew in upland regions in altitudes of 750–1,000 meters above sea level. Some of these wild prototypes still grow in the uplands of Iraq.

Two types of wheat were grown in the Neolithic period: einkorn and emmer. Wild forms of einkorn ranged from the Balkans to western Iran. Emmer was found in northern Mesopotamia, eastern Turkey, Iraq, Syria, Israel, and Jordan. Barley occurred in the same area, although wild barley has a wider range, from central Asia to the Atlantic. However, early farming was not based on barley alone but on a combination of barley and wheat. Barley was domesticated by 7000 B.C. Emmer also was domesticated by at least 7000 B.C., and the earliest domesticated einkorn wheat has been dated at around 6500 B.C.

It seems likely that such crops were collected by hunting-gathering peoples who gradually depended more and more on this source of food and began to plant their seeds and cultivate them, pulling up weeds and driving away birds and foraging animals.

How were these cereals first prepared for food? Carleton S. Coon believes that porridge of some kind preceded the making of bread, which required a communal oven. Porridge is easier to prepare than bread and is eaten throughout the Middle East. A maize porridge was eaten by the Indians of South and Central America. The California Indians, who gathered wild seeds, also made porridge.

Early farming was a form of simple horticulture; its principal tool was the digging stick. More advanced horticultural societies had hoes and made use of terracing and techniques of fertilization. At a still more advanced level, that of agriculture, Old World farmers had animal-drawn plows and dug irrigation channels to fertilize their fields.

Domestication of animals

Domesticated animals are animals under the control of human beings, who may introduce artificial selection by determining the choice of mates. This eventually results in genetic changes, such as size and other features. The first animal to be domesticated, long before the Neolithic period, was the dog. It was mentioned in Chapter 10 that the oldest evidence for the domesticated dog so far comes from the Yukon, Alaska, 30,000 or more years ago. People had to have a rather assured control over their environment and food supply to forego killing off such animals. The most important animals to be domesticated by Neolithic people—sheep, goats, cattle, and pigs—inhabited the same upland regions of the Near East where wild barley and wheat were found.

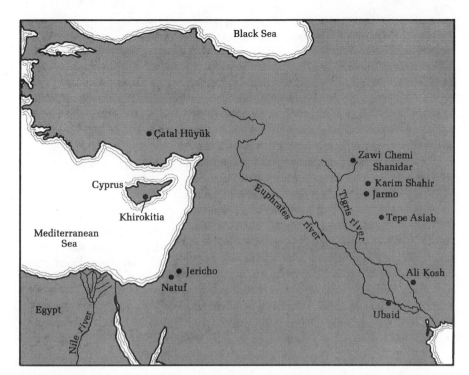

The domestication of sheep and other animals may have developed independently in several places in Asia Minor and Europe, for the idea of domesticating seems to have spread faster than the domesticated animals themselves. Both in the Baltic area and in Iraq there are gradual transitions from wild to domesticated forms of pigs. Similarly, cattle apparently developed from wild aurochs, both on the southern shore of the Bosphorus and in Schleswig-Holstein (Herre 1963:242).

On the basis of calibrated radiocarbon dates, cattle and pigs are said to have been domesticated in both Greece and the Near East by around 7000 B.C. Sheep were first domesticated in the Near East or Turkey at about 7500 B.C. The earliest evidence of goat domestication is at Asiab in the Near East around 8000 B.C. There is later evidence of domesticated goats at Jarmo, Ali Kosh, and Sarab in the Near East at around 7000 B.C. and of domesticated onagers at Jarmo around 7000 B.C. Dogs were domesticated earlier in Mesolithic times, both in Europe and in the Near East. The horse was not domesticated until around 4000 B.C. in the steppes of the Ukraine, while asses were domesticated in Lower Egypt in the fourth millennium B.C. (Protsch and Berger 1973).

How can archaeologists tell whether some animal bones were from wild or domesticated forms? Sometimes size is an indication. Domesticated animals tend to be smaller than wild ones. Moreover, the bone structure tends to be less solid. Polarized light may reveal features of bone structure that distinguish domesticated from wild forms. The horns of domesticated goats often differ in appearance and in cross section from those of wild goats. The corkscrew shapes of Near Eastern goat horns are not found in wild forms. There are also distinguishing features in the horns of wild and domesticated sheep.[2]

Reasons for domestication

Why did human beings first start to domesticate plants and animals? The most likely purpose of most animal domestication was to keep a ready supply of meat around. At any rate, sheep were not domesticated for their wool, since wild forms have little of it; wool developed in the course of domestication. Similarly, cows were not domesticated for their milk, since wild forms do not produce much milk. One hypothesis is that cows were first corraled and kept on hand for sacrificial purposes, since cows often have been regarded as sacred animals. While there may have been some such nonutilitarian purposes in animal domestication, the practical advantages evidently became recognized, at least in the Near East.

Apart from milk, meat, hides, and wool, domesticated animals transported plant nutrients to the village through their manure and helped to fertilize the fields.

V. Gordon Childe put forth what was called the *oasis theory* of domestication. According to this view, in postglacial times there was widespread desiccation in western Asia and North Africa, during which humans and other animals were drawn to the banks of streams and shrinking springs because of their need for water. Childe assumed that men already were domesticating plants by this time. The animals attracted to the oases could graze on the stubble of their fields. Since people could tolerate such beasts and might even protect them from predators, the animals became tame and used to human beings. The advantages of this symbiotic relationship led men to perpetuate it.

This seemed to be a reasonable hypothesis, but Robert J. Braidwood pointed out that there had been at least three earlier interglacial periods with similar climatic features. These should have had the same effect of driving humans and animals into oases with resulting domestication, but such did not occur. Besides, there is no evidence for unusual climatic change in southwestern Asia in the early period of animal domestication (Braidwood 1975:95–97).

Braidwood's own explanation was that by about 8000 B.C., men in the hills around the fertile crescent had come to know their environment so well that they began to domesticate the plants and animals they had formerly been gathering and hunting. Led on by "increased experimentation" and

---

[2] See the illustrations in Leonard et al. 1973:81–84.

"increased receptiveness," they made the shift to food production. The hilly flanks of the fertile crescent became a nuclear zone from which the new patterns spread to other groups. This zone of origin happened to be rich in the plants and animals that became domesticated.

Lewis R. Binford criticized Braidwood's theory for the vagueness of such would-be explanatory terms as "increased experimentation" and "increased receptiveness," which do not really provide an explanation for what happened. Binford has proposed a more demographic approach. He assumes that population growth took place in the more successful Mesolithic settlements, leading to a splitting off of daughter groups that impinged on marginal, less-sedentary populations. It was in this marginal zone that the development of food production was likely to be most advantageous. According to this view, domestication of plants and animals would not take place in the more advanced and prosperous settlements but in the less-secure, marginal ones (Binford 1968). A hypothesis of this sort has the advantage of being testable to some degree in the archaeological record; some attempts have been made to apply the Binford model to early levels of domestication in southwestern Asia (Flannery 1969).

Kent V. Flannery pointed out that plants and animals sought by Mesolithic collectors in the Near East were available at different seasons in different regions and altitudes. There were dates in the lowlands; acorns, almonds, and pistachios in the foothills; and grapes, apples, and pears in the northern mountains. Even in preagricultural times, some items were exchanged in trade, such as obsidian, used in flaked tools, and asphalt for setting and hafting flints. Some regional specialization seems evident. This made possible the removal of wild seeds from mountain slopes to lowlands, to niches where they did not naturally grow. Artificial selection was now possible, since people could select for characters that were not beneficial to the plant under normal conditions. In other words, plant domestication was now under way (Flannery 1965).

Some of the oldest samples of domesticated grain dated so far have come from marginal regions remote from the present ranges of the wild plants. In keeping with Binford's hypothesis, Flannery (1969:81) writes: "It is possible, therefore, that cultivation began as an attempt to produce artificially, around the *margins* of the 'optimum' zone, stands of cereals as dense as those in the *heart* of the 'optimum' zone."

The emphasis on population pressure to account for the switch to agriculture has been carried further by Mark N. Cohen (1977). Cohen draws attention to the near-simultaneity of this development in different parts of the world. This was not simply due to the happy discovery and subsequent spread of ingenious inventions. It can only be accounted for, according to Cohen, by steadily increasing population growth, for a hunting-gathering basis of subsistence cannot support large or dense populations. Farming is not an easier or more secure way of life and does not produce food of better quality. "Agriculture has in fact only one advantage over hunting and gathering: that of providing more calories per unit of land per unit of time and thus of supporting dense populations; it will thus be practiced only when necessitated by population pressure" (Cohen 1977:15).

Knowledge about the properties of plants and seeds is widespread among hunting-gathering people. Hence the switch to agriculture could easily have taken place at different times and places, when people were forced to produce more food from a unit of space. This not only involved a change in diet to less-preferred foods, but it also required more work. Although some hunting-gathering groups might have tried to limit their own population growth, they would then have been at a competitive disadvantage with those that did not. Hence population pressure was inexorable and the development of agriculture inevitable. Such, at least, is Cohen's argument.

It used to be assumed that hunting-gathering peoples are more anxious about food supplies and less well fed than village farmers. A conference of anthropologists who had worked with present-day hunting-gathering groups was held at the University of Chicago in 1966. Their findings were presented in a published volume (Lee and De Vore 1968). One of their conclusions was that meat generally plays a minor role in the diet of such peoples, constituting from 20 to 40 percent. Vegetable foods, fish, and shellfish make up the bulk of the diet. (Exceptions occur among peoples such as the Eskimos who lack vegetable foods.) Even though they live in poorly favored marginal regions, the hunting-gathering peoples of the present day do not seem to suffer from food shortages. They know where available roots, berries, or nuts are apt to be found and usually do not have much anxiety about where their next meal is coming from. Two or three hours of work may suffice to provide the day's food. (Again, there are exceptions, as among Eskimos or northern Algonquians, especially in wintertime.)

Hunting-gathering peoples often live longer than one might expect. In a Bushman group numbering 466, there were 46 persons over 60 years of age (Lee and DeVore 1968:36). The ways of life of hunting-gathering peoples of the present day who live in the most ill-favored parts of the world cannot be representative of the pre-Neolithic hunting-gathering life. The Old World hunters lived in much more favorable environments, and they must have been better fed than the hunters of today.

However, despite the advantages of a hunting-gathering way of life, it did give way to agriculture in the course of time. Domestication of plants took place in different parts of the world, not only in the Near East but also in southern and eastern Asia and in the New World.

At a Neolithic site called *Koldihawa*, in Uttar Pradesh, India, indications of rice (both wild and domesticated) have been dated older than 4500 B.C., which, if confirmed, would be the world's oldest known domesticated rice (Jacobson 1979:483).

In the preceding chapter, reference was made to a Mesolithic stone assemblage known as Hoabinhian, found in all parts of mainland southeast Asia. Hoabinhian tools such as adzes and ground-stone knives were found in Spirit Cave in northern Thailand, excavated by Chester F. Gorman of the University of Hawaii. The cave has also yielded remains of domesticated plants dated by radiocarbon at about 7000 B.C., contemporary with early plant domestication in the Near East. The plants from Spirit Cave are quite different, however, including leguminous beans, bottle gourds, and cucumbers. Pepper, betel, and water chestnut also were found. Cord-marked pottery appeared soon after the domesticated plants. A similar Mesolithic culture with cord-marked pottery seems to have existed around 8000 B.C. in northern China, Taiwan, and Japan, where pottery existed long before it appeared in the Near East. Kwang-chih Chang believes that the early plant domesticators in eastern Asia were probably fishermen who had a settled way of life. He suggests that the first domesticated plants were used mainly for containers, such as bamboo trunks and bottle gourds. Plants also were used for cordage in making fish nets and lines. Bamboo, bottle gourds, and tubers such as yam and taro probably played a minor role in subsistence at first, supplementing a diet consisting mainly of fish, shellfish, and wild animals (Chang 1970). Rice was not domesticated until much later, but there is evidence that rice was cultivated in Thailand prior to 3500 B.C.

Plant domestication in eastern Asia

Mesoamerica may be said to include the territory from northern Mexico to northwestern Costa Rica. In this area, between approximately 7000 and 2000 B.C., there were many groups with variants of the Desert Tradition who hunted small game and collected wild plants. Very gradually plant collection was transformed into cultivation. Two archaeological sites involving cave deposits best document this transition: one in the mountains of Tamaulipas on the northeastern fringe of Mesoamerica and the other in the Tehuacán Valley of southern Puebla in the heart of Mesoamerica. The two regions are about 400 miles apart. Metates and manos for grinding seeds were found at both sites. These became standard equipment used in grinding corn for tortillas.

It is interesting that the same plants do not appear to have been domesticated in the same periods at these two sites. There was wild maize (Indian corn) at Puebla in 5000 B.C.; but there was no maize in Tamaulipas until around 2500 B.C. Pumpkins were cultivated at Tamaulipas between 7000 and 5000 B.C. but do not appear at Puebla until 3000 B.C. Squash was known in Puebla in 6000 B.C. but not until 2000 B.C. at Tamaulipas. It seems likely that different plants began to be cultivated by different groups. Later, with the development of Mesoamerican culture and increased interaction between communities, there was an interchange of cultivated plant species. Finally, a complex of plants became widely diffused, particularly

Domestication of plants in the New World

Evolution of corn in the Tehuacán Valley, Mexico. At far left is a small cob of wild corn dated at around 5000 B.C., followed by early domesticated cobs dated at around 4000 B.C., 3000 B.C., and 1000 B.C. At far right is a modern form of corncob dating from around the time of Christ. All are shown in four fifths of natural size (MacNeish 1974).

maize, pumpkins, squash, beans, chili peppers, tobacco, and bottle gourds. Cotton appeared at both Puebla and Tamaulipas around 1700 B.C.

The principal plants developed in Neolithic times in the Old World—barley, wheat, millet, and rice—did not appear in the New World, where the main crops, instead, were maize, beans, and squash. These plants and the techniques of their cultivation were quite different from the plants and methods of cultivation in the Old World. This shows that plant domestication was discovered by the American Indians, not taught to them by some superior invaders from abroad.

It is true that three New World plants are found also in the Old World: cotton, the sweet potato, and the gourd. Some proponents of trans-Pacific diffusion have argued that cotton must have been brought across the sea to the Americas in pre-Columbian times. This cannot be ruled out as a possibility, but it has not been proven.

Sweet potatoes were grown in Polynesia and Melanesia, as well as in the New World. Some authorities believe that the plant originated in the New World and spread to the Pacific Islands; others claim that the diffusion worked the other way around.

The early date of the gourd at Tamaulipas would seem to rule out the possibility of trans-Pacific diffusion. Gourds may have drifted across the ocean in pre-Columbian times.

Mesoamerica was not the only center of New World domestication. Domesticated beans from Peru have been dated by radiocarbon as far back as between 8500 and 5500 B.C. In 1970 a cave near Ayacucho in the Andes of Peru yielded corncobs that have been dated between 4300 and 2800 B.C. It has also been shown that maize agriculture was present in Ecuador about 5,000 years ago. Bitter manioc was cultivated in tropical Venezuela and adjacent regions. Its consumption depended upon techniques for squeezing poisonous prussic acid from the roots—another original American Indian invention. In the Andean highlands, potatoes were grown. It is possible that corn was first domesticated in Peru. But Mesoamerica was the center from which the important maize-beans-squash complex diffused to North America. Maize had spread to the North American Southwest by around 2500 B.C. Within 2,000 years, maize was being cultivated from Canada to Florida in the eastern half of North America, as well as in the Southwest, and along the western coast of South America as far south as northwestern Argentina.

An important difference between Old World and New World agriculture is that it was not accompanied in the New World by much domestication of animals. A few animals were domesticated in the Americas: guinea pigs and muscovy ducks in Peru, turkeys and bees in Mexico. Llamas were employed as pack animals in Peru; their wool and that of the vicuña and alpaca were used for textiles. Dogs had probably been brought over by emigrants from Asia.

There were no indigenous wild horses or cows to be domesticated in the New World. The horses of Pleistocene times had become extinct; these animals were not known to American Indians until their introduction by Europeans. American buffalos do not seem to be amenable to domestication. As a result, the Indians had no animals to serve for traction, and they developed no wheeled vehicles or plows. Fortunately, the American crops were of a sort that did not require plow cultivation; digging sticks usually were sufficient.

Summary

Plants were domesticated in both the Old World and the New around 8000 or 7000 B.C. By 2,000 years ago most people in the world lived by farming, which replaced the earlier hunting-gathering mode of subsistence.

There was little domestication of animals in the New World, but some Old World species were domesticated by the eighth millennium B.C., including cattle, sheep, goats, and pigs.

The switch from hunting-gathering to farming may have been due to population pressure, but this is still a subject of debate.

Suggestions for further reading

A valuable and stimulating collection of articles is assembled in Stuart Struever, ed., *Prehistoric Agriculture* (New York: The Natural History Press, 1971); see especially the papers by Binford and Flannery. See also Peter J. Ucko and G. W. Dimbleby, eds., *The Domestication and Exploitation of Plants and Animals* (Chicago: Aldine, 1969).

V. Gordon Childe's oasis theory is set forth in his classic work, *Man Makes Himself* (New York: Mentor Books, 1936, 1951), pp. 67–69. A recent expression of Robert J. Braidwood's views appears in the 8th edition of his *Prehistoric Men* (Glenview, Ill.: Scott, Foresman, 1975).

The role of population pressure as the determining factor in the switch to agriculture is set forth in Mark Nathan Cohen, *The Food Crisis in Prehistory. Overpopulation and the Origins of Agriculture* (New Haven: Yale University Press, 1977). For different views about the significance of population pressure, see Fekri A. Hassan, "Determination of the Size, Density, and Growth Rate of Hunting-Gathering Populations" and Bennet Bronson, "The Earliest Farming: Demography as Cause and Consequence," both in Steven Polgar, ed., *Population, Ecology, and Social Evolution* (The Hague: Mouton, 1975), pp. 27–52 and 53–79.

On the subject of population control, see Brian Hayden, "Population Control among Hunter/Gatherers," *World Archaeology* 4 (1972): 205–21, and William T. Divale, "Systemic Population Control in the Middle and Upper Palaeolithic: Inferences based on Contemporary Hunter-Gatherers," *World Archaeology* 4 (1972): 222–37.

Early evidence of plant domestication in Thailand is presented in Chester F. Gorman, "Hoabinhian: A Pebble-Tool Complex with Early Plant Associations in Southeast Asia," *Science* 163 (3868) (1969): 671–73.

For developments in the New World, see Gordon R. Willey, *An Introduction to American Archaeology*, vol. I: *North and Middle America* (Englewood Cliffs, N.J.: Prentice-Hall, 1966), pp. 78–92.

The main pioneer research on early plant domestication in the Tehuacán Valley was done by Richard S. MacNeish, whose article, "Ancient Mesoamerican Civilization," which originally appeared in *Science* 143 (1964): pp. 531–37, is reprinted in Struever, *Prehistoric Agriculture*, pp. 143–56. For good illustrations and text, see Jonathan Norton Leonard and the Editors of Time-Life Books, *The First Farmers* (New York: Time-Life Books, 1973).

CHAPTER 13

Neolithic patterns

The development of horticulture led to various alterations in the ways of life in both the Old World and the New, but these changes came about gradually. Long after farming was first begun, hunting and gathering must have continued to be the main sources of subsistence, with horticulture only a sideline. Even after farming became a major source of food, seminomadic conditions persisted when soil resources were depleted, forcing a shift to new quarters. For example, a Neolithic settlement in the Rhineland consisting of 21 households is estimated to have been occupied seven times during a 450-year period. Sites like this were inhabited for about ten years and then abandoned to give the soil time to regenerate itself. Nevertheless, the potential for permanent settlement based on food production was strengthened in the Neolithic period.

Horticulture also facilitated the preservation of food. Grain could now be stored for the future. Hunters have no special problem if their region is rich in game, but if it is not and if they have no techniques for salting, drying, or preserving meat, they are out of luck. Perhaps the Eskimos were fortunate to live in a natural icebox in winter; their food could be cached out of reach of dogs and wolves for later consumption. The Blackfoot and other Indian tribes of the Plains pounded dried lean meat, sometimes mixed with berries and bone marrow, to make pemmican, which they stored in buffalo-skin containers. Although hunting peoples such as these devised various ways of preserving meat, it is a common practice for hunters to divide their game right after the kill and eat it within a short time. Then, the hunters must be off again for more. The addition of easily stored grain to the human diet gave added security.

There also were hazards in increased sedentary life, however. In preagricultural times, no epidemic-forming parasites could have had man as their only host. Human populations were small and scattered. Congregation in villages, however, meant that garbage dumps and human feces provided new sources of infection, as did the domesticated animals that were often carriers of the human types of salmonella, ascaris worms, hookworm, and other parasites that spread through fecal matter (Polgar 1964:204–5).

Although humans thus became exposed to new diseases, the developments of Neolithic times seem to have favored their survival, since there was a population explosion in the Old World during the Neolithic. Skeletal remains from Neolithic burial sites greatly outnumber those of preceding periods, despite the relatively short duration of the Neolithic.

Neolithic housing in the Near East and Europe

When sedentary life was made more feasible, people could begin to give more attention to their dwellings, building more substantial houses than hunting-gathering peoples are usually apt to do. The material used depended on what was locally available and on the climatic conditions. In the Near East, for example, at the Turkish site of Çatal Hüyük, which is described in more detail later, houses were often made of rectangular, sun-dried mud bricks, reeds, and plaster. There was little use of stone at Çatal Hüyük, for it is not found locally in the alluvial plain. The houses were closely huddled together, perhaps for defense. Çatal Hüyük rather resembles a Southwest American Indian pueblo, including the feature that entrance to a house was made by ladder from the roof.

The houses of Khirokitia in Cyprus were large, domed, circular dwellings, like beehives, with stone foundations and mud-brick walls. Entrance was through wooden framed doors sunk slightly below ground level. Some of these houses had a second story resting on square limestone pillars.

Apart from dwellings, Neolithic villages also contained grain storage pits or granaries and ovens. Ovens were not only important for the baking of bread, but they also served as prototypes for the pottery kiln and later the smelting furnace.

It is understandable that in the wooded regions of Europe much of the Neolithic housing was made of wood. The Danubian farmers built long houses with gabled roofs. Somewhat similar wooden structures were built by the Swiss Lake Dwellers.

At Skara Brae in the Orkney Islands, off northern Scotland, trees that could provide wood did not flourish because of the strong winds that sweep over the islands. The islanders hollowed out a settlement in the sand dunes made largely of stone with a roofing of whalebone rafters. There were narrow entrances only four feet high with stone doors. The houses were furnished with stone beds, softened with heather and skins, and had stone "dressers" with shelves. These houses were connected by roofed alleyways, forming a tightly knit community.

Circular house foundations at Khirokitia, Cyprus.

Since the houses of Skara Brae were built of stone and were later covered by sand dunes, they have been remarkably well preserved. They give an impression of coziness and seem more "advanced" than one might expect of such a marginal Neolithic community. Neolithic homes in more favored regions, such as Çatal Hüyük, were even more comfortable.

Housing in the New World

Permanent housing also became practical in the New World with the development of horticulture, and we find some understandable parallels to Old World architecture, based on the limitation of possibilities. Only certain kinds of materials are useful in building construction, and there is a limited number of functionally effective ways in which they can be put together. Such features as doors and lintels in stone and adobe houses are understandable from this point of view. Inca houses were generally rectangular, thatched, and gable roofed. They usually had no windows, but some late Inca buildings had them. The Pueblo Indians of the North American Southwest built closely massed apartment-house-like structures of adobe, stone, and wood, which resembled the houses of Çatal Hüyük, while the Iroquois Indians of the eastern woodlands of North America constructed longhouses, which bore some similarities to those of the Neolithic Danubian peasants of eastern Europe. As in the Old World, the builders in each area were limited by the materials at hand. Rectangular adobe bricks were units of building construction in coastal Peru. The only people to use lime mortar were the Maya of Mesoamerica.

Later, we shall see that still more parallels to Old World architecture appeared in the higher centers of civilization in Mesoamerica and Peru, where city life developed.

Stonework

The term *Neolithic*, or *new stone*, refers to the fact that the stone tools used during this period were different from those found in the Paleolithic. Neolithic tools included ground-stone axes and adzes, hafted to handles. Similar tools were used in Mesolithic Europe. Axes and adzes made

Neolithic axes.

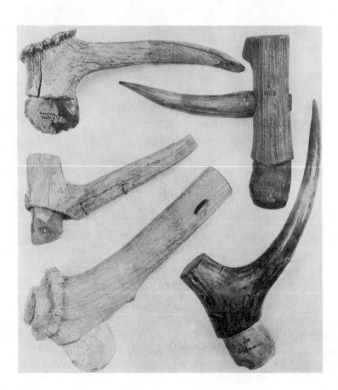

possible the carpentry involved in the construction of Danubian longhouses, doors, beds, and other furniture. Such tools could be made of granular stone instead of flint and were fashioned by rubbing and grinding. This is a more laborious, time-consuming process than flaking, but the resulting tool is more durable and effective. Axes and adzes were sometimes drilled to provide for a shaft or handle. In early Neolithic times, this was probably done with a bow drill, drilling from both sides. Querns, rubbing stones, mortars, and pestles are common Neolithic tools used for preparing cereals. Sickles and polished stone bowls are also commonly found. Ground-stone tools came into use in the New World at comparable cultural levels.

Weaving was a by-product of the domestication of plants and animals, utilizing the fibers of plants such as flax or of animals such as sheep wool. The making of basketry and matting must have preceded weaving; it is sometimes hard to distinguish between them in archaeological remains. Woven textiles, characterized by being made from spun or twisted threads, depend upon some spinning technique. An old and widespread device for this purpose is the spindle, a thin rod usually made of wood, equipped with a weighted whorl of wood or clay. Some twisted fiber is fastened to the spindle, which is then dropped toward the ground, rotating, while the spinner draws out the thread and adds more fiber.

Weaving

Zapotec women in Mexico weaving with belt looms.

Weaving can be done without a loom in a way similar to making woven baskets, but finger weaving is a slow process. The invention of a loom in the Neolithic period greatly facilitated the making of textiles. Woven garments thenceforth supplemented or replaced animal skins for clothing. There is abundant evidence of woven clothing at Çatal Hüyük, where fur and animal skins (especially leopard skins) were also worn. Neolithic Egyptian graves have yielded textiles. The material most often occurring in early Neolithic sites is flax. Domestication of cotton evidently came later, first attested to in the Indus Valley civilization of the third millennium B.C.

Weaving also developed in the New World. Domesticated cotton was used for textiles in Peru by 2000 B.C. The preceramic site of Huaca Prieta, dated at around that time, gives evidence of finger weaving; the loom was not yet known. By about 1,000 years later, mantles uncovered at Paracas show that the loom had been invented. Looms and spindle whorls for spinning were also used throughout Mesoamerica. The most widespread form of New World loom was a belt or backstrap loom in which the horizontal or slightly tilted loom was attached to the weaver by a belt around her back while the other end was tied to a post or a tree.

Because of the dryness of the climate, much Peruvian weaving has been preserved and may be seen in museums throughout the world. Peruvian textiles show impressive workmanship of great variety. The Peruvians had one advantage over all other American Indians: the use of wool obtained from llamas, alpacas, and vicuñas. The highlanders in the Andes, where the weather can be very cold, had a practical motivation to prepare warm clothing. As already noted, cotton was also known from early times.

The use of the loom spread through the areas of higher civilization in the New World—to Bolivia and Ecuador and even to some of the tropical forest peoples, such as the Jivaro. Weaving also diffused to the Pueblo area in the North American Southwest. Apparently as an independent invention, weaving developed among the tribes of the northwestern coast of North America, who devised a suspended-warp upright loom. Textiles were made from spruce roots, wild hemp, and cedar bark. So-called Chilkat blankets were made of mountain-goat wool, spun and twined over a core of cedar-bark string.

Pottery

Pottery is not always found in Neolithic sites. It is absent, for example, from the lower strata of excavations at Jarmo and Jericho. It occurs in some nonagricultural sites. Some of the oldest-dated pottery, estimated at about 12,600 years ago, comes from Kyushu in southern Japan, before agriculture was introduced.

Some nomadic hunting-gathering peoples, such as the Bushmen and the Eskimos, have pottery. Generally, however, pottery is inappropriate for such people, being rather heavy, bulky, and breakable, and skin or

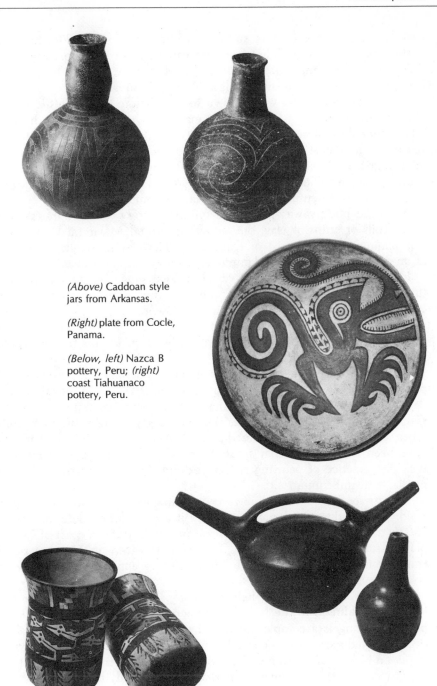

(Above) Caddoan style jars from Arkansas.

(Right) plate from Cocle, Panama.

(Below, left) Nazca B pottery, Peru; *(right)* coast Tiahuanaco pottery, Peru.

basketry containers are more suitable. With settled village life, however, pottery can be very useful. Large jars can then be used to store grain; dishes, mugs, cooking pots, and other vessels can be made. Thus, pottery is usually found in abundance in later Neolithic sites.

The properties of clay were known to men before the Neolithic period. Clay figurines, sometimes fired, were made by Upper Paleolithic hunters. Clay generally requires some treatment before it can be worked. If it is too dry, water must be added. If it is too sticky, it may be tempered by adding grit, sand, shell, or other material. Such tempering also helps to prevent cracking when the vessel is fired. Clay is usually mixed and kneaded before working to ensure uniform texture or composition.

Neolithic pottery was not made on the potter's wheel but was built up of coils or strips of clay, one above the other. Making a large pot in this manner may take two or three days. The clay must always be kept at an appropriate degree of dampness, not too wet and not too dry.

Firing involves exposing the vessel to heat long enough (above 500° C) to drive out its water content. This was first done in open fires, but later kilns or ovens were built for the purpose.

Since pottery is porous, water kept in a jar may seep through. Glazing was invented in the Near East to give the ware a smooth, waterproof finish.

The earliest Neolithic pottery was not decorated, but in the late Neolithic period, vessels were painted in southern Turkey. Red-on-cream ware is dated at around 5500 B.C. Finely made, dark burnished ware comes from Çatal Hüyük. Pots of various sizes and shapes, including anthropomorphic types, and painted with various designs, including imitations of basketry, have been found at Hacilar in southern Turkey, dated at around 5200 B.C. The practice of painting pottery extended from Iran to the Balkans in the sixth millennium B.C.

What may be the oldest known pottery in the New World comes from Valdivia, Ecuador. Gordon Willey gives it a radiocarbon date of 3000 to 2500 B.C. Pottery from Puerto Hormigas on the Caribbean coast of Colombia is dated at around 2900 B.C. The earliest pottery in Mesoamerica is from around 2300 B.C., while, in Peru, pottery appears at some sites at around 1800 B.C.

Gordon F. Ekholm, who believes that pottery originated in the Old World and diffused to the New World across the Pacific, has argued that pottery making is a complex technical process that is not likely to have been invented more than once (Ekholm 1964:495). Against this view, which implies a lack of inventiveness on the part of the American Indians, there may be cited the list of inventions that appeared only in the New World before the coming of Columbus. Erland Nordenskiöld and others have drawn up a lengthy inventory of such items, which include the following, among others: the hammock, the method of removing poisonous prussic acid from manioc and thus producing edible tapioca, the Peruvian whistling jar, the cigar, the cigarette, the tobacco pipe, the enema syringe, the rubber ball, and the toboggan (Nordenskiöld 1930:23–24). If the Indians could invent these things that were not invented anywhere else, they could probably have invented the items in dispute, such as pottery. We have already seen that they domesticated uniquely New World plants such as maize, potatoes, and pumpkins. To these may be added tomatoes, peanuts, lima beans, kidney beans, cacao (for chocolate), agave (for pulque), and avocados. American Indians discovered the properties of coca (for cocaine) and rubber. So they were not uninventive.

Pottery making does, however, seem to have diffused from Siberia to North America between 3000 and 1000 B.C. By the latter date, Woodland peoples in eastern North America were using conchoidal-based, cord-marked, unpainted pots just like those used in Siberia. Other items, such as the adze and harpoon, are believed to have diffused from Siberia at around the same time. Thus, we have at least two areas of pottery diffusion in the New World, one in the peripheral northern and eastern zones and one in the centers of high civilization and their surrounding fringes. None of this pottery was shaped on the potter's wheel, an invention not made by the American Indians. But much American pottery is very beautiful, particularly the strikingly painted Nazca ware of Peru and the sophisticated ceramics of the Maya and the North American Southwest.

Trade

It used to be thought that there was little trade in Neolithic times, since each community was apt to be self-sufficient—able to meet its own needs for food, clothing, and other necessities. Whatever trade was engaged in was apt to concern only luxuries, nonessentials (Childe 1953:74). However, there is now evidence that trade began early in Neolithic times and covered considerable distances. Obsidian was traded in the eighth century B.C., and in Neolithic times there was trade in other substances, such as salt and sulfur. Most of the raw materials used at Çatal Hüyük, apart from clay, reeds, and some wood, seem not to have been available locally. Timber had to be brought down from the hills, obsidian from volcanoes, marble from western Anatolia, stalactites from caves in the Taurus Mountains, and shells from the Mediterranean. This was evidently a society depending heavily on trade from many different sources. Çatal Hüyük also seems to have been characterized by considerable specialization and division of labor. In these respects Çatal Hüyük anticipated the stage of civilization.

Megalithic cults

One feature of the European Neolithic was the development of *megalithic* (large stone) cults. By now men had learned how to move and set up large, sometimes enormous stones. This must have involved the cooperation of many persons. Food resources were evidently plentiful enough to divert time from the food quest to this difficult work.

The simplest megalithic structure is the *menhir*, a single standing stone. Sometimes a row of menhirs is formed in an orderly line; this is called an *alignment*, many of which are found in Brittany, some extending for a mile in length. Sometimes menhirs are arranged in a circle or horseshoe formation, as at Avebury and Stonehenge in England and at Hagar Qim in Malta. Sometimes menhirs are shaped to form a long, communal grave, known as a *passage grave*.

In the first edition of this book, following a traditional interpretation, the northern European megalithic cults were described as being derived from the Mediterranean. It was assumed that this cult was spread by seafaring people, since passage graves are found near the coasts of Spain, Brittany, Ireland, and Denmark. A Mediterranean origin for the cult is now held to be unlikely, however. This change of opinion was brought about by revisions in radiocarbon dates through the new bristlecone calibration technique discussed on page 35. As a result, the megalithic tombs of northern Europe are now found to be older than the pyramids of Egypt, and Stonehenge is believed to have been built before the Mycenaean civilization of Greece began.

According to new radiocarbon dating, Stonehenge was built in different stages, beginning around 2800 B.C. and completed after 1100 B.C. "The megalithic chamber tombs of Spain and Portugal date from 3800 to 2000 B.C. The British and Irish tombs date from just after 3800 to 2000 B.C. and the Scandinavian tombs from before 3000 B.C. to, say, 1800 B.C." (Daniel 1980:87).

Colin Renfrew has presented a new explanation for the development of European megalithic tombs. He points out that they are generally located in Atlantic coastal regions that were long occupied by sedentary Mesolithic peoples before practices of farming were introduced. These were successful, viable communities, but the introduction of agriculture must have given them even more security than they already enjoyed. This made possible greater population density and population increase. Conflict between local groups over land resources probably ensued. In such a situation it is of adaptive value for members of a community to feel a sense of solidarity; participation in a megalithic cult could have provided the sense of common participation that the situation required (Renfrew 1973:142–45).

Stonehenge

The most famous megalithic structure is Stonehenge on the Salisbury Plain in England, dating back nearly 4,000 years. The bluestone menhirs that make up one of the concentric circles must have been transported from the Prescelly Mountains of Wales, which are 130 miles away as the crow flies. But, of course, their transportation could not have followed a straight course. The stones are believed to have been moved largely by sea on raft floats and overland by a system of rollers, altogether over a distance of 240 miles. Eighty or more of these bluestones weighed up to five tons each.

Even larger and heavier are the sarsen stones that form the most imposing segments at Stonehenge. Large stone lintels were somehow hoisted up and laid across some of the pairs of menhirs. The sarsens, which average 30 tons, were moved from 20 miles away. One estimate of the work involved in setting up this awesome structure is that it must have required about 1.5 million man-days of physical labor, to say nothing of the planning and brainwork involved.

The purpose of this enormous effort has long been a subject of speculation. An astronomer, Gerald S. Hawkins, has offered the most probable explanation: that Stonehenge served as a kind of astronomical observatory, providing sighting points for sunrise at the longest and shortest days of the year and also for midpoints at the times of equinoxes. The arrangement of the stones also made possible prediction of eclipses of the moon. The structure of Stonehenge is so perfectly adapted for such observations that it would be hard to consider its layout a matter of chance. Stonehenge must have been conceived, designed, and set up by men who had learned a good deal about the orderly movements of the sun and moon. Another proponent of the idea that Neolithic Britons had a scientific understanding of astronomy is Alexander Thom (1971).

Some authorities (for example, Ellegård 1981) find it so hard to credit the "barbarians" of that time with such sophisticated astronomical knowledge—far in advance of contemporary Egypt and Mesopotamia—that they have rejected this interpretation. But it seems hard to do so. Rather, we should probably revise our assumptions about the people of prehistoric times who often seem to have been capable of remarkable inventions, deductions, and discoveries. We need not assume that the builders of Stonehenge were purely rational in their motives. Religion was probably mixed up with their science; very likely the sun and moon were their gods. But

Stonehenge.

it must have been reassuring for the people of Stonehenge to know that their gods were so reliable and that it was possible to predict to the day when the solstices would come and the moon fall under eclipse (See Hawkins 1965).

In the preceding pages we have reviewed some general features in both the Old World and the New of cultural patterns commonly found in societies at the Neolithic level: plant and animal domestication, housing, ground-stone tools, weaving, pottery, and trade. To get a more integrated conception of some particular Neolithic communities, let us consider in more detail four Old World Neolithic settlements: Ali Kosh in Iran, Jarmo in Iraq, Çatal Hüyük in Turkey, and Pan-po in northern China.

Ali Kosh, Iran

Ali Kosh was a small village, with probably fewer than 100 inhabitants, located on the Deh Luran plain east of the Tigris River in Iran (see the map on p. 193). Between approximately 7500 and 6750 B.C., according to radiocarbon dating, it was inhabited by people who collected wild plants but also had some domesticated wheat and barley. Moreover, they herded sheep and goats. Their culture is reminiscent of Karim Shahir, the earlier Mesolithic community farther north, which gave evidence of incipient animal domestication (see p. 186).

Between 6750 and 6000 B.C. there was a slight increase in the number of sheep and in the amount of domesticated wheat and barley, along with a reduction in the amount of wild legumes collected. The multiroomed houses of Ali Kosh increased in size. Domed brick ovens and brick-lined roasting pits were found at this level, and there is now clear osteological evidence of domestication in goats, the animals most often eaten. But hunting continued, to judge from remains of gazelle, onager, and wild cattle, and there was fishing and collection of aquatic resources: catfish, carp, water turtle, mussels, and river crabs (Hole, Flannery, and Neely 1969).

Jarmo, Iraq

A contemporary site (around 6750 B.C.) with similar features was Jarmo, in the hills of northeastern Iraq. There were about 25 rectangular mud houses in this village with perhaps 100 or 150 inhabitants. These people had flint sickles for reaping barley and wheat. The wheat is considered to be about halfway between wild and fully domesticated forms. There were mortars for grinding grain and ovens for parching it. Dogs, sheep, and goats were domesticated. There are not many bones of wild animals, but some hunting was still being done, and the Jarmo people also ate large quantities of snails. They made clay figurines, bracelets of stone and bone, and well-made cups, bowls, and palettes of ground stone. There is evidence of matting or basketry, impressed in the mud floors (Braidwood 1975:127–30).

A remarkably sophisticated Neolithic settlement, dating from around 6500 or 5700 B.C., has been found at Çatal Hüyük on the plateau of Anatolia in Turkey. The settlement covered 32 acres. The people here raised crops (barley, wheat, peas) and had sheep and cattle. Pottery was made. The plastered, mud-brick houses were laid out in a rather orderly manner, rectangular in shape and grouped around courtyards. Some of the houses, which may have been shrines or temples, contain the earliest murals found on man-made walls.

A large bull, six feet long, rather reminiscent of the big bulls at Lascaux Cave, covers one of the walls. It is surrounded by very small human figures. (Many pairs of bulls' horns, some set in plaster, have also been found at Çatal Hüyük, suggesting the existence of a cult of the bull, like that which developed later at Crete.) Deer are also depicted in the murals, together with human hunters holding bows. The most impressive of the murals shows about a dozen men grouped in three rows performing a dance. Some hold bows, one beats a drum, and some are jumping. This is a lively scene, well executed. These paintings were applied with a brush on white plaster, the colors including red, pink, mauve, black, and yellow. There are also wall paintings of giant vultures attacking human bodies. This may imply a practice of exposure of corpses to vultures, as is done by the present-day Parsis of India. The defleshed bones were assembled for secondary burial beneath the floors of the houses.

Handicrafts were varied, including, among other things, beautifully made wooden bowls and boxes, basketry, pins, knives, and obsidian mirrors.

There is a good deal of sculpture, including many seated goddesses,

Çatal Hüyük, Turkey

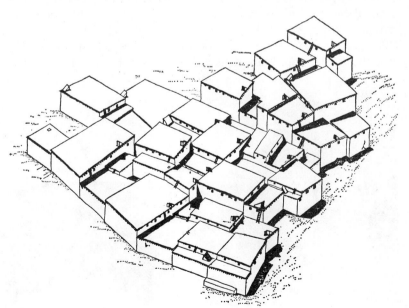

Schematic reconstruction of a section of Level VI at Çatal Hüyük.

sometimes depicted giving birth. They tend to be rather fat, like Upper Paleolithic Venuses. Similar statuettes came from other Neolithic sites in the Near East, including Hacilar and Jarmo (Mellaart 1967).

Pan-po, northern China

Wheat and barley were domesticated in northern China in Neolithic times. The use of wheat and barley must have diffused eastward from southwestern Asia, moving along the southern edge of the steppes. But the grain that became most popular in northern China was millet, which may have been domesticated locally. Cattle also were introduced, although the Chinese never took to drinking milk.

Neolithic settlements developed in a region in northern China where three great rivers come together—the Huangho, Fenho, and Weishu—and where three modern Chinese provinces adjoin—Honan, Shansi, and Shensi. In these three provinces two early Neolithic cultures flourished: Yangshao and, somewhat later, Lungshan. More than 1,000 Yangshao sites have been found, dating between approximately 6000 and 4000 B.C. There are over 400 of these sites in the Wei Valley.

The following are some of the characteristic traits of the Chinese Neolithic: cultivation of millet and rice; domestication of pigs, cattle, sheep, dogs, and chickens; construction of stamped-earth and wattle-and-daub structures; domestication of silkworms and possible loom weaving of silk and hemp; cord-marked pottery and ceremonial ware; use of jade; and scapulimancy (divination by means of cracks in shoulder blades) (Chang 1968:86–87).

An extensively excavated Yangshao settlement is Pan-po in Shensi Province, dated by radiocarbon from around 4600 to 4000 B.C. or perhaps earlier. During the early period about 600 people lived there, in about 200 houses. There were over 200 deep storage pits in the village. Millet was the staple crop. Only dogs and pigs seem to have been domesticated;

Yangshao Neolithic pottery.

Pots at Pan-po Neolithic site, northern China

deer hunting evidently provided the bulk of the meat consumed. Most of the dwellings were round or oblong semisubterranean houses with thatched roofs. Clay was used to make cupboards, benches, and ovens. In the center of the village was a plaza with a large communal structure, around which the smaller houses were ranged in a circle, with the doors facing the center. North of the dwelling area was a village cemetery. Six pottery kilns have been found on the outskirts. Most of the ware was coarse household pottery, but finer painted vessels used for funerary purposes were buried with the dead. The potter's wheel does not seem to have been used.

In later years Chinese communities sought to defend themselves through protecting walls. Pan-po was similarly security conscious but found protection in a different way—by means of a moat around the village. The village was also divided by a deep ditch. The purpose of this feature is less evident. It is thought to have perhaps separated two clans or groups of families, but this is only speculation.

Despite the ditch, the planned layout of Pan-po with it communal building and the common cemetery, suggest a consciousness of community, perhaps along clan or lineage lines. The Chinese ancestor cult may have its origin in this early period, although there is more definite evidence of such a cult in the later Lungshan stage. This tightly knit community seems to have been largely self-sufficient, but there is evidence of trade in the remains of seashells and stone materials, such as jade, from distant regions.

Settlements of the Lungshan stage were spread out over a much wider area than the earlier Yangshao. The house construction was similar to that at Pan-po, but the villages were larger and more permanent, occupied over longer periods of time. It has been inferred that the Yangshao people practiced slash-and-burn horticulture and had to shift their settlements occasionally, but by Lungshan times agricultural methods had improved, perhaps with the adoption of irrigation, fallowing, use of fertilizers, or other practices. Lungshan villages had permanent walls of stamped earth, indicating a need for fortification. All this suggests population increase, movement of farming peoples to new areas, and increased conflicts between communities.

There is some evidence of craft specialization. The potter's wheel was then in use. Since some of the black ceramics, characteristic of the Lungshan culture, were finely made, pottery may have become a specialized craft. Some settlements also produced fine work in jade. There is more evidence of status differentiation than in the more egalitarian Yangshao settlements, as seen in distinctions in burial practices and the concentration of jade artifacts at isolated spots in one site. Scapulimancy was practiced, and there is now evidence of an ancestor cult (Chang 1968:128–29).

Although it shared some of the same domesticated plants, animals, and other features as the Southwest Asiatic Neolithic, the Chinese Neolithic seems to have had its own characteristic style from early times.

World view of Neolithic farmers

Can anything be said of how life appeared to the humans of Neolithic times, of what values and attitudes they shared? It may seem too speculative to raise such a question, for we are dealing with a period before the appearance of written records, and one can only make deductions of doubtful validity. Nevertheless, the question seems worth trying to answer, for the Neolithic was an important transition point for humanity from a hunting-gathering way of life to one based on agriculture and the domestication of animals. The changes in human patterns of subsistence must have involved the adoption of quite different daily routines and the cultivation of virtues different from those of hunting-gathering peoples.

We are probably safe in saying that patience and perseverance were necessary Neolithic virtues. This is not to say that hunters and gatherers did not also have these qualities. The hunter stalking his prey, the Eskimo waiting by the blowhole of a seal must also maintain great patience and perseverance. But the technological developments of the Neolithic surely enhanced such tendencies. It takes more time and patience to make a ground-stone adze than a flake tool; many days, many stages go into the making of a textile garment or a clay vessel. Neolithic people learned to adopt a routine way of life involving a round of chores. While the hunter lives more in the present, the farmer must think ahead and sow seeds to be harvested in a later season.

Hunter and farmer focus their attention on different things. The hunter is alert to spoor and tracks, slight disturbances in the soil; he must know the characteristics of different kinds of wild animals. The farmer is more concerned about the sun, rainfall, and the changes of seasons. The quite individualistic religion of hunting-gathering North American Indians such as the Ojibwa (Chippewa) focused on health, so vital to a hunter, while the more collective religion of the agricultural Hopi, with its cycle of calendrical ceremonies, focused on rainfall and fertility of the fields. One may say that the farmer learns to think in calendrical seasonal terms and to study the movements of the sun, moon, and stars for clues to the proper times for planting, harvesting, and other stages in the agricultural cycle.

Despite all his hard work, the farmer cannot count on success. Drought, frost, hail, windstorms, floods, locusts, fire, and other acts of nature may ruin his crop. He has to wait for the seeds to grow and must depend on the gods for conditions favorable to growth. He repeats practices that have worked before. Conservatism and patience seem to be encouraged by such a life, and, perhaps also, a mystical attitude toward nature, the Earth Mother, and other deities on whom the farmer depends.

At the same time, Neolithic people had reason to develop a growing self-confidence. Childe has suggested that the making of pottery reacted on human thought:

> The lump of clay was perfectly plastic; man could mold it as he would. In making a tool of stone or bone he was always limited by the shape and size of the original material; he could only take bits away from it. No such limitations restrict the activity of the potter (Childe 1953:79).

Clay and pottery thus became symbols of the process of creation.

Neolithic community life involved much group cooperation. This may be true of hunters, too, as in the case of animal drives or surrounds, such as the communal buffalo hunt of the North American plains. But Neolithic community cooperation seems to have been more sustained. This is suggested by the relatively ambitious architecture at such settlements as Çatal Hüyük and Pan-po.

Settled village life facilitates the accumulation of property. Nomadic hunters must travel light, but farmers can acquire bulky objects such as stone mortars and pottery storage vessels. Land ownership also becomes a possibility which may militate against the community cooperation just mentioned. When hunters or pastoralists quarrel, families can separate and go different ways. This is less easy for farmers who are anchored to the soil and who must learn to keep their feelings in check if they wish to get on with their neighbors. It has been hypothesized that farmers are therefore more apt to engage in covert witchcraft practices than are nomadic pastoralists. In a study of four African tribes containing both pastoralists and agriculturalists, there appeared to be some partial confirmation of this hypothesis (Edgerton 1971:288–92). However, there are pastoral tribes and hunting-gathering societies that have much concern about sorcery. Since farmers must settle local disputes or else engage in feuds that disrupt community life, there tends to be some development of local government. The tendencies in Neolithic village life toward private property, incipient social stratification, and government control were to develop further in the civilizations of the Bronze Age.

Diffusion of Neolithic patterns

There were Neolithic communities in eastern Europe by the sixth millennium B.C.; in central Europe, by the fifth; and in England, by the fourth.

Meanwhile, Neolithic cultures also spread across North Africa. In climate and in culture, the African Mediterranean coast ressembled that of Europe. Racially, too, there was much similarity. The Berbers, ancient peoples of North Africa, are Caucasoids. Some of their more isolated groups in the Atlas Mountains have retained an essentially Neolithic way of life down to recent times.

Much of North Africa today, particularly the deserts of Libya and the great Sahara Desert, is bleak and inhospitable. But, before 2000 B.C., the land was well watered. This is indicated by the presence of bones of many animals that could not live there now: giraffe, hippopotamus, elephant, antelope, and others. (Ancient isolated trees still survive in soil where seeds no longer grow, and stunted crocodiles inhabit desert pools they could not have reached by waddling overland.)

Neolithic pastoralists once lived in the Tassili Plateau in the central Sahara in Algeria, where they painted beautiful frescoes on rock walls. The first settlers brought sheep and goats; a later wave had herds of cattle, which are depicted with realism and elegance on the rock. Also shown are scenes of men hunting rhinoceros and hippopotamus, girls of Ethiopian type with sugerloaf hair style and white robes, and a woman with a row of pots, cooking food.

Neolithic patterns also moved eastward from the Near East into South Asia through Iran, Baluchistan, and Afghanistan. Archaeologists have recently been excavating prepottery Neolithic sites at Mehrgarh on the Bolan River, at the foot of the Bolan Pass, one of the main passes that leads from Afghanistan into what is now Pakistan. They have tentatively placed the beginnings of the prepottery settlement at some time before 6000 B.C. Barley, einkorn, and emmer wheat were domesticated here. Cattle, rather than sheep or goats, were the main domesticated animals. This Neolithic culture evidently laid the groundwork for the development of the Bronze Age Harappa civilization.

Pastoralism

Pastoralism is a way of life that developed in semiarid grasslands, deserts, and steppes in which dependence on animal husbandry became the main basis of the economy and plant cultivation of lesser or little importance.

Different kinds of animals have been herded by pastoralists in different parts of the Old World: reindeer by the Lapps of northern Europe, cattle in Africa, camels in Arabia and the Sahara Dessert, and herds of mixed composition in many areas.

Pastoralists often engage in some agriculture as a sideline. This is true, for example, of the Marri Baluch of Baluchistan, among whom there are groups that may temporarily abandon farming if their herds grow large enough. Robert Pehrson (1966:14) writes:

> Once the herd reaches about one hundred animals, its value is so great that other considerations become secondary compared with the welfare of the herd, and unless very favorably situated the camp then breaks loose from its village nucleus, migrating widely in search of pasture and water.

The migrations of pastoral tribes, however, are not usually erratic and random. Nomads often follow traditional routes in cycles that may require several years to complete. Or else an annual cycle, known as *transhumance*, may be observed, which involves having different winter and summer camps. Thus, pastoralists in the western part of the Indian subcontinent drive their herds up to the mountains in summer, down to the plains in winter. Cattle herders in the Upper Nile Valley have different grazing grounds in dry and wet seasons.

Cattle-herding pastoralists often engage in fighting and raiding. This has been noted for various African cattle-raising groups and for such peoples as the ancient Aryans.

Occupation of the steppes

The vast steppes of central Asia were sparsely inhabited in Neolithic times and did not become important highways for East-West cultural diffusion until horseback riding developed. Some sendentary agriculturalists lived along the fringes of the steppes. In the Ukraine, remains of what has been called the Tripolye culture (circa 3000–1700 B.C.) have been uncovered. This differs from later cultures of the steppes in not being nomadic. The Tripolyans lived in wattle-and-daub huts arranged in a circle. They raised wheat, barley, and millet and bred horses, cattle, goats, sheep, and pigs. There is no evidence that a plow was used. The largest Tripolyan village excavated so far had as many as 200 houses grouped in five concentric circles. But farming without metal plowshares is difficult in such terrain, and villages of this sort were exposed to attacks by nomads, which increased after horse riding became widely practiced.

Summary

The sedentary village life that increased in Neolithic times made it possible to store and preserve food. More permanent housing appeared. There were new methods for making stone tools. Axes and adzes were made of granular stone instead of flint and were ground rather than flaked. Weaving was a by-product of the domestication of plants and animals, making use of plant fibers and sheep's wool. Looms were invented in both the Old World and the New. Pottery is also a common feature of Neolithic sites, although missing in some of the earlier levels. This pottery was not usually made on the potter's wheel but slowly built up with coils or strips of clay. Some trade took place between villages. There is evidence that Neolithic patterns of culture diffused from the Near East across North Africa and into Europe. At the same time, there was an eastward diffusion, with Neolithic patterns moving into South Asia through Iran, Afghanistan, and Baluchistan. A pastoral economy often developed in grasslands, deserts, and steppes, in areas not suitable for farming.

Suggestions for further reading

Although some of its findings have been shown to be wrong, V. Gordon Childe's *Man Makes Himself* (New York: Mentor Books, 1936, 1953) is again recommended. It is a stimulating work.

Also recommended are: Ralph Linton, *The Tree of Culture* (New York: Alfred A. Knopf, 1955), especially chapters 13–18; James Mellaart, "Roots in the Soil," in *The Dawn of Civilization: The First World Survey of Human Cultures in Early Times*, ed. Stuart Piggott (New York: McGraw-Hill, 1961), pp. 41–64, and *Çatal Hüyük: A Neolithic Town in Anatolia* (New York: McGraw-Hill, 1967); G. Rachel Levy, *Religious Conceptions of the Stone Age and Their Influence upon European Thought* (New York: Harper Torchbooks, 1948, 1963). Much of this work is of an imaginative, speculative nature and may be vulnerable to critical objections, but it assembles much valuable information.

On technology, see R. F. G. Spier, *From the Hand of Man: Primitive and Preindustrial Technologies* (Boston: Houghton Mifflin, 1970).

On Tassili, see Henri Lhote, *The Search for the Tassili Frescoes: The Story of the Prehistoric Rock-Paintings of the Sahara*, trans. from the French by Alan Houghton Brodrick (New York: E. P. Dutton & Co., 1959), handsomely illustrated. See also Lhote's "The Fertile Sahara," in *Vanished Civilizations of the Ancient World*, ed. Edward Bacon (New York: McGraw-Hill, 1963), pp. 11–32. On the megalithic cults: Colin Renfrew, *Before Civilization. The Radiocarbon Revolution and Prehistoric Europe* (New York: Alfred A. Knopf, 1973).

For a fascinating encounter between astronomy and archaeology, see Gerald S. Hawkins, in collaboration with John B. White, *Stonehenge Decoded* (New York: Doubleday & Co., 1965).

On early China: Kwang-chih Chang, *The Archaeology of Ancient China* (New Haven, Conn.: Yale University Press, 1968); William Watson, "A Cycle of Cathay," in *The Dawn of Civilization*, ed. Piggott, pp. 253–76. On pastoral nomads: E. D. Phillips, "The Royal Hordes: The Nomad People of the Steppes," ibid, pp. 301–28. Also recommended: Marshall D. Sahlins, *Tribesmen* (Englewood Cliffs, N.J.: Prentice-Hall, 1968).

CHAPTER 14

The development of civilizations

We have seen that some Neolithic communities, such as Çatal Hüyük, developed some rather sophisticated culture traits and had sizable populations. Pottery was made; in Çatal Hüyük and probably elsewhere fresco paintings were executed. These communities were moving in the direction of what has vaguely been called "civilization." Perhaps they could be said to have already reached that level, but that would depend on one's definition of the term.

Civilization has sometimes been equated with urbanism or city life, though with the added implication of a more polished way of life—"civil," "urbane" behavior, in contrast with the roughness and naïveté of rural yokels.

Criteria of civilization

A difficulty with using city life as a criterion for civilization is that it is hard to determine at just what point a town becomes a city. During the Predynastic period and much of its early history, Egypt seems to have been a country of villages and market towns with no cities except for temporary capitals. John A. Wilson (1951:34) writes that "Probably one would have to come far down into history—possibly down to the 18th Egyptian Dynasty before one could be sure of a city in the modern sense." Minoan Crete, also, did not represent a true city culture.

The presence of a writing system has also been suggested as the distinguishing mark of civilization. It is true that Sumer, Egypt, the Indus Valley, and Crete all had writing systems in the Bronze Age period, but the pre-Columbian Incas of Peru possessed no writing, although they did have

221

city life, metallurgy, and other features commonly associated with civilization.

Since the advanced cultures of the Old World developed in what has been called the Bronze Age, between approximately 3500 and 1500 B.C., it is tempting to use bronze metallurgy as an indicator of civilization; but such metallurgy was unknown to the Aztecs of Mexico, although they knew how to work copper and gold.

Another yardstick for civilization is the presence of a state, a ruling governmental body. A state and city life seem to be related. In a tribal society, kinship units provide agencies for social control; but, in a city, many men are strangers and informal social sanctions are harder to apply. A superordinate governmental agency becomes necessary if social order is to be maintained.

We need not insist on a single criterion for the level of "civilization." In addition to those already cited, some other common features of civilizations may be mentioned: the building of monumental constructions with mass labor, class stratification, division of labor and craft specialization,

Centers of Old World civilization.

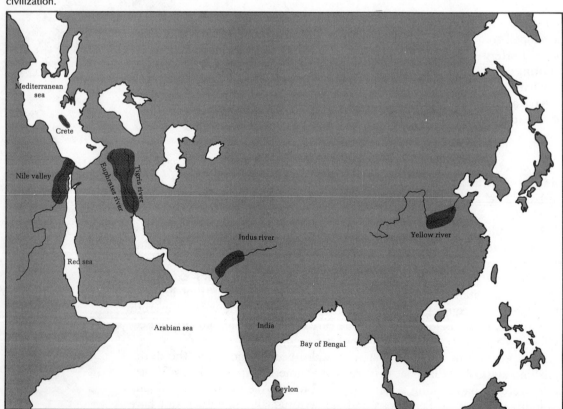

development of trade and communications, development of warfare, and advances in knowledge in such fields as mathematics, astronomy, and calendrical calculations. These topics, among others, will be elaborated upon further in this chapter.

Courses toward civilization have probably differed greatly in different regions. Yet there have often been striking parallels in such cultural advances, so that the civilizations of Mexico and Peru, although largely independent in their development, not only showed many similarities to one another but both resembled the Bronze Age civilizations of the Old World in many respects as well.

One important precondition of civilization is the productivity of agriculture, which makes large concentrations of population possible. Some new inventions facilitated increased agricultural production.

Agricultural productivity

Early farming was of the type known as *swidden cultivation* or slash-and-burn horticulture. This process involves clearing a patch of land by burning, planting crops and tending them for a year or more, and then abandoning the plot so that its fertility may be renewed. New plots are opened up in the same way; earlier ones, once abandoned, may be reopened once their fertility is restored. This kind of cultivation must have developed independently in many forested regions. It is still widely practiced in different parts of the world today among tribal groups in India, the Congo, the Amazon, and Oceania and among peasants in Mexico and Southeast Asia.

Swidden cultivation is usually done on a small scale, often with plots of an acre or less. The population density in societies practicing this type of cultivation tends to be low; settlements are small, seldom with more than 250 persons. This type of horticulture does not encourage political unification, although it may occur.

New farming techniques

Some new developments in Bronze Age times increased agricultural productivity. One was the invention of the ox-drawn plow, which was used in Mesopotamia by 3000 B.C. The ox-drawn plow appeared in Egypt and the Indus Valley at about the same time, perhaps due to diffusion of the idea from Mesopotamia. With a plow drawn by oxen, men could put a much greater area of land under cultivation than before, with less time and effort involved.

Oxen also pulled carts with solid wooden wheels in Bronze Age centers and were sometimes used for trampling grain as a form of winnowing.

Another aid to agriculture was the use of metal sickles for reaping, which were in evidence by 3000 B.C. Another was the pickax, a prominent tool in Sumer, where a seeder plow that dropped seeds into newly plowed land through a kind of funnel was also developed.

Large granaries have been found in the remains of Old World centers of civilization, which show that a sizable surplus of grain could be stored. These granaries provide direct evidence of the enhanced productivity of agriculture in the Bronze Age.

Irrigation

Still another contribution in this direction was the development of irrigation. It may be noted that the civilizations of Mesopotamia, Egypt, and the Indus Valley all developed in rather dry regions through which rivers run.[1]

In Mesopotamia, there are the Tigris and Euphrates Rivers; in Egypt, the Nile; and in the Indus Valley, in what is now Pakistan, there are the Indus River and its tributaries. The dryness of the climate in these regions would naturally encourage the development of irrigation networks to tap the river waters. In northern China, where the Bronze Age Shang dynasty civilization developed, the climate has been described as semiarid. Here, too, irrigation was resorted to on a large scale.

The earliest of these civilizations dependent upon irrigation developed in Mesopotamia, a flat, treeless plain, where irrigation had to be employed if farm communities were to survive. But only one of the two great rivers in this region lent itself well to irrigation. The Tigris had too deep a bed to be easily tapped by canals. The Euphrates, however, had a high bed and was flanked by banks that rose high above the surrounding plains. The high level of this river made it well suited for irrigation.

The first settlements beside the Euphrates must have had relatively simple canals, but as the riverside communities expanded, an increasingly complex irrigation network developed with various smaller channels leading off from the larger ones and reaching fields progressively farther away from the river. This system of irrigation greatly enhanced the productivity of agriculture and made it possible for the Mesopotamian farmer to harvest two crops a year. He was no longer dependent on rainfall as the upland Neolithic farmers had been or as were the swidden agriculturalists of central Europe. His settlement also was more permanent; the Mesopotamian farmer no longer had to move his village or his fields from time to time.

There were similar developments in parts of the New World. Irrigation systems were developed in coastal Peru about 2,000 years ago, making it possible for farmers to raise two or more crops a year. Peruvian farmers also made use of guano—bird droppings—for fertilizer. In the highlands, terraces with strong retaining walls were built to provide level fields and

---

[1] The Indus Valley, however, is thought to have been more fertile and better watered at the time of Harappa and Mohenjo-daro than it is at present.

to prevent erosion. This more productive kind of cultivation can be called agriculture rather than horticulture.

Irrigation was also practiced in the Valley of Mexico and in the North American Southwest in pre-Columbian times. A device used by the Aztecs to increase food productivity was the *chinampa*, a man-made islet composed of reeds, mud, and rotting vegetation that supported beds of topsoil. Although *chinampas* have been called "floating gardens," they were anchored by willow trees planted at their edges. *Chinampas* provided excellent soil, allowing for three harvests a year.

Through such devices as irrigation, terracing, and *chinampas*, agricultural productivity increased, allowing for greater concentrations of population.

An irrigation network requires some centralized supervision to prevent **Social control** the outbreak of quarrels over access to the water. This may have been one of the reasons for the development of political organization in the early city-states of Sumer. Moreover, large cooperative undertakings were required to build, maintain, clean, and repair the canals and to combat the danger of floods to which Mesopotamia was subject. Such efforts had to have some direction, and this may have been one of the functions of the nascent city government.

Monumental constructions and mass labor

In each of the earliest centers of Old World civilization, one finds massive structures that must have required the organization and direction of large work gangs. In Egypt there are the pyramids; in Mesopotamia, the ziggurats; and in the Indus Valley cities, the large mounds, or *citadels*, as they have been called. The purpose and significance of these great structures differed in the respective societies, but they all attest to the ability of a centralized power to exact hard labor from large numbers of people. Some authorities have argued that this labor need not have been particularly burdensome and that it may have been done in small doses during spare times after the harvest. Be that as it may, these huge constructions embody many man-hours of work. Herodotus was told that 100,000 men worked on the Great Pyramid. Even if we grant this to be an exaggeration,[2] it is clear that a great labor force was required. About 2.3 million stones went into the making of the Great Pyramid (completed about 2600 B.C.), with an average weight of 2.5 tons, although some weigh 15 tons and there are also some granite slabs that weigh nearly 50 tons.

The ziggurats of Mesopotamia and the mounds of the Indus Valley cities were made of piles of sun-dried brick; so they are less awesome constructions as far as their logistics is concerned. Yet they are impressive

---

[2] A recent estimate is that only about 4,000 men were employed at a time.

Pyramids of Giza, Egypt.

structures, too. The ziggurat at Ur was 68 feet high, topped with a shrine to the moon god. It could be seen 15 miles away across the flat plain. A ziggurat at Uruk has been estimated to have required a full-time labor force of 1,500 men working for five years. The walled citadel at Mohenjo-daro in the Indus Valley was up to 50 feet high and contained several public buildings. Here, again, a large labor force under the supervision of overseers must be assumed.

It may be that collective work on the irrigation canals provided the model for later large-scale enterprises. The needs of defense were involved in some cases, glorification of the state or its religion in others. Palaces and royal tombs were built to honor kings or pharaohs and to emphasize their power and wealth.

Comparable phenomena took place in the New World. Great pyramids appeared in Mesoamerica and Peru. The massive Inca fortifications at Sacsa-huamán are reminiscent of Old World defense works.

Class stratification

There is archaeological evidence to show that the Old World centers of civilization had class stratification. There are considerable differences, for example, in the size of Indus Valley homes, some being large, with many rooms, while there are also cramped rows of what have been called workingmen's quarters. Sumerian cities also had class stratification. S. N. Kramer (1963:77, 89) states that the population consisted of four categories: nobles, commoners, clients, and slaves. Nobles owned large estates; the poor lived in humble quarters.

A similar situation appears at the later 14th century B.C. Egyptian site of Tell el-Amarna, where there were royal palaces, lavish homes of court nobility, well-appointed middle-class dwellings, and also the cramped quarters of the poor.

Slavery was a recognized institution in both Egypt and Sumer. Some Egyptian rulers from the 15th century B.C. on brought large numbers of Asiatic captives back from their wars. Many were employed in quarries and mines; others became house slaves.

There were special laws in Mesopotamia regarding the treatment of slaves. The latter were usually captured prisoners of war, but in Mesopotamia one might also become a slave through failure to pay debts, or one might sell a wife or child into slavery to avoid bankruptcy. But freemen who became slaves in this way could be ransomed and freed, and their period of slavery was meant to be temporary, limited by law to three years. It can be seen from this that slavery in Mesopotamia was a somewhat different institution from slavery in the United States before the end of the Civil War, where slavery was usually a lifelong inherited condition associated with a particular racial group.

In Peru, in the New World, the emperor, called the Inca, was regarded as the son of the Sun, a divine being. His tribesmen, especially his closest relatives, made up the nobility, just below which came the *curaca*, or provincial nobles, who provided the lesser officials of the government.

The common people were distinguished from the nobles by dress. They were not allowed to wear the finer wool of alpaca and vicuña, but only llama wool. They could not wear gold and silver ornaments. In matters of food and drink they were also restricted, and they were not allowed to hunt.

Each Maya city-state was ruled by a man who was believed to be divine and was supported by councilors and various other officials. These men were of the upper class, not subject to taxation. The common people provided tribute of such items as vegetable produce, cotton cloth, game fowls, fish, cacao, copal for incense, honey and wax, and strings of jade, coral beads, and shells (Morley 1956:158). There was also class stratification among the Aztecs at Tenochtitlán, with a class of nobles at the top and one of slaves at the bottom.

Division of labor   The civilizations of Mesopotamia, Egypt, the Indus Valley, Mexico, and Peru were characterized by the development of division of labor. During the Neolithic period there seems to have been relatively little division of labor. Men did the hunting and worked in the fields, while women wove cloth and made pottery. There was relatively little craft specialization.

V. Gordon Childe's explanation for the proliferation of specialties during Bronze Age times in the Old World was that the heightened productivity of agriculture ensured a grain surplus and thus allowed some segments of the population to engage in specialized nonagricultural tasks. It was no longer necessary for all able-bodied workers to till the fields. New technological advances also spurred the division of labor. Another way of looking at these phenomena is to stress the growing social inequality and political centralization as causative factors. A ruling class could exert pressures in the formation of a surplus and also in the direction of craft specialization. Among the Inca of Peru, for example, the grain and produce provided by the commoners were placed in government storehouses from which the state could withdraw goods as needed. Particular specialists, such as female weavers, were state supported.

Metallurgy

One of the new specialists was the metallurgist, whose complex craft involved technical knowledge, which was often kept secret. The smelting of ores under high temperatures, the preparation of casts, hammering, and annealing all required extensive training. The smith was widely regarded as a kind of miracle worker, skilled in magic; it was to his own interest to maintain this reputation.

The making of bronze tools was an important development in what has come to be known as the Bronze Age. Bronze is an alloy of copper and tin, which is harder than copper alone. Mineral resources of copper and tin are not usually found together. It has been suggested, therefore, that men learned to work copper before they made bronze tools and that a Copper Age should be interposed between the Neolithic and the Bronze Age.

The oldest known work in bronze comes from Ban Chiang in northeastern Thailand, where bronze spearheads, anklets, and bracelets were found which have been dated at around 3000 B.C. In the Near East, bronze came a little later, and in China about 1,000 years later than in Thailand.

Metallurgy also developed in the New World. As far back as around 3000 B.C. there were Indians in northern Wisconsin making spear points, knives, and other objects from cold-hammered copper; but this was not metallurgy, for the metal was not smelted.

The first true metallurgy in the New World was developed in Peru by around 700 B.C. In the Chavín period, various gold ornaments were made, including pendants, tweezers, crowns, pins, and spoons. The Peruvians learned how to make bronze, something not attained by the Aztecs, although knowledge of metallurgy diffused from South America to Mesoamerica. Platinum, which was not worked in Europe until A.D. 1730, was made into ornaments by the Indians of Colombia and Ecuador. The American Indians did not have an Iron Age.

The lost-wax process of casting, which was known in Mesopotamia, was practiced in Peru, Central America, and Mexico. This is a relatively complex invention, since it depends upon a prior knowledge of the properties of wax, fired clay, and molten metal. Let us say that you wish to make a dagger; first, you make a dagger of wax and then coat it with clay, leaving a hole to the outside. The clay is then fired and turned into pottery; the wax melts and pours out through the hole, leaving a dagger-shaped hollow in the interior. Molten metal is then poured in through the aperture. It fills up all the available space and takes on the dagger shape. After the metal has cooled and hardened, the pottery mold is broken; the dagger may then be filed and polished.

The Incas were able to make remarkable objects of gold and silver, including life-sized gold statues of their rulers and replicas of local plants and animals in gold. Unfortunately, the Spaniards melted most of this artwork down into gold bullion.

Pottery

Another new specialist in the Old World Bronze Age was the potter. It is probable that in the preceding Neolithic period the womenfolk of a particular household usually made their own pots and jars, building up the walls by hand with strips or coils of clay. In the Bronze Age, however, there were professional potters who exchanged their wares for other goods.

This specialized trade resulted from yet another technological innovation: the potter's wheel, which first appeared in Mesopotamia in the fourth millennium B.C. In this technique, the potter centers a damp lump of clay on a horizontal revolving wheel that may be rotated either by hand or by pumping a foot pedal. A rim of clay is formed by holding the hands steadily together on the circumference of the clay lump and quickly raising up the side walls as the wheel revolves.

Mastery of the potter's wheel is not easy; training and practice are required to learn this art. But, once the knack has been acquired, a potter can produce pottery vessels on the wheel much more quickly than by the old coil-strip method. Moreover, wheel-made ware is more finished in appearance, being more perfectly round and smooth.

Priesthood

Priests were also specialists. In Egypt there were various classifications of priests whose services at the temple were complemented by other specialized personnel: singers, musicians, astrologers, interpreters of dreams. Although Egyptian and Sumerian religions differed considerably in content, both saw a great expansion of the priesthood and the development of huge temple complexes during the Bronze Age. In both areas, temples owned land. It has been estimated that at one point temple lands amounted to about one fifth of all Egypt. The temples of Sumer were not only places of worship but also elaborate centers of production, with workshops for weavers, tailors, sculptors, goldsmiths, carpenters, and other specialists. The temples also provided formal education (although there were private secular schools as well in Sumer), and the priests formed the principal group of educated men, often skilled in writing, mathematics, and medicine, as well as in ritual. Some of the Egyptian priests were similarly learned.

The priesthood was also an important institution in the higher civilizations of the New World.

Most hunting-gathering societies in North and South America had shamans or medicine men rather than priests. The shaman is generally concerned with individual crises, such as sickness; he attempts to make contact with the supernatural world through trance, magic, divination, or other means. The priest, who is engaged in ritual of a more collective, organized variety, is an official of a cult or church from which his authority derives.

In Mesoamerica the emergence of the priest has been dated at 900 B.C., when the first large-scale religious structures were built. Ultimately, ceremonial centers appeared throughout Mesoamerica, all under the supervision of priest-intellectuals who were set apart from the rest of the people by distinctive dress and special knowledge. Part of this special knowledge was a system of writing first developed by the Olmecs or Zapotecs, ancestral to the Maya script. Ceremonial centers were associated with trade; they were also market centers. Priests were involved in economic affairs in another respect; as specialists in calendrical knowledge they could advise farmers when to plant crops. And, of course, they led the rituals and sacrifices that persuaded the gods to bring rainfall, fertility, and success in war. The priests were thus high-ranking specialists whose services became indispensable and who were able to maintain a dominant position in the societies of Mesoamerica for many hundreds of years.

Other specialties

With the development of writing systems, the scribe appeared in Egypt and Sumer, having knowledge and training that gave him relatively high status. This is reflected in an Egyptian text dating from perhaps the 11th Dynasty (late third millennium B.C.) in which a father urges his son to study hard to enter this profession. The father contrasts the easy and prestigious work of the scribe with the demanding, unpleasant labors of the smith, stonemason, barber, and farmer.

We learn from this text that the barber was another specialist, one low in the hierarchy:

> The barber shaves from morning till night; he never sits down except to meals. He hurries from house to house looking for business. He wears out his arms to fill his stomach, like bees eating their own honey (Woolley 1965:170).

Weaving was a hereditary specialty in Mesopotamia, where guilds and workshops developed. Indeed, there were separate guilds for spinners, dyers, and fullers.

Other specialists referred to in early texts include brickmakers, carpenters, goldsmiths, and jewelers.

Not only were there many kinds of specialists, some of a hereditary nature, but these occupations were often ranked high or low in relationship to others. Some, like the higher scribes and priests, had high status; others, like barbers and sweepers, ranked low. Here we see the development of class or caste differentiation.

Peasantry

We do not usually think of the peasant as a kind of specialist, but they are now coming to be seen as dependent on urban life, in which respect they differ from tribal groups that practice agriculture.

There were no peasants before the development of civilization. George M. Foster has written:

> When settled rural peoples subject to the jural control of outsiders exchange a part of what they produce for items they cannot themselves make, in a market setting transcending local transactions, then they are peasants. We see peasants as a peripheral but essential part of civilization, producing the food that makes urban life possible, supporting (and subject to) the specialized classes of political and religious rulers and the other members of the educated elite (Foster 1967:6).

Does the peasant way of life bring about a particular "style of life" or world view? Some writers have thought so. Robert Redfield found some common attitudes and values implicit in the literature about Greek, Polish, Chinese, Kurdish, and Guatemalan peasants. There is a practical, utilitarian attitude toward nature combined with a religious view, a deemphasis of emotion and a preference for security rather than adventure, a desire for children and for wealth (Redfield 1957:39).

Foster (1965) has further described the peasant view of life as involving "The Image of Limited Good," meaning that peasants conceive of their world as one in which all the desired things of life exist in finite quantity, always in short supply. The peasant sees no way of increasing the total supply of goods; therefore, a family can improve its position only at the expense of others. Foster sees peasants as exhibiting extreme caution and reserve, a reluctance to reveal true strength and position. There is an avoidance of display.

Generalizations such as those made by Redfield and Foster may be rather vague, and perhaps they do not apply to some particular peasant societies; but they do suggest that the peasant way of life encourages a different world view from those of—say—merchants or equestrian nomads; it emphasizes different attitudes and values. Thus we see the development of civilization as fostering differentiations in personality along with specialization and division of labor.

Trade and communication

Since Bronze Age specialists were now producing various kinds of goods, it is evident that trade was concomitantly increasing. Trade was both local and far ranging. It has been mentioned that Mesopotamia, Egypt, and the Indus Valley all had to import copper and other metals from elsewhere. Egypt and Mesopotamia both imported wood, and Sumer and the Indus Valley imported stone. Since these were all commodities of basic importance, foreign trade was clearly a necessity. Improved means of transport had to be developed to meet such needs.

Although wheeled vehicles such as the ox cart existed, they were not suitable for long journeys, and there were few roads in Bronze Age times. The light, two-wheeled chariot drawn by asses or horses was geared to the uses of warfare rather than trade. It was not known to the Egyptians until the invasion of the Hyksos in 1730 B.C. Pack asses were relied upon mainly for overland transport, although camels were also used. Water transport, however, was much preferred in the valleys of the Nile and the Tigris and Euphrates. Sailing ships also plied the Mediterranean, bringing luxury goods such as silver, lapis lazuli, and other precious stones, as well as oil, myrrh, and resin. Ships that carried such cargo over long distances had to be larger and more strongly built than the simpler craft of Neolithic times. The Bronze Age, then, saw various advances in communication— improvements in shipping and navigation and the domestication of animals used in transportation, such as the donkey, camel, and horse.

Abundant evidence of contact between distant communities appears in the archaeological record. Seals made in the Indus Valley have turned up in Sumer, and Egyptian beads, palettes, and stone tools have been found in the Syrian port of Byblos. Texts are available of treaties made between the Egyptian Pharaoh and the King of the Hittites in the 15th century B.C. Despite much trade and communication, however, these different societies remained distinct in culture, each with its own writing system and its characteristic styles of art and architecture.

An important, early, "international" port was Ugarit, also known as Ras Shamra, in northern Syria. In the second millennium B.C. there was

Decorative plaque made of shell on lapis lazuli depicting mythical episodes, found in the Royal Tombs at Ur.

a trading colony there from Crete, importing Minoan pottery. Trade goods from Mycenaean Greece and Cyprus passed through Ugarit. In this region we can see a blending of various art styles—Egyptian, Mesopotamian, and Greek.

Sir Leonard Woolley (1953) described a similar port of trade, Al Mina, situated less than 100 miles north of Ugarit. Here, there were Cretan, Hittite, and Egyptian influences. Writing of Ugarit and Al Mina, another observer (Revere 1957:54) has suggested:

> The geographic proximity and exposed strategic location of these eminently important trading centers must force us to the conclusion that during centuries of the second millennium Hittites and Egyptians were tacitly agreed to respect the neutrality and inviolability of each other's *epineion*.

The original form of trade exchange in the early Bronze Age must have been barter, but, in time, a medium of exchange became established, first in grain and later in metal. As early as 2400 B.C., silver was a recognized medium of exchange in Mesopotamia, with a fixed ratio to grain, one *mina* of silver equaling 60 *gur* of grain in value. The development of such a standard further facilitated international trade. In Mesopotamia both internal and international trade ultimately became protected by legislation relating to rates of interest, debt, safe conduct for merchants in foreign countries, and related matters.

It should not be assumed that all these merchants were free agents concerned only with profits for themselves. Polanyi (1957) has presented evidence that Babylonia in Hammurabi's time had a "marketless" economy in which prices were fixed.

In Egypt, where trade was dominated by the pharaoh, merchants seem to have had even less freedom of action.

Trade and communications also developed in the New World. Compared with Mesoamerica, however, there was relatively little trade in Peru, despite the Incas' excellent system of roads. The roads were built for military purposes so that the army could strike quickly. The main road from north to south served no economic purpose; most of the trade was between coast and highland. Cotton and fish from the coast were exchanged for llama wool and potatoes from the highlands. But private travel and trade were restricted under the Inca. There was no standard medium of exchange, and most of the barter that took place was in regional markets.

Although movement and trade were limited, some systems of communication were highly developed in Peru. Relay runners were stationed at intervals along the highways so that the rulers at Cuzco could be quickly informed of any disturbance in the provinces. Watch-fire signals were also used.

Mesoamerica did not have road systems as good as those of Peru, but there was more trade, partly because of the great ecological diversity of the region. Different valleys, mountains, and lowlands produced different kinds of products.

Much Mesoamerican trade took place in connection with temples. There was trade in shells, feathers, cotton, rubber, and other goods from different parts of Mexico.

Warfare

One by-product of the development of civilization was a steady increase in the scale of warfare. With larger concentrations of population, the number of persons involved in a siege increased. More men could be drawn into battle. The Bronze Age workers who were conscripted to build pyramids or ziggurats could also be conscripted to fight. Meanwhile, metal weapons—spears, swords, helmets, shields, and other accouterments—increased the efficiency of war.

The Sumerians seem to have been the first to organize drilled armies

Section of Royal Standard of Ur.

in which there were different types of soldiers—infantry, spearmen, and charioteers. These are depicted in the Royal Standard of Ur (circa 2700 B.C.). Most of the early fighting among the Sumerian city-states seems to have been over possession of water and land resources; later, there was fighting for control of trade routes. The Royal Standard shows orderly phalanxes of helmeted foot soldiers and chariots with solid wheels drawn by onagers. To be effective the Sumerian phalanxes must have been drilled to act in unison. Phalanxes were named and had special insignia. No doubt efforts were made to establish *esprit de corps* in such units.

Drilled armies of increasing size became a common institution in Mesopotamia. Akkadian troops waged distant campaigns, with Sargon (2872–2817 B.C.) leading a standing army of 5,400 men.

Being protected by natural boundaries of desert and sea, Egypt was relatively well protected from outside attack, but around 1730 B.C. it was invaded by the Hyksos, nomadic warriors who ruled the country until around 1570 B.C. The Hyksos had the advantage of a secret weapon unfamiliar to the Egyptians, the horse and chariot, which had long been used in Mesopotamia. They also had a composite bow built up of layers of wood, sinew, and horn glued together, which was more effective than the bows used in Egypt. The Hyksos wore body armor and had new types of swords and daggers. All these factors gave them the upper hand over the almost naked and poorly armed Egyptians, from whom the Hyksos proceeded to exact tribute, while living apart in fortified camps.

After the Egyptians had acquired the use of the new military devices, they succeeded in driving out the Hyksos. Not content with that, a new imperial spirit developed in the ruling dynasty. Under Thutmose III (1490–1436 B.C.) Egyptian armies invaded Palestine and Syria. This resulted in changes in the composition of troops. Although conscription had been practiced formerly, the Egyptian farmers had always been needed on the land to produce their crops; but now a standing army was required in Syria. The problem was solved by forming foreign mercenary troops. In Syria, the Egyptian forces came up against the Hittites, who were said to have had 3,500 chariots at the battle of Carchemish, although this may have been an exaggeration. Thus, warfare raged back and forth through the Near East, with different nations rising and falling—Hittites, Assyrians, Persians, and others. There was also large-scale fighting in the New World, as will be shown in Chapter 16.

Infectious diseases

In addition to an increase in the scale of warfare, another unfortunate by-product of civilization was an increase of infectious diseases. Hunting-gathering people, being relatively isolated, are not apt to be infected by such diseases, but for that reason they do not develop immunity to them either. When city life developed, with its attendant problems of waste and sewage disposal and the presence of larger masses of people, there were greater possibilities for the transmission of infections and, ultimately, for the development of immunity as well. "In order for a pathogen to survive, it must be able to exist until new hosts appear. Many of the infectious diseases such as measles and influenza, present in modern populations, require an interacting community on the order of 500,000 individuals or more in order to be maintained" (Amerlagos and McArdle 1975:4). The early cities were not large, but the city dwellers were in contact with other communities, so the possibilities for infections increased.

Writing

The earliest Sumerian and Egyptian written texts date from the last quarter of the fourth millennium B.C. Since writing of quite different types appears in the two societies at about the same time, one conclusion could be that the invention of writing was made independently in both Mesopotamia and Egypt. Some authorities, however, hold that the Mesopotamians were the first to develop a writing system and that the *idea* of writing, if not the specific system, spread from Sumer to Egypt. The people of the Indus Valley also had a distinctive writing system at the time they had trade relations with Sumer. Here, again, it is possible that the idea of writing was derived from Mesopotamia. The Cretan writing systems, which date from the first half of the second millennium B.C., are also different from those of the other Bronze Age centers and so is that of ancient China, dating from about the same period. It is known that various culture patterns diffused from Egypt to Crete and from the Near East to China; so the idea of writing may have diffused as well. At any rate, each of these Bronze Age centers had its own form of writing. Evidently, man's way of living had come to require some system of keeping records and transmitting information in relatively permanent form.

Writing at Sumer was done on clay tablets. The cuneiform (wedge-shaped) inscriptions were made by a stylus, often a reed, while the clay was still damp. The earliest clay tablets at Sumer contain lists of things stored at the temple and give the number of cows, sheep, and other items owned. From this concern for bookkeeping, it has been held, a writing system ultimately developed. In early Egyptian writing, however, the underlying need seems to have been the communication of orders and the recording of royal accomplishments. In ancient Mesopotamia, where merchants played an active role, most of the clay tablets were business contracts; in Egypt, on the other hand, writing mainly recorded the commands and achievements of the pharaoh and preserved valued spells and magical formulae. Large numbers of texts have been preserved in both Mesopotamia and Egypt. The Mesopotamians baked important clay-tablet contracts; the firing process made them practically indestructable. But many unfired, sun-dried clay tablets also have been unearthed in good condition, still legible. The Egyptians sometimes carved inscriptions in stone, which, of course, survived; but so did many writings on papyrus, the Egyptian paper made from the papyrus reed. Rolls of papyrus have often remained well preserved because of the dryness of the Egyptian climate.

Not all the ancient writing systems have been deciphered. Scholars can read Egyptian hieroglyphics, Mesopotamian cuneiform tablets, and the ancient Chinese script, but the Indus Valley writing remains largely indecipherable (Clausen and Chadwick 1969; Burrow 1969). One of the Cretan writing systems, known as *Linear B,* was decoded in 1952; its language proved to be Greek. Another Cretan script, *Linear A,* has not yet been deciphered.

The earliest writing systems are pictographic in character, consisting of a series of pictures or pictograms. The pictures stand for concepts, not specific sounds; so, if they are clear enough, they may be understood by people speaking different languages. A weakness of such a system is that abstract ideas are hard to convey in this form of writing.

A later stage of writing is ideographic, in which the individual symbols are called *ideograms.* One symbol may stand for various things; a round disk is not only the sun but may also represent heat, light, day, and other concepts. When seen in context, the right meaning may be understood, just as we immediately know what is meant when we see a skull and crossbones on the label of a bottle. This system may express abstract ideas, but it may also lead to confusion. Should the picture of a foot be interpreted to mean foot, walking, standing, or what? One way of coping with such ambiguities was the insertion of classifying signs, indicating the category of objects to which the word belonged—birds, gods, or whatnot. Sumerian scribes placed such markers before or after the more ambiguous symbols; such signs are known as *determinatives.*

The oldest known Mesopotamian and Egyptian scripts are not purely ideographic, although they may have been so in earlier stages of their development. The first writings known already contain phonetic elements and so are referred to as mixed or transitional—presumably on their way to becoming phonetic scripts, although some of the early "transitional" scripts lasted for 3,000 years or more.

When concepts were hard to represent in pictograms, a phonetic principle might be employed. To express *I,* one might draw an eye; they sound alike. The Sumerian word *ti* meant both arrow and life. The latter, more abstract term could be expressed by the picture of an arrow.

Phonetic writing, the last stage, may be either syllabic or alphabetic. The most important form in the development of the modern world has been alphabetic writing, in which letters represent single sounds. This is the most simplified, efficient writing system. The alphabet has between 22 and 26 signs, in contrast to about 460 Egyptian hieroglyphs, 600 Babylonian characters, and 400 in the Indus Valley script. Kroeber has drawn attention to the fact that the alphabet was invented only once. Although there are many alphabets in the world today that look quite different from one another, all are traceable to a single source, some Semitic people, perhaps the Phoenicians in southwestern Asia before 1000 B.C. (Kroeber 1948:313, 514).

In Mesoamerica, in the New World, the Olmecs, Mixtecs, Zapotecs, Aztecs, Totonacs, and Maya had writing systems. That of the Maya, which may have developed from the Olmec system of writing, was the most advanced. It was an ideographic script. Only about 10 percent of the Maya glyphs have been deciphered.

Zapotecs, Totonacs, Aztecs, Mixtecs, and Maya made a kind of paper from beaten bark, strips of which, covered with writing, could be fashioned into a book folded in an accordianlike fashion. Only three of these books, or codices, remain from the Maya region, of which one, the Dresden Codex, concerns mathematics, astronomy, and calendrical matters, among other things.

It is curious that the Incas did not develop a system of writing, since in some respects, such as metallurgy and political organization, their civilization was more advanced than those of Mesoamerica. So complex a society with such tight political control demanded some system of record keeping. In the case of the Inca, this need was met by strings of knotted cords called *quipus*. (See p. 274.)

Mathematics

Besides developing writing systems, the civilizations of the Bronze Age also increased knowledge of mathematics, although this advance was uneven. In Mesopotamia much was known about algebra, geometry, and arithmetic. (The Babylonians were familiar with the "Pythagorean theorem," squares, cube roots, and multiplication tables.) But in Egypt there was relatively little knowledge of these subjects, despite the very accurate calculations involved in the construction of the pyramids. The Egyptians had a decimal system of numeration, while the Mesopotamians had a sexagesimal system, with units of 60. This applied to weights, so that 180 grains made a shekel, 60 shekels equaled a *mina*, and 60 *mina* were a talent.

Both decimal and sexagesimal systems have influenced our modern ways of reckoning. The Mesopotamian system survives in our way of dividing the circle into 360 degrees, the hour into 60 minutes, and the minute into 60 seconds.

The Dresden Codex shows that the Maya had developed much astronomical knowledge and a remarkable mathematical system. The latter was a vigesimal system, based on the number 20. The number one was indicated by a single dot; two, by two dots; three, by three; and four, by four. The number five was indicated by a bar; six, by a bar with a dot above it; seven, by a bar with two dots; and so on. Ten was indicated by two bars, one above the other; 11, by two bars with a dot above them. Fifteen was indicated by three bars. Twenty was symbolized by a shell (the symbol for zero) with a dot above it.

The invention of zero and position numbering was an independent invention of the Maya, paralleling the invention of the zero in India but dated even earlier in time. This, of course, weakens the possible significance of diffusion from the Old World as a source of higher civilization in Mesoamerica.

Astronomical and calendrical calculations

Many nonliterate peoples with a simple technology have some knowledge about the phases of the moon and the movements of the stars. We have already noted the extraordinary achievements made along these lines by the builders of Stonehenge.

Some knowledge about the yearly cycle is useful to farmers who have to plan ahead, sow seed at a propitious time, and harvest their crops at the right moment. In the Bronze Age, astronomical and calendrical calculations were facilitated by the development of writing and mathematics, which made it possible to keep records of astronomical phenomena, to note the lengthening and shortening of days, and to record other cyclic manifestations. Such calculations could be made by educated priests in Egypt and Mesopotamia, who not only used the information for immediate agricultural purposes but also had to determine fixed dates for the celebration of annual festivals, which generally had some relationship to the agricultural cycle.

The astronomical knowledge of the time was mixed up with astrological notions about the influence of gods and planets on human life. Nevertheless, many accurate observations were made and recorded. Because of their superiority in mathematics, the Babylonians had greater knowledge of astronomy than the Egyptians. They studied the risings and setting of the moon and of Venus, and the lengths of day and night in different seasons. The Babylonians do not seem to have developed any scientific theory about these phenomena, but they did embark on a preliminary phase of scientific investigation: the systematic recording of observations.

The Babylonians had a calendar of 12 lunar months of 29 or 30 days each. The months were divided into four seven-day weeks, with one or two additional feast days thrown in. The Babylonian calendar was thus like ours in some respects, although there was some awkwardness in the fact that the lunar calendar did not jibe with the yearly solar one; hence it was necessary to insert an intercalary month now and then to reestablish uniformity.

The ancient Egyptian calendar was the forerunner of the one in use today, since their year consisted of 365 days with 12 months of 30 days plus 5 additional days. This was the time usually involved from one inundation of the Nile to the next. The year was divided into three seasons of four months each. The early Egyptians did not insert an intercalary day every four years as we do today; so their calendar, like that of the ancient Mesopotamians, became more inaccurate with time. Egyptians of a later period, however, found a fixed astronomical peg for their calendar in the heliacal rising of Sirius, which used to occur just before the annual flooding of the Nile. It was the Egyptians who first broke up the day into 24 hours, dividing day and night into 12 segments each. They invented a water clock, which remained the best timing device until the medieval European invention of the mechanical clock.

In the New World the Maya had an accurate calendrical system, but one involving elaborate astrological concepts of the relationships between gods and divisions of time. There were auspicious and inasupicious periods, just as in the astrological systems of the Old World. Both the Maya and the Aztecs distinguished a 52-year cycle. The Aztecs believed that the world might come to an end after such a cycle was finished. When this proved not to be the case, there was much celebration.

Maya astronomical observatory at Chichén Itzá, Yucatán, Mexico.

The priests had to keep track of the calendrical round and its astrological concomitants in order to perform the correct rituals and to offer appropriate sacrifices to the right god at the right time. It seems likely that this calendrical knowledge, together with the knowledge of writing and mathematics, was largely limited to the priesthood.

Cross-cultural regularities in the development of civilizations

In the preceding pages some general attributes of civilizations have been discussed. These civilizations all developed from a Neolithic level of cultural development but represent something quite different from the Neolithic way of life. There seem to be no marked indications of social inequality in Neolithic settlements, even in such advanced ones as at Çatal Hüyük. In the Chinese Neolithic site of Pan-po there are communal buildings and cemeteries and evidence of an apparently egalitarian, tightly knit community. These two communities may not be representative of all Neolithic settlements, and there must have been much variation, but, generally, they seem to differ from the higher civilizations in the ways mentioned. With the development of urban life there may have been a deemphasis of kinship ties accompanied by greater, class stratification and political centralization.

Some writers see the formation of a state as the crucial integrating factor in these developments, since the state is the warmaking unit that levies taxes and corvée labor and builds fortifications and monumental constructions. But how did the state come into being?

Different explanations have been offered. Karl A. Wittfogel's view is that political centralization was related to the practice of irrigation. He calls the ancient civilizations of Mesopotamia, Egypt, India, China, and Peru "hydraulic societies." Wittfogel (1957) holds that control over the irrigation network in these societies gave the state a despotic domination unchallenged by other centers of power. The monumental constructions raised in each of these "oriental despotisms" testify to the power of the state and the religion associated with it.

Although Wittfogel's ideas seem convincing, some criticisms have been made of the hydraulic theory. There are despotic societies that have had no connection with irrigation and there are societies that make much use of irrigation but have not become despotic. The ancient Hohokam society of the American Southwest built an elaborate irrigation system, but there is no evidence of a ruling class. There were also large irrigation works in ancient Ceylon but no evidence for the hypothesized hydraulic bureaucracy. In reviewing these objections, William P. Mitchell (1973:533) suggests a reformulation: ". . . it is not irrigation itself, but the centralized coordination of irrigation activities that has important social consequences."

Robert McCormick Adams (1966:66–69) argues that irrigation developed on a large scale in Mesopotamia only *after* the appearance of strongly centralized state systems. This criticism has in turn been challenged by William Sanders and Barbara Price (1968:177–88), who believe that conflict over water resources in both Mesopotamia and Mesoamerica stimulated a demand for central authority to supervise the irrigation network, as Wittfogel suggested. Wittfogel's theory is more applicable to some societies than to others; it works best with societies in dry regions through which rivers run, such as the Nile, the Tigris and Euphrates, and the Yellow, but it cannot be applied so well to the tropical lowland Maya area.

With regard to Peru, Lanning (1967:181) states that "We cannot . . . say that irrigation led to the centralization of authority but rather that, once authority was centralized, it became possible to build and maintain irrigation systems."

Another theory about the origin of the state is that of Robert L. Carneiro, which holds that population increase in a successfully developing agricultural society must lead to rivalry over land resources in a geographically circumscribed setting, such as the coastal valleys of Peru, which are hemmed in by mountain walls, desert, and the sea. In a more open settlement, groups can bud off and exploit more distant land resources, thus avoiding conflicts; but this cannot be done when land resources are limited by circumscribed bounds. In the latter case there will be conflict between groups until one of them becomes superordinate over the others and is able to exact tribute or taxes. The defeated groups, unable to escape, must accept subordinate status; thus, class stratification and political centralization emerge. A group that dominates a single valley may later branch out and try to control other valleys. In Peru this process eventually culminated in the far-flung Inca empire (Carneiro 1970).

Again, this seems a plausible explanation, but D. E. Dumond (1965) has pointed out some exceptions to Carneiro's thesis. There are societies, such as the Ifugao of the Philippines and the Chimbu of the New Guinea highlands, that had high population densities and also presumably had circumscribed boundaries but did not develop political integration. Conversely, the Maya lowland area lacks circumscribed boundaries, but city-states developed there.

Elman R. Service (1975) and some other writers have derived the formation of states from chiefdoms that have redistributive systems. *Redistribution* refers to a system of economic exchange in which goods are funneled to a central place of storage and then distributed by a central authority such as a chief. Service believes that sedentary chiefdoms are apt to be located in regions with variegated natural resources, such as a mountain valley with access to a coastal region. Such a situation facilitates the exchange of diverse products and the development of economic specialization. An influential chief may coordinate such economic activity through a system of redistribution, which further promotes his political importance. Service argues that primogeniture (inheritance by the oldest son) is an almost universal feature of chiefdoms. In this way, political authority in a chiefdom is perpetuated. Such authority is usually combined with a religious role, so that the chief is also a priest or associated with a priesthood.

The chief's followers may be mobilized to build large constructions like burial mounds or pyramids (Service 1975:chap. 4). It is in these terms that Colin Renfrew (1973) has explained the construction of megalithic structures in Neolithic Europe. Marvin Harris, who shares most of these views, remarks: "Under certain circumstances, the exercise of power by the redistributor and his closest followers on the one side and by ordinary food producers on the other became so unbalanced that for all intents and purposes the redistributor chiefs constituted the principal coercive force in social life. When this happened, contributions to the central store ceased to be voluntary contributions. They became taxes. . . . And redistributors ceased to be chiefs. They became kings" (Harris 1977:76).

Karl Polanyi claimed that the ancient kingdoms made use of systems of redistribution.

> The kingdom of Hammurabi in Babylonia and, in particular, the New King-dom of Egypt were centralized despotisms of a bureaucratic type founded on such an economy. . . . A vast number of storehouses was ready to receive the produce of the peasant's activity, whether he was cattle breeder, hunter, baker, brewer, potter, weaver, or whatever else. . . . This was the system practiced in ancient China, in the empire of the Incas, in the kingdoms of India, and also in Babylonia. In these, and many other civilizations of vast economic achievement, an elaborate division of labor was worked by the mechanism of redistribution (Polanyi 1957:51–52).

According to Leslie A. White (1959) the distinguishing feature of cultural evolution from one stage to another, such as from the Neolithic level to that of "civilization," is the increase in energy made available to man. Hunters and gatherers rely on their own human power. Animal domestica-tion in Old World Neolithic communities added animal power as a source of energy for human exploitation, but still more sources of energy were available for human use in Bronze Age civilizations. This does not explain how or why particular Neolithic communities developed into urban centers of civilization while others did not, but it provides an index of cultural evolution: increase in available energy resources.

The many parallels in the development of Old World and New World civilizations give an impression of orderly sequences in cultural evolution, of cross-cultural regularities. Julian H. Steward (1955b) has presented a scheme for conceptualizing the development of complex societies, subdi-vided into certain stages: Pre-Agricultural Era, Incipient Agriculture, Forma-tive Era, Era of Regional Development and Florescence, and Period of Cyclical Conquests. Thus, the *Formative Era* is one in which basketry, pottery, weaving, metallurgy, and construction are developed and in which there is a growth of population, relative peace, and wide diffusion of culture between centers of civilization. In the *Era of Regional Development and Florescence* there are theocratic states with a priestly intelligentsia and class stratification. The *Period of Cyclical Conquests* is marked by increasing militarism, urbanization, and building of fortifications.

Some writers have attempted to apply this scheme, or similar ones, cross-culturally to different societies, sometimes with changes in the terminology for eras or stages (Steward et al. 1955; Braidwood and Willey 1962). Such a program involves the construction of typologies, fitting societies at particular stages into appropriate pigeonholes, which can be compared cross-culturally. Although the search for laws or cross-cultural regularities is an essential aim of anthropology, this process sometimes may do violence to the unique characteristics of particular societies. Despite the many similarities in the civilizations noted in this chapter, there were also many differences. The following chapter deals with such differences.

Summary

A culmination of Neolithic sedentary life based on farming was the development of urbanism. City life is one of the principal criteria of civilization. Among the others are a writing system, bronze metallurgy, division of labor, class stratification, and the formation of a state. Most of these components appeared in the advanced Old World centers of culture in the Bronze Age, between around 3500 and 1500 B.C. in Sumer, Harappa, and Egypt and also, a little later, in China of the Shang dynasty. There were parallel developments in the advanced cultures of the New World, among the predecessors of the Aztecs and Inca in Mesoamerica and Peru.

City life depends upon increased agricultural productivity, which resulted from such farming techniques as the ox-drawn plow, metal sickles for reaping, the pickax, and use of irrigation.

Political centralization characterized the Bronze Age civilizations. The building of monumental structures such as pyramids and ziggurats were manifestations of the new state system, as was an increase in warfare. In contrast to the preceding Neolithic period, there was considerable division of labor, including such specialists as metallurgists, potters, priests, weavers, goldsmiths, and peasants. In keeping with this specialization, there was an increase in trade and communication. Writing systems appeared in all the Old World Civilizations and in Mesoamerica, although not among the Inca of Peru. In all these areas, moreover, there were developments in mathematics and in astronomical and calendrical calculations.

Writers such as Wittfogel, Carneiro, Service, and Steward have pointed out apparent cross-cultural regularities in the development of civilizations. At the same time it seems that each of the centers of civilization retained a distinctive culture.

Suggestions for further reading

Once again, V. Gordon Childe's *Man Makes Himself* (New York: Mentor Books, 1951) is recommended.

Sir Leonard Woolley, *The Beginnings of Civilization; History of Mankind: Cultural and Scientific Development*, vol. 1, pt. 2 (New York: Mentor Books, 1965) is a learned, thick compendium of information, available as an inexpensive paperback.

Stuart Piggott, ed., *The Dawn of Civilization: The First World Survey of Human Cultures in Early Times* (New York: McGraw-Hill, 1961) is a beautifully illustrated collection of articles by authorities in the field. See also Jeremy A. Sabloff and C. C. Lamberg-Karlovsky, eds., *The Rise and Fall of Civilizations: Modern Archaeological Approaches to Ancient Cultures. Selected Readings* (Menlo Park, Calif.: Cummings Publishing Co., 1974).

For theories about the origin of the state, see Elman R. Service, *Origins of the State and Civilization. The Process of Cultural Evolution* (New York: W. W. Norton, 1975); Ronald Cohen and Elman R. Service, eds., *Origins of the State: The Anthropology of Political Evolution* (Philadelphia: Institute for the Study of Human Issues, 1978); and Henri J. M. Claessen and Peter Skalnik, eds., *The Early State* (The Hague: Mouton, 1978). See also Jeremy A. Sabloff and C. C. Lamberg-Karlovsky, eds., *Ancient Civilization and Trade* (Albuquerque: University of New Mexico Press, 1975).

The irrigation hypothesis concerning the development of "hydraulic societies" is set forth in Karl A. Wittfogel, *Oriental Despotism. A Comparative Study of Total Power* (New Haven, Conn.: Yale University Press, 1957).

For a brief survey of writing systems, see David Diringer, *Writing* (New York: Praeger Publishers, 1962).

A very interesting account of cuneiform writing and related topics is available in Edward Chiera, *They Wrote on Clay: The Babylonian Tablets Speak Today* (Chicago: The University of Chicago Press, 1938).

For references on Egypt, Sumer, Harappa, and Shang China, see the Suggestions for Further Reading at the end of Chapter 15.

For references on Peru and Mesoamerica, see the Suggestions for Further Reading at the end of Chapter 16.

Four centers of Old World civilization

In the preceding chapter, some general attributes of civilization were discussed. But the centers of Old World civilization were not all alike. While patterns may have diffused from one region to another, each society maintained its own culture and style of life. The languages and writing systems of Sumer, Harappa, Egypt, Crete, and China were all different from one another. Egyptian architecture was not like that of Mesopotamia or Crete, despite the communication between these centers. Greeks visited Egypt, but they did not borrow or imitate the pylon, pyramid, or obelisk, nor did they start to mummify the dead. Some of these centers of civilization were ahead of their contemporaries in some respects, behind in others. The metalwork and handicrafts of the Indus Valley cities were not so good as those of Sumer, but their city planning and concern with sanitation were far advanced. Egyptian knowledge of medicine was superior to that of Mesopotamia, but the Mesopotamians were ahead in mathematics and astronomy. The advance of civilization was thus not uniform. Besides, the significance of a particular invention may have differed from one society to another. We have noted that the earliest use of writing in Mesopotamia was in connection with bookkeeping, while in Egypt it was used for the transmission of orders and the recording of royal achievements.

Some anthropologists, for example Julian Steward, have focused on regularities in cultural evolution and have drawn attention to similarities in the evolution of culture in different parts of the world. But while the search for laws and regularities is one of anthropology's most important concerns, another approach also has its value: to see a particular culture as a configuration that may be unique in some respects. In this way, Ruth

Benedict contrasted the culture of the Pueblo Indians of the Southwest with other American Indian cultures, while Henri Frankfort showed how Egyptian culture differed from that of Sumer in its dominant institutions and values.

In this chapter, we shall briefly examine four centers of Old World civilization, with the focus on what was especially characteristic of each.

Sumer

The names Mesopotamia, Sumer, and Babylonia have appeared a number of times in the preceding two chapters. The reader may have assumed that these are interchangeable terms; sometimes this is so, but sometimes it is not. Mesopotamia refers to a geographical region, the area of the Tigris and Euphrates Rivers. Sumer was the land where the Sumerian civilization developed in the lower half of Mesopotamia, an area of approximately 10,000 square miles, "roughly identical with the modern Iraq from north of Baghdad to the Persian Gulf" (Kramer 1963:3). The history of Sumer may be said to end and that of Babylonia to begin about 1750 B.C., when Hammurabi conquered Sumer and established a larger Mesopotamian kingdom, stretching from the Persian Gulf to the Habur River, far to the northwest of Babylon.

In the third millennium B.C., Sumer was made up of about a dozen walled city-states. Some of the most important ones (Eridu, Ur, Larsa, and Uruk) were in sight of one another without being separated by any natural boundaries. Since they were expanding, land-hungry settlements, it is not surprising that warfare was endemic in Sumer. The appearance of a cluster of cities not far from one another presents a picture quite different from that of the Indus Valley, where the two main cities were nearly 400 miles apart, and also from Egypt, where city life developed more slowly.

The city-states of Sumer did not come into being all at once. It is now believed that the first settlers in this area were not Sumerians, for the names of the most important cities—Eridu, Ur, Larsa, Isin, Adab, Kullab, Lagash, Nippur, Kish—are not of Sumerian origin. The rivers also must have been named by people of a different linguistic stock. Moreover, many words used by Sumerians—words for farmer, herdsman, fisherman, plow, furrow, palm, date, metalworker, smith, carpenter, basketmaker, weaver, leatherworker, potter, mason, and perhaps merchant—also seem to be of non-Sumerian origin (Kramer 1963:40–41).

We do not know who these earlier settlers were or how they were supplanted by the Sumerians, but it is evident that they, rather than the Sumerians, were the first civilizing force in the area. They have come to be known as the Ubaid people, after the site of Tell al-Ubaid near Ur, which was inhabited about 4000 B.C.

The Sumerians themselves are believed to have entered the region around 3500 B.C., perhaps from Iran, whence their predecessors may also have come. Even if they did not invent some of the innovations formerly attributed to them, the Sumerians had the resourcefulness and intelligence to adopt and further develop Ubaid patterns of living. In the centuries that followed, their language replaced that of the Ubaid people as the dominant speech of southern Mesopotamia.

The Ubaid period was followed by a stage called *Uruk* (circa 3500–3000 B.C.), after the city of Uruk, the Erech of the Old Testament. During this period large ziggurats and imposing temples were built. Each Sumerian city-state had a temple dedicated to its main god, who was conceived to own and protect the land under his jurisdiction.

Part of the temple land, which may be called common, was worked by all the people for the welfare of their god, temple, and community. The temple provided seeds, tools, and draft animals for this labor. The stores of grain thus produced were kept at the temple for various uses: sacrifice to the god, food for his priests and other temple personnel, and rations for the workers, who were also subject to military service and corvée labor on irrigation ditches.

From this information we get the initial impression of a centralized ruling bureaucracy associated with a dominant religion exercising unchallenged control over a subject populace. But this picture needs to be modified; it does not tell the whole story. First of all, the temple did not own all the land. Some land was rented out to sharecroppers; the rest was the private property of individuals. Nor was private property a negligible institution. Kramer (1963:75) writes:

> . . . there are quite a number of documents from Lagash as well as from other sites which indicate quite clearly that the citizens of the city-states could buy and sell their fields and houses, not to mention all kinds of movable property.

Moreover, the temple was not the only source of political power, although it may have been so at first. The continual warfare of city-states led to the elevation of military leaders. The prototype of the king may have been elected at first or appointed by an assembly; but eventually a hereditary kingship developed, and the palace became a center of power equal to, or greater than, the temple. This may be seen by the mass burials in the Royal Tombs at Ur, clear evidence of the king's despotic power which developed during the Early Dynastic period (2900–2370 B.C.), following the Uruk.[1] Yet this tyranny did not last. Both Kramer and Frankfort have described Sumerian society as being relatively democratic. If this was so, it may have been partly due to the fact that there was more than one power center. Perhaps palace and temple balanced one another, with neither side gaining complete control over the people for long. Moreover, the institution of private property made possible other channels of power and

---

[1] Late Uruk is also known as the Protoliterate period, since it contains the first evidence of writing.

Ur, with the ziggurat in
the background.

Reconstruction of
ziggurat at Ur, ca. 2000
B.C.

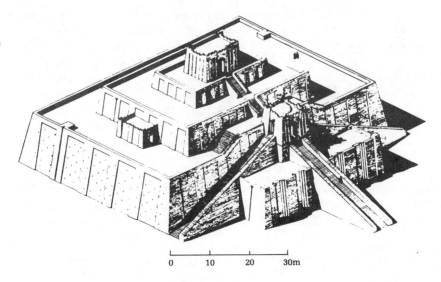

0   10   20   30m

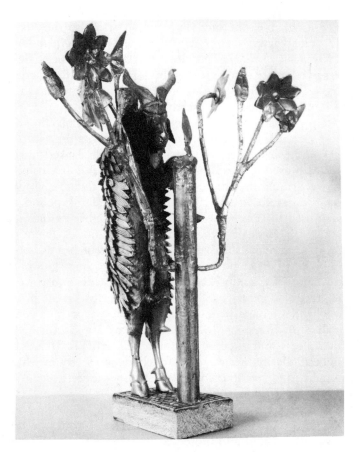

Figurine of a goat made of wood overlaid with gold, silver, shell, and lapis lazuli, found in the Royal Tombs at Ur, Mesopotamia.

prestige than either temple or palace. It seems likely that a relatively free and open society existed much of the time in Sumer; otherwise it would be hard to explain the dynamic character of this most inventive, creative culture.[2]

Sumer produced not only the first writing but also the first schools of which we have evidence. Several "textbooks" have been uncovered at Shuruppak, dating from about 2500 B.C. Practice tablets with exercises have also been found, sometimes with corrections made by the teachers. At Mari an early schoolroom with rows of baked-brick benches was excavated. There are also texts that describe the boredom of school attendance and the severity of teachers' canings. Not everyone went to these schools, incidentally; there is good evidence that the students generally came from well-to-do or politically important families.

Since Sumer was the first civilization to develop city-states and a system

[2] Some idea of this creativeness may be gained by scanning the Table of Contents in Kramer (1959), which lists a long row of "firsts."

of writing, it is not surprising that it was also the first to produce a set of codified laws, that of Ur-Nammu, who ruled in Ur about 2100 B.C., 300 years before Hammurabi of Babylon, whose code of laws is better preserved, more complete, and better known to the modern reader. Sumerians developed the lost-wax process of casting metals. Their contributions to military tactics have already been noted.

Sumer was also the first civilization to develop the principle of the true arch, dependent upon the keystone, while its neighbors were still making use of the less-efficient corbel arch, which lacked a keystone. The true arch was used in the Royal Tombs at Ur and also in private dwellings.

A charming invention of the Sumerians, which had its practical utility, was the decorated seal. Beginning in the Uruk period, carved stone seals were used to stamp the equivalent of a signature on moist clay tablets or to place a mark of ownership on merchandise. There would seem to be no need to make such things into objects of beauty, but that is what the Sumerians did, engraving mythical themes or scenes of everyday life with great precision and delicacy. The seals attest two things: the importance of private property in Sumer and the development of an aesthetic sense.

The Sumerians seem to have gone out of their way to excel. In an analysis of Sumerian texts, Kramer has argued that a competitive drive for success and superiority was a leitmotiv in their culture. This again suggests that Sumer was a relatively open society in which there was some mobility and freedom within its stratified order.

Egypt

The civilization that grew up along the banks of the Nile River was relatively isolated and protected by deserts to the east and west. Invaders would have had to spend about a week crossing desert country to reach the Nile. Although this journey could be made, it would have been difficult for large invading forces in the days before the Hyksos launched their attack with horses and chariots. Egypt was also protected to the south by difficult terrain beyond the First Cataract and by the Nubian deserts. Approaches could be made from the Mediterranean, but sea travel did not attain importance until large, seaworthy craft were built. In the beginning, at least, Egypt was relatively safe from invasion, unlike the exposed city-states on the plains of Sumer.

In the Predynastic period, between approximately 4500 and 3200 B.C., there were farming communities strung along the valley of the Nile, some of which produced well-made pottery. The people lived in huts made of grass and reeds. These settlements seem to have been quite self-sufficient. There were no large population clusters.

Conditions changed around 3200 B.C., when the Two Lands, North and South Egypt, were unified by the semilegendary king Menes, who may have been Narmer, a ruler from the South. Menes (Narmer), founder of the First Dynasty, became the first pharaoh of a united Egypt. His conquest of the north was memorialized on a carved palette in which the King was depicted standing over and striking a fallen enemy. Corpses, bound prisoners, and severed heads are shown.

A notable aspect of the Narmer palette is the presence of a Mesopotamian art motif: two fabulous beasts ("serpo-pards") face one another with long, intertwined necks. In the late Predynastic period, some other Mesopotamian culture traits had already appeared in Egypt. One of the most important of these was the use of bricks, similar in size and shape to Mesopotamian bricks and laid in the same fashion. Still more important was the use of writing. To be sure, early Egyptian hieroglyphs were quite different from cuneiform writing. This seems to have been a case of stimulus diffusion; probably the idea of writing, rather than the characters themselves, spread from the one society to the other.

More clear-cut evidence of Mesopotamian contact is supplied by three Sumerian cylinder seals found in Egypt. The custom of using cylinder seals was temporarily adopted. The first monumental architecture also began to appear. It is interesting that we find no evidence of a reverse current; there seems to have been no Mesopotamian borrowing from Egypt at this time.

The period following the unification of Egypt was one of rapid culture change, perhaps due partly to the new political organization and partly to the novel ideas coming in from abroad.

The pharaoh who ruled Egypt was believed to be a living god, not simply an agent of the gods. One cannot tell whether this idea was generally accepted at first or whether the notion was gradually instilled into the population. At any rate, it does not seem to have been effectively challenged for a period of about 2,500 years. During his lifetime the pharaoh was conceived to be the god Horus. When he died, he became the god Osiris and his son became Horus; so there was always a Horus on the throne.

The king was the head of both church and state. In both cases, he delegated his powers to lesser authorities, priests and government officials, who acted on his behalf throughout the kingdom. There was usually no independent counterpoise to the state; the influence of the merchant class was much weaker than at Sumer. The word *merchant* does not appear until the second millennium B.C., when it designates the official of a temple privileged to trade abroad (Frankfort 1956:118). Most foreign trade was under the direction of the king, who also dominated internal trade. Although merchants existed, they had little power and influence. There seem to have been no Egyptian laws regulating trade. For that matter, there were no publicly displayed legal codes corresponding to those of Mesopotamia, for justice ultimately lay in the hands of the god-king who did not need to make his legal system explicit to his subjects.

A god-king requires fitting monuments. Pyramids and colossal royal tombs were logical consequences of such a regime. The first giant pyramid-and-tomb complex was built around 2750 B.C. for King Djoser (or Zoser) by

Step pyramid at
Sakkarah, Egypt, built
around 2750 B.C.

his vizier, Imhotep, evidently a man of genius. At Sakkarah, Imhotep built a step pyramid and a funerary temple made of small stone bricks, laid as mud bricks were laid, with paneling in the style of brick tombs. The step pyramid was not faced to give a smooth slope from top to bottom as was done later. This was the first stone structure of such imposing size. Nothing like it had ever existed before; it must have convinced at least some Egyptian peasants that their rulers were truly gods.

The Great Pyramid of Khufu (or Cheops) at Gizeh was built not much later, being completed around 2600 B.C. It is still the largest stone structure in the world. Inside the pyramid there was an intricate network of passageways leading to two burial chambers. All this was accomplished without the benefit of any wheels, pulleys, or cranes; only ramps, rollers, and levers were used.

The period of massive pyramid building lasted about 400 years, although smaller pyramids continued to be raised during the next four centuries. Later, during the New Kingdom (1567–1085 B.C.), mortuary temples were constructed instead.

Two things are striking about Egyptian culture: one is the speed with which culture change took place after the unification of north and south; the other is the stability of culture after the first creative outburst gave way to a more conservative way of life. Both cultural stability and change pose problems for analysis. The stability of Egyptian culture is perhaps the most remarkable, since it extended over such immense periods of time. We can contrast it with our own history when we reflect that the Declaration of Independence was signed a little over 200 years ago and that Columbus came to the New World less than 500 years ago. We reckon the years of our history in the hundreds; but ancient Egypt's runs to almost 3,000 years, during most of which time (at least from our point of view) the culture does not seem to have changed very much. This conservatism may be due partly to the country's relative isolation, partly to the restraining influence of a state in which political control, religion, and commerce were all centralized in the hands of a single ruling group.

This is not to say that there were no shifts in power, conflicts, or crises in all that time. During what has been called the First Intermediate Period, toward the end of the third millennium B.C., the nobles became relatively independent of the pharaoh and decided to appropriate the Pyramid Texts, which had originally been meant for the use of god-kings alone. They wanted to take advantage of the funeral rituals that insured deification in the afterworld. "Every man a king," at least after death, seems to have been their slogan.

There were other oscillations of power. Reference has been made to the invasion of the Hyksos and the imperial expansion that followed their expulsion. There were times when the priesthood, enriched by the rulers' foreign conquests, seemed to pose a threat to the pharaoh's authority. There was the effort by Ahkenaton, or Ikhnaton (1369–1353 B.C.), to bypass the priesthood, abolish the old religion, and establish an exclusive cult of the sun-god Aton. But traditional customs seem to have persisted most of the time. Strict conventions governed the arts, religious observances, and priestly prerogatives up to the time of Cleopatra.

Egypt had some influence on other early Old World civilizations. Part of the splendor of ancient Crete may be attributed to Egypt, for there seems to have been considerable contact between Egypt and Crete during the Twelfth Dynasty (about 2000–1785 B.C.). Stone bowls of Early Dynastic style and an Egyptian statue of the Twelfth or Thirteenth Dynasty have been found at Knossos. Scarab seal stones have also been discovered in Crete.

Apart from such legacies as the pyramids, the Sphinx, and the royal tombs, Egypt made some important practical contributions to the later culture of the world: paper made from papyrus, the making of glassware, and methods of tanning leather still in use today. But, compared with Sumer's many innovations, this list is brief, despite Egyptian civilization's enormous span of time.

Harappa

Not as much is known about the Indus Valley civilization, now commonly called the *Harappa culture*, as about the civilizations of Sumer and Egypt. This is partly because the very existence of this civilization was not known until the 1920s, by which time the cultures of Mesopotamia and Egypt had already been extensively investigated. Then, too, scholars have learned to read Mesopotamian cuneiform and Egyptian hieroglyphs, and abundant texts are available in clay, papyrus, and stone; but there are no Indus Valley texts. The only available writing is on seals and on pottery fragments, and the script has not yet been deciphered.

The Harappa culture overlapped in time with the civilizations of Sumer and Egypt but was not quite so old. It was formerly dated back to around 3000 B.C., but recent radiocarbon dates suggest that 2500 B.C. would be more accurate. This civilization seems to have collapsed between 1900 and 1500 B.C. Its span was thus shorter than that of either Sumer or Egypt. Although some attractive figurines have been found at its two principal cities, Harappa and Mohenjo-daro, its art was not so rich or abundant as those of the other two centers of civilization. But the territorial expanse of the Harappa culture was more far-flung than that of either Sumer or Egypt, covering more than 1,200 miles by 700 miles in extent. This whole area, however, may not have been occupied simultaneously. The Indus Valley civilization was not limited to the banks of the Indus and its tributaries but extended far south along the coast of the Arabian Sea to the present state of Gujarat, as far east as Delhi, and as far to the northwest as northern Afghanistan.

Harappa and Mohenjo-daro were nearly 400 miles apart. They had fairly large populations, one estimate for Mohenjo-daro being 40,000. About 80 settlements have been found so far. One of the more recently excavated sites, Kalibangan in northwestern Rajasthan, India, is a major city like Harappa and Mohenjo-daro. Another large Harappan site, perhaps the largest one found to date, was discovered in 1979 at Dhoraji in the state of Gujarat. Seven Harappan sites have also been found in recent years in northern Afghanistan. What is striking is the uniformity of this culture. These communities had standard sizes of bricks, uniform weights and measures, and very similar pottery throughout.

The cities were not just agglomerations of houses but gave evidence of careful city planning. The streets were straight and intersected at right angles like American city blocks. There were drains in the streets, showing an unusual attention, for that time, to the problems of sewage disposal. Drains led down from individual houses into the public sewers. Almost every house had its own well, but there were also public wells.

As in Sumer, the houses did not have windows in their outer walls; light and air came from a courtyard around which the rooms were grouped. The houses had two stories, with a steep staircase of masonry leading to the upper floor. Some homes had only two rooms, others were large and elaborate—an indication of class differences.

Many people in India at the present time are vegetarians, but the presence of burned animal bones in Indus Valley sites shows that beef, mutton, poultry, and fish were eaten in those days. Cows, humped zebu, buffaloes, sheep, elephants, cats, dogs, and other animals were known to the Indus Valley folk. They raised wheat, barley, and peas. Moreover, they seem to have been the first people to grow cotton, and it is likely they traded it in Sumer. At any rate, there is evidence of trade with the contemporary cities of Mesopotamia, for seals of Indus Valley type have been found in Sumerian cities.

There are many similarities between the Indus Valley settlements and those of Sumer. The crops and domesticated animals were largely the same; so was the style of house building. Copper and bronze ornaments were found in both areas, although their workmanship was finer in Mesopotamia. Women's vanity cases found in Harappa are similar to those of Sumer, and similar eye shadow and face paint were used. Pottery was made on the potter's wheel in both areas.

Seistan, a region on the border of Iran and Afghanistan, was evidently a channel through which trade passed between East and West around the middle of the fourth millennium B.C. (Dales 1973:163). This may have been one of the routes through which western ideas reached the Indus Valley.

Halfway between Sumer and Harappa is the city site of Tepe Yahyā in Iran, which contains writing tablets in the Proto-Elamite language dated at 3560 B.C. (± 110 years). Tepe Yahyā is thus earlier than Harappa by several centuries, but it flourished for more than ten centuries and overlapped the early Harappa period. Tepe Yahyā was rich in soapstone or steatite and must have been a center of trade in this commodity, which was used for making bowls (of similar design) in both Sumer and the Indus Valley and also for seals in the latter region. There were other intermediate sites through which trade may have taken place. As in both Mesopotamia and the Indus Valley, Tepe Yahyā had a large mound about 60 feet high. This site suggests the way in which urban culture may have moved eastward to the Indus Valley region; it may help to explain some of the parallels in culture between Sumer and the Harappa civilization (Lamberg-Karlovsky 1971). There were, however, some differences between Mesopotamian and Indus Valley cultures. Harappan bronze axes and similar tools were inferior in workmanship, lacking sockets for handles, which had long been known in Sumer. The arch, first invented in Mesopotamia, did not appear in Indus Valley architecture, nor did round columns. On the other hand, town planning and sanitation were more highly developed in Harappa and Mohenjo-daro, where there was also much more use of fired brick than in Sumer. The writing systems of the two cultures were different. There are no stores of clay tablets in the Indus Valley like those of Mesopotamia. The Indus Valley script appears in brief inscriptions on small steatite seals on which there are also well-made figures of animals in bas-relief. These seals have been found in abundance in the homes of both rich and poor—over 1,200 were found in Mohenjo-daro alone. Perhaps every citizen had one as a kind of identification, or perhaps they were used in trade to mark merchandise. Their exact purpose is still not known.

The Indus Valley cities differ from those of Egypt or Mesopotamia in having no identifiable temples or monumental sculpture. This does not mean that Indus Valley people had no places to worship. There is a large bath at Mohenjo-daro that may have had some religious functions. It looks rather like a modern rectangular swimming pool, with steps going down

Indus Valley seals.

into the water. Perhaps it was only a place to bathe and nothing more, but bathing has religious connotations in India today—especially at traditionally sacred places such as the Ganges River at Banaras. Since this is such a widespread custom in India, it is evidently very old and may date back to Indus Valley times.

To the west of both Harappa and Mohenjo-daro was a fortified mound made of piles of sun-dried brick, with a facing of fired brick about 50 feet high. On top of the mound at Mohenjo-daro, the bath and a large granary were built. Harappa had granaries with a total floor space of over 9,000 square feet, similar to that of Mohenjo-daro, with rows of small houses nearby where the workers may have lived.

The smaller communities of the Indus Valley had the same grid layout of the larger cities and the same kind of drain system and house type.

Statuettes give us some idea of the clothing worn. There was a shawl-like cloth worn over the left shoulder and under the right arm and a lower garment like the cotton *dhoti* now worn by men in India. Finger rings, bangles, bracelets, and anklets have been found and earrings of gold, silver, and copper. Bronze razors were used.

A metal saw with a toothed edge has been found at Mohenjo-daro, the first true cutting saw in the archaeological record.

The artwork of the Indus Valley is on a small scale, consisting of the seal carvings and the small statuettes and figurines that include many realistic carvings of bulls and female clay figures that may represent mother goddesses. There is a bronze figure of a naked dancing girl with rows of bangles on her arm.

Small carts were modeled in clay, perhaps as children's toys. They closely resemble ox carts used in southern Asia today. There were many animal figurines, some with movable parts pulled by strings—a bull with a nodding head, a monkey with movable arms, and pottery rams on wheels with a hole through the neck for a drawstring.

Large numbers of dice have been found, some of which are like the cubic dice of the present day with dots from one to six on their respective sides. They differ from modern dice only in the ways in which the dots are arranged. Marbles were also used, as in Sumer and Egypt.

The Harappans had to import many materials from elsewhere: gold from southern India or Afghanistan; turquoise, silver, and lapis lazuli from Afghanistan or Iran; copper from Rajasthan or Afghanistan; and jadeite perhaps from Tibet. That they traded with Sumer is suggested by Harappan seals that have been found in Mesopotamia. They may have exported cotton, the earliest remains of which have been found in the Indus Valley. Timber and ivory were probably exported.

The Indus Valley civilization must have had a well-developed political system, judging from city planning and the standardization of the size of bricks and of weights and measures. Both Wheeler and Piggott believe that it must have been an autocratic regime, but this is an inference derived from the archaeological remains; there are no texts to demonstrate it.

These communities seem to have had a relatively high standard of living. Many of the homes were fairly large in size. But, in spite of the appearance of comfort and the unusual attention given to sanitation, the life expectation seems to have been short. Judging from the skeletons found in Harappan cemeteries, few people lived much beyond 30 years of age; most were dead by the age of 40.

Harappan culture seems to have existed without much change for hundreds of years and then declined between 1900 and 1500 B.C., at least in the more northerly areas. Many explanations have been offered for this decline. One attributes it to the progressive desiccation of the landscape due to deforestation, overgrazing, and, perhaps, changes in rainfall and climate.

Another theory is that the coastal area of the Arabian Sea is an active geological zone that has been gradually rising for thousands of years. Some areas that were formerly islands are now part of the mainland, and some former seaports are now located inland, far from the coast.

It is also believed that Mohenjo-daro and other Indus Valley settlements suffered from flooding and deposits of silt and may have become engulfed in mud.

The period of decline is traditionally associated with the entry into the Indian subcontinent of the Aryans, the nomadic, cattle-herding people who came down through the mountain passes in the northwest. In the Vedas, ancient hymns of the Aryans, there are references to their conquest of large, walled cities. It may be that these were the cities of the Indus Valley. The Aryans cannot have wiped out the Indus Valley people, who must have been numerous, but they were evidently strong enough to establish themselves before long as the dominant power in northern India.

The civilization that subsequently developed in northern India must have represented a blend of the two cultures; the ancient civilization of the Indus Valley and the culture of the pastoral herders.

Shang China   Civilization flowered in China during the Shang Dynasty, a little before 1500 B.C. Here, again, we find a riverine civilization. It developed in the

Shang bronze vessel.

northern part of Honan Province north of the Huangho, or Yellow River. Excavations made at Anyang, a Shang capital city, have thrown much light on this advanced Far Eastern culture.

Here we find the traditional characteristics of a civilization: city life, a system of writing, a state organization, use of bronze, monumental constructions, class stratification, division of labor, widespread trade and communication, development of warfare, and increased knowledge of astronomy and calendrical calculations. Since these features all appeared rather suddenly, a good deal later than the development of civilization in the Near East, it seems likely that at least some aspects of Shang culture resulted from diffusion of ideas from the West. On the other hand, Shang culture seems to have developed naturally from the already complex Lungshan Neolithic described in Chapter 13. In that chapter it was noted that the use of barley and wheat probably diffused eastward along the southern edge of the steppes and that cattle were introduced in Neolithic times.

The writing system, ancestral to modern Chinese, was quite different from that of Sumer, Egypt, or the Indus Valley, although it followed similar principles. This may be another instance of stimulus diffusion, although in this case the distance from the Western centers of civilization is great.

Some of the new metal tools of the Shang period, such as socketed axes, resemble those of Europe. Shang ritual bronze vases and urns are famous for their craftsmanship. Their style seems to owe nothing to the West. Moreover, early Chinese bronzework had a local peculiarity: the regular practice of adding lead to the alloy. Chariots were used in late Shang times, very similar to those of Indo-European peoples to the west. Some Shang art motifs are thought to be traceable to Sumer. Li Chi (1957:26–29) cites an intertwined serpent motif as one example. He also mentions an unusual jar cover shaped like a flower pot with a "phallic" handle similar to jar covers found in Jemdet Nasr and Mohenjo-daro.

Early Chinese culture may thus have been influenced by new ideas spreading from the West, but it seems to have been quite selective and to have developed in relative isolation with a characteristic style of its own. Some useful culture patterns were slow in reaching China or in being accepted, such as the use of bricks in architecture. Bricks were not introduced until the time of the Han Dynasty (206 B.C.–A.D. 220). The Chinese did not make use of stone in building construction, although stone was available. Roof tiles, which we think of as characteristically Chinese, date from the Chou period (1027–256 B.C.).

In Shang times, houses were built on raised platforms of pounded earth. The soil was held in on all sides by a broad frame; loose earth was then poured in and beaten. The walls of house compounds were made in the same manner.

Village walls were already characteristic of the Neolithic Lungshan period. In Shang times, large city walls were built. The one at the Shang capital of Ao is estimated to have required the work of 10,000 men for

Shang bronze mask.

18 years (Chard 1969:259). Wall building was the type of monumental construction favored by the Chinese. Some Shang cities had an inner wall within which lived the aristocracy. Later, in the Ch'in Dynasty (221–206 B.C.), the 1,400-mile Great Wall of China was built to keep out the barbarians.

The Shang capital at Anyang had special sections or quarters for bronze metallurgists, stoneworkers, and specialists who made bone tools such as arrowheads, hairpins, and ladles. Objects of jade were also made.

There is evidence of class stratification and political centralization. The population was divisible into three groups: aristocracy, craftsmen, and peasants. Shang "royal tombs" show patterns similar to those of Sumer and Egypt, servants of the king being killed and buried with their master. Horses and chariots were also interred with the dead ruler. Sacrificial victims were buried when buildings were constructed.

The use of bronze was limited to the upper class. Metal was not employed for agricultural tools. The peasants used stone reaping knives and still lived at a Neolithic technological level. Chariots driven by members of the ruling group were fitted with bronze ornamentation. Bronze ritual vessels were made for and buried with upper-class owners.

Much of our knowledge about Shang culture comes from oracle inscriptions. The early Chinese resorted to divination to get advice from the supernatural world. The Neolithic Lungshan people practiced scapulimancy. They exposed the shoulder blade of a cow to fire and then examined the cracks that appeared in the bone to find answers to their questions, just as a modern tea-leaf reader interprets the arrangement of the tea leaves in a cup to foretell the future.

Scapulimancy was practiced in the Shang period with some innovations. Turtle shells were now used as well as animal bones, and the questions to be answered were first scratched onto the bone before it was heated. More than 100,000 pieces of oracle bones have been recovered. Most of their inscriptions are brief; the longest ones have little more than 60 words and most have only 10 or 12. Nevertheless, these earliest Chinese writings are most informative because they tell us something about the concerns, hopes, and anxieties of the people. Certain themes recur. One concerns sacrifices. To what spirits should I offer sacrifice? What should I offer, and when? Another category deals with announcements to the spirits. Spirits were told about war raids, the numbers of captives, sicknesses, and other important matters. Evidently the spirits were expected to help in these matters in some way. Questions were also asked about impending journeys, what route to take and where to spend the night.

Many questions concerned hunting, indicating that this activity occupied an important place in the life of the Shang aristocracy. Some bone inscriptions give the results of the hunt, perhaps to show that the oracle had been correct. One inscription records that 348 animals were killed on one occasion. Another lists a kill of 162 deer, 10 boars, 1 rabbit, and 114 animals of an unidentified species. Elephants are sometimes mentioned. Both elephants and rhinoceroses are depicted quite realistically in the form of bronze vessels of the Shang period. China evidently contained many tropical animals at this time, including also tiger and leopard.

Li Chi (1957:25) holds that it is no coincidence that an animal style of art flourished at this time. It testifies to the hunting traditions of the ruling Shang group.

The Shang Dynasty came to a close when it was overthrown by a Western tribe, the Chou, whose dynasty lasted from 1027 to 256 B.C. Culture patterns established during the Shang period were perpetuated in the Chou Dynasty. Indeed, in spite of the many upheavals China has experienced, Chinese culture has shown much continuity from Shang times down to the present.

Summary

The four regions discussed in this chapter are areas where *pristine* states, as opposed to *secondary* states, developed. This distinction was made by Morton H. Fried:

> By the former term is meant a state that has developed *sui generis* out of purely local conditions. No previous state, with its acculturative pressures, can be discerned in the background of a pristine state. The secondary state, on the other hand, is pushed by one means or another toward a higher form of organization by an external power which has already been raised to statehood (Fried 1960:729).

It is evident that many parallel features characterize these four cultures. All meet the general criteria for civilization set forth in Chapter 14, although cities were late in developing in Egypt. All four civilizations emerged in river valleys where irrigation enhanced agricultural productivity and where rivers also provided avenues for trade and communication. Trade was necessary in such regions, which often lacked essential materials. Wood, metal ores, and stone had to be imported into the valleys of Egypt and Mesopotamia. Although trade made possible the emergence of a merchant class, it was sometimes conducted primarily by the state, as in Egypt. Either way, agricultural productivity and trade facilitated economic specialization. Agricultural productivity also spurred an increase in population in each of these areas, and probably warfare as well, in the period just before the emergence of the state (Webb 1975:186–87). All four cultures were marked by the appearance of monumental constructions, class stratification, and division of labor, and each had a system of writing.

In spite of these numerous parallels, there were distinguishing features in each of the four cultures. Egypt was more politically centralized than Sumer. Art was less developed in Harappa than in Egypt, Sumer, and Shang China, and there seem to have been no imposing temples there, as there were in Sumer and Egypt. There is more evidence of city planning in the Indus Valley than in Sumer. Hunting apparently played a larger role in Shang China than in any of the other three civilizations.

The common features shared by these four centers of civilization also appeared in Peru and Mesoamerica. Once again, however, there were also distinctive features in each of these centers of New World civilization, as we shall see in the following chapter.

Suggestions for further reading

Sumer

The best guide to Sumerian culture is Samuel Noah Kramer, who has written several books and articles about Sumer. One of these is a popular, well-illustrated introduction, *Cradle of Civilization* (New York: Time, Inc., 1967). Kramer's list of Sumerian "firsts" appears in *History Begins at Sumer* (New York: Doubleday-Anchor Books, 1959). See also *The Sumerians: Their History, Culture, and Character* (Chicago: University of Chicago Press, 1963). All are well written.

An early, absorbing account of archaeological discovery is C. Leonard Woolley, *Ur of the Chaldees: A Record of Seven Years of Excavation* (Harmondsworth, Middlesex: Penguin Books, 1940); a later, more up-to-date version appears in *Excavations at Ur: A Record of Twelve Years' Work* (London: Ernest Benn, 1955). A learned work that deals more with the later Mesopotamian cultures (Babylonia, Assyria) than with Sumer is A. Leo Oppenheim, *Ancient Mesopotamia: Portrait of a Dead Civilization* (Chicago: University of Chicago Press, 1964). For an imaginative interpretation, contrasting the Egyptian and Mesopotamian civilizations, see Henri Frankfort, *The Birth of Civilization in the Near East* (New York: Doubleday-Anchor Books, 1956).

Egypt

For a brief, well-illustrated popular account, see Lionel Casson, *Ancient Egypt* (New York: Time, Inc., 1965).

A more advanced general survey is available in John A. Wilson, *The Culture of Ancient Egypt* (Chicago: University of Chicago Press, 1951).

A classic early study of Egyptian religion, which contains much textual material, is James Henry Breasted, *Development of Religion and Thought in Ancient Egypt* (New York: Harper & Row, 1959 [1912]). A thoughtful, more recent treatment of the same subject is Henri Frankfort, *Ancient Egyptian Religion: An Interpretation* (New York: Harper & Row, 1961).

On the early Egyptian state, see J. J. Janssen, "The Early State in Ancient Egypt" in Henri J. M. Claessen and Peter Skalnik, eds., *The Early State* (The Hague: Mouton, 1978), pp. 213–34.

For interesting information on the Egyptian priesthood, see Serge Sauneron, *The Priests of Ancient Egypt*, trans. Ann Morrissett (New York: Grove Press, 1960).

Linton's chapter on Egypt in *The Tree of Culture* (New York: Alfred A. Knopf, 1955), pp. 400–24, is also recommended.

Harappa

A good general work on Indian prehistory is Stuart Piggott, *Prehistoric India to 1000 B.C.* (Harmondsworth, Middlesex: Penguin Books, 1950).

More recent surveys may be found in the following works by Mortimer Wheeler, *Early India and Pakistan, to Ashoka* (New York: Praeger Publishers, 1959), pp. 93–117; "Ancient India," in *The Dawn of Civilization: The First World Survey of Human Culture in Early Times*, ed. Stuart Piggott (New York: McGraw-Hill, 1961), pp. 229–52; and *Civilizations of the Indus Valley and Beyond* (New York: McGraw-Hill, 1966).

See also Walter A. Fairservis, Jr., *The Roots of Ancient India. The Archaeology of Early Indian Civilization* (New York: Macmillan, 1971). Good illustrations of Mohenjo-daro are available in Dora Jane Hamblin and the Editors of Time-Life Books, *The First Cities* (New York: Time-Life Books, 1973, chap. six).

Shang China

For both the Chinese Neolithic and Shang China, see Kwang-chih Chang, *The Archaeology of Ancient China*, rev. ed. (New Haven, Conn.: Yale University Press, 1968). See also John Hay, *Ancient China* (London: Bodley Head, 1973).

For the early state in China, see Timoteus Pokora, "China," in Henri J. M. Claessen and Peter Skalnik, eds., *The Early State* (The Hague: Mouton, 1978), pp. 191–212.

An early work which is still of value is Herrlee Glessner Creel, *The Birth of China: A Study of the Formative Period of Chinese Civilization* (New York: Frederick Ungar Publishing, 1937 [3rd printing, 1954]).

Surveys are available in Linton, *The Tree of Culture*, pp. 520–37; Kwang-chih Chang, "China," in *Courses toward Urban Life: Archaeological Considerations of Some Cultural Alternates*, Robert J. Braidwood and Gordon R. Willey, eds. (Chicago: Aldine, 1962), pp. 193–210; Chester S. Chard, *Man in Prehistory* (New York: McGraw-Hill, 1969); and William Watson, "A Cycle of Cathay," in *The Dawn of Civilization*, ed. Piggott, pp. 253–76. The latter is well illustrated.

CHAPTER 16

Two centers of New World civilization

When the Spaniards arrived in the New World, the Aztecs held control over most of Mexico, while the Incas ruled Peru and adjacent regions. The Europeans were surprised by the high level of civilization that they found in both areas. Archaeological research has since shown that there were much earlier centers of civilization in Mexico and Peru before the periods of Aztec and Inca domination.

Just as there are problems about the extent of Mesopotamian influence on the development of civilization in Egypt and the Indus Valley, there are parallel questions about contact between Mesoamerica and Peru. To what degree did each center of civilization develop independently? And was there any contact between the civilizations of the Old World and the New? Early in the 20th century a British anthropological school led by G. Elliot Smith, William J. Perry, and W. H. R. Rivers held that Egypt had significantly influenced the cultures of the New World, introducing metallurgy, pyramid building, a cult of the sun, and other aspects of advanced culture; but this school of thought is now defunct. There have also been supporters of the idea that there was a trans-Pacific diffusion of culture traits from Japan, China, or Southeast Asia to the New World.

Some have claimed that the pottery of Valdivia, Ecuador, was influenced by the Jomon pottery of Japan (Estrada and Meggers 1961; Ford 1969). Others have argued that the Chavín culture of Peru was influenced by trans-Pacific contacts from China (Jett 1978:611–12). Still others find significance in the similarities of serpent columns and balustrades in the architecture of Chichén Itzá in Yucatan and serpent balustrades in the Borobodur in Indonesia (Ekholm 1953:84). These suggestions of trans-Pacific diffusion

267

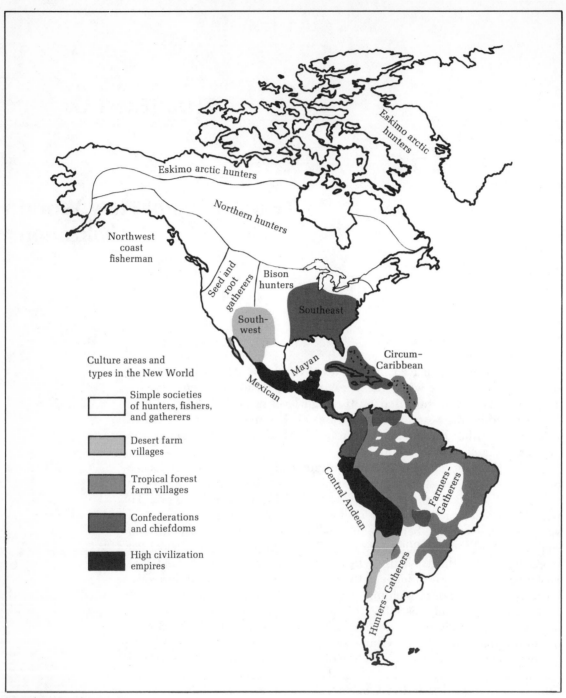

Map showing culture areas and types of society in pre-Columbian North and South America.

are certainly tantalizing, but this school of thought still remains a minority view. We are left with the question of Mesoamerican influence on Peru and vice versa. Here we are dealing with contiguous areas, not separated by immense distances of ocean; it seems much more likely that there was some diffusion between these two regions.

In Chapter 14 reference was made to the Olmecs, who built the first large religious structures in Mesoamerica and made use of a system of writing ancestral to the Maya script. The period of Olmec influence in Mesoamerica (1500–400 B.C.) is a little earlier but partly contemporary with the spread of the Chavín culture in Peru (900–200 B.C.). Some authorities, such as James Ford (1969) see indications of Olmec influence in the Chavín culture, while others contend that cultural evolution in the two New World regions was independent and parallel. Let us first consider the course of cultural evolution in Peru. Later in this chapter we will review analogous developments in Mesoamerica.

Early civilization in Peru

Advanced cultures developed in both the highland and coastal regions of Peru. The coastal area is very dry, having an extremely low rainfall, but the rivers that come down from the Andean mountains create fertile strips of land leading to the sea. The eastern slopes of the Andes are covered by tropical forests.

The coastal valleys fit Carneiro's circumscription model for the development of a state, since there are usually deserts on either side of the valley, and on the west is the Pacific Ocean. To some extent, although less than in Mesoamerica, the terrain fits Elman Service's description of the kind of setting amenable to the development of a chiefdom, with a diversity of environmental resources from the mountains and the coast, leading to trade and specialization. Wittfogel's irrigation hypothesis is also applicable here, since the coastal farmers tapped the river waters to irrigate their fields. It seems understandable, through a combination of these reasons, that political centralization developed in such a setting, so that a particular river valley could be controlled by a single chiefdom. Later, larger states dominated several valleys.

The Initial period in Peru (1800–900 B.C., following Willey 1971) is marked by the first appearance of pottery and woven cloth. This corresponds to the early part of Steward's Formative era (see p. 244). Village life based on the cultivation of maize, squash, beans, guavas, chili peppers, and sweet potatoes was already established by 1800 B.C. in the coastal valleys, supplemented by the rich resources of the sea. The guinea pig, a source of meat protein, had been domesticated by 1800 B.C. The llama, however, first appeared in the Initial period, along with the domestication of manioc and peanuts on the coast (Lanning 1967:88–89).

Ceremonial centers were a feature of the Initial period, containing large platform mounds such as Las Haldas in the north-central coast and La

Florida near Lima. Kotosh in the highlands contains a structure called the Temple of the Crossed Hands, which is held to be the earliest temple in Peru. There is evidence of llama sacrifice at one coastal temple (Bankes 1977:132).

Chavín

The Early Horizon (900–200 B.C.) is the period marked by the Chavín culture mentioned earlier, named after the temple site of Chavín de Huántar in the northern highlands of Peru. Remains of guinea pigs, llamas, fish bones, and marine shells were found in a Gallery of Offerings here.

This temple and other manifestations of Chavín culture are characterized by an elaborate art style, in which jaguar or puma attributes such as fangs and claws are given to human figures, snakes, and eagles.

> Serpent heads are also frequently disposed on all parts of the body of the principal animal or human represented in a sculpture. The style is graceful, flowing, essentially curvilinear, and intricately and rhythmically balanced. A characteristic mode is an eye with an eccentric pupil, and this, together with the grimacing, fanged mouths of the animals, demons, or gods, gives a somewhat sinister, baleful aspect to the Chavín figures (Willey 1971:116).

One wonders whether the religion associated with this complex could have been influenced by the use of hallucinogenic drugs, for the psychedelic San Pedro cactus has been identified in Chavín textiles and funerary pottery (Furst 1976:109).

The Chavín art style in pottery, textiles, and stone sculpture spread widely in both highland and coastal regions, mainly in northern and central Peru, but also reaching parts of the south. It is believed to represent the diffusion of a religious cult, not imposed by military conquest, for garrisons and fortifications are not associated with the style. But the widespread diffusion indicates that regional barriers were breaking down at this time and that goods and ideas were being exchanged between north and south, highland and coast (Lanning 1967:102–3).

The Early Intermediate period

Evidence for inter-regional wars appears in the succeeding Early Intermediate period (200 B.C.–A.D. 600), marked by the first cities that held over 5,000 persons: Tiahuanaco and Pucara in the Titicaca Basin and Huari in the upper Mantaro Basin. There must have been a population increase concomitant with the extension of irrigation and terracing. Different art styles now characterized separate regions, suggesting a kind of "nationalistic" tendency. Moche pottery from the northern coast is readily distinguishable from the Nazca pottery of the south, and there are other regional distinctions.

Relief carving on the
Raimondi stone, Chavín
de Huántar.

During the Middle Horizon, from around 600 to 1000 A.D., there was a spread of the Tiahuanaco art style from what is now highland Bolivia to the southern parts of Peru. There is impressive stone sculpture and architecture at Tiahuanaco, notably the so-called Gateway of the Sun, the central figure of which is a deity with a rectangular face, a headdress with serpent rays, and a jaguar mouth reminiscent of the Chavín style. On either side of this deity are rows of running winged figures holding staves. These elements and other associated features also appear in the artwork of Pachacamac on the central coast of Peru. The Tiahuanaco style is also found in southern Bolivia and the far southern coast of Peru. "In all of these territories," writes Gordon Willey, "the implantation of Tiahuanaco remains is complete enough to imply actual colonization and, perhaps, conquest and dominance of local peoples" (Willey 1971:160).

The city of Huari had trade relations with Nazca on the southern coast, and its sphere of influence extended to the northern coast and highlands as well. Willey believes that the widespread state control of foodstuffs, such as marked the later Inca empire with its storehouses, highways, and garrisons, first came into being during the Middle Horizon (Willey 1971:764). John H. Rowe (1967:312) attributes the eventual collapse of Tiahuanaco and Huari to the hostility of the rural peoples who lived around them, reminiscent of the hostility of the rural population to the cities in the later Roman empire.

Although city life declined in southern Peru, it flourished on the northern coast during the Late Intermediate period, from around A.D. 1000 to 1476. The capital of the Chimu kingdom was at Chan Chan, near the present-day city of Trujillo. Different estimates have placed its size at between 6 and 11 square miles. There are 10 large, rectangular, walled enclosures in the center of the city, containing palacelike buildings, pyramids, tombs, and stone-lined reservoirs. There are also evidences of craft specialization and social stratification. Chan Chan was later conquered by the Incas and incorporated into their empire.

Stela, Tiahuanaco, Bolivia.

The Incas

The relatively brief period of Inca political domination has been termed the Late Horizon (A.D. 1476–1534). The Incas were Quechua-speaking highlanders who began to expand during the reign of Pachacuti Inca Yupanqui (1438–1471), purportedly their ninth ruler. Their capital was at Cuzco, a much smaller town than Chan Chan. The Incas seem to have been remarkably efficient in military and administrative matters. They systematically conscripted men for military service and corvée duty. Armies were able to move quickly over the excellent roads that tied the empire together. Thus, in less than 100 years, the Incas came to rule over more than 6 million people, including not only all of Peru and Bolivia, but also parts of Ecuador in the north and Chile to the south.[1] Steward and Faron have argued that the boundaries of this long, narrow empire (with an average width of only 300 miles) were, at least in part, environmentally determined. "The whole Inca subsistence pattern and the sociopolitical structure were highly adapted to an irrigation area and could not be supported in a tropical rain forest like that of the Amazon Basin, in a steppe country like the Gran Chaco, or a mediterranean climate like that of Chile" (Steward and Faron 1959:116). The authors point out that within the Inca realm there were settled agrarian peoples who had long been adjusted to state regulations; to replace one set of rulers for another involved no great change for them.

Decorated city walls at Chan Chan, northern coast of Peru.

At the head of the Inca sociopolitical hierarchy was the emperor, known as *the* Inca, or *Sapa* (supreme) Inca, a sacred person associated with the sun, from whom he claimed descent. Among the last emperors before the Spanish conquest, the Inca's principal wife was his own eldest sister, but he had many secondary wives as well. Descendants of the emperors formed an aristocracy, within which there were distinctions and gradations. These could be determined by the kind of earplugs an Inca nobleman wore—whether gold or silver. (Commoners could not wear either kind.) The Inca tribe in general formed an upper class within the empire, ruling over the lesser tribes, but some non-Incas were admitted into the elite group, including *curacas*, or provincial nobles. These were former rulers who had either been defeated in war or else had peacefully submitted to Inca domination. They were allowed to exercise political authority, as formerly, but under Inca control. Their sons were required to live in Cuzco as hostages and to receive the formal education given to young Inca men.

The commoners tilled the soil for the upper classes and for the state religion as well as for themselves, providing grain and other produce; they were liable to military and corvée service, working on roads, irrigation ditches, terraces, fortifications, and other public-works projects. The nobles, who generally lived in the capital at Cuzco, were exempt from such work and service. The nobles were allowed to hold landed estates, to receive formal education, and to marry more than one wife—privileges not granted the common people.

The Inca religion in Peru was state supported. The priests were fed by the labor of the common people; special storehouses were set apart to supply the religious order. The priesthood formed a hierarchy, at the top of which was a High Priest, who was always a brother, uncle, or other close relative of the emperor. As in Mesoamerica, church and state were closely interlinked.

---

[1] Estimates of the population under Inca control have ranged from as high as 37 million to as low as 3 million. The most recent, by Richard P. Schaedel, is about 8 million. See Schaedel 1978, p. 294.

There were priestesses as well as priests. Government officials visited each village from time to time to select some of the more attractive girls of about ten years of age for special training and government service. Known as "Chosen Women," these girls filled various roles. Some became concubines of the emperor or were given by him to members of the nobility as secondary wives. Some became priestesses of the Sun cult and weavers attached to temples, and some were killed in sacrifice. The Incas, however, did not indulge in large-scale human sacrifice as the Aztecs did. They took it out on the llamas instead. A white llama was offered every morning at the Temple of the Sun in Cuzco. On special ceremonial occasions hundreds or thousands of llamas were killed. One form of Inca divination was based on the examination of the entrails of sacrificed llamas.

A curious parallel with Christian practices was the Inca custom of confession of sins to priests, who exacted penance, usually a period of fasting or prayer. After penance was completed, the sinner washed in a stream to be purified.

The Inca polity depended upon a system of redistribution which exacted sacrifices from the commoners but provided benefits as well. In each province land was set aside for the state and for the religion. The crops harvested there were deposited in special storehouses.

> The food from the religious storehouses served to support the numerous priesthood, and for the sacrificial and ceremonial purposes. The government's store was drawn on for support of the nobility and all state officials, artisan craftsmen, the army, and all other nonreligious nonproducers. In the latter category were the aged, infirm, and widows. The state storehouses also served as insurance against unforeseen calamities and "acts of God"—earthquake, storms, and other causes of crop failure (Mason 1957:178).

As mentioned earlier (p. 239), it is curious that the Incas did not develop a system of writing, since the government had need to keep records of the numbers of men available for corvée duty, stored materials, and other items. Instead of a writing system, the Incas made use of knotted cords called *quipus*. A *quipu* had a main cord from a few inches to over a yard in length, to which were attached smaller colored strings knotted at intervals. Knots and colors had particular ascribed meanings. The knots could stand for numbers counted in a decimal system. The color may have indicated the category of items to be counted. In this way, a census was kept. At Cuzco, where the *quipus* were stored, it could be known how many families or how many men of fighting age lived in such-and-such community. The number of llamas, sandals, and other items could be quickly ascertained for particular regions.

A group of specialists memorized these *quipu* records, including historical accounts. Unfortunately, the system by which they worked has not been preserved.

The state controlled marriage, making it obligatory for girls to marry

Machu Picchu, late Inca
settlement.

by 18 and men by 25 years of age. Those who passed the deadline were
paired off by a government official. Once a year there was a mass marriage
at Cuzco for betrothed couples. The emperor performed the wedding cere-
mony; representatives of his did the same in provincial towns of the realm.
The state provided each bride and groom with two sets of clothing; the
community gave them a house. Marriages were endogamous within the
community. Divorce was not allowed. People born with particular physical
deformities were required to marry persons with the same kind of deformities.

Only married men were obliged to perform corvée service. One form
of such service was to serve as runners. Messages were carried along the
public roads by relays of men, sometimes carrying *quipus*. The runners
were stationed in posts at intervals of about a mile and a half along the
road. "Even fresh sea fish was said to have been relayed daily to the Lord-
Inca; the shortest distance to Cuzco from the sea was 130 miles" (Von
Hagen 1957:200).

The Incas worshiped a creator god, Viracocha, and also the Sun and the Moon, who was the Sun's wife. The god of Thunder was appealed to for rain. Various places and objects were worshiped as *huaca*, a term which originally meant sacred shrine but was later applied to any object that was felt to have religious significance. The state ingeniously manipulated religious traditions to its own advantage. When a new province was defeated, its principal *huacas* were taken to Cuzco, where they served as hostages, but this also gave the conquered people a sense that Cuzco was their capital. At the same time, the worship of the Inca gods was established in the province (Rowe 1946:273).

Strict punishments were applied to criminal offenses, particularly those against the state. There was a prison in Cuzco containing wild animals, to which condemned prisoners were sent.

In the realm of the arts, the Incas were most proficient in weaving, metallurgy, and the use of stone in architecture. Textiles from the coast have been better preserved than Inca cloth, but Peruvian weaving is generally of high quality and very tightly woven. "Ordinary modern shirting has about 60 cross threads per inch; the Peruvians often crowded 250, occasionally 500, threads into that space" (Leonard 1967:125). Some of the Chosen Women specialized as weavers, making clothes for the Inca and the aristocracy.

The Incas knew how to make bronze tools, which have appeared throughout the region they controlled. But it was their work in gold that most impressed the Spanish chroniclers, especially the building complex known as the "Golden Enclosure" in Cuzco, in which there was a golden cornfield. Cieza de León tells of "the garden where the clods [of earth] were pieces of fine gold, and it was artificially sown with cornfields which were of gold, as well as the stems of the leaves and the [corn] cobs. Besides all this they had more than twenty llamas of gold with their young, and the [Indian] shepherds life-size, with their slings and crooks to watch them . . . all made of gold" (Von Hagen 1957:146).

Massive stone walls built by the Incas at Cuzco, Sacsahuaman, and elsewhere were constructed without mortar, with the large stone blocks fitting so closely together that a knife blade cannot be inserted between them. Some of the stones in the fortress wall at Sacsahuaman are 20 feet high. To assemble these stones and to fit them together was a remarkable feat of engineering.

One more achievement of the Peruvians may be mentioned: their accomplishments in surgery. This includes the early coastal people, perhaps more than the Incas. At any rate, the Peruvians performed such operations as amputations and the trepanning of skulls. They used forceps and tourniquets and bandaged with gauze and cotton. The purpose of the trepanning, whether medical or magical, is not known, but over 10,000 trepanned skulls have been found in Peru, and their appearance shows that this difficult operation was often successful.

In Mesoamerica there is a great diversity of altitude, climate, and vegetation confined within a relatively small geographical range, with a high chain of volcanic mountains descending to savannas, humid tropical forests, and deserts.

The Olmecs

The first indications of complex culture appear in the steamy lowlands of Tabasco and Veracruz. This culture, which has been labeled Olmec, began to appear around 1500 B.C., when there were villagers raising maize and perhaps some manioc. They also relied on fishing, but not much on hunting, and they made thin-walled pottery.[2] A feature of Mesoamerican prehistory is the speed with which presumably egalitarian farming communities like these gave rise to class stratification and ceremonial centers. There is evidence of such trends at the site of San Lorenzo Tenochtitlán between around 1200 and 900 B.C. Large human heads made of basalt have been found, with headgear resembling modern football helmets. These, along with other kinds of stone sculpture, are termed *monuments*. At San Lorenzo there are 65 stone monuments in all, plus 10 more nearby. All were carved in basalt from the Tuxtla Mountains, 60 kilometers away; and some weigh many tons.

It must have required a sizable labor force to move the large stones from that distance. Yet San Lorenzo was not a very large community. There were over 200 mounds, most of which were probably platform bases for houses. Coe and Diehl (1980a:29) estimate that the population probably never amounted to more than 1,000, but they add that the outlying support area must have been much greater. They also suggest that San Lorenzo may have been a gigantic unfinished effigy mound in the shape of a bird with outstretched wings, flying east, comparable to the Poverty Point Mound in Louisiana.

Not only is there evidence for ceremonialism but also for warfare at San Lorenzo. There are signs of cannibalism in the burnt and broken bones of human skeletons, most of which were adults, perhaps captives. (A figure on one stone monument apparently holds two bound prisoners.)

The people of San Lorenzo had to import various items that were not locally available. In addition to the basalt for their monuments, ground stone tools, metates and manos, they also imported serpentine schist, magnetite, and ilmenite. Obsidian came from the highlands of Guatemala and also from central and western Mexico. Specialization is indicated in the manufacture of the metates and manos, objects of serpentine and schist, obsidian, and pottery. Over 700 pottery figurines were found at San Lorenzo. Some depict ball players with different kinds of helmets, the earliest indica-

---

[2] Pottery has also been found in the Maya area in northern Belize near the Caribbean dated at around 2000 B.C.

Olmec head.

tion of the Mesoamerican rubber ball game. There are also fat figurines, one-eyed gods, and dwarfs.

It is rather surprising to find so complex a culture in such an unpromising environment. The humid tropical lowlands do not lend themselves to Wittfogel's hydraulic hypothesis for the development of a state. Certainly there is no need for irrigation in such a region. This has led some theorists to suggest that advanced culture really began in the more arid highlands, where irrigation was practiced, and later spread to the Olmec area. But so far the latter seems to have temporal priority. Several authorities, believe that Olmec culture was the source of all later Mesoamerican civilization.

The "symbiotic" hypothesis of Sanders and Price (1968:188–91) which is generally applicable to Mesoamerica (but particularly to central Mexico, according to them) may help to account for the advanced culture of the Olmec. Zones with contrasting environments, such as lowland and highland, benefit by mutual exchange and trade; when such symbiosis is combined with competition, cooperation, and population growth, a favorable milieu is established for the evolution of civilization.

At first glance, Carneiro's circumscription hypothesis for the evolution of a state does not appear to apply to the Olmec area. Carneiro contrasts circumscribed regions like the Nile Valley and the valleys of Peru with the Amazon Basin, which seems to be much like the Olmec lowlands. There are no real circumscribing boundaries, for people can always move further upriver or fan out along tributaries. But Coe and Diehl cite a passage where Carneiro points to an exceptional condition. Sixteenth century travelers in the Amazon region noted that there were fairly large villages on the river which were set close together and had social stratification and a paramount chief that controlled many communities. Carneiro explains this anomaly in terms of a concentration of resources, which amounts to a kind of circumscription. He argues that certain riverside areas which are annually flooded provide exceptionally good land for farming that obviates fallowing, while at the same time the river abounds in fish, turtles, caiman, manatees, and other resources. So productive an area would naturally be attractive to outsiders and worth defending by those who settled there.

> Eventually crowding occurred along many portions of the river, leading to warfare over sections of river front. And the losers in war, in order to retain access to the river, often had no choice but to submit to the victors. By this subordination of villages to a paramount chief there arose the Amazon chiefdoms representing a higher step in political evolution than had occurred elsewhere in the basin (Carneiro 1970:736–37).

Coe and Diehl believe that this is what happened in the Olmec area. They argue that the Olmec elite had economic, political, and religious powers not shared with commoners. Their economic power was crucial; it involved both control over scarce resources and the elite's role in redistribution. San Lorenzo was particularly well situated in having more river levee land suitable for farming than other areas. The authors believe that land ownership, as in later Mesoamerica, was in the hands of kin groups. Any group that controlled a choice stretch of land would have a more secure subsistence base than others and would be able to play a leadership role in trade, hosting fiestas, and forming alliances. Moreover, the power derived from trade and redistribution was accompanied by political and religious power, for Olmec chiefs were thought to have had more access to the supernatural world than ordinary folk. The giant stone heads are held to have been portraits of actual chiefs. Thus Coe and Diehl believe that the circumscription hypothesis best accounts for the rise of the San Lorenzo Olmec, their engagement in war, and the development of a chiefdom or state organization (Coe and Diehl 1980b:147–52).

The occupation of San Lorenzo ended around 900 B.C., when the stone monuments were deliberately mutilated and buried. But Olmec culture continued at the site of La Venta, which had been occupied for perhaps a few hundred years. This site, located on a small island, eighteen miles from the Gulf of Mexico, contains the same kind of large basalt heads with thick lips and "football" helmets that were found at San Lorenzo. It was evidently a ceremonial center arranged in an orderly symmetrical style on a north-south axis with a large pyramidal mound rising above it. On either side of a central court there were platforms which have yielded mosaic pavements, each consisting of about 485 blocks of green serpentine, set in colored clays, to form a large conventionalized jaguar mask. A third mosaic pavement of this type was found just north of the pyramid. Since these pavements were buried soon after being completed, they are believed to have been offerings. On top of one of them were placed twenty jade and serpentine celts laid out in the form of a cross, with a concave hematite mirror placed at the intersection.

Beautifully carved pieces of jade are a striking feature of the La Venta site and of Olmec culture in general. A recurrent theme in Olmec art is a were-jaguar, or a weeping baby with jaguar features, perhaps a rain god. Objects in this style have a wide distribution in Mesoamerica, especially in southern lowland Mexico and to the west in the state of Guerrero. Michael Coe believes that the Olmecs penetrated these regions in a search for jade, obsidian, and other commodities. He suggests that the Olmecs followed two main routes: one to the west, to Guerrero, and another across the isthmus of Tehuantepec and along the Pacific Coast down through Guatemala and El Salvador, perhaps reaching as far south as Costa Rica (Coe 1968:100–103). Large boulder sculptures have been found in El Salvador, carved in the Olmec style, while Olmec cave paintings have been found in Guerrero.

The La Venta center came to an end about 400 B.C., with the same mutilation of monuments that marked the end of San Lorenzo. In addition to San Lorenzo and La Venta, there is a third Olmec site at Tres Zapotes, located 100 miles northwest of La Venta. Once again, there are colossal stone heads and large mounds, one almost 450 feet long. A noteworthy discovery at Tres Zapotes was a broken stela that had been set up behind a stone altar in the fashion of later Classic Maya stelae. It depicts a stylized were-jaguar mask on one side and has an inscription on the other which makes it the oldest dated monument found so far in the New World. Matthew Stirling, the archaeologist who found the stela in 1939, recognized it as having the Long Count System of bar-and-dot numbers used in later Classic Maya times (see p. 239). The date given has been determined as referring to 31 B.C. in our own calendar. A date of 98 B.C. appears on a small jade statuette. These dates are earlier than the oldest one known for the Maya lowlands: A.D. 292, from a stela at Tikal. Coe has suggested that the Olmecs may have been speakers of the Maya language, variants of which are spoken in the Olmec heartland, although he concedes that the Zapotecs of Oaxaca may have had more to do with the invention of writing in Mesoamerica than the Olmecs, for their writing system may date as far back as the fifth century B.C.

At any rate, Olmec influence in the Maya area is indicated at the site of Izapa on the Pacific coastal plain of Chiapas in southeastern Mexico, near Guatemala. There are 80 pyramids at Izapa, arranged around courts and plazas, containing carved stelae with altars. Coe considers the Late Formative art of Izapa to be transitional between Olmec and early Mayan art; but instead of the rounded three-dimensional sculpture of the Olmec, the Izapa carvings are relatively flat, in low relief, done in a baroque style like that of the later Classic Maya (Coe 1968:118–22). Both Olmec and Maya carvings show scenes of warfare, with rulers trampling prisoners. The Olmecs and Maya also shared the rubber ball game and some religious paraphernalia such as pottery incense burners and sharp instruments for the ceremonial letting of blood. Both the Olmecs and Maya valued jade, which they coated with red cinnabar or hematite. There is also evidence of trade between the Olmecs and speakers of non-Mayan languages. In Oaxaca there are representations of were-jaguars, the St. Andrew's cross, and other Olmec symbols.

Basing his argument on recent ethnographic examples, Kent V. Flannery has presented a model to account for the diffusion of such patterns:

> data from several parts of the world suggests that a special relationship exists between consumers of exotic raw materials and their suppliers, especially when the suppliers belong to a society which is only slightly less stratified than that of the consumers. First, it seems that the upper echelon of each society often provides the entrepreneurs who facilitate the exchange. Second, the exchange is not "trade" in the sense we use the term, but rather is set up through mechanisms of ritual visits, exchange of wives, "adoption" of members of one group by another, and so on (Flannery 1974:79).

Flannery goes on to argue that the elite of the inferior group may imitate the behavior of the elite of the superior group and take over their religious practices and symbolism in the process. Such elite groups were apt to be hereditary. Flannery cites two juvenile burials at La Venta that were accompanied by various items of jade. In view of their youth, one must assume that their status was ascribed rather than achieved.

Flannery's hypothetical reconstruction helps to account for the diffusion of Olmec patterns from the lowland to Central Mexico, Oaxaca, and Guatemala and is in keeping with a statement by Sanders and Price (1968:120):

> All over central and southern Mesoamerica shortly after 1500 B.C. population growth had reached a level that permitted and encouraged the development of a chiefdom level of social structure. The geographical diversity of the area was a major stimulus towards trade, on one hand, and cultural diversity on the other. The result was the emergence of a variety of regional cultures in constant mutual contact.

There has been a good deal of inconclusive argument among Mesoamerican specialists about whether the Olmec political system should be called a chiefdom or a state. It does seem evident, however, that the Olmec sites could not be called cities; their populations were too small.

Teotihuacán

The scene now shifts from the Olmec lowlands to Teotihuacán in the highlands of central Mexico, where a true urban civilization and a state

Pyramid of the Sun,
Teotihuacán.

were in evidence by the end of the second century A.D. The population
of Teotihuacán is estimated to have then been around 45,000; by around
A.D. 500 it may have had 125,000 inhabitants.

Teotihuacán occupies a strategic location on the best route between
the Valley of Mexico and the Valley of Puebla and is accessible to the
lowlands of the Gulf Coast. Although the area is rather dry, the plain is
suitable for farming, having rich alluvial soil watered by springs. Irrigation
was probably practiced as well. An adequate food supply was thus available
for the city's large population. Many of the farmers probably lived in the
city itself. There was a large market where produce from other regions
was available.

Teotihuacán has a very orderly layout, grouped around a main north-
south avenue, intersected by another main street running east-west. At
the point of their intersection there was an administrative, marketing, and
religious center now known as *The Citadel*. The two huge pyramids of
the sun and moon were located on the north-south avenue. Streets were
arranged on a grid system. In the residential area there were one-storey
apartments grouped around a patio, each with its own drainage system.
Frescoes were often painted on plastered walls.

Apart from dwellings, more than 500 craft workshops have been found

Bas-relief at
Teotihuacán.

at Teotihuacán, most of them concerned with the manufacture of obsidian tools. (This valley was formerly a source of obsidian for the Olmecs). At some points in the city there is a concentration of Maya and Zapotec pottery, suggesting the possibility that there were foreign enclaves or colonies.

From the murals and figurines one can learn something about the religious beliefs and practices of the time. Among the deities worshiped were Tlaloc, the rain god; Quetzalcoatl, the feathered serpent, and Xipe, the flayed god. There is some evidence of ritual cannibalism. Teotihuacán is believed to have been a pilgrimage center as well as a center for trade. Products from Teotihuacán are widespread in Mesoamerica. And yet, despite its large population and great influence, the city collapsed around 700 A.D. for reasons not yet understood.

For a few centuries before its collapse, Teotihuacán maintained close ties with an outpost colony at Kaminaljuyu, located in the suburbs of present-day Guatemala City in the highlands. An acropolis of Teotihuacán style was constructed there, and pottery and other materials bear the stamp of Teotihuacán workmanship, but there are Maya ceramic remains as well. It seems likely that there was a military takeover here. Some Mesoamerican specialists believe that the Teotihuacán example provided a model for imitation by the lowland Classic Maya in secondary state formation and urbanism. The larger Maya centers like Tikal (which also shows Teotihuacán influence) may have drawn inspiration from Kaminaljuyu and Teotihuacán. There was evidently a good deal of trade between the lowland Maya area and Teotihuacán. Pottery from Tikal has been found in Teotihuacán, and green obsidian blades were placed in Tikal graves. Quetzal feathers and jaguar pelts may also have been exported (Coe 1980:73).

At the same time that the Maya area was being influenced by Teotihuacán, a similar influence was being exerted at El Tajín in the present state of Veracruz, 900 miles away. In both the Maya area and at El Tajín there was sculpture depicting human sacrifice, warriors, and the rubber

Pyramid of the Moon,
Teotihuacán.

ball game. There were other contemporary centers of civilization at Monte
Alban in Oaxaca, and at Xochicalco and Cholula in central Mexico.

Classic Lowland Maya civilization

The Classic period (A.D. 250 to 900) marked the florescence of Maya
culture in the lowlands, characterized by hieroglyphic writing; codices; position numerals; an elaborate calendar; large pyramidal structures; corbel vault-
ing; buildings of limestone masonry, often grouped around plazas; stone
stelae with inscriptions; courts for the rubber ball game; fine sculpture;
bas relief; frescoes; and elegant polychrome pottery. Although many of
these traits may have been derived from Olmec or other sources, they
acquired a particular splendor among the Maya of this period.

The Maya area made up the southernmost section of Mesoamerica,
stretching from Tabasco and Chiapas in Mexico to parts of Honduras
and El Salvador and including the Yucatán Peninsula, Belize, and Guatemala. The total area makes up about 100,000 square miles, covering a
larger territory than any other Classic Mesoamerican culture. This is still
the region where speakers of Mayan languages live today. It is customary
to divide the Maya area into northern, central, and southern zones. The
first two are lowland regions, while the southern zone includes the highlands

Pyramid at Xochicalco.

of Guatemala. Classic Maya civilization flourished mainly in the humid, forested central area at such centers as Palenque, Bonampak, Uaxactún, Tikal, Piedras Negras, Copán, and Quiriguá. The northern zone is a more arid lowland region containing the sites of Uxmal, Chichén Itzá, Kabah, Labná, Dzibilchaltún, Mayapán, and Tulum.

It was formerly assumed that the population of the lowlands was never very sizable, probably amounting to no more than 30 people per square mile, about the same as in modern Yucatán (Morley 1956:46). But more recent estimates give a much higher density.

> Norman Hammond has counted eighty-three major sites in the southern portion of the Yucatán, separated by an average distance of only 15 kilometers (9.3 miles). . . . At its maximum during the 9th century A.D., Tikal may have had as many as 40,000 inhabitants in its rural perimeter while the overall regional density has been estimated at 250 people per square mile. This would make the Petén as thickly populated as modern-day Europe (Harris 1977:87).

Supporting the earlier estimates was the assumption that Maya farming was of the slash-and-burn variety that cannot long support dense populations. But recent air flights over the lowlands have revealed evidence of ridged fields resembling the *chinampas* of the Aztecs. Canal networks and reservoirs have also been discovered. In addition to corn, beans, and squash, the Maya probably also exploited root crops and also breadfruit trees, which are often found around Maya ruins today.

There are various indications, then, of greater sophistication in Maya farming practices than was formerly supposed (see Siemens and Puleston 1972; Turner 1974; Matheny 1976; Turner and Johnson 1979). However, Michael Coe (1980:84) is skeptical of the high estimates of population density. He believes that Tikal, the largest Classic Maya site, had a dispersed population, with a little more density near the center, where dwellings of aristocrats and bureaucrats were located. There was no orderly grid layout of streets, as at Teotihuacán.

Maya architecture at Labná, Yucatán. Compare the corbel arch here with the corbel arch at Mycenae, ancient Greece, page 296. A corbel arch differs from a true arch in lacking a keystone. The corbel arch was used in the Old World before the invention of the true arch.

High steep pyramids grouped around a plaza mark the center of Tikal (see photo, p. 22). Priests and administrators usually lived near the center in Maya settlements. Diego de Landa, the 16th century Spanish chronicler of Maya customs, wrote: "In the middle of the town were their temples with beautiful plazas, and all around the temples stood the houses of the lords and the priests, and then (those of) the most important people . . . and at the outskirts of the town were the homes of the lower class" (Landa 1941:62).

Class stratification in Maya society is suggested by the frescoes of Bonampak which depict warriors wearing elegant head-dresses, capes of jaguar skin, and jade ornaments. Graves of the elite are said to yield larger, more robust skeletons than commoner graves in the outlying areas. Maya lineages were stratified. Inheritance of property went through the patrilineal line. Nobles or members of the highest lineages owned private lands and held political positions. Stelae erected between the seventh and ninth centuries A.D. at Piedras Negras on the western border of the Petén contain representations of rulers, identified by name glyphs, with sometimes the name glyphs of the ruler's wife and children. The Maya were interested in recording dynasties, with their dates chiseled in stone.

A remarkable expression of the near-deification of a ruler is a tomb dug into the heart of the pyramidal Temple of the Inscriptions at Palenque, Chiapas, not far from Piedras Negras. The tomb, discovered in 1952, contains a marvelously carved stone slab, over 12 feet long by 7 feet wide,

Maya stela at Quiriguá,
Guatemala.

that covered a stone sarcophagus. Here lay a ruler, surrounded by jade ornaments, with a piece of jade in his mouth and a jade mosaic mask over his face, with eyes made of shell and obsidian. On the basis of hieroglyphic analyses this ruler has now been identified as a man named Pacal, meaning *Shield,* who ruled Palenque from A.D. 615 to 683, after which he was succeeded by a son.

There was a good deal of warfare in Classic Maya times. At Becan there was a moat, a mile in circumference, and Tikal was also fortified. Some war captives became slaves; others were sacrificed, either by having their hearts torn out or by being beheaded.

During the first half of the ninth century the Maya stopped putting up commemorative stelae. Palenque and other western lowland centers were the first to be abandoned, around A.D. 810, later followed by others toward the east. By A.D. 900 all of the southern lowland centers had disintegrated. Various explanations have been offered for this collapse, including warfare, drought, overpopulation, soil exhaustion, peasant rebellions against the elite, and epidemics of new diseases. (For an ecological analysis, see Deevey, Rice, Rice et al., 1979).

In the northern part of the Yucatán Peninsula there was an invasion of peoples from Mexico. Mexican motifs appear in sculpture at Kabah dating from the eighth and ninth centuries, and there was a stone platform for use as a skull rack at Dzibilchaltún at this time. The Mexican rain god Tlaloc appears on incense burners in the cave of Balankanche near Chichén Itzá, dated by radiocarbon at A.D. 860. From the late 10th to the late 12th century the Toltecs dominated the great center of Chichén Itzá.

The center of Toltec power was at Tula, 40 miles northwest of Teotihua-

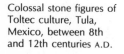

Colossal stone figures of Toltec culture, Tula, Mexico, between 8th and 12th centuries A.D.

cán. The Toltecs ruled an area north and west of the Valley of Mexico. During the period of their domination at Chichén Itzá, they built temples and other structures similar to those at Tula, including long colonnaded courts, feathered-serpent columns, and bas-relief panels of eagles and jaguars eating human hearts. In front of a temple, as at Tula, lay the *chacmool* figure of a reclining man whose stomach held an offering plate. But Maya features also persisted, such as representations of Chac, the long-nosed god.

The Toltecs abandoned Chichén Itzá in A.D. 1224, not long after the collapse of Tula itself. Political power in Yucatán then shifted to the large walled city of Mayapán, which held about 12,000 people and covered about two square miles. This was not an orderly planned city like Teotihuacán but a crowded, jumbled settlement, lacking ball courts and prominent temples. This city was destroyed in 1441.

The Aztecs

As we have seen, the center of political power in Mesoamerica frequently shifted from one region or tribal group to another. The last group of rulers to hold power over a wide area before the coming of the Spaniards were the Aztecs or Mexica. The Aztecs were latecomers in the Valley of Mexico, who had come down from the North, relative barbarians compared to the older settlers. Around 1325 the Aztecs settled at Tenochtitlán on the west side of Lake Texcoco, where they engaged in trade, warfare, and the making of alliances. Their rise to power closely paralleled that of the Inca in time. Like the Inca, they built upon previous cultural advances; they claimed to be the successors of the Toltecs. The word *Toltec* was then synonymous with *civilized*, and the artisans at Tenochtitlán were called *toltecas*.

The Aztecs themselves specialized in fighting, but despite their legendary ferocity they did not succeed in building an organized political empire like that of the Inca. In the century before the arrival of the Spaniards in 1519, the Valley of Mexico was dotted with city states, most of which were conquered by the Aztecs. But the victors did not exercise close political supervision over the conquered settlements. Some were allowed to retain their original rulers, and others were given an appointed chief, but all had considerable autonomy. The main requirement was that each city-state must pay taxes, send military contingents, and submit law suits to higher Aztec courts. By 1519 the Aztecs ruled over an area stretching between the Gulf of Mexico and the Pacific, covering much of present-day Mexico with the exception of some independent or semi-independent territories, such as Tlaxcala, where Cortés found ready allies in his advance toward Tenochtitlán.

Cortés' success in gaining allies was furthered by the Aztec practice of making sacrificial victims of soldiers captured in war. The Aztecs believed that their gods had to be offered human hearts in order to keep the universe going. This provided motivation for their raids on neighboring tribes. Sometimes thousands of victims were killed at a time at the pyramid temples of Tenochtitlán.

The main pyramid temples were found in a central area of the city enclosed within a wall. There was a large double-temple pyramid for Huitzilopochtli, god of warfare and the sun, and Tlaloc, god of rain. There were also temples for Quetzalcoatl, the feathered serpent; Xipe Totec, the flayed god of spring and renewal; and Tezcatlipoca, Lord of the Smoking Mirror. Outside this center there were elegant palaces of the nobles, plazas, and market places.

Tenochtitlán and a sister community, Tlatelolco, were built on an island and adjacent islets in the lake, joined to the mainland by three long causeways. Two aqueducts brought water from the mainland, while *chinampas* supplied agricultural produce. The city was a kind of Venice, with canals taking the place of streets. "Not a wheel turned or a pack animal neighed; transport was on the backs of men or in the bottoms of boats" (Vaillant 1956:218). The Aztecs had no use for boats larger than dugout canoes, for they were not seafaring people. In his final attack on Tenochtitlán Cortés had thirteen large sloops built to attack the smaller craft on Lake Texcoco, while his foot soldiers and cavalry advanced over the causeways to converge on the city.

The population of Tenochtitlán-Tlatelolco in 1519 has been estimated to have been about 600,000. The urban area was divided into four main quarters, each having a temple complex and each being ruled by a warrior chief. The quarters were further subdivided into wards. When they first advanced on the capital city, the Spanish soldiers were much impressed by its appearance. "When we saw so many cities and villages built both in the water and on dry land, and this straight, level causeway, we couldn't restrain our admiration. It was like the enchantments told about in the books of Amadis, because of the high towers, *cués* [temples], and other buildings, all of masonry, which rose from the water" (Díaz 1956:148).

Tenochtitlán was much more of a real city than the Inca capital of Cuzco, and there was much more trade. The market at Tenochtitlán was judged by Cortés to serve 60,000 buyers and sellers daily. Since produce sold at the market was taxed, one was not allowed to buy and sell apart from the marketplace. The market had judges to decide disputes. There were separate sections or streets for different wares: pottery, herbs, game birds, textiles, and jewelry. Slaves were also sold. As in Peru, there was no money, and most exchange was by barter. But cacao (chocolate) beans were used to some extent as a medium of exchange, as were lengths of cloth.

Among the Aztecs, merchants known as *pochteca* formed a special favored class. They lived in a separate quarter of the city and worshiped a god of their own. They were not concerned with the trade of the marketplace but with long-distance trade in luxury goods, slaves, and valued raw materials, such as animal skins, precious stones, and the feathers of wild birds. The *pochteca* had the privilege of having their own law courts, in which all law cases concerning them were tried. They formed an endogamous group, membership in which passed from father to son.

The Aztecs had moved, in less than 200 years, from an egalitarian to a stratified social order. But upper-class rank was attained through achieved rather than ascribed status. Warrior chiefs were rewarded for deeds in battle by wealth, landed estates, and high rank, and they could wear splendid clothing and jewelry not allowed to common persons. Priests also had positions of distinction, being divided into different categories according to specialized functions. Children of the upper class attended schools attached to temples and learned the Aztec pictographic system, as well as rhetoric and divination.

Commoners had to pay taxes and perform military service or corvée duty when required, building roads, bridges, and temples. Children of commoners also went to a school, which was less strict than that for the upper class. The training emphasized military and religious instruction. The commoners were higher than slaves, who formed a separate class; but slavery was not permanent, and a slave could buy his freedom and own private property and land. One might become a slave in punishment for a crime or through indebtedness.

At the head of the sociopolitical order stood the emperor, seconded by a kind of vice emperor, who was the supreme judge in martial and criminal law; he moved into the palace to replace the emperor when the latter left the city. The emperor also consulted with a four-man advisory committee. Succession to the imperial rule was within a particular lineage, the successor being chosen by a small group of oligarchs. The succession often passed from brother to brother before moving to the next generation.

As heirs of previous Mesoamerican civilization, the Aztecs did not contribute much that was new. Twin temples with double staircases were innovations. Much Aztec sculpture and architecture is impressive. Miguel León-Portilla (1963) has written about Aztec philosophical speculations, which emphasized the uncertain and transitory nature of human life and the value of intuition and poetic inspiration. There was also a fatalistic concern with astrology and the reading of omens. "He who was born under the sign two *tochtli* would be a drunkard, and he who was born under the sign four *itzcuintli* would be prosperous and rich even if he never did anything" (Soustelle 1970:113).

It was foretold that the god Quetzalcoatl would return from the east on a particular day of the 52-year cycle. This was the day when Cortés landed on the coast with his men, news of which was quickly conveyed to Moctezuma, the Aztec emperor, by his couriers. Moctezuma's ambivalence and indecision about how to deal with this deity helped to bring about the end of Aztec rule.

Summary   Civilization developed at about the same time in Mesoamerica and Peru from around 900 B.C. Some anthropologists, such as James Ford, see a link between the two areas and indications of Olmec influence in the Chavín culture of Peru, while others hold that the two centers developed independently. The two centers share much geographical diversity, with high mountain ranges and lowlands, providing for an exchange between people of different ecological regions. Carneiro's circumscription hypothesis for the development of the state seems to be more applicable to the Peruvian valleys than to the Olmec lowlands, and yet Coe and Diehl claim that this model does fit the Olmec situation. The Peruvian terrain lends itself well to Wittfogel's hydraulic hypothesis. The Olmec lowlands do not do so at all, but the Mexican highland valleys do. Some writers argue that civilization first developed in the highlands, but so far the Olmecs seem to have priority as the first builders of an advanced culture in Mesoamerica, with pyramidal mounds, sophisticated artwork, writing, and a calendrical system. They did not, however, have cities, and perhaps they cannot be said to have created a pristine state.

Teotihuacán, on the other hand, was a true city which dominated central Mexico and had outposts in Guatemala that influenced Classic Lowland Maya culture. It had the salient characteristics of a civilization discussed in the two preceding chapters, including class stratification, division of labor, economic specialization, trade, and the building of monumental constructions. Teotihuacán may have had a population of 125,000 by around A.D. 500. The city was laid out in a very orderly way with a grid system of streets.

In Peru and Bolivia there were large cities at about the same time: Tiahuanaco, Pucara, and Huari. Tiahuanaco influence appears on the coast, just as Teotihuacán influence can be seen at Kaminaljuyu in Guatemala, and in both cases a kind of colonialism seems to have been involved.

Chan Chan on the northern coast of Peru was a large city of the Late Intermediate period (A.D. 1000–1476), covering more than 6 square miles and laid out, like Teotihuacán, in an orderly pattern.

The Incas and Aztecs were both latecomers, embarking on a program of expansion and conquest at about the same time, building on the accomplishments of their respective predecessors. The Incas conquered Chan Chan and incorporated it into their empire. The Aztecs claimed to be the heirs of the Toltecs, who were synonymous with advanced civilization. They made use of the previously developed Mesoamerican calendrical and writing systems. The Incas, on the other hand, had no writing system but only the use of *quipus* for keeping records. However, the Incas seem to have been much more successful in organizing and unifying their empire. Aztec political centralization was less secure, partly due to the Aztec practice of fighting and raiding to get victims to sacrifice to their gods. The Incas had little human sacrifice.

Tenochtitlán was more of a true city than Cuzco, characterized by much more economic specialization and trade. Both empires were marked by class stratification, with an emperor at the summit. Despite the power of the Inca and Aztec governments, both collapsed before the determined assaults of relatively small armies of Spanish soldiers equipped with superior military technology, including crossbows, guns, cannons, and mounted cavalry.

Suggestions for further reading

Brief descriptions of Inca culture are available in both George Peter Murdock, *Our Primitive Contemporaries* (New York: Macmillan, 1934) and Elman R. Service, *Profiles in Ethnology* (New York: Harper & Row, 1971). Murdock's book also contains an account of the Aztecs, while Service's has one on the Maya.

On the archaeology of the Peruvian area, see Edward P. Lanning, *Peru Before the Incas* (Englewood Cliffs, N.J.: Prentice-Hall, 1967) and Gordon R. Willey, *An Introduction to American Archaeology*, Volume Two: *South America* (Englewood Cliffs, N.J.: Prentice-Hall, 1971, especially chap. 3). For good photographs of Peruvian sites, including airplane views, see Paul Kosok, *Life, Land and Water in Ancient Peru* (New York: Long Island University Press, 1965).

An early account of Inca ways by a man who was part Inca and part Spanish is given in Garcilaso de la Vega's *The Incas. The Royal Commentaries of the Inca*, translated by Maria Jolas from the critical annotated French edition of Alain Gheerbrant (New York: Orion Press, 1962). See also J. Alden Mason, *Ancient Civilizations of Peru* (Harmondsworth: Penguin Books, 1957), and John H. Rowe, "Inca Culture at the Time of the Conquest," in *Handbook of South American Indians*, ed. Julian H. Steward, Smithsonian Institution, Bureau of American Ethnology, Bulletin no. 143, vol. 2 (Washington D.C., 1946), pp. 183–330.

Two historical works that deal with the Spanish conquest of the Incas are: Burr Cartwright Brundage, *Lords of Cuzco. A History and Description of the Inca People in Their Final Days* (Norman: University of Oklahoma Press, 1967); and John Hemming, *The Conquest of the Incas* (New York: Harcourt Brace Jovanovich, 1970).

For Mesoamerica a general text is available: *Prehistoric Mesoamerica* by Richard E. W. Adams (Boston: Little, Brown, 1977). See also the earlier work by William T. Sanders and Barbara J. Price, *Mesoamerica. The Evolution of a Civilization* (New York: Random House, 1968); and Kent V. Flannery, ed., *The Early Mesoamerican Village* (New York: Academic Press, 1976). Also recommended is Muriel Porter Weaver's *The Aztecs, Maya, and Their Predecessors* (New York: Seminar Press, 1972).

For the Olmecs, see Michael D. Coe, *America's First Civilization* (New York: American Heritage, 1968); Michael D. Coe and Richard A. Diehl, *The Land of the Olmec*, 2 vols. (Austin: University of Texas Press, 1980).

A well-illustrated book is *Teotihuacán* by Karl E. Meyer (New York: Newsweek Books, 1973).

On Maya civilization: Michael D. Coe, *The Maya*, rev. ed. (London: Thames and Hudson, 1980); Richard E. W. Adams, ed., *The Origins of Maya Civilization* (Albuquerque: University of New Mexico Press, 1977); and T. Patrick Culbert, ed., *The Classic Maya Collapse* (Albuquerque: University of New Mexico Press, 1973).

On the Aztecs, see George C. Vaillant, *The Aztecs of Mexico: Origin, Rise and Fall of the Aztec Nation* (Baltimore: Penguin Books, 1956); Jacques Soustelle, *Daily Life of the Aztecs,* translated from the French by Patrick O'Brian (Stanford, Calif.: Stanford University Press, 1970); and *The Bernal Díaz Chronicles,* translated and edited by Albert Idell (New York: Doubleday-Dolphin Books, 1956).

CHAPTER 17

Movements of peoples, cultures, and ideas

The centers of Old World civilization continued to influence surrounding peoples, sending out feelers of trade and communication and engaging in war and diplomacy. For example, from before 3000 B.C. to around 1650 B.C., there was frequent trade between Egypt and Crete, where a wealthy, sophisticated mercantile civilization developed. The Minoan palace at Knossos had over 1,000 rooms, some decorated with lively frescoes. Here, again, we have bronze tools, a state, class stratification, a writing system, and the other usual attributes of civilization.

Cretan influence was felt on the mainland of Greece, where the Mycenaean civilization developed between approximately 1700 and 1100 B.C. Impressive stone chambers and tombs were built by the Mycenaeans in which modern excavators have found fine pottery, gold, and silverware.

Meanwhile, new centers of civilization developed in India and the Far East. Cities appeared in the Ganges Valley in India east of the Indus between 1000 and 500 B.C.

The vast steppe regions between Europe and China, formerly something of a barrier between East and West, became more open with the introduction of horseback riding soon after the 14th century B.C. Covered wagons had also been invented by this time, which facilitated a nomadic way of life; pottery models of such wagons have been found in a few sites on the steppes. Archaeological information about some of the equestrian nomads of the steppes comes from mounds or barrows where princely chiefs were buried. The magnificence of the artwork in such burials shows that this was not a "primitive" society; it was clearly in touch with advanced urban centers. Indeed, this kind of pastoralism seems to require some contact

Great tomb at Mycenae, Greece. Note similarity of the corbel arch to the Mayan arch at Labná shown on page 286. This is an example of parallel development in architecture in two unrelated cultures.

with cities and towns, since pastoralists need metal tools, cloth, grain, and other goods which they cannot produce themselves and can acquire only through barter, trade, pillage, or domination.

Horseback riding gave the nomads remarkable mobility, enabling them to attack settled communities and, if need be, quickly withdraw. It happened that many pastoral tribes in the western steppes spoke Indo-European languages. Between 1900 and 1000 B.C., waves of Indo-European migrants and raiders moved down into Europe, the Near East, and southern Asia, dominating several areas of advanced civilization. The Aryans moved down across northern India. The Mitanni and Iranians occupied Iraq and Iran. The Hittites entered Anatolia. Later nomadic invasions occurred at the other end of the steppes, toward the east, when the cities of China were overrun and temporarily ruled by four great invasions of nomadic tribes: the Ch'i-tan, the Jurchen, the Mongols, and the Manchus. Although they were tremendously disruptive, the nomadic tribes of the steppes also provided channels for the diffusion of culture traits between East and West.

China continued to be an important source of cultural diffusion. Bronze implements were imported into Japan in the third century B.C., while writing was brought to Japan from Korea in about A.D. 450. There was a sophisticated civilization in Japan by the seventh century A.D. This civilization owed much to China, not only in the realm of material culture but also in the spheres of philosophy and religion. The first Buddhist temples in Japan were built around A.D. 600.

In Southeast Asia there appeared societies that were also influenced by China but that owed still more to Indian civilization, as may be seen

in the elaborate monuments of Borobudur in Central Java (late 8th century
A.D.) and Angkor Wat in Cambodia (first half of the 12th century A.D.).

The development of iron metallurgy had many consequences for the
civilizations of the Old World, in some ways quickening, in others destructive. Iron objects have been found in Bronze Age sites; but iron was not
used much until around 1400 B.C., when some tribesmen in Armenia learned
how to work the metal more effectively. About 200 years later the knowledge
of ironworking began to diffuse rather quickly, so that iron tools finally
came to be used not only by agriculturalists but also by many pastoral
nomads and hunting-gathering peoples, who often acquired them through
trade. The knowledge of ironworking was introduced to Egypt from Asia
Minor in the first millennium B.C. and diffused south of the Sahara to

**The development
of ironworking**

High centers of African
culture.

tribes in both West and East Africa. But this knowledge never reached Australia, Polynesia, or the New World until the coming of Europeans.

Although the furnaces of early times were unable to liquefy iron, the ore could be reduced to a spongy mass filled with slag, which had to be pounded out while the metal was white-hot. Early metallurgists also found that the hardness and flexibility of the metal could be increased by heating it with wood and repeatedly hammering and bending it. Bellows were used to keep the fire at a high temperature.

Once these techniques were mastered, the resulting iron tools proved to be tougher and more useful than those made of bronze. Moreover, iron was much more abundant and readily available. Its use is often said to have had a democratizing effect, for copper and bronze were for the upper classes but iron was used by the common people. There were iron hoe blades, plowshares, sickles, and knives in Palestine before 1000 B.C. From around 700 B.C., iron axes were used to clear forests in Europe. Greek and Roman farmers had iron shovels and spades, scythes, hooks, and other implements. Iron shears for shearing sheep and iron saws, tongs, hammers, and chisels were known from around 500 B.C. Pulleys and lathes were also known in the early Iron Age.

All these useful inventions aided the common man and greatly raised his standard of living. Unfortunately, however, iron was also used for improved weaponry—swords, daggers, and spears. Barbarous tribes thus equipped were able to assault the centers of former Bronze Age civilizations. The Dorian invasion led to Greece's Dark Age (circa 1100–750 B.C.), during which communities reverted to a self-sufficient agrarian and pastoral economy, trade relations were broken, and traditions of literacy lost. During the centuries that followed, new states rose and fell in various parts of the Old World.

Advanced cultures of Africa

Until recently, it was not widely known that civilization had developed in Africa south of the Sahara before the period of European colonization. Most of these African societies had no writing systems, but they did possess other attributes of civilization, such as city life, metallurgy, class stratification, and the development of a state apparatus. Some of the societies had extensive roadbuilding; in Kenya there were roads extending for 500 or 600 miles.

The diffusion of ironworking greatly facilitated the development of culture south of the Sahara. A center for this diffusion from around the third century B.C. was Meroë, in the land of Kush, on the southern edge of Egypt. Meroë had large iron-smelting works. Since it lay on caravan routes leading to the Abyssinian highlands and ports of the Indian Ocean, iron goods were transported eastward, but they may also have moved westward to Nigeria across North Africa. People in the western Sudan, at any rate,

Ife bronze head.

were working iron in the last centuries before our era, having learned the process either from a northerly source or from Meroë.

Iron tools helped to open up the forests for settlements and cultivation. They also aided tribes that had them to defeat those that lacked iron weapons. This gave the peoples of Ghana an initial advantage over their neighbors. Ghana became a centralized state by A.D. 800. Mali, another western savanna state, existed from the 13th to the 16th century. These communities had trade links with North Africa and the Mediterranean by camel caravans. Mali imported silks, damascened blades, and horses from the Mediterranean and Egypt.

Evidence of high civilization comes from the beautiful bronze portrait heads of Ife and Benin, made between the 13th and 18th centuries A.D., in what is now southern Nigeria, by the lost-wax process of casting.

While advanced cultures were developing in West Africa, a similar process was underway in East Africa. In the west, commerce was carried via camel caravans across the Sahara, while on the east coast, trade came from across the Indian Ocean from Arabia, India, and even China. In the excavations of one East African port, the archaeologist G. Mathew found some glazed stoneware that had probably come from Thailand, a mass of Chinese porcelain of the Sung to early Ming periods (circa A.D.

The conical tower at the Zimbabwe ruins.

1127–1450), some coins from Mesopotamia and Persia, and beads from India.

There was a demand in India for the iron of East Africa, considered superior to Indian iron in the making of swords. Gold was exported to India from southeastern Africa.

Most famous of the lost cities of Africa is Zimbabwe, a 60-acre inland city in southern Rhodesia (now renamed Zimbabwe), which existed from around the 6th to the 17th century A.D. and had stone walls with a height of 30 feet and a thickness of 20 feet. Basil Davidson (1959) believes that this was a mining civilization whose development was linked to the coastal trade. Its inhabitants were probably Bantu-speaking peoples. Less than 200 miles away is the roughly contemporary site of Mapungubwe, which has yielded many objects of plate gold.

One of the most remarkable and dramatic phases of man's advance across the globe was the peopling of the Pacific Islands. This was a relatively late migration, having to depend upon the development of adequate means of navigation, the outrigger canoe, and other seaworthy craft. (Some Polynesian canoes were over 100 feet long and 6 or more feet wide). The migration had to proceed in easy stages, since the ocean is vast and islands are often hundreds or thousands of miles apart. Some, like New Zealand or Easter Island, were from 1,000 to 1,800 miles away from the nearest other inhabited island.

Occupation of the Pacific Islands

Where did these people come from? How could they travel for hundreds of miles without sight of land and without knowing where they were going? These questions have been much debated ever since the 17th- and 18th-century discoveries of the Polynesian islands by Europeans. All sorts of explanations have been offered. One, for example, was that the Polynesians were the surviving inhabitants of a former continent that sank below the sea and left only scattered islands above the surface.

One authority, Andrew Sharp, believes that the long voyages of the Polynesians must have been largely accidental, made in canoes blown off course. Without instruments of navigation, the Polynesians had to steer by the sun by day and by the stars at night; but the heavenly bodies were often hidden by clouds. Sea currents were changeable. The early voyagers cannot have set out on deliberate expeditions to distant, unknown islands; they must have been blown there by unexpected storms and then been unable to find their way home again. Sharp gives an example of a late 17th-century canoe that was lost at sea for 70 days and traveled for 1,000 miles. The people in the canoe had no idea where they were (Sharp 1957:15).

This seems to be a minority view among anthropologists. Those who disagree with Sharp concede that accidental, storm-driven voyages must have often occurred, but they believe that deliberate expeditions also took place. This is suggested by the fact that dogs, pigs, and the various domesticated plants used for food by the Polynesians were transported to distant islands. The men and women who made these trips had all the necessities for beginning life over again in a new setting. Some of these voyagers were exiles, either going voluntarily or else being driven off by a more powerful faction. While many such parties must have disappeared, some did land on distant islands such as Hawaii and Easter Island.

Also seen as a minority view is the variant of the accidental voyage theory set forth by Thor Heyerdahl. His notion is that some Peruvians were carried out to sea on a raft and drifted to the islands of Polynesia. Instead of coming from Asia, as most anthropologists hold, they came

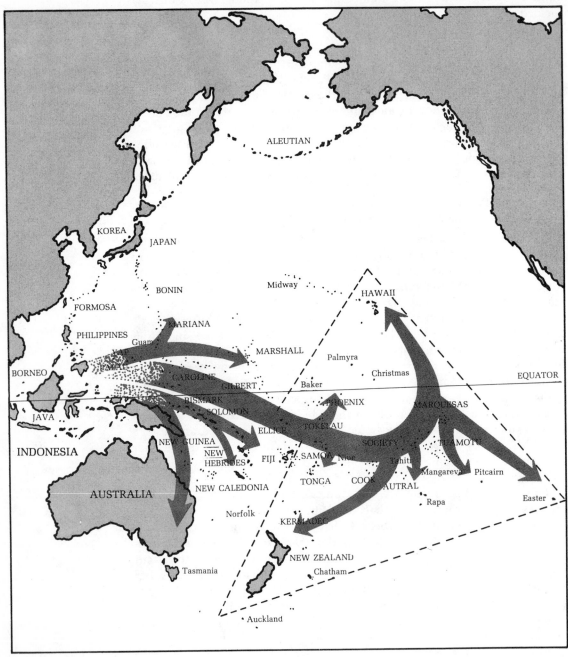

Map showing routes in
the peopling of the
Pacific.

from the New World. He has presented some cultural and linguistic evidence for this view. For example, the sweet potato is found in both Polynesia and Peru. In the Quechua language of Peru, the sweet potato is called *kumar*, while in Polynesia it is called *umara, kumala,* or some variant. Heyerdahl believes that the sweet potato is an indigenous American plant that was transported to Polynesia by Peruvians. But it could have been the other way around. Several botanists have claimed an Old World origin for the sweet potato, as for most other Polynesian plants. The breadfruit, pandanus, yam, and sugarcane all came from Southeast Asia, while the taro may have originated in southern Asia. (Suggs 1960:23). The few domesticated animals of Polynesia—the dog, pig, and jungle fowl—also have an Old World origin.

The Malayo-Polynesian language has ties with the Old World, not with the New. It is spoken as far west as the large island of Madagascar, near the southeastern coast of Africa, and as far east as Easter Island, 2,000 miles from the coast of Peru. The Malayo-Polynesian language stock includes the languages of Polynesia, Micronesia, Melanesia, Indonesia, and the Philippines; and it is related to some languages spoken in Thailand and Taiwan. Thus, the evidence of botany, biology, and linguistics seems to point to Southeast Asia as a point of origin for the Polynesians. There is similar evidence in material culture. For example, a type of adze used in southern China in Neolithic times, and not found elsewhere in Asia, is very similar to the Polynesian adze.

Robert C. Suggs believes that the expansion of the Shang state in northern China some time before 1600 B.C. was a catalyst that resulted in emigration among coastal peoples in southern China who had a Neolithic horticultural and maritime culture. These emigrants are believed to have settled first in the Philippines, later moving through Melanesia and Papua. The Marianas Islands are thought to have been settled by migrations from the Philippines.

According to radiocarbon dating New Caledonia and Fiji were inhabited by around 800 B.C. or earlier. The Society Islands and the Marquesas were occupied around the second or third century B.C. The Society Islands in the heart of Polynesia may have been the point from which Hawaii, New Zealand, and other islands were settled. Hawaii became inhabited around the second century A.D.; Easter Island, in the fourth century; and New Zealand, not until around A.D. 1000.[1]

The culture carried through these islands was a Neolithic one based on root-crop horticulture, breadfruit, and fishing. Bark-cloth clothing was made from the paper mulberry. Evidently this culture was well adapted to its tropical island environment, since population generally built up in the islands. But this led to warfare and sometimes emigration. There was

---

[1] The foregoing reconstruction is based on Suggs (1960). Some quite different radiocarbon dates are given in Ferndon (1968:100). According to Ferndon, an early occupation date for Fiji comes as late as 46 B.C.

Samoan woman.

much fighting in Polynesia; the natives of Tonga built forts with moats, walls, and lookout towers, while the Samoans had fortified villages. Chiefs acquired high status. Rules of primogeniture determined relative rank. Some chiefs gave expression to their status by directing the building of large ceremonial structures. Megalithic architecture appeared in Tahiti, the Marquesas, Hawaii, and Easter Island.

Ideas of sacredness became attached to chiefs, expressed in the concepts of mana—impersonal supernatural power—and taboo. A chief was believed to be too sacred to be touched by an ordinary person; even his belongings, charged with mana, were taboo to others. This resulted in a certain degree of awe-inspiring isolation from the common people. These are some aspects of the culture encountered by Europeans in the 17th and 18th centuries.

Having advanced so far eastward across the Pacific, did the Polynesians ever go farther and reach the New World? It is possible; some scattered Polynesian objects have been found in South America, but their archaeological context has usually been uncertain.

Global interchanges of plants, animals, and germs

When Europeans began to explore North and South America, they discovered that although some of the plants and animals were familiar, many were unknown to them. Moreover, some important domesticated animals of the Old World, such as cattle, sheep, and horses, were not to be found.

Many American Indians were farmers raising such crops as maize, beans, squash, and manioc, but they did not have barley, wheat, and millet; nor did they raise oranges, grapes, or sugar cane. Some plants, such as cacti, are exclusively American. The white potato was a native of Peru. Other native American plants were avocadoes, peanuts, pumpkin, tomatoes, papaya, guava, pineapples, chile pepper, cocoa, rubber, and tobacco. Before long these all became well known in the Old World, while at the same time Old World plants and animals were introduced into the Americas.

On his second voyage, Columbus brought to Española the seeds and cuttings of various European plants, including wheat, chickpeas, onions, radishes, and sugar cane. Orchards with European fruits were started. Some of the new crops flourished, while others did not. Oranges, lemons, and figs did well in the West Indies; so did bananas, brought over in 1516 from the Canary Islands. Although grape vines failed to grow in the Antilles, a suitable Mediterranean climate for grapes and wine production was found in Peru and Chile during the 16th century. The same regions were suitable for the planting of olive trees, which began in 1560.

The Spaniards raised wheat and had their customary bread and wine for meals, while most American Indians in Mesoamerica and Peru continued to eat maize. Pork was the main meat first consumed by the Spaniards; the pigs they introduced flourished in the new environment. The horses ridden by Spanish cavalry awed and frightened the native Americans who had never seen such large animals before. This was one factor that helped to secure the victories of Cortés and Pizarro. In the colonial period that followed, horses became useful in cattle raising in both North and South America. Like pigs and horses, cattle flourished in their new habitat. According to Crosby (1972:85), "there were probably more cattle in the New World in the 17th century than any other type of vertebrate immigrant." They provided not only meat but also hides and tallow used for candles. There was a great demand for leather in Europe. In the late 16th century many thousands of hides were sent annually to Spain.

Europeans introduced the wheel into the Americas, with wagons drawn by horses or oxen. Mules and burros were useful as pack animals. Sheep, goats, chickens, and cats were also brought over from Europe. In pre-Columbian times woolen clothing was known only to Andean peoples like the Incas, but after the Spanish conquest sheep wool became available elsewhere in the New World. Similarly, the white potato of the Andean highlands was not known in North America but was brought to New England from Europe in 1718 (Crosby 1972: chapters 1 and 3).

Adapting to European introductions such as the horse and gun, some Indian tribes in both North and South America radically changed their means of subsistence and way of life. Toward the end of the 18th century, the Cheyenne Indians of the North American Plains had acquired enough horses to give up their settled villages for nomadic buffalo-hunting. Something similar happened on the plains of South America, after the Spaniards introduced the horse. In this case, instead of the buffalo, the Indians hunted wild cattle, which had originally been brought over by the Spaniards. Mounted Tehuelche bands in Patagonia became larger than aboriginal bands; some included about 500 persons. Collective hunting, making use of the surround, was employed by the horsemen, as on the Great Plains of North America, and there was warfare between different Indian bands (Steward and Faron 1959:408–24). Just as the Indians of the Great Plains made tools, clothing, and dwellings from buffalo hides, bones, and sinew, the South American tribesmen did the same with wild cattle.

While Old World plants and animals brought about great changes in the Americas, the introduction of New World cultigens revolutionized subsistence patterns in Europe, Africa, and Asia in the post-Columbian era. Maize, the Indian corn, became an important crop in southern Europe, from Portugal to the Balkans. Yugoslavia and Rumania are now among the largest maize producers in the world. The potato was accepted in cooler regions like Ireland, where it was introduced in the late 16th century and where it was a staple crop until the disastrous potato blight and famine caused a mass migration of Irish to America in 1846–50. Russia is the world's largest potato producer today.

Manioc was taken over in Africa, which now produces half of the world's supply. It is also an important crop in South India. India is the world's leading producer of peanuts and one of the leaders in production of maize, while China is the largest producer of sweet potatoes and also a high-ranking producer of maize (Crosby 1972: chap. 5). Thus native American crops, unknown to the Old World before the voyages of Columbus, became vital ingredients in the agriculture of Europe, Africa, and Asia.

Rubber was another American Indian discovery that later had a great variety of uses. In 1528 Cortés brought some Aztec players of the Mesoamerican rubber ball game to the court of Charles V in Spain, where they played several demonstration games. This may have been the origin of modern team sports such as volleyball, soccer, baseball, and football. Team sports like shinny, hockey, and lacrosse were played in the pre-Columbian New World but were not known in the Old World before this time (Borhegyi and Borhegyi 1963; Stern 1948).

The development of new crops brought about changes in the organization of production. The Portuguese started the sugar plantation system in Brazil and became the main supplier of sugar to Europe in the 16th century but soon met with successful competition from English and French New World plantations. The plantation system was also applied to other crops such as cotton, rice, indigo, tobacco, and coffee. To meet the needs of this new form of economy, between 8 and 10.5 million slaves were brought from Africa to the New World by 1850 (Crosby 1972:213).

The smoking of tobacco was a widespread American Indian custom which was quickly taken up by Europeans and spread to all parts of the world with remarkable speed. The custom of smoking was introduced by the Spaniards to the Philippine Islands and thence to China in the 17th century, when maize and the sweet potato were also first grown there. (The Spanish peso, minted in Central and South America, was then standard currency in China).

Opium, formerly used as a medicine, was now smoked for the first time. The Manchu government tried to prohibit the import of opium and sometimes destroyed shipments of it, but by the early 19th century the opium trade had become an important component of the British East India Company's business. The Company shipped Chinese tea and luxury goods such as silk and porcelain to Europe and the American colonies, but there were few goods for them to trade with China—mainly wool and some cotton from India—and the Company consequently suffered from a drain of silver in payments. The East India Company's solution to this problem was opium, the main source of which was in Bengal, where the Company had a monopoly of the crop. In the late 1830s about 40,000 chests of opium a year were exported to China. In 1838, 9 out of 10 people in Kwangtung and Fukien provinces were said to have become addicts. The total number of smokers was estimated to have been somewhere between 2 and 10 million (Hsü 1975:223–24). Conflict over this trade led to the Opium Wars of 1839–42 and 1856–60 between England and China.

So far, we have considered plants and animals that were carried intentionally from one part of the world to another after the discovery of America. But there were also seeds transmitted unwittingly across the seas in clothing or merchandise. New grasses and other plants made the Atlantic crossing in this way, while European rats occupied ships and disembarked in the New World. Finally, we must consider disease.

One of the reasons why remarkably small armies of Spaniards were able to conquer much greater forces in Mexico and Peru and were able to maintain political control in those regions is that the native Americans were soon decimated by diseases introduced by the Europeans, for which the Indians had not yet acquired immunity. These effects were most strongly felt during the first 100 years of contact. The worst of the new infections was smallpox, which swept through Mexico, Central America, the Caribbean Islands, and Brazil in the 16th century. Measles and typhus were also introduced. The population of central Mexico may have dropped by about 8 million as a result.

The New World may have been able to retaliate against the Old through the agency of syphilis. Venereal syphilis does not seem to have been known in Europe before 1493, but traces of the disease are identifiable in pre-Columbian American Indian bones. There were epidemics of syphilis in Spain, France, Italy, Germany, Holland, and England during the 1490s. But although some authorities trace this disease to the Americas, there is another school of thought which holds that venereal syphilis is only one syndrome of treponematosis, a world-wide disease which was already present in a mild form in Europe before 1492. The conflicting hypotheses about the origin of syphilis are discussed by Crosby (1972: chap. 4).

In conclusion then, the discovery of Columbus helped to unify the world and to bring about global transferences of plants, animals, and germs from one region to another. Culture patterns and systems of social organization were often changed in the process.

New trends in religion

We saw earlier that civilization brought with it marked social inequality, political centralization, and increase in warfare, and that the development of ironworking by 1000 B.C. led to an improvement in weaponry and still more destructive fighting. Perhaps these considerations help to explain the appearance of new trends in Old World religions during the sixth century B.C. In many of these religions there was a world-renouncing, other-worldly emphasis, a pessimistic view of life, and a stress on the need for personal salvation. In Buddhism and Jainism, monastic orders were founded to help persons withdraw from worldly concerns and focus on spiritual matters. These religions were often founded by a particular teacher who set forth a body of doctrine about the right way of life. Since these religions generally appeared in the more advanced civilizations, the movements were often literate, and the doctrines of the master and his disciples could be put in writing as sacred texts. Most of the sixth-century religions had a strong concern with ethics. This applies to movements in such disparate regions as China, India, the Near East, and Greece. Confucius, Lao-Tse, Gautama Buddha, Mahavira, Zoroaster, Jeremiah, Ezekial, Isaiah, and Pythagoras seem to have been roughly contemporaneous. They often differed considerably from one another in their teachings, but all were concerned with ethical problems. New religions developed from the teachings of Gautama Buddha (563–483 B.C.); Mahavira (599–527 B.C.), founder of Jainism; Confucius (551–479 B.C.); Lao-Tse (604–531 B.C.), founder of Taoism; and Zoroaster (circa 660–583 B.C.), founder of Zoroastrianism. Some of these religions, such as Buddhism, were proselytizing cults which ultimately influenced millions of persons.

It is instructive that something similar to the Golden Rule appeared in many of these religious traditions. Diffusion may have been involved in some cases; in others it may have been a matter of independent invention. The concept is not always quite the same in different religious contexts; sometimes there are subtle differences. For example, the later Christian statement of the Golden Rule in Matthew 7:12 reads: "So whatever you wish that men would do to you, do so to them; for this is the law and the prophets."

In the *Analects* of Confucius (15:23) we read: "Is there any one maxim which ought to be acted upon throughout one's whole life? Surely the maxim of loving-kindness is such—Do not unto others what you would not they should do unto you."

Here the difference is in the positive phrasing of the Christian text—to do unto others—as opposed to the negative phrasing in the Confucian advice: "Do not unto others what you would not they should do unto you."

Six centuries later, similar views were expressed in the teachings of Jesus, and six centuries after that, in the doctrines of Mohammed.

Since Buddhism, Christianity, and Islam were all proselytizing religions, their influence was not confined within one country but swept across large portions of the world. Buddhism originated in India but was carried to Ceylon, Nepal, Tibet, the countries of Southeast Asia, China, and Japan. Christianity originated in the Near East and diffused through Greece, Rome, and the rest of Europe, and, later, after the great period of exploration, to the New World and other portions of the globe. Islam spread westward from the Near East across North Africa, temporarily gaining a foothold in Spain and finding converts among tribesmen of the African savannas. The religion of Mohammed moved northward and eastward to become established in Turkey, Iraq, Iran, large sections of the Indian subcontinent and the Eurasian steppes, and parts of China and most of Indonesia.

Summary

Although the topics dealt with in this chapter are disparate, they share a common theme: the extension of culture patterns from one part of the world to another, either in migration, as in the case of the Polynesians, or through culture contact, trade relations, or military conquest. Contact between previously distinct and separate regions like the Old World and the New may result not only in culture changes but also in exposure to new diseases for which either the explorers or the natives lack immunity.

In some cases the global changes discussed in this chapter were disastrous, such as the development of the opium trade in China, the American slave trade, and the smallpox epidemics in the New World. The development of iron-working, which of course had many useful applications, also led to an increase in warfare and the collapse of some centers of Old World civilization. A new invention, like nuclear fission, may have potentialities for both progress and disaster.

In some cases, the introduction of new patterns gave added strength to the receiving cultures. European domesticated animals such as the horse, cow, sheep, and goat, and Old World cultigens such as barley and wheat revolutionized subsistence patterns in the New World, while maize, manioc, potatoes, and other New World plants greatly benefited the nations of Europe, Africa, and Asia.

This chapter illustrates the point that racial or linguistic barriers are no deterrent to the transmission of new ideas, whether these have to do with subsistence patterns or with religious doctrines like those of Buddhism, Christianity, and Islam.

Our planet has not yet become politically or culturally integrated, but ever since Neolithic times, despite the frequent collapse of civilizations, there has been a progressive intermeshing of peoples, cultures, and ideas across the geographical and political boundaries of the world.

Suggestions for further reading

As a general source of information on the diffusion and spread of Old World cultures, see Ralph Linton, *The Tree of Culture* (New York: Alfred A. Knopf, 1955). For Africa, see Basil Davidson, *The Lost Cities of Africa* (Boston: Little, Brown, 1959). For Polynesia, see Robert C. Suggs, *The Island Civilizations of Polynesia* (New York: Mentor Books, 1960); Andrew P. Vayda, ed., *Peoples and Cultures of the Pacific: An Anthropological Reader* (New York: Natural History Press, 1968).

On the global interchanges of plants, animals, and diseases, see Alfred W. Crosby, Jr., *The Columbian Exchange. Biological and Cultural Consequences of 1492* (Westport, Conn.: Greenwood Publishing, 1972).

On the sixth century B.C. new trends in religion, see under "Historical Religion" in Robert N. Bellah, "Religious Evolution," in *Reader in Comparative Religion: An Anthropological Approach*, ed. William A. Lessa and Evon Z. Vogt, 3d. ed. (New York: Harper & Row, 1972), pp. 43–45. See also Edward Rice, *The Five Great Religions* (New York: Four Winds Press, 1973).

PART FIVE

Biological variation in modern *Homo sapiens*

CHAPTER 18

The concept of race

As human beings occupied different geographical regions of the world and adapted to new environments, they often became characterized by physical variation. Some authorities see in various Upper Paleolithic skeletons the foreshadowings of present-day racial groups. For instance, Cro-Magnon man of the Dordogne region in France has been held to be a European Caucasoid, or "white." Seven skeletons found at Choukoutien, China and dated at about 10,000 B.C. were considered by Carleton S. Coon to have had Mongoloid traits. Coon also asserts that some Upper Pleistocene skeletal remains found at Kanjera, Lake Victoria Nyanza, have Negroid traits. Of course, such racial attributions may be hazardous, since none of the soft parts—hair, skin, or eyes—can be preserved or deduced from the fossil remains.[1] Most physical anthropologists regard the differentiation of present-day racial groups as being relatively recent. This brings us to the question: What is a race? What, if anything, do race differences signify?

A race may be defined as a human population whose members have in common some hereditary biological characteristics that differentiate them from other human groups. Putting it in more genetic terms, a race is a breeding population that differs from others in the frequency of certain genes. Membership in a race is determined only by hereditary biological

Race defined and questioned

---

[1] This is not to say that race cannot be deduced from skeletal material. This often has been done successfully; see Krogman 1962. The remote age adds to the difficulties in the case of the Kanjera finds. Coon's views are set forth in Coon 1962.

Racial types: Australian aborigine; Mongoloid, Siberian; Mongoloid, Eskimo; African Negro (Swaziland).

Samoan man; Caucasian woman (India); Papuan Negro; and White man (Ireland).

traits and has no necessary connection with language, nationality, or religion, although language, nationality, and religion often act as isolating mechanisms that may maintain to some extent the distinctiveness of a racial group. There is no such thing as an Aryan race, a French race, or a Muslim race.

Some anthropologists even argue that there is no such thing as race at all; "races," in their view, are merely products of human imagination and reason that correspond to no reality in the world of nature. This extreme opinion has long been advocated by Ashley Montagu (1964); but it has

been adopted by a number of other physical anthropologists, including Frank Livingstone, Jean Hiernaux, and C. Loring Brace.

One reason these writers reject the race concept is that there is no agreement among physical anthropologists about how many races there are.

An early attempt at racial classification was made by Linnaeus, who first classified man as a primate. Linnaeus distinguished some subdivisions

Early notions about race

of the human species, of which four were based on geographical areas—American, European, African, and Asiatic—while others were more fanciful, such as an alleged *Homo monstrosus*, and *Homo ferus* or wild man, suggested by speechless wild children who had sometimes been found wandering in the woods of Europe. A later taxonomist, Johann Friedrich Blumenbach (1752–1840), rejected the latter two categories and added a fifth geographical variant, Malayan. These were the first leading racial classifications; many more were to be drawn up in succeeding generations.

Racial variations were often interpreted as degenerations from a primordial type. Both Blumenbach and Buffon believed that Adam and Eve were white, and Oliver Goldsmith argued that white was the original natural color of man. Goldsmith thought that proof of this lay in the fact that the babies of other races were born light skinned. In the late 18th century, Samuel Stanhope Smith asserted that humans had originated, fully civilized and white, somewhere in Asia, but some offshoots had developed dark skin due to the effects of heat. A contemporary, John Hunter, claimed that savage living conditions generally led to dark complexion (Jordan 1968:514). On the other hand, James Cowles Prichard, in 1813, asserted that Adam had been a Negro, and that in the process of civilization, man had been slowly turning white. Although these theories differed from one another, a common thread that ran through them all was the conviction of white superiority held by the white theorists.

Those who followed the monogenetic tradition of descent from Adam and Eve had to account for the racial diversity which had developed since. Not all thinkers accepted this view, however. Some 18th-century writers believed that different races were the products of separate acts of creation. Voltaire, who held polygenetic views, thought that Negroes were not capable of achieving an advanced civilization. Some American defenders of slavery held that blacks and whites were separate species. An obvious weakness of this notion was that the two races could interbreed and produce fertile offspring. Nevertheless, there were several proponents of what came to be known in Europe as the "American school," founded by a physician and anatomist, Samuel George Morton. Between 1830 and 1851, Morton acquired a collection of 968 skulls from different parts of the world. He developed certain standard measuring practices involving about a dozen separate measurements, including that of the cranial capacity. Skull measurements of this sort became standard procedure in the physical anthropology of the rest of the 19th century and the early decades of the 20th. Members of the American school thought that Negroes and whites belonged to separate species and that Negroes were inferior to whites. But despite their implicit support for slavery, polygenetic views did not prevail in the South, since they challenged biblical authority. Fundamentalists could find support for the inferior position of blacks in Noah's curse on his third son, Ham, whose descendants were destined to be the servants of servants. This was believed to refer to the Negro race.

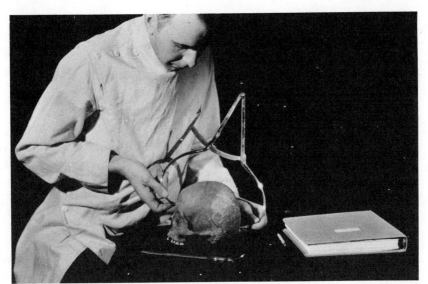

Measurement of head length of skull.

Skull measurement

Racial prejudice took a new turn in 19th-century Europe; it sought scientific justification. By measuring skulls or estimating cranial capacities, some 19th-century scholars tried to find evidence for the superiority of the whites. It is curious that some of the first work of this kind had an intra-European scope and was concerned with trying to demonstrate the superiority of either broad- or narrow-headed persons. Paul Broca, who founded an anthropological society in Paris in 1859, believed that city dwellers had rounder, broader heads than people who lived in the country and that round-headed Frenchmen of Gallic ancestry were superior to narrow-headed Nordics. An opposing view was held by Otto Ammon, who believed that narrow-headed Nordics were essentially superior to broad-headed Europeans of Alpine stock. Ammon measured the skulls of army recruits in Baden and found that men from the city of Baden tended to have narrower heads than those from the rural districts around the city. This led him to conclude that there is a selective migration of the more intelligent and adventuresome narrow-headed persons from the countryside to the city, leaving behind on the farms a plethora of peaceful, dull-witted, broad-headed peasants.

It was unfortunate for Ammon's theory that an Italian scholar, Livi, found just the reverse situation in southern Italy, where the rural population around Naples turned out to be prevailingly narrow-headed, while a higher incidence of broad-headed persons was found in the city of Naples itself.

The situation in both cases can be explained by the fact that cities attract a heterogeneous population from different parts of Europe and not just from the immediate area. The countryside around Baden has an old, stable population of broadheaded Alpines, but in Baden itself there are narrow-headed Nordics from northern Europe and narrow-headed Mediterraneans from southern Europe; hence, there is a higher incidence of narrowheadedness in the city than in the surrounding countryside. A similar situation exists in southern Italy, where the stable, rural Mediterranean population is prevailingly narrow-headed. But in the city of Naples there are more central Europeans of Alpine stock and, hence, a higher incidence of broad-headedness than in the surrounding countryside.

There is no longer a school of thought that champions the broad-headed or narrow-headed person as superior. It is nice to know that a racist view can become extinct. At the time, however, such views were taken seriously. Vacher de Lapouge, another member of this school, believed that since the enterprising narrow heads automatically rise to the top, they form an upper-class aristocracy, ruling over the submerged broad heads. He predicted an ultimate class war between these two groups and wrote that "I am convinced that in the next century millions will cut each others' throats because of one or two degrees more or less of cephalic index."[2] De Lapouge was right that in the next century millions would cut each others' throats, but he was wrong about the reasons for it.

The notions of Broca, Ammon, and De Lapouge may seem funny to us now, but there was a serious consequence in their head-measuring activities. Racist thinking now sought scientific justification. Broca, Ammon, De Lapouge, and others used methods that were held to be scientific and thus brought the question of racism into the arena of science. Moreover, after the publication of Darwin's *Origin of Species* and the growing acceptance of the idea of evolution, a new type of sanction for the notion of white supremacy appeared. Some writers argued that the whites were the most highly evolved and least apelike of the various races and had the largest skulls and brains.

Franz Boas in *The Mind of Primitive Man* and Otto Klineberg in *Race Differences* countered these arguments. If one selects certain traits for comparison, they pointed out, a case may be made for the whites being more highly evolved than Mongoloids or Negroids; but it depends upon the traits selected. If one chooses other traits for comparison, Negroids may be seen to be less apelike than whites or Mongoloids. In their dark pigmentation, prognathism (facial protrusion), receding forehead, and low, broad nose, the Negroes seem to be more apelike than the other two major racial groups. But Negroes have some traits that show them to be less apelike than Caucasoids and Mongoloids: in particular, the thickness of their lips. Man differs from the other primates in having everted lips in which the mucous membrane can be seen as a continuous red line. The Negroes have the thickest, most everted lips among present-day racial groups. Their hair form is also least apelike, for tightly curled or kinky

---

[2] Quoted in Klineberg (1935:7). An almost identical quotation is attributed by Jacques Barzun to Alfred Fouillée (Barzun 1937:176).

hair is not found among apes and monkeys. The whites are the most apelike of the three major racial stocks in having more body hair and more of a brow ridge than either Negroids or Mongoloids. However, one cannot say that any one of these three groups is the most highly or least highly evolved (Klineberg 1935:34; Boas 1938:100–102).

Racists have sometimes made the claim that whites have larger or more advanced brains than nonwhites. Comparative studies have sometimes shown slight differences in cranial capacity between racial groups, but these do not seem to be significant. One comparative study of the cranial capacities of whites and blacks gives the mean capacity of 1,179 white male skulls as 1,517.49 cubic centimeters and that of 661 black male skulls as 1,467.13 cubic centimeters. Thus, the white skulls are larger, but the difference between the two series is only 50.36 cubic centimeters. Some series of nonwhite skulls have yielded larger cranial capacities than the white series with which they were compared (Simmons 1942; see also Klineberg 1935:83–87; and Fox 1968).

Brain size and morphology

It must be kept in mind that in many of the non-European groups the stature is smaller than that of whites. An increase in head size accompanies growth in stature. Since diet affects stature, the more favorable nutrition of European and American whites may affect brain size, but this would not necessarily indicate greater intelligence on their part. Many outstanding persons have had quite small brains. Within the normal human range, mere size is not an indicator of intelligence.

Some American racists have argued that whites have more highly developed frontal lobes than blacks do and that the brains of whites show more fissuration and sulcification. Robert Bean is cited for an early study (1906) in which he claimed that Negroes tend to have smaller frontal lobes than whites. A later study by Franklin P. Mall did not confirm Bean's findings. He separated the brains of about 100 Negroes and whites into three groups according to the richness of their convolutions. The brains of the whites were not found to be more complex. Mall also weighed the frontal lobes of all the brains. He found that the brains of Negroes were somewhat lighter than those of the whites, but the Negro frontal lobes were relatively as heavy. Mall (1909) emphasized the great variation to be found among the brains of both racial groups. J. H. Kohlbrugge has written:

> The comparison of convolutions and sulci does not present constant racial differences. . . . Each variation can be found in different races if one has enough data. . . . Among a group of brains belonging to different races, no one is capable of distinguishing one which corresponds to an Australian from a European, nor one of a genius from that of a man of average intelligence (quoted in Comas 1961:308).

Still another work on brain morphology cited in racist literature is F. W. Vint's "The Brain of the Kenya Native" (1934). The reason this brief article is referred to in such publications is that Vint, who made a study of 100 brains of Kenya natives, concluded, among other things, that the pyramidal cells of the supragranular cortex are smaller in the brains of Kenya natives than in the European brains described by Von Economo. Racist writers who have made use of these findings consider it to be significant that the African Negro brains studied had thinner supragranular layers of the cortex than Europeans brains. But these writers ignore some qualifications made by Vint himself. He pointed out that his collection of brains came from individuals who, while alive, were generally of poor physique. Vint (1934:216) wrote: "The high incidence of spirochaetal diseases, yaws and syphilis, must be taken into consideration in any deduction drawn from the findings in this series of brains." The racist writers who cite Vint's study make no reference to this caveat. Moreover, none of the 100 brains came from members of the so-called "educated class." If generalizations are to be made about the brains of blacks and whites, certain variables should be held constant, if possible, such as previous condition of health, freedom from disease, and the former educational levels of the subjects. One should be certain, moreover, that the techniques used in fixing the brains, preserving and preparing them for examination, are the same for both groups of specimens. This may not be the case when one investigator reports on the brains of one racial group, while another reports on the brains of a different group.

Intelligence testing

In current racist literature, much is made of the fact that whites generally do better than blacks in intelligence tests given in the United States. This fact has long been known, but the most generally held interpretation among psychologists and other social scientists is that the poorer performance of blacks on such tests reflects poorer educational facilities for blacks and a more generally depressing, inhibiting social environment. IQ scores do not reflect native intelligence. Many studies have shown that when children are moved from orphanages to satisfactory foster homes their IQ scores often shoot up. And IQ scores may also drop if the individual's environment is restrictive and unrewarding.

Klineberg has shown that an individual's performance on intelligence tests is affected by many factors besides intelligence, such as familiarity with the language in which the test is given, motivation, rapport with the investigator, and level of education. He showed that northern blacks did better than southern blacks in intelligence tests given to army recruits in World War I. For that matter, northern whites also did better than southern whites. Evidently these differences reflect more adequate educational facilities in the North. What is more, some groups of northern blacks did better than southern whites. Indeed, on the Beta tests, the blacks of Ohio did better than the whites of 27 other states (Montagu 1963:111).

In a much-debated article, "How Much Can We Boost I.Q. and Scholastic Achievement?", Arthur R. Jensen (1969) claims that efforts in compensatory education such as the Head Start program have failed to raise the level of scholastic performance among blacks; their inability must therefore be due to a genetic deficiency in intelligence. Some of Jensen's critics have replied that most programs in compensatory education have not been effectively administered; their alleged failure need not imply any genetic inadequacy on the part of blacks.

Jensen and other writers with a racist orientation assert that, when blacks and whites of comparable status and educational level are tested, whites still come out ahead. But in what sense is status comparable? Negroes were slaves little more than 100 years ago, and in the intervening years they have faced barriers of poverty and prejudice. The U.S. Census of 1940 showed that only 2.2 percent of blacks had finished 4 years of high school; only 1.1 percent had finished 4 or more years of college. These low figures cannot be due to intellectual deficiency; more significant, no doubt, has been the low-caste position of the blacks, their poverty, and a consequent lack of motivation. This is suggested by some more figures: in 1965 Negro men held a little over 1 percent of the white-collar jobs available to men and 2 percent of the "male technician" jobs available (Rovere 1965:126). The 1940 statistics on school and college attendance showed that there has been little time in which to establish traditions of scholarship and concern with higher education among American blacks. Some more recent figures, however, show a decided improvement. "Between

1967 and 1972 the number of blacks enrolled in colleges doubled to 727,000; 18 percent of all blacks aged 18 to 24 were attending college in 1972, compared with 26 percent of whites (*Time*, June 17, 1974:19–20).

In an article criticizing the Jensen article, C. Loring Brace and Frank B. Livingstone draw attention to reported effects of malnutrition on IQ, which should affect many lower-class American blacks. Jensen is able to dismiss this variable by claiming that there is little extreme malnutrition in the United States—a debatable point. Brace and Livingstone also comment: ". . . we fail to see, after pointing out that environment can change IQ by as much as 70 points, he [Jensen] can make the statement that 'in short it is doubtful that there is any significant environmental effect on IQ' " (Brace and Livingstone 1973:429).[3]

To understand the low IQ scores and the high rates of divorce, delinquency, and crime among American blacks, often cited by racists, we must look at the social environment and past history of the American black, including the years of slavery and their aftermath, years of poverty and prejudice. One need hardly invoke race to account for such phenomena.

It is striking that despite the prejudices they have encountered, American blacks have often been outstanding in the fields where they have been accepted, especially in literature, music, the entertainment world, and athletics.

Racial classifications

Many anthropology textbooks in recent years list three major racial stocks: Caucasoid, Negroid, and Mongoloid. The Caucasoids are the so-called whites, who seem to have originated in western Europe and who specialized in light pigmentation, so that some of the more northerly Europeans have light skin, blue eyes, and blond hair, although "Mediterranean" Caucasoids, found on both sides of the Mediterranean and extending eastward through the Near East into India, have dark hair and dark eyes.

The Negroids include the African Negroes; some writers have grouped the dark-skinned peoples of Melanesia with them as "Oceanic Negroes." Negroes generally have dark pigmentation; dark hair and eyes; a broad, low-bridged nose; thick, everted lips; and kinky or curly hair.

The Mongoloids include the Japanese, Chinese, and other peoples of eastern Asia, the Eskimos, and all the American Indians down to the tip of South America. They are therefore grouped around the Pacific Ocean. Mongoloids generally have straight black hair and dark eyes, with yellowish skin pigmentation. They often have broad cheekbones, low nose bridges, and eyes characterized by an epicanthic fold, a flap of skin that covers the inner pink margin of the eye near the nose. Facial and body hair are usually sparse.

---

[3] Despite some shifts of emphasis, Jensen has restated his original thesis without essential change in *Bias in Mental Testing*, 1980.

In addition to the three large categories of Caucasoids, Negroids, and Mongoloids, various other groups can be distinguished that have some distinctive physical characteristics. The Bushmen of South Africa are lighter skinned than the Negroes, although they have tightly curled hair of Negroid type, which in their case is often clustered in little clumps on the skull—"peppercorn" hair. They have short stature. Women sometimes have the condition known as *steatopygia*, a marked enlargement of the buttocks.

The Ainu of northern Japan differ from Japan's Mongoloid majority in having a lot of body and facial hair of a wavy type and large brow ridges.

The Australian aborigines have dark brown skin, abundant body and facial hair, large jaws, and heavy brow ridges. The Vedda of Ceylon and some of the dark-skinned peoples of southern India resemble the Australian aborigines in many respects.

The Polynesians are rather large brown-skinned people who seem hard to classify under any of the three major racial groupings.

In some racial classifications, the groups just mentioned are listed as separate races, apart from the three major ones. Other authorities lump some of them together as subdivisions of the larger ones. For example, Ralph Beals and Harry Hoijer (1965:218) characterized the Ainu, the Vedda, "Dravidian" Indians, and the Australian aborigines as possible Archaic Caucasoids.

The Melanesians and Papuans used to be classified with the Negroes of Africa, since they have dark skin, dark eyes, and, often, kinky hair. But they are a long way from Africa, although there are some intermediate Negroid or Negrito peoples, the Andaman Islanders of the Indian Ocean, who have short stature, like the Pygmies of the Congo. There are also many dark-skinned, but not Negroid, peoples in southern India, and there are Negritos in the Malay Peninsula.

The question arises: Do the African Negroes and the Melanesians have a common ancestry? Was there once a dark-skinned population somewhere in South Asia that split into two wings, with one moving down into Africa and the other toward New Guinea? Or were there simply two distinct groups of human beings that developed in some ways along parallel lines? We will later consider the hypothesis that dark pigmentation confers some benefits in tropical areas. This might also be true of kinky or curly hair and broad nostrils. If these features have survival value in the tropics, it is understandable that they could develop in different tropical areas of the world through the operation of natural selection.

A similar question of classification concerns the African Pygmies and Southeast Asiatic Negritos. The Pygmies of the Congo are short-statured Negroes. There are also short people of Negroid appearance in the Andaman Islands, in the Malay Peninsula, and in parts of New Guinea and the Philippines. Do these scattered groups represent surviving members of an early, short-statured Negro population? Or are they different populations

"Mongoloid spot."
Mongoloid babies often
have a bluish spot near
the base of the spine
which later disappears.

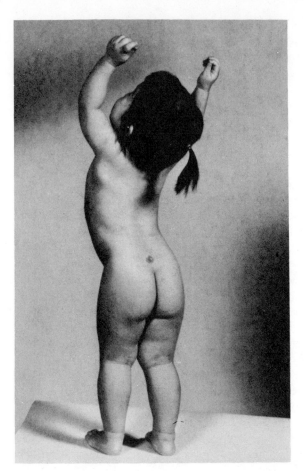

that have developed along similar lines? Coon (1962:4n) has argued that the Melanesians and Africans are not genetically related since they differ completely in the composition of their blood groups. Blood-group studies also would seem to show that there is no genetic relationship between the African Pygmies and the Papuan Negritos. However, Birdsell claims that blood-group similarities or differences cannot indicate genetic relationships or lack of them. As we shall see in the next chapter, blood groups are influenced by natural selection. Particular blood types may have adaptive value in particular environments. Birdsell believes that the Oceanic Negritos are, after all, genetically related to the African rain-forest people (Birdsell 1972:444–45; see also Giles 1973:239).

These, at any rate, are the problems of lumping or splitting—of grouping together or separating—that face racial taxonomists. Hence the disparity in the numbers of races listed in different texts. Some authorities list only three. Coon distinguishes five major races. Stanley Garn (1961) lists 32.

Coon and Garn believe that these discrepancies do not weaken the validity of racial classification. They point out that there are large groups, which they call *geographical* races, and smaller ones, which they call *local* and *microgeographical* races. Garn and Coon (1955) argue that racial classifications have value for the study of evolutionary mechanisms at work in man's adaptation to different environments. However, it is a weakness that different numbers of races are singled out by different writers.

Another reason why opponents of the race concept criticize current racial categories is that the latter are based primarily on observable and measurable phenotypic traits that give little indication of underlying genotypes. Even so, there are often greater physical differences within a given race than between any two. For example, the world's tallest and shortest peoples are both classified as Negroid.

Europe has been the scene of recurrent invasions and migrations. This makes it hard to postulate a "pure" Nordic or other racial stock in Europe. In the United States, there has been much interbreeding between blacks and whites. Bentley Glass and C. C. Li (1953; Glass 1955) have calculated from blood-group distributions that North American Negroes have about 31 percent white ancestry. In a later publication, Glass reduced this figure to about 28 percent. In any case, the percentage is substantial. On the basis of a genetic probability table, Robert P. Stuckert (1976) has concluded that over 36 million whites in the United States are descendants of persons of African origin and that the majority of persons with African ancestry are classified as white. Should we then abandon the term *race?*

To review some of the points made so far: A race was defined as a human population whose members have in common some hereditary biological characteristics that differentiate them from other groups. Some anthropologists deny the validity and usefulness of the race concept, partly because there is no agreement among physical anthropologists as to how many races there are. Moreover, there is much overlapping, and there has been much interbreeding among human populations.

It is undeniable, however, that a blonde Swede, an African Negro, and a Chinese Mongoloid look quite different from one another. How can we explain the development of such observable differences?

Pigmentation and environment

Skin color is the most noticeable racial trait. It is degree of pigmentation that most clearly distinguishes Negroes and whites. This is illustrated in John Howard Griffin's book, *Black Like Me* (1960). Griffin, a white man, had his skin darkly pigmented through a combination of taking oral tablets and exposing his body to ultraviolet rays. With a dark skin, he then traveled about in the South, where he was automatically accepted as a Negro by whites and blacks alike.

There has been much speculation to account for the extremes of pigmentation found in human beings. Such extremes are also found in some wild animals, such as black bears and white polar bears. They are more common, however, in domesticated forms of cows, horses, pigs, sheep, dogs, and so on. Since man domesticated himself before he domesticated other animals, Franz Boas suggested that such variations in pigmentation, as well as other "racial" differences, may in some way be due to domestication or the experience of living in an artificially protected environment (Boas 1938:99). It may be argued that black and white forms of animals would be too noticeable for safety in many environments and that mutations in these directions would be disfavored, but under the protection of domestication, such mutations could occur without penalty.

A more widely held view among physical anthropologists is that degree of pigmentation is related to climate. Those who advance this view sometimes cite Gloger's rule, which holds that races of birds and mammals living in warm, humid regions have more melanin pigmentation than races of the same species living in cooler, drier regions. This "rule" was at first meant to account for the color of fur and feathers and had more to do with the effects of humidity than of temperature. But dark-skinned human beings are also found in warm, humid regions, although not all occupants of such regions have dark skins. Dark pigmentation occurs mainly among people who live within 20 degrees of the equator. It may therefore provide some selective advantage in tropical regions. What advantages can it have?

It is somewhat paradoxical to note than black skin absorbs more heat than white skin. It has been shown that "black Yoruba skin reflects only 24 percent of incident light whereas untanned European skin reflects as much as 64 percent" (Loomis 1973:259). Black skin in the tropics must therefore possess some advantages that more than offset the disadvantage of absorbing more heat than white skin.

Negroes and whites differ in the amount of melanin in the skin. The melanin serves to absorb ultraviolet rays. People with very light skin not only suffer more from sunburn than dark-skinned persons but they also have a higher incidence of skin cancer, especially in sunny southerly areas. Man was originally a naked tropical animal. Mutations in the direction of dark pigmentation would evidently have been favorable for human beings living in the tropical zone where solar radiation is most intense and subject to little seasonal change.

There are some difficulties with this theory, although they are not necessarily damaging to the basic principle. One difficulty is that many African Negroes live in jungle areas where they are not much exposed to sunlight. Another difficulty is that the American Indian inhabitants of tropical South America and most of the peoples of Indonesia and Southeast Asia are relatively light skinned. The first objection has been met by a historical reconstruction that has not been exactly demonstrated but that seems plausible: that is, the African Negroes are relative newcomers to the jungle area, having formerly lived in more open savanna country. Coon (1954) has argued that the African Negroes cannot have made their homes in the forest much before the time of Christ. If the ancestors of the modern Negroes lived in grasslands south of the Sahara during Pleistocene times, dark pigmentation would have been advantageous for them. He also points out that there are other bare-skinned animals living in the same environment that are either black or dark gray in color, such as the elephant, rhinoceros, hippopotamus, and buffalo.

There are two ways of accounting for the relatively light pigmentation of American Indians in tropical South America. One is that they are relatively late arrivals in this region. The other is that those who live in the tropical forest area are not exposed to much sunlight, while those who live in the highlands wear much clothing and broad-brimmed hats. The light-skinned inhabitants of Indonesia and Southeast Asia are also believed to be relatively recent immigrants of post-Neolithic times (Brace 1964:118–19).

The solar-radiation theory seems plausible. But we must also try to account for the development of light pigmentation. It has been suggested that light pigmentation is favorable in clouded northerly areas, since it allows more ultraviolet rays to penetrate the skin and build up vitamin D. Dark-skinned persons in northerly areas run the risk of rickets. Negroes suffer more from rickets than do members of other races. Not enough vitamin D is absorbed through the skin from exposure to sunlight. One experimenter, A. F. Hess, took 6 white and 6 black rats and placed them on a rickets-inducing diet, low in phosphorus. When he exposed the rats to a critical amount of ultraviolet light, all the white rats remained healthy, while the black rats developed rickets. The farther north one goes, the less the availability of ultraviolet radiation in wintertime. Light pigmentation would thus seem to be adaptive in a northern environment and dark pigmentation less adaptive (Loomis 1973:253–55). This argument seems convincing. C. Loring Brace, however, has another suggestion; he believes that the use of clothing originated in western Europe. Neanderthals and their successors had to wear clothes to stay alive during the periods of intense cold weather in Europe. The abundance of scrapers dating from the beginning of the Würm glaciation suggests that animal skins were prepared for clothing, and we know from the presence of bone needles that Upper Paleolithic Europeans made clothes. Once this pattern began, the presence or absence of melanin in the skin became relatively immaterial (although some parts of the body were still exposed to ultraviolet rays), and mutations in the direction of pigment loss could occur without ill effects. We may assume that this development would be apt to occur whenever human beings wear clothing, but clothes have been worn longest in the area where the lightest-skinned people are found (Brace 1964:115–17). These speculations seem reasonable, although the absence of proof gives them a tentative character.

Body build and environment

Another "rule," like that of Gloger, referred to in zoology is Bergmann's rule, which holds that the smaller-sized races of a species are found in the warmer parts of its range, while the larger races are found in the cooler parts. Julian Huxley has written that most small or moderate-sized species of birds and mammals vary in size with latitude and become larger the nearer they are found to the poles. He writes:

> Thus, for each degree of north latitude, the linear dimensions of puffins increase by over one percent; with the result that puffins from their furthest north in Spitzbergen have nearly doubled the bulk of puffins from their furthest south on the coast of Brittany. The biological reason for this is that absolutely larger bodies have a relatively smaller surface, and so lose heat less readily (Huxley 1957:43–44).

Another such rule is Allen's "rule," which holds that animals in colder regions tend to have shorter protruding body parts and limbs than those in warmer regions, thus exposing less body surface to heat loss.

How well do these rules apply to humans? In some ways not so well,

Eskimos have a short, squat body build adaptable to a cold climate.

since humans have a culture with which they modify their environment. They may wear clothes, build a shelter, or crouch beside a fire. Climatic forces do not bear upon human beings as directly and inexorably as they do upon puffins. Nevertheless, Coon, Garn, Birdsell, and others have argued a case for the influence of climate on body build among humans.

The Eskimos are short, not tall, and Coon, Garn, and Birdsell point out that they have chunky bodies, thick chests, short legs, and short fingers and toes. Their bodies are thus well constructed to preserve heat. In contrast, the Nilotic Negroes of the Sudan are tall and lanky; they have long, narrow chests and long arms and legs. Such a body build would be unfortunate in the Arctic, but is well suited to a hot, dry environment where it is well adapted to shed heat. Not all Negroes have this type of body build. The so-called Forest Negroes are more rugged and stockily built and have shorter legs, and the Pygmies of the Congo are, of course, very short in stature. The Nilotic Negroes, however, are generally long and slender. Cau-

These Nilotic African Negroes have a tall, lanky body build adapted to a hot, dry climate.

casoids who have lived for many generations in the same environment as these Negroes have a similar body build. Moreover, many of the mammals that inhabit hot, dry deserts and savannas, such as giraffes, camels, and cheetahs, are also built along lean lines. The Australian aborigines who live in the hot, dry desert regions of northern and central Australia, as pointed out by Coon, Garn, and Birdsell (1950:37), have slender body builds.

Here, one begins to wonder, however. The Australian aborigines, until recently, never wore clothing. Perhaps their slenderness might be appropriate to the heat of the day, but how would it protect them from the coldness of the night? The aborigines sleep naked on the ground, between fires, under conditions that cause extreme discomfort to Europeans.

It must be said that Bergmann's "rule" has been criticized, not only in its applicability to humans but also in application to animals in general. To quote one critic, Charles G. Wilber:

> The barren ground caribou is given as larger than the more southern forest species. The extensive migrations back and forth of these animals should not be ignored and the greater severity of cold in the subarctic forests is a pertinent factor. The penguins of the extreme south are said to be larger than those nearer the equator. But, large and small penguins are found together in some antarctic areas. In all these examples when one examines the basic data, the differences in size and weight are relatively trivial and do not in any clear manner give overwhelming cold survival value to the heavier forms . . . (Wilber 1960:108).

Besides, asks Wilber, what about the roly-poly hippopotamus, rhinoceros, and elephant in the tropics?

These criticisms seem to place the burden of further proof on the climatic determinists. Their views have other weaknesses. It is awkward for their theory, for example, that two tribes at Tierra del Fuego, the Ona and Yahgan, differ greatly in stature—the Ona being tall and the Yahgan short. One can straighten things out, perhaps, by arguing that the Yahgan (or the Ona) are relative newcomers into the area, but there is no good evidence for either case. In tropical Africa one can find both very tall and very short human beings, just as one can find both pygmy chimpanzees and normal-sized ones and pygmy as well as large hippos.

Bergmann's and Allen's "rules" imply the operation of natural selection in the development of body builds appropriate to particular environments. But some recent laboratory studies on the effects of heat and cold on pregnant rats and their offspring suggest that more direct effects of temperature may be involved. Heat stress results in an increase of limb length compared to that in control animals, while cold stress reduces some skeletal dimensions (Riesenfeld 1973; Siegel, Doyle, and Kelley 1977).

Adaptation to high altitudes

Human beings have adapted to different altitudes, as well as to different climatic zones. Nepalese, Tibetans, and Indian inhabitants of the Andean

Plateau, or Altiplano, have had long periods of exposure to high altitude. Such peoples often suffer discomfort when traveling to the lowlands, while lowland peoples may become quite ill on exposure to high altitude and often experience a reduced capacity for sustained work. There is evidence that lowland peoples suffer some reduction in fertility when living at high altitudes. Spaniards living in the Andes found it difficult to have offspring. Indians who have lived for many generations at high altitudes do not suffer from infertility; they have a high birth rate, but the death rate for females is unusually high. Postnatal growth is slow when compared with other populations. This may be related to the *hypoxia*, or oxygen deficiency, experienced at high altitudes, since hypoxia also affects growth in a number of other animals besides man. Adaptation to high altitude may affect body build in relation to large chests and lowered diaphragms, allowing for larger lungs.

Mountain peoples have a high concentration of red cells and hemoglobin in their blood, and their lung capillaries are dilated to facilitate pulmonary circulation. The heart tends to be large. Similar physiological responses have been seen in rats transported from lowlands to mountain settings. Such rats showed an increase in red cells and hemoglobin and enlargement of the heart. Exposure to hypoxia stunted their growth, which also occurs among human natives of the Peruvian Andes. There was no inhibition of pregnancy among the tested rats, but 25 percent of the females had abnormally stunted fetuses, and the litters were smaller than those bred at sea level. High altitude, then, poses various problems of adaptation; 17,500 feet seems to be the highest level at which humans can live permanently. However, about 25 million people do live in the high Andes and in the Himalayas, and more than 10 million live above 12,000 feet (Baker 1969; Hock 1970).

Summary

A race may be defined as a human population whose members have in common some hereditary biological characteristics that differentiate them from other human groups. A problem with this concept is lack of agreement about how many races there are. There are differences of opinion about splitting or lumping racial groups in the case of the Negroid peoples of Africa and Melanesia or the African Pygmies and southeast Asiatic Negritos. Moreover, there has been a good deal of interbreeding among the world's racial stocks.

Some theories to account for group differences in pigmentation and body build were examined. Since dark pigmentation occurs mainly among people who live within 20 degrees of the equator, it may have some selective advantage in tropical regions, especially in providing protection against solar radiation. Bergmann's rule and Allen's rule may help to account for differences in body build between squat, compact Eskimos and tall, slender Nilotic Negroes. But these hypotheses, although plausible, have received cogent criticism.

Efforts by racists to demonstrate the innate superiority or inferiority of particular racial groups through the means of intelligence tests or other instruments have not been successful, largely due to a failure to consider the effects of environmental influences.

Suggestions for further reading

On the general subject of race and ability, see Franz Boas, *The Mind of Primitive Man*, rev. ed. (New York: Macmillan, 1938); Otto Klineberg, *Race Differences* (New York: Harper & Row, 1935).

The classic work on the "Negro problem," which might better be called the white-and-Negro problem, is Gunnar Myrdal, with the assistance of Richard Sterne and Arnold Rose, *An American Dilemma: The Negro Problem and Modern Democracy* (New York: Harper & Row, 1944). For a more recent study, see Charles E. Silberman, *Crisis in Black and White* (New York: Random House, 1964).

On the historical and comparative aspects of slavery, see Frank Tannenbaum, *Slave and Citizen: The Negro in America* (New York: Alfred A. Knopf, 1947).

For a psychological or psychoanalytic study of the American Negro, see Abram Kardiner and Lionel Ovesey, *The Mark of Oppression: Explorations in the Personality of the American Negro* (Cleveland and New York: World Publishing Co., 1962).

On the Jensen article, see Martin Deutsch, "Happenings on the Way Back to the Forum: Social Science, I.Q., and Race Differences," *Harvard Educational Review* 39, no. 3 (1969): 523–57, and other articles in the same issue. See also C. Loring Brace and Frank B. Livingstone, "On Creeping Jensenism," in *Man in Evolutionary Perspective*, ed. C. Loring Brace and James Metress (New York: John Wiley and Sons, 1973), pp. 426–37; Lee Willerman, Alfred F. Naylor, and Ntinos C. Myrianthopoulos, "Intellectual Development of Children from Interracial Matings," ibid., pp. 438–42; Sandra Scarr-Salapatek, "Book Reviews: Unknowns in the I.Q. Equation," ibid., pp. 458–67.

On the American Negro, see also Thomas F. Pettigrew, *A Profile of the Negro American* (Princeton, N.J.: Van Nostrand Reinhold, 1964); George E. Simpson and J. Milton Yinger, *Racial and Cultural Minorities* (New York: Harper & Row, 1953). See also Martin Deutsch, Irwin Katz, and Arthur R. Jensen, eds., *Social Class, Race, and Psychological Development* (New York: Holt, Rinehart, & Winston, 1968).

For historical background on British and white American attitudes toward the Negro, see Winthrop D. Jordan, *White over Black: American Attitudes toward the Negro, 1550–1812* (Chapel Hill: University of North Carolina Press, 1968); William Stanton, *The Leopard's Spots: Scientific Attitudes toward Race in America, 1815–59* (Chicago: University of Chicago Press, 1960). See also chapter 4, "Rise of Racial Determinism," in Marvin Harris, *The Rise of Anthropological Theory: A History of Theories of Culture* (New York: Thomas Y. Crowell Co., 1968), pp. 80–107.

The case for the climatic determinism of racial features in man is best set forth in Carleton S. Coon, Stanley M. Garn, and Joseph B. Birdsell, *Races: A Study of the Problems of Race Formation in Man* (Springfield, Ill.: Charles C. Thomas, Publisher, 1950); and in Carleton S. Coon, "Climate and Race," in *Climatic Change*, ed. Harlow Shapley (Cambridge, Mass.: Harvard University Press,

1954). "Climate and Race" is reprinted in Morton H. Fried, ed., *Readings in Anthropology*, vol. I: *Readings in Physical Anthropology, Linguistics and Archaeology* (New York: Thomas Y. Crowell Co., 1959), pp. 103–20.

For a criticism of such theories, see Weston La Barre, *The Human Animal* (Chicago: University of Chicago Press, 1954), chap. 8.

For some stimulating hypotheses about the development of diversity in humans, see C. L. Brace, "A Nonracial Approach towards the Understanding of Human Diversity," in *The Concept of Race*, ed. Ashley Montagu (London: Free Press, Collier-Macmillan, Ltd., 1964), pp. 103–52. The latter book presents the views of those who are critical of the race concept.

CHAPTER 19

The concept of cline and the study of single-trait distributions

Frank B. Livingstone (1964:47) has written, "There are no races, there are only clines." A *cline* is a geographical transition from higher to lower incidence of a biological trait, a gradient in the frequency of a trait over a geographical range. Julian Huxley's example of the size of puffins, cited in the preceding chapter, would be an example. One can follow a gradient in size from large to small as one goes from pole to equator. To take a human illustration: As one moves from northern to southern Europe, one notices a decrease in the frequency of blue eyes and blond hair among the inhabitants. If one took blood samples from the people in the same area, one would find different frequencies of certain blood groups, but cline maps of their distributions would not resemble these for eye color or hair color. For example, gene *b*, the gene for blood group B, progressively increases in frequency from West to East. (See the map on p. 336.)

There is a tendency in present-day physical anthropology to study the distribution of genetically determined single traits. When these are plotted, they often do not coincide very well with traditional racial groupings. Serological studies provide some of the best examples. Knowledge of the different blood groups has great practical importance in relation to blood transfusion. For this reason, abundant records about blood groups are available from populations all over the world. We can therefore trace the distribution of blood factors A, B, O, Rh, and others in different human populations. Let us consider some of these distributions.

The blood types A, B, AB, and O are the earliest known and most fully studied. If a person has the chemical factor A in his or her blood, **The ABO blood groups**

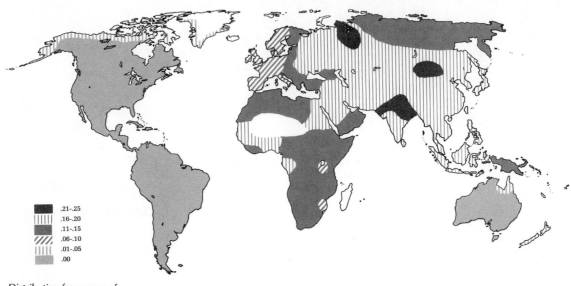

.21-.25
.16-.20
.11-.15
.06-.10
.01-.05
.00

Distribution frequency of
gene *b*.

it is said to belong to blood group A. If the blood has another chemical factor called B, it is assigned to blood group B. If blood has both factors, it belongs to blood group AB. If blood has neither A nor B, it belongs to blood group O. An individual inherits one blood-group gene from each parent, so there are six possible genotypic combinations: OO, AA, AO, BB, BO, and AB. Since neither A nor B is dominant over the other, their combination results in the blood group AB. But O is recessive to both A and B. Thus both AA and AO result in the phenotypic blood group A, and both BB and BO result in the phenotypic blood group B, making four main blood types.[1]

These blood groups have been distinguished because they may not be compatible in blood transfusions. Transfusion of A blood into a person of blood group B, or vice versa, may result in the clumping or disintegration of blood cells. This also happens if an O recipient receives blood of another type. It used to be thought that persons of blood group O were "universal donors" who could give blood to patients of any type, while AB individuals were "universal recipients" who could receive blood of other types without injury. This is not always the case, however; so blood given in tranfusions is usually of the same type as that of the person receiving the blood.

Turning now to the anthropological significance of the blood groups, it has been shown that they are not evenly distributed throughout mankind.

---

[1] There are two forms of A, which slightly complicates matters, but this does not negate the above.

.51-.60
.41-.50
.31-.40
.21-.30
.11-.20
.01-.10
.00

Distribution frequency
for gene *a*.

Although the gene for O is recessive, blood group O has the highest frequency in human populations. Most American Indians belong to blood group O. There is very little B among North and South American Indians, but some northern tribes, the Blackfoot and Flathead Indians of Montana, have surprisingly high percentages of A.

There is a high incidence of A in western Europe and high concentrations of B in northwestern India, Pakistan, and northern China and Manchuria. These distributions do not accord very well with traditional racial classifications. The Caucasoids of northwestern India and Pakistan have blood types like those of the Chinese and unlike those of western Europe, while the Mongoloids of eastern Asia have a different blood type from that of most American Indians.

The significance of these distributions is not yet understood. The factors for A and B have not been brought about by recent mutations, since the apes also have them, or substances very similar to them, and it is likely that the blood groups are older than *Homo sapiens*. Natural selection may have influenced their distribution. It has been shown that there is some association between blood group O and susceptibility to duodenal and gastric ulcers, and between blood group A and susceptibility to stomach cancer. It is also possible that the different blood groups have been selectively affected by plagues and epidemics.

The chemical factor known as Rh is present in the blood of about 85 percent of Caucasoids. Those who have it are said to be Rh positive. The

The Rh factor

15 percent who lack this chemical substance are said to be Rh negative. The significance of the Rh factor lies in the damage to embryos that may occur during prenatal development in Rh-negative women married to Rh-positive men. Mother and fetus have separate circulatory systems, but it sometimes happens that some of the fetus' blood filters through into the mother's bloodstream. Since the fetus manufactures the Rh substance derived from its father's genetic combination (the Rh-positive condition being dominant over the negative), the mother's blood produces antibodies that may subsequently filter into the fetus' body and damage its blood cells. The danger is greater in the case of third, fourth, or later pregnancies, by which time the mother may have produced more antibodies, which may then attack the fetus at an earlier stage of development, when it is more vulnerable. This resulting ailment is known as *erythroblastosis fetalis*. Fortunately, it is relatively rare and may be controlled by a vaccine if it is given to the mother within a few days after her first delivery.

It is interesting that American Indians have no Rh-negative genes; hence, they do not suffer from *erythroblastosis fetalis*. Rh negative is also absent among Polynesians, Melanesians, and Australian aborigines. Its incidence is apparently low among peoples of the Far East. African Negroes and American Negroes have about half the incidence found among whites. The highest known concentrations of Rh negative are among the Basques of northern Spain and southern France and among some isolated village communities in Switzerland. It may be that Rh negative originally developed as a mutation in Europe and subsequently spread to other areas of the world.

Much work is currently being done in the analysis of blood chemistry. Various other blood factors have been discovered, such as the MNSU system, the Duffy system, the Diego system, and others. Mapping of the frequencies of these systems will throw more light on the genetic relationships of different human populations.

The sickle-cell gene

Sicklemia is a condition in which a person's red blood cells, when deprived of oxygen, assume a crescent or sickle-shaped appearance instead of the usual round form. This may be seen when a drop of the person's blood is left to stand on a glass slide. The condition of sicklemia is determined by genetic factors and may exist in either a homozygous or heterozygous form. In the former case, the individual produces only the sickle-cell type of hemoglobin in which oxygen is transported to the various cells of the body. Such individuals suffer from anemia and usually die before maturity. Heterozygotes have both a sickle-cell gene and a normal gene. Since such persons have a fair amount of normal hemoglobin, they may not suffer from anemia, although they sometimes do. In a population in which the sickle-cell allele is present, there are also "normal" homozygous persons who do not have the gene.

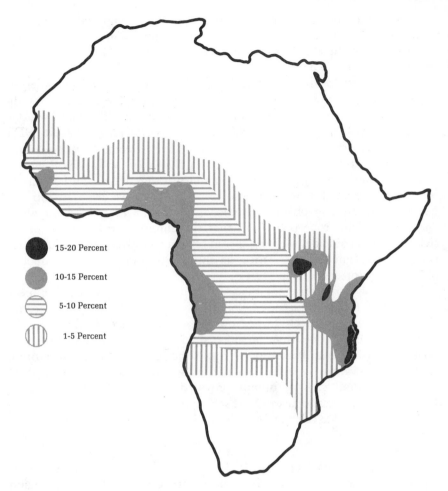

Distribution of sickle-cell gene. Frequency of the sickle-cell gene is plotted in percent on the map of Africa. High frequencies are confined to a broad belt in which malignant tertian malaria is an important cause of death.

15-20 Percent

10-15 Percent

5-10 Percent

1-5 Percent

Since anemic homozygous individuals usually die without reproducing, one would expect the incidence of the sickling gene to diminish through natural selection; but there are parts of Africa where the gene has an incidence of over 20 percent. Although it has not been found among the Bushmen of South Africa, the sickle cell is present in most African Negro populations and in about 10 percent of American Negroes. The sickling gene is also found in parts of Sicily, Italy, Greece, Turkey, Arabia, and India, but it is not known to be present in the peoples of eastern Asia, Melanesia, Polynesia, Australia, or the American Indians.

The wide distribution and the sometimes high incidence of the sickling gene suggest that it has some selective advantage. The gene is generally found in malarious tropical regions; apparently the sickle-cell trait provides some protection against falciparum malaria. Just how it does so is not understood, but investigations in Africa have shown that heterozygous persons have much more resistance to the disease than do normal homozygous ones. Anemic homozygous persons die out; normal homozygous ones get malaria. It is the heterozygous persons, therefore, who are favored by natural selection in malarial areas.

This accounts for the persisting incidence of the sickle-cell gene, despite the selective pressures against it. One would expect the incidence of the gene to decline among American blacks who do not live in malarial regions. One would also expect it to decline in Old World regions where DDT campaigns have helped to eradicate malaria. Meanwhile, it has some survival value in the tropics, although it also poses the threat of anemia.

Livingstone (1958) has shown how man has fostered the spread of malaria in Africa through his own cultural advance. Here we have an intricate network of factors involving technology, population increase, mosquitoes, and genes. Livingstone points out that the cline in the frequency of the sickle-cell trait coincides with the spread of yam cultivation. Such cultivation is relatively recent in West Africa, having had to wait for the introduction of iron tools for clearing the forest.

The major local carrier of malaria, *Anopheles gambiae*, cannot breed in water that is brackish, shaded, polluted, or has a swift current. In former times there were relatively few favorable breeding places in the forest for this mosquito, since the trees provided shade and there were few stagnant pools. But, when man began to cut down the forest and establish farming settlements, swamps were formed, the shade cover was removed, and villages, ponds, and garbage dumps provided attractive breeding grounds. Population increase also favored the spread of malaria. It was in this setting, then, that the sickle-cell mutation became favored by natural selection.

Thalassemia

A type of anemia known as *thalassemia* is also common in malarious regions. In this case, the areas involved are the Mediterranean region, Asia Minor, India, Thailand, and Indonesia. Here, again, individuals who are homozygous for the gene that causes the anemia are apt to die young, but those who are heterozygous seem to receive some protection from malaria, although the evidence for such protection is not so clear as it is for the sickling gene.

Lactase deficiency

Mammals suckle their young, whose first food is milk. Some human infants, however, cannot digest milk, since they do not have enough lactase, the enzyme that breaks down lactose. Lactose is the milk sugar which provides about 40 percent of the caloric value in human milk.

In the United States many adults drink milk, which we consider to be a natural, healthful drink for human beings. But in the past dozen years or so it has become evident that this is not a general human trait. In most parts of the world people lack the lactase enzyme after four years

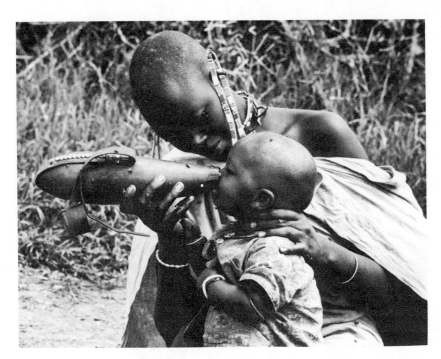

Masai mother feeding her child cow's milk from a gourd. The Masai are a pastoral tribe in East Africa.

of age. If they drink milk, such persons suffer from flatulence, belching, cramps, or diarrhea. Since this lactose intolerance is also characteristic of most adult mammals, it is evidently the normal human condition, while milk drinking among adults is the exception.

Lactose tolerance among adults has been found in about 90 percent of northern Europeans. Lactase deficiency, or lactose intolerance, has been reported for more than 75 percent of Thais, Koreans, and Chinese tested and for more than 75 percent of such West African tribes as the Hausa, Yoruba, and Ibo. Australian aborigines, Greenland Eskimos, and many American Indian groups have also been rated high in lactase deficiency. The problem for investigation, then, is not why some people cannot digest milk but, rather, why so many Europeans and Americans are able to. This ability is evidently related to the domestication of cattle, which took place by around 7000 B.C. in both Europe and the Near East, while goats were domesticated in the Near East around 7500 B.C. It is not known when such animals began to be milked, or when adults began to drink the milk, but it has been hypothesized that in such human populations mutations may have occurred which served to prolong the production of lactase into the adult state. Through natural selection, such individuals and their off-spring would have benefited from the increased nutrition thus provided. Lactose tolerance seems to be transmitted genetically and is dominant.

In support of this hypothesis is the distribution of lactase deficiency found in Africa. Two northern pastoral tribes, the Fulani of Nigeria and the Tussi of Uganda, have a rate of 78 or 80 percent lactose tolerance and in this respect resemble northern Europeans. But, as noted earlier, the Hausa, Yoruba, and Ibo of Nigeria have more than 75 percent lactose intolerance. The Yoruba and Ibo never acquired cattle, since they inhabit an area infested with tsetse flies. The Fulani live farther north in an area free of the tsetse fly, where they have raised cattle for hundreds of years. The Fulani drink the fresh milk of their cattle and sell a kind of yogurt in local markets, which can be digested by lactase-deficient persons.

Most of the slaves taken to America were West Africans like the Yoruba and Ibo, who were lactose intolerant. American blacks have about 70 percent lactose intolerance, which is lower than that of West Africans, probably because of gene flow from whites (McCracken 1971; Kretschmer 1972).

This chapter has dealt with an approach in current physical anthropology that places an emphasis on the study of single-trait distributions and clines. The value of studying clines and frequency distributions lies in the possibility of uncovering the selective factors that affect the incidence of the trait in question. Thus, we have seen how, in certain regions, natural selection has favored such apparently deleterious genes as those that cause sicklemia and thalassemia. The study of clines opens up real problems for research in physical anthropology. In contrast, the classification of races seems to be a rather sterile procedure. When plotting the distribution of single traits, it is often seen that they cross traditional racial groupings. The ABO blood groups, for example, are found in different "races," although sometimes in different frequencies. The distribution of the sickle cell also crosses racial lines. It was formerly believed to be a "Negroid" trait, but we now know that the sickling gene is not limited to Negroes; nor is the gene for thalassemia limited to Mediterranean Caucasoids.

Summary

A *cline* is a gradient in the frequency of a biological trait over a geographical range. Maps may be made to illustrate such gradients, as in the frequency of gene *a* or gene *b* or the sickling gene. Such distributions do not coincide well with traditional racial groupings. Clinal patterns indicate that deleterious genes may sometimes have a selective advantage. The sickle-cell trait seems to confer some protection against a form of malaria, and the same is true of the gene for thalassemia. Many physical anthropologists therefore believe that the concept of cline is more useful for research purposes than the race concept.

Suggestions for further reading

Two articles by Frank B. Livingstone are recommended: "On the Nonexistence of Human Races" in *The Concept of Race*, ed. Ashley Montagu (London: Free Press, Collier-Macmillan, Ltd., 1964), pp. 46–60; and "Anthropological Implications of Sickle-Cell Gene Distribution in West Africa," *American Anthropologist*

60, no. 3 (1958): 533–62. Also see C. L. Brace, "On the Race Concept," with discussion and comment by Carleton S. Coon, Earl W. Count, Stanley M. Garn, Julian Huxley, Ashley Montagu, and Andrzej Wiercinski, *Current Anthropology* 5, no. 4 (October 1964): 313–20. See also Eugene Giles, "Culture and Genetics," in *Human Evolution: Readings in Physical Anthropology,* 3d ed., ed. Noel Korn (New York: Holt, Rinehart & Winston, 1973), pp. 234–47.

On the human blood groups, see William C. Boyd, *Genetics and the Races of Man* (Boston: Little, Brown, 1950); "Four Achievements of the Genetical Method in Physical Anthropology," *American Anthropologist* 65, no. 2 (1963): 243–52.

On lactase deficiency, see Norman Kretschmer, "Lactose and Lactase," *Scientific American* 227 (1972): 70–78.

CHAPTER 20

Retrospect and prospect

From about 60 million to 30 million years ago our ancestors seem to have been small tree-dwelling creatures somewhat like tarsiers, living in small social units. During the Miocene epoch, about 20 million years ago, they became larger in body size and more apelike. Some time within the succeeding 10 million years our ancestors came down to the ground and assumed a semierect and later a fully erect posture with bipedal locomotion. With the exploration of a savanna environment there was probably an increase in group size for the sake of protection against predators. By 2.5 million years ago our ancestors had been using stone tools for some time, and probably also tools of wood, bone, and horn. By 500,000 years ago, as *Homo erectus*, they must have acquired a language. They had thick chinless jaws and heavy brow ridges. Some of these hominids moved northward into new areas in Europe and northern China, cooking their food and keeping warm with fire and sometimes making their homes in cave shelters. Although human beings had by then been using tools for many hundreds of thousands of years, the technology had not changed very much up to this point.

Around 40,000 years ago, our ancestors, now classifiable as *Homo sapiens sapiens*, had more domed foreheads than their predecessors, discontinuous brow ridges, and well-developed chins. These people hunted big game with improved tools, such as spear-throwers and harpoons, and some of them painted animals on the walls of caves. During this period human beings were spread out from Europe through Siberia, and some of them had probably crossed the Bering Straits land bridge into North America. By

Retrospect: A brief review

345

40,000 years ago, some arrived in Australia; around 24,000 years ago still others entered Japan.

Human beings began to domesticate plants and animals in the Near East around 8000 B.C. and in Mesoamerica and Peru at around the same time or a little later. In Southeast Asia and northern China there was also domestication of plants and animals. Then, from Neolithic beginnings in Egypt and the Near East, the Indus Valley, northern China, and elsewhere, there developed that complex of traits which we call *civilization:* city life, the presence of a state, a writing system, bronze metallurgy, class stratification, division of labor, craft specialization, development of trade and communications, and advances in knowledge in mathematics, astronomy, and calendrical calculations. Remarkably similar parallel developments took place in both Mesoamerica and Peru.

From the plateau of civilization developed the complex culture we share today. But our present way of life has been significantly shaped by the development of modern science from the 17th century on and also by the Industrial Revolution which first began in England during the last third of the 18th century. The Industrial Revolution, including factory production of goods, was intimately involved with a commercial revolution characterized by a market system responsive to laws of supply and demand. The leading societies of today, whether they be labeled capitalist, socialist, or communist, are all industrial societies depending upon the factory production of goods.

Indications of adaptive success

Looking back from our present position, however precarious that may be, we humans may congratulate ourselves on the long way we have come since the time of our small arboreal ancestors of 50 million years ago. Apart from mankind's achievements in science, technology, and the arts, which only members of our own species can appreciate, the success of *Homo sapiens* may be gauged in the same ways in which adaptive success in other species is assessed. One criterion for that is the extent of territory covered by the species and the number of ecological niches it has been able to enter. On that score, *Homo sapiens* rates well. Originally tropical primates, human beings are now found in all geographical environments, including tropical forests, grasslands, deserts, northern boreal forests, and polar lands. Our nearest relatives, the apes, have been left behind in circumscribed tropical regions.

Human beings have adapted to the varied environments of the earth by means of culture rather than through somatic adjustments. Instead of growing a fur coat in the Arctic, like a seal or polar bear, the Eskimo kills the seal and the polar bear and makes tailored fur clothing. He uses seal blubber in a lamp to cook seals and to keep his igloo lighted and warm. Culture is our homeostatic mechanism for keeping the environment sufficiently stable for comfort. We now have air-conditioned homes in the desert; scientists have even been able to live for weeks in laboratories under the sea.

Another indication of the adaptive success of a species is the size of its population. On these grounds, too, we must be judged successful. In Mesolithic times the world's population probably numbered between 5 million and 10 million persons. There were population explosions in the succeeding Neolithic and Bronze Age periods, and by the beginning of the Christian era there were about 300 million people. By A.D. 1650 there were about 500 million. This was followed by another population boom, which has been maintained ever since, so that at present there are about 4 billion people in the world. This crowding of our planet is becoming one of mankind's biggest problems. At the same time, it does testify to the adaptive success of *Homo sapiens*.

Culture and natural selection

Since humans depend so much on culture, it is sometimes asked whether natural selection still operates in *Homo sapiens* today. After all, cultural innovations and remedies can often counteract the effects of genetic failings. The disease of diabetes mellitus, for example, results from a genetic deficiency in the secretion of insulin, a hormone needed for the utilization of blood sugars, but diabetes may be treated by regulating the diet or by periodic injections of insulin. Thus protected, diabetics need suffer no ill effects, although their genes remain unchanged. Natural selection no longer weeds out diabetics, with the result that the general incidence of the defective genes must be increasing. As long as preventive treatment is available, however, no harm results.

It has been suggested that persons with a genetic predisposition toward diabetes may actually have had a selective advantage during hunting-gathering times, when food intake was irregular and obesity was rare (Neel 1962). It is under conditions of modern life that diabetes becomes dangerous; at the same time man had learned how to cope with this danger.

However, this single example does not demonstrate the current inefficacy of natural selection. Indeed, the preceding chapter contained a good illustration of its present relevance; selective factors favor the heterozygous condition of the sickling gene in those parts of Africa where falciparum malaria is prevalent. This is a relatively recent phenomenon which depended upon the clearing of forests for yam cultivation. The last chapter also contained a discussion of lactose tolerance which developed along with pastoralism in parts of the Old World. Here, again, we can detect the operation of natural selection at work in relatively recent times.

Eugenic measures

Apart from natural selection, human beings also influence the hereditary composition of the population through their own selective actions. Amaurotic idiocy results from inheritance of a rare recessive gene. Someone who has learned that he or she carries such a gene is faced with the dilemma of whether to marry, and, if so, whether to have children. Genetic counseling is available to such persons, who may be advised not to have offspring. More than 1,600 human diseases are caused by genetic defects. New hospital techniques have made it possible to detect about 40 of these hereditary ailments early in pregnancy. Preferably around the 16th week of gestation, a sterile needle is inserted into the amniotic cavity to tap a sample of the fluid that surrounds the fetus. Various laboratory tests are then made of this material to determine the genetic makeup of the fetus. Abortions are recommended in some cases, such as Tay-Sachs disease, which leads to blindness, retardation, and death in infancy (Friedmann 1971).

Many genetic disorders, such as hemophilia, are sex-linked and could be prevented if one could control the sex of one's offspring. This is a possibility for the future. A team of British scientists has developed techniques for determining the sex of very early rabbit embryos, which might ultimately be done with humans too (Rosenfeld 1975:158–59).

Predictions have been made about the future possibilities of genetic engineering in directly acting on DNA to counteract genetic defects. For the time being, however, the best protection for individuals and families against adverse genetic inheritance seems to be more widespread knowledge about genetics and biology.

A promising recent development is the experimental work being done in gene splicing, in which DNA from two different organisms is combined, thus forming recombinant DNA. A number of commercial laboratories have been launched to make use of gene splicing techniques in the manufacture of bacterially produced interferon to combat cancer, and of synthetic insulin to control diabetes.

Present and future environmental hazards

Although population increase was cited earlier as an indication of adaptive success in our species, it also represents a threat to our survival. The world's population is now doubling within a period of 35 years, but the rate is even faster in the less-developed nations. Among the dangers attending this boom are the prospects of famine, epidemics, and urban crowding.

In 1800 there were only 50 cities in the world with a population of over 100,000, while today there are almost 2,000 such cities. And some of them are huge: Shanghai has about 11 million people, Tokyo about 9 million, and London and New York about 8 million each. With so much urban congestion, air and water pollution are inevitable. For example, there has been an increasing concentration of lead in our water, air, and food, with the attendant threat of lead poisoning. The level of lead in the atmosphere today is very much higher than it was in the days of early hominids, who are estimated to have had about two parts per million of lead in their bones, whereas human bones today have about 2,000 parts per million of lead. A report was made at meetings of the American Association for the Advancement of Science in January 1981 describing an experiment carried out in two towns near Boston. Children were asked to give their baby teeth, when they lost them, to their teachers. The lead content of the teeth was then assayed, and the children were divided into two groups: high-lead and low-lead. Next, IQ tests, sentence repetition tests, and other measures were given, in which the high-lead group performed significantly less well than the low-lead one. Moreover, encephalograms found some evidence of brain alterations among high-lead students.

Bronchitis and emphysema are common ailments aggravated by the air pollution in our cities. Chemicals, pesticides, and organic wastes pollute water supplies, while the widespread use of automobiles contributes to smog and air pollution. Although such facts have received much publicity and are well known, people are not leaving the cities. Jobs keep them there, and in any case cities have always been associated with civilization and advances in human life. Besides, pollution is not limited to urban centers, for the spraying of agricultural fields with pesticides also pollutes rural lakes and streams.

So far, however, most city dwellers have managed to survive well enough. In some cases successful efforts have been made to salvage lakes and streams and to reduce air pollution. But with the continuing increase in city life and growing population, the problems will continue. In addition to that, of course, human beings of the foreseeable future will face the dangers of war, including the possibilities of nuclear explosions and radiation fallout. Although life has never been easy for *Homo sapiens*, it could get worse.

Homo sapiens of the future

Some writers have speculated about the future appearance of members of our species. Some see *Homo sapiens* of the 21st century as a large-brained, hairless creature with a frail constitution, but this seems to be simply a reverse caricature of our stereotype of the Paleolithic caveman: burly, bearded, hairy, and small brained. In all these respects, some have assumed, humans of the future should differ from this ancestral type.

The idea that future humans will have huge heads and brains has no support in the fossil record, for the cranial capacity of *Homo sapiens* has not increased since Paleolithic times. Our brains now seem to be large enough for all practical purposes. One tendency that does seem likely to continue, however, is increased round-headedness. Our early hominid ancestors had long narrow skulls; since then skulls have been getting rounder.

Human beings have become taller in the course of evolution, and the human life-span has lengthened, at least in some nations. Can we project these tendencies in the future?

Body size

In the course of our evolution we have considerably increased in body size from the prosimian stage of 50 million years ago. This increase may be seen as another indication of adaptive success. Such increases have occurred in different classes of animals in the course of evolution. A large animal has advantages for defense and attack and may also be faster than smaller ones. A larger animal "will, on an average, have more cells in the body, with increased opportunity for complication or differentiation of tissues and organs; under some conditions, such as cold climate for warm-blooded animals, it will have improved thermal efficiency" (Simpson 1967:151). But large size is not always adaptive; indeed it has sometimes presaged extinction, as in the case of the dinosaurs which evolved from small lizardlike reptiles. Changes in climate or other aspects of the environment may make such giants vulnerable. Mammals, especially some of the larger forms, tended to decrease in size after the Pleistocene (Simpson 1967:137).

As discussed in Chapter 18, there seem to be selective advantages for different types of human body build in different environments. But within the same environment there may develop changes in size in response to changing conditions. What evidence is there for changes in size in human populations during the past few hundred years? For one thing, the suits of armor in our museums give the impression that medieval knights were short of stature compared to Europeans or Americans of today. Earnest A. Hooton (1946:532) rejected this conclusion, however, suggesting that the surviving suits of armor had probably been outgrown by their owners. Anyway, he argued, ordinary serfs may have been taller than their masters. Better evidence, though limited to one region, comes from measurements by Karl Pearson of skeletal remains from 17th century London. The average human body length was estimated at five feet, five inches. In more recent years, especially since World War II, there is no doubt that an increase in stature has taken place in both Europe and the United States. In 1960, 13-year-old boys in Glasgow, Scotland, were found to be four inches taller than 13-year-olds had been 40 years before, and they weighed 14½ pounds more, while girls were 3¼ inches taller and weighed 16½ pounds more (Dubos 1965:78).

In the past 30 years Americans have been getting taller and taller. Children tend to be taller than their parents. This development has had all kinds of repercussions in the field of business. Shoe companies have been making more shoes of larger size. Hotels have been installing more long-sized beds. Movie theaters have been installing wider seats to fit the broadening American posterior. This increasing size is probably due to improvements in nutrition—vitamin-enriched breads, cereals, and other foods. The mixing-up of populations attendant upon industrialization may also have led to genetic diversity and hybrid vigor, leading to taller stature. This suggestion was made by Harry L. Shapiro (1974:63–66), who notes that inbreeding, which was common in medieval European populations, tends to reduce stature, whereas population mixture and gene flow may lead to taller stature. The tendency to grow taller is not limited to Caucasoids, for since World War II, the same thing has been happening in Japan where, again, children are often taller than their parents. If this tendency persists, it may work a revolution in the architecture of the low-ceilinged Japanese home.

But the trend toward larger size will not be worldwide. In many parts of the world large size would be disadvantageous under present conditions. In the underdeveloped and overpopulated countries of Asia, people are often undernourished. Large body size with its demands for larger food intake would be an unfortunate development in these areas. The advent of economic prosperity in such regions, however, might well be accompanied by an increase in body size, like that now seen in the United States, Europe, and Japan. However, if worldwide population increase continues, it may ultimately be of selective advantage for our species to become smaller again, to reduce competition for the available food resources of our planet—unless, of course, scientists find the means to greatly increase those resources.

Rate of maturation

Another current change, concomitant with size increase, is that boys and girls now reach sexual maturity much earlier than they did a generation or two ago. In the United States the average age at *menarche*, or first menstruation, is now 12.9 years, with much individual variation. A generation ago the mothers of these girls began to menstruate a year or half a year later than their daughters do now. As in the case of height, better nutrition may be involved in this change, for girls of lower socioeconomic groups tend to mature later. The amount of hard work required in childhood may also be a factor. That is suggested by a study of height and age at menarche among girls in rural Poland. Farming girls, required to do more manual work, were found to begin menstruation later (a little over age 14) than girls of nonagricultural groups, who menstruated earliest, before age 14; while girls of a farmer-worker category were intermediate in that respect. The girls of the agricultural group were also a little shorter and lighter than those of the farmer-worker and nonagricultural groups (Laska-Mierzejewska 1970).

A problem facing us today is that while individuals reach sexual maturity earlier, the educational process and the period of adolescent dependency are lengthening. There is something wrong with this situation, as the tension among so many adolescents in our society attests. Societies of the future will have to work out some solutions to these difficulties.

Longevity

What about longevity? Will people of the future live to be 100 or 200 years old? That seems possible in view of mankind's increasing knowledge about biology and medicine. Looking back at our evolutionary record, it seems that the human life-span has increased over time. Based on a study of skeletal material it has been estimated that the average age at death for the australopithecines was 18.0 for *A. robustus* and 22.9 for *A. africanus*. During Paleolithic and Mesolithic times the average life-span was around 30 years. As late as 1931 India had an average length of life of less than 27 years, but by 1900–1902 the United States already had an average life-span of 61.5 years, and it is now more than 70 years. Thus environmental conditions clearly influence longevity.

One would expect, then, that at least some groups of *Homo sapiens* of the future will have a good chance for a longer life, especially considering the increased knowledge of medicine and biology. Permanent immunization against most diseases is now considered possible, and it is thought that the human life-span could be lengthened by 50 years. Rejuvenation of the brain by injections of DNA is also contemplated (McHale 1969:109). Organ transplants are among the manifestations of increasing medical skill, and artificial organs may be developed in the future. Heart, kidney, spleen, pancreas, and duodenum have all been successfully transplanted. Organ and tissue banks, like blood banks, have also been started. Artificial kidney machines are in use. Pacesetters operating on small mercury batteries have a wide distribution (McHale 1969:103–4). A recent report claims that about 20,000 patients a year are now given pacemakers and that nearly 500,000 Americans have had poor heart valves replaced by artificial ones. Lasers have been used in hundreds of operations to repair defects in the retina. Great advances have taken place in ear surgery to correct hearing loss, and electronic hearing aids have been greatly improved. Medical aid to embryos, as in cases of Rh-positive babies with Rh-negative mothers, is being rapidly advanced. All these relatively recent developments should add to human effectiveness and longevity, while some of the debilitating effects of old age will be simultaneously reduced.

Because of faith in the medical science of the future, Robert C. W. Ettinger has carried on a campaign for the quick-freezing of the dead. Future scientists will presumably know how to revive these ancient frozen corpses, who may then be thousands of years old. That would be longevity indeed! Persuaded by Ettinger's argument, several people have requested the freezing process in their wills. The first volunteer was a psychology professor from California, who is now stored at a temperature of –320 F (Rosenfeld 1975:63–66).

Perhaps human beings of the future who will thaw out these refrigerated Rip van Winkles will turn out to be not so different from us in physical appearance. But their culture will surely be quite different. Perhaps, when they hear the story of the defrosted survivors, they will look back with sympathy on our barbarous time, as today we look back at the era of *Homo erectus*.

Summary

About 50 million years ago our ancestors were small, tree-dwelling primates. They grew larger in the Miocene epoch, about 20 million years ago, and later became terrestrial bipeds with upright posture. By about 2.5 million years ago our ancestors were tool-users, and by about 500,000 years ago they had acquired a language. By about 40,000 years ago our ancestors, now classifiable as *Homo sapiens sapiens,* were spreading out across the globe and had entered the New World. By 40,000 years ago some human beings reached Australia, while others entered Japan about 16,000 years later.

Homo sapiens sapiens can be accounted an evolutionary success on the basis of the number of ecological niches or geographical environments in which our species has flourished, and on the basis of population growth. It is estimated that there were between 5 and 10 million persons in Mesolithic times, and 500 million in A.D. 1650. There are about 4 billion today.

However, the present crowding of our planet poses problems for our future existence on it. The world's population is now doubling within a period of 35 years. There has been a great increase of cities in the past 100 years, with the attendant problems of air and water pollution. Nevertheless, despite famine, depressions, wars, and the threat of war, the human species has been managing fairly well. There has been a recent increase in body size in some countries, such as the United States and Japan, where life expectancy is longer than it used to be, and remarkable advances in medicine have made it possible to prolong life and to enhance its satisfactions.

Suggestions for further reading

Theodosius Dobzhansky, *Mankind Evolving: The Evolution of the Human Species* (New Haven, Conn.: Yale University Press, 1962). René Dubos, *Man Adapting* (New Haven: Yale University Press, 1965). Albert Rosenfeld, *The Second Genesis: The Coming Control of Life* (New York: Vintage Books, 1975). Albert Damon, ed., *Physiological Anthropology* (New York: Oxford University Press, 1975). Solomon H. Katz, ed., *Biological Anthropology* (San Francisco: W. H. Freeman, 1975); see particularly Part V, "The Challenge of the Present."

Glossary,
references cited,
illustrations

Glossary

Absolute dating. Giving a date in terms of specific years.

Acheulean. Lower Paleolithic tool tradition containing hand axes, cleavers, and flakes produced by the Levallois technique.

Adze. A cutting tool with the blade set at right angles to the handle.

Aegyptopithecus zeuxis. A fossil hominoid primate from the Egyptian Fayum dating from the Oligocene period.

Agglutination. Clumping of red blood cells.

Agriculture. A system of food production that makes use of plow and draft animals (Old World) or of fertilizers, terraces, irrigation, or *chinampas* (pre-Columbian New World).

Albumin. A protein found in blood plasma or serum, muscle, the whites of eggs, milk, and many plant tissues and fluids.

Alignment. A row of menhirs.

Alleles. Partner genes at the same locus on a pair of chromosomes.

Amphibians. A class of cold-blooded vertebrates intermediate in some respects between fishes and reptiles.

Anemia. A deficiency of red blood cells or hemoglobin.

Anthropoid. A member of the suborder Anthropoidea, or used as an adjective referring to that suborder.

Anthropoidea. The suborder of Primates containing the higher primates, such as monkeys, apes, and human beings.

Antibody. A protein substance that attacks invading foreign proteins within the body.

Ape. See **Pongids.**

Arboreal. Tree-dwelling.

Archaeology. A main division of cultural anthropology that deals with past cultures through excavation and analysis of their remains.

357

Archaic Tradition. North American Indian way of life dating from around 8000 B.C. depending on a broad-spectrum food exploitation, including the use of shellfish, hunting, and collecting.

Artifact. A worked or man-made object.

Assemblage. The material, including artifacts, found in an archaeological site.

Atlatl. See **Spear-thrower.**

Aurochs. Wild cattle ancestral to modern domesticated cattle.

Australopithecines. Hominids of the late Pliocene and early Pleistocene epochs with small cranial capacity and upright posture.

Australopithecus. A hominid genus of the late Pliocene and early Pleistocene epochs, divided by some authorities into two species: *africanus* and *robustus.*

Azilian. A European Mesolithic culture.

B

Bâton de commandement. Name given to Upper Paleolithic objects of bone and horn that may have been used for straightening arrows or spears.

Bergmann's "rule." An assertion that the smaller-sized races of a species are found in the warmer parts of its range, while the larger races are found in the cooler zones.

Big-Game Hunting Tradition. The first clearly distinguishable culture in the New World, associated with the hunting of bison, mastodon, camel, and horse.

Bipedalism. Upright locomotion on two feet.

Biperipheral traits. Cultural traits found only in the most northerly hunting-gathering groups of North America and in southerly South American tribes. These are believed to be among the earliest traits brought over from the Old World into the New World.

Blade. A sharp-edged flake with long, parallel sides, at least twice as long as they are wide. A characteristic stone tool of the Upper Paleolithic period in the Old World.

Blade core. A piece of flaked stone from which blades are struck off.

Blood group. A classification of types of red blood cells, determined by their reactions to particular antibodies.

Bola. Round stone balls connected with cords, thrown to entangle an animal.

Boomerang. Australian throwing-stick used in hunting.

B.P. Before the present.

Brachiation. A means of locomotion through trees by arm swinging from branch to branch, practiced especially by gibbons and siamangs.

Brachycephalic. Broad-headed.

Broad-spectrum food exploitation. The practice of exploiting a great range of different plant and animal food resources within a particular environment.

Bronze Age. A period of advanced civilization and urban life in parts of the Old World from around 3500 to 1500 B.C.

Burin. A chisel-like stone tool used in the Upper Paleolithic period for working bone, ivory, antler, and wood.

C

Calibration. Rectification.

Canine fossa. A hollow in the cheekbones on either side of the nose in modern man.

Carbon-14. See **Radioactive carbon dating.**

Carnivorous. Meat-eating.

Catarrhine. Old World anthropoid, having a dental formula that includes only two premolars in each jaw on either side, as opposed to the platyrrhine New World monkeys which have three premolars in each jaw on either side.

Catastrophism. 19th-century belief that the earth had periodically undergone violent upheavals that extinguished previous organic forms, which were replaced by newer ones.

Caucasoid. A term for the "white" race.

Ceboidea. The Primate superfamily containing the New World monkeys.

Cephalic index. The ratio of the width to the length of the skull:

$$\frac{\text{Width of skull}}{\text{Length of skull}} \times 100$$

Cercopithecinae. A subfamily of Old World monkeys such as baboons, macaques, and rhesus monkeys.

Cercopithecoidea. The Primate superfamily containing the Old World monkeys, including both the Cercopithecinae and the Colobinae.

Cerebellum. A large, dorsally situated part of the brain.

Chacmool. A life-size reclining figure of a man with an offering plate on his stomach, associated with Toltec and Aztec temples.

Chiefdom. A political system intermediate between a tribe and a state, in which a chief customarily belongs to a particular dominant lineage.

Chinampa. A man-made islet, anchored by willow trees, constructed by pre-Columbian Aztecs of Mexico to support topsoil for growing crops.

Chopper. Earliest type of stone tool, with a jagged cutting edge formed by striking off a few flakes.

Chromosome. A structure in the nucleus of a cell containing the genes.

Chronometric dating. A method of dating that provides a date in terms of numbers of years.

Civilization. Advanced form of culture associated with agriculture, metallurgy, division of labor, class stratification, formation of a state, and city life.

Class. A classification more inclusive than an order and less inclusive than a phylum.

"Classical" Neanderthal. A type of Neanderthal having a thick skull, heavy brow ridges, low elevation of the skull, and not much of a chin.

Cline. A gradient in the frequency of a trait over a geographical range.

Codex (plural, **codices**). An ancient manuscript. The codices of pre-Columbian Mesoamerica were made of folded strips of beaten bark paper.

Cognitive anthropology. A branch of anthropology, more particularly of anthropological linguistics, that is concerned with the ways in which the speakers of particular languages classify and conceptualize phenomena. Sometimes known as ethnoscience.

Colobinae. A subfamily of leaf-eating Old World monkeys, such as langurs and colobus.

Competitive exclusion principle. The proposition that two species with similar food habits cannot long occupy the same ecological niche.

Composite tool. A tool consisting of different parts and made with different materials.

Coprolites. Fossils of feces.

Core tool. A flaked stone tool making use of the original core of stone from which flakes have been struck.

Corvée labor. Forced unpaid labor exacted by the state.

Coup de poing. See **Hand axe.**

Cranial capacity. The volume of the cranial vault, which gives an idea of brain size. Measured in cubic centimeters.

Cranium. The complete skull that encloses the brain.

Cultural anthropology. With physical anthropology, one of the two main divisions of anthropology; it includes the fields of linguistics, ethnology, and archaeology, all of which have to do with the study of cultures.

Cultural diffusion. The spreading of a culture trait from one society to another.

Cultural evolution. The development of culture through progressively more complex stages with increases in the energy available to human beings.

Culture. The shared behavior learned by members of a society; the way of life of a group of people.

Cuneiform. Wedge-shaped characters inscribed in clay.

Cytoplasm. The material in a cell that is outside the nucleus.

D

Datum point. A fixed point established at or near an archaeological site as a reference point for excavations.

Dendrochronology. An absolute dating technique involving the analysis of annual growth layers or rings of trees in a particular area.

Dental formula. A statement of the number of each kind of teeth in the tooth series occupying half of the upper and lower jaws.

Descriptive linguistics. A branch of linguistics concerned with the analysis of a language as a synchronic system, its phonemes, morphemes, and rules of syntax. Also called structural linguistics.

Desert Tradition. An American Indian way of life dating from around 8000 B.C. involving adaptation to arid regions in the Great Basin, the Southwest, and Mesoamerica.

Determinative. A marker or sign used to clarify ambiguities in an ideographic system of writing.

Diastema. A gap in a tooth series for admission of the canine tooth from the other jaw.

Diffusion. See **Cultural diffusion.**

Digging stick. An implement used by food gatherers to dig up roots and tubers; the main tool used in simple horticulture for making a hole in the ground to deposit seeds.

Diurnal. Active during the daytime, in contrast to nocturnal.

DNA. Deoxyribonucleic acid, made of sugar-phosphate chains, capable of self-replication.

Dolichocephalic. Narrow-headed.

Dominant. Referring to an allele that is expressed phenotypically even if the alleles are heterozygous.

Dryopithecines. Apes of the Miocene epoch dating from around 15 million years ago.

Dryopithecus. Genus of Miocene apes.

Dryopithecus **(or Y-5) pattern.** A tooth pattern having five cusps with a Y-shaped groove running between them, found in the lower molars of dryopithecine apes and modern chimpanzees, gorillas, and man.

E

Eocene epoch. A geological period between approximately 58 and 36 million years ago.

Epicanthic fold. A fold of skin covering the inner margin of the eye near the nose, often found in Mongoloids.

Ethnocentrism. The tendency to negatively judge and evaluate other ways of life in terms of one's own culture.

Ethnology. A main division of cultural anthropology that deals with the study of living cultures.

Eugenics. Doctrines concerning the improvement of hereditary traits in human beings through the control of mating and reproduction.

Eutherian mammals. Mammals that have a placenta for nourishment of the embryo during the intrauterine period.

Evolution. The development of more complex forms of life from simpler forms. Descent with modification.

F

Family.   A classification more inclusive than a genus and less inclusive than an order.

Femur.   Thighbone.

Fetus.   The developing organism within the maternal uterus, especially after attaining the basic structural plan of the species, from the second or third month after conception until birth.

Fission-track dating.   Dating of mineral or glass material containing uranium through analysis of damage tracks caused by the spontaneous fission of uranium-238 nuclei.

Flake tool.   A tool made from a flake struck from a core of stone.

Flotation.   Technique for recovering small plant remains and bits of bone by deposition in a watery medium.

Fluorine analysis.   A way of gauging the relative ages of bones found in the same layer of soil from the amount of fluorine the bones have absorbed from the soil.

Folsom point.   A fluted stone projectile point made by big-game hunters of North America around 10,000 B.C.

Foramen magnum.   A hole in the base of the skull through which the spinal cord connects with the brain.

Fossil.   The remains of an ancient form of life, often mineralized.

Founder effect.   The establishment of a new breeding population by a small group which is unrepresentative of its parental stock in genetic features.

G

Gene.   A unit of heredity in a particular position on a chromosome.

Gene flow.   The exchange of genes between populations.

Gene frequency.   Relative incidence of an allele in a population.

Gene pool.   The sum total of the genes in a breeding population.

Genetic drift.   Changes in allele frequency through isolation of a group from its larger population.

Genetics.   The study of biological heredity and variation.

Genome.   The sum total of DNA contained in the chromosomes of a cell.

Genotype.   The genetic makeup of an organism, the complete set of genes inherited from parents.

Genus.   A classification within and less inclusive than a family, more inclusive than a species. Human beings belong to the genus *Homo* and to the species *sapiens.*

Geology.   The study of the earth and its changes over time through the analysis of its different layers and their fossil contents.

Gigantopithecus.   A genus of large apes that lived in India in the Pliocene epoch, about 5 million years ago, and more recently in southern China, during the Lower Pleistocene.

Gloger's "rule."   Races of birds and mammals living in warm, humid regions have more melanin pigmentation than races living in cooler, drier regions.

Graver.   A pointed or sharp-edged cutting tool.

Grooming.   The practice among primates of combing through fur with hands and teeth.

H

Hand axe.   A pear-shaped unhafted stone core tool widely used in the Lower Paleolithic period.

Heterodont.   Having different kinds of teeth for different functions, as among mammals, in contrast to the homodont tooth pattern of reptiles.

Heterosis.   See **Hybrid vigor.**

Heterozygous.   Having alleles of different types.

Hieroglyphic.   A form of writing in which ideograms are combined with phonetic elements.

Historical linguistics.   The diachronic study of languages over time.

Hominid.   A member of the family Hominidae, or used as an adjective referring to that family.

Hominidae.   The family that includes human beings and their precursors, such as *Homo erectus* and the australopithecines.

Hominoid.   A member of the superfamily of Hominoidea, or used as an adjective referring to that superfamily.

Hominoidea.   The Primate superfamily that includes both apes and human beings.

Homo africanus.   Term used by John T. Robinson for *Australopithecus africanus.*

Homo erectus.   A form of hominid that lived between 1.5 million and 100,000 years ago, represented by such examples as Java man and Peking man.

Homo sapiens (sapiens).   Modern man.

Homodont.   Having teeth of the same type, as among reptiles, in contrast to the heterodont tooth pattern of mammals.

Homozygous.   Having alleles of the same type.

Horizon.   A period in which a characteristic set of artifacts was used.

Horticulture.   A system of food production lacking the use of plow and draft animals and utilizing a simple technology, principally a digging stick.

Huaca.   A sacred object in Peru.

Humerus.   The long bone of the upper arm.

Hunting-gathering.   A means of subsistence without horticulture or agriculture, depending upon the collection of plants, nuts, and fruits and the hunting of animals.

Hybrid.   Offspring of two plants or animals of different breeds, species, or genera.

Hybrid vigor, or **heterosis.**   A condition of Darwinian fitness manifest by a plant or animal, resulting from the crossbreeding of distinct varieties, in which the organism proves to be superior to either parental strain.

Hybridization.   See **Gene flow.**

Hydraulic society.   An advanced agricultural society making use of irrigation and tending to have a high degree of political centralization.

Hylobatinae.   A subfamily of apes that includes gibbons, concolors, and siamangs.

I

Ideogram.   An individual symbol in an ideographic system of writing.

Ideographic.   A form of writing in which the symbols, or ideograms, may stand for various concepts.

Independent invention.   The discovery of the same invention by two or more different persons or in two or more different cultures.

Industry.   In archaeology, the artifacts of a particular kind made by the same people at the same time, found at an archaeological site.

Insectivorous.   Insect-eating.

In situ.   The position and setting in which a fossil or artifact was found when first discovered.

Interglacial.   A period between glaciations.

Ischial callosities.   Calloused areas on the buttocks of Old World monkeys and some apes.

Isolating mechanism.   Any circumstance that prevents reproduction or an exchange of genes.

K

Kingdom.   The primary division of living forms into animals and plants.

Kitchen midden.   A refuse heap, often consisting largely of shellfish.

Knuckle-walking. Means of locomotion in gorillas and chimpanzees in which the long arms bear the weight of the animal in quadrupedal locomotion.

Kuru. A degenerative disease affecting the nervous system, carried by a latent virus among the Fore of New Guinea. It was probably spread by cannibalism involving the consumption of brains infected by the virus.

L

Lactose. A sugar present in milk.

Lactose intolerance. An inability to digest milk in the years after childhood due to a lack of the enzyme lactase.

Leister. A trident-shaped spear with a point flanked by two prongs, used for spearing fish in the Upper Paleolithic period in Europe.

Levallois technique. A way of making flake tools by first trimming and preparing the core from which they are detached.

Linguistics. The study of languages.

Living floor. Area of former human activity at an archaeological site.

Locus. The position of a gene on a chromosome.

Loess. Wind-blown dust from glaciers.

Lost-wax process (or *cire perdu* **method**). Method of casting metal objects in molds shaped of wax, coated with clay.

Lumbar curve. Curve in the lumbar region of the spine, characteristic of human beings but not of apes.

M

Maglemosian. A coastal culture in northern Europe during the Mesolithic period.

Mammals. The class of warm-blooded vertebrates to which human beings belong.

Mandible. The lower jaw.

Mano. A stone held in the hand to crush grain on a metate.

Mastoid process. A triangular-shaped process of the temporal bone behind the ear in human beings.

Megalithic cults. Cults involving large stone structures.

Meganthropus palaeojavanicus. A hominid, possibly australopithecine, from Java, dated at nearly 2 million years ago.

Meiosis. The cell-division process of reproductive cells.

Melanin. Pigmentation in the skin of human beings.

Menhir. A single-standing megalith, or large stone.

Mesoamerica. The area between northern Mexico and Costa Rica.

Mesolithic. The period between the Paleolithic and Neolithic dated in Europe between 12,000 and 5000 B.P.

Mesopotamia. The area of the Tigris and Euphrates Rivers, extending from the mountains of Asia Minor to the Persian Gulf.

Metallurgy. The technology and process of making metal objects.

Metate. A slab of granular stone on which corn or other seeds are ground.

Microlith. A small stone tool made from a blade which has been snapped into fragments, including arrowheads, scraping, cutting, and boring tools, often hafted to handles of bone or antler.

Miocene epoch. A geological period between approximately 23.5 million and 5 million years ago.

Mitosis. The process of division in cells other than reproductive cells.

Mongoloid. Racial classification including Chinese, Japanese, and American Indians, peoples grouped around the Pacific Ocean.

Monkey. A member of the suborder Anthropoidea apart from the apes and human beings, divided into two subfamilies, one of Old World and one of New World monkeys.

Monogenesis. Belief in a single origin of the human species, as in the story of Adam and Eve.

Mousterian. A Middle Paleolithic industry associated with Neanderthals.

Mutation. A change in the structure or the chemistry of a gene.

N

Natural selection. A process of selection that takes place in nature without anyone's intentional control (as opposed to artificial selection by breeders); the mechanism of evolution suggested by Darwin whereby organisms with adaptive advantages tend to survive and reproduce their kind more successfully than those that lack such adaptations.

Neanderthal. A late Pleistocene type of *Homo sapiens* that preceded modern humans.

Negrito. Short-statured Negroid peoples, such as the Andaman Islanders and the Semang of the Malay Peninsula.

Negroid. Racial grouping of dark-skinned African and Melanesian peoples.

Neolithic. The New Stone Age period in which plants and animals were domesticated in the Old World, dated between around 10,000 and 5500 B.P. in the Near East.

Net reproductive success. Success in natural selection determined by the number of offspring that have survived to reproduce.

Nocturnal. Active at night, as opposed to diurnal.

Nomadism. Movement from place to place without fixed residence.

Nucleus. The central part of a cell containing the chromosomes.

O

Oasis theory. Explanation for the domestication of animals through their enforced proximity to man at oasis regions in desiccated areas.

Obsidian. Volcanic glass.

Obsidian hydration. A method of chronometric dating based upon measurement of the amount of hydration in a piece of worked obsidian.

Ocher, or **ochre.** An earthy iron ore, usually red or yellow, used as a pigment and often found in prehistoric graves both in the Old World (as in the Upper Paleolithic) and in the New.

Oldowan tool. See **Chopper.**

Olfactory. Referring to the sense of smell.

Oligocene epoch. A geological period between approximately 23.5 million and 35 million years ago.

Oligopithecus. An Oligocene primate found in the Fayum, Egypt.

Omnivorous. Eating a diversified, unspecialized diet.

Onager. A wild ass, domesticated by the Sumerians in the Bronze Age.

Opposable thumb. A thumb that can touch the other digits of the hand.

Order. A classification less inclusive than a class and more inclusive than a family. Human beings belong to the order of Primates in the class of mammals.

Oreopithecus bambolii. An anthropoid primate of Miocene times in Europe, probably a brachiator.

Orthogenesis. A belief in a constant and seemingly goal-directed tendency in the evolution of organisms.

Osteology. The study of bones.

P

Paleoanthropology. The study of early stages of human biological and cultural evolution based upon the resources of geology, biology, physical anthropology, archaeology, and other disciplines.

Paleocene. A geological period dating between approximately 65 million and 58 million years ago.

Paleolithic. The Old Stone Age, dating from the first use of tools to around 12,000 B.P.

Paleontology. The study of forms of life of past geological periods from their fossil remains.

Paleomagnetism. A method of chronometric dating based on shifts in the earth's magnetic poles.

Palynology. Pollen analysis, carried out primarily to determine the kinds of plants present at an early site.

Passage grave. A collective megalithic burial chamber characteristic of Europe from Mesolithic to Bronze Age times.

Pastoralism. A means of subsistence relying heavily on domesticated herding animals.

Peasants. Agriculturists who are connected with a state or city life but who mainly engage in subsistence farming on a family basis and do not hire labor or specialize in cash crops.

Pelvis. The hip bones and sacrum.

Pemmican. Dried meat used by North American Indians, made of pounded dried meat mixed with melted tallow and sometimes seasoned with berries.

Peppercorn hair. Hair clustered in clumps on the skull, as among the Bushman of South Africa.

Phenotype. The observable appearance of an organism.

Philtrum. A median groove in the upper lip in human beings.

Phylum. A major subdivision of a kingdom, more inclusive than a class.

Physical anthropology. A field that deals with humans as physical organisms and with human evolution and variation; with cultural anthropology, one of the two main divisions of anthropology.

Pictographic writing. The earliest kind of writing system, consisting of pictures that stand for concepts.

Pithecanthropus erectus. The designation given by Eugène Dubois to the first find of *Homo erectus* remains, discovered in Java in 1891.

Placenta. An organ in the maternal uterus from which embryos of eutherian mammals get nourishment and oxygen.

Pleistocene epoch. A geological period between approximately 1.8 million and 10,000 years ago.

Pliocene epoch. A geological period between approximately 5 million and 1.8 million years ago.

Pochteca. Aztec merchants engaged in long-distance trade.

Pollen analysis. Analysis of pollen from an archaeological site to reconstruct ecological conditions of that time.

Polygenesis. A belief in multiple origins of the human species.

Pongids. Apes, members of the family Pongidae within the superfamily Hominoidea, including the chimpanzee, gorilla, orangutan, gibbon, and siamang.

Ponginae. A subfamily of apes that includes the orangutan, chimpanzee, and gorilla.

Population genetics. A branch of genetics concerned with calculating the gene frequencies of breeding populations.

Postcranial. Referring to the skeletal parts below the head, or cranium.

Potassium-argon dating. A dating technique for determining the age of rocks in volcanic areas from the ratio of radioactive potassium to argon.

Potsherd. Clay fragment.

Predator. An animal that lives by eating other animals.

Prehensile. Grasping. A characteristic of the primate hand and foot. Some South American monkeys have prehensile tails.

Prehistory. The period before the advent of systems of writing.

Primates. The order of mammals that includes lemurs, tarsiers, monkeys, apes, and human beings.

Prognathism. Forward protrusion of the facial region and jaws.

Pronograde. Locomotion on all fours, with trunk in horizontal position.

Propliopithecus. A hominoid fossil of the Oligocene epoch in the Fayum, Egypt.

Prosimian. A member of the suborder Prosimii.

Prosimii. The suborder of primates containing the lower primates, such as lemurs and tarsiers.

Q

Quadrupedal. Locomotion on all fours.

Quern. A milling stone for grinding grain.

Quipu. A collection of knotted strings used by the Inca of Peru for keeping records.

R

Race. A human population whose members have in common some hereditary biological characteristics that distinguish them from others.

Racism. The explanation of a people's behavior in terms of genetic endowment, usually associated with a belief in the innate superiority and inferiority of particular groups.

Radioactive carbon dating. A dating technique to determine the approximate age of organic material from the amount of carbon-14 (C^{14}) it contains.

Ramapithecine. A member of the genus *Ramapithecus*.

Ramapithecus. A possible hominid, or a hominoid having hominid-like dental features, dated between 8 and 14 million years ago.

Ramus. Ascending portion of the lower jaw.

Random mating. Mating resulting purely from chance without any bias due to selection.

Recessive. Referring to a gene that is not expressed phenotypically, except when the alleles are homozygous.

Relative dating. A form of dating that does not give an absolute date but establishes a chronological sequence in placing some items earlier or later than others.

RNA. Ribonucleic acid, which is found in both the nucleus and cytoplasm of a cell.

S

Sacrum. Group of fused vertebrae at the bottom of the vertebral column that joins with the pelvis to form the pelvic girdle in human beings.

Sagittal crest. Crest on top of the skull from front to back for the attachment of muscles that move the jaw; found in male gorillas and chimpanzees.

Savanna. A tropical or subtropical grassland zone, between forests and deserts, containing scattered trees.

Scraper. A stone tool used in such activities as scraping hides.

Sedentism. Pattern of settled residence.

Seriation. A method of relative dating by ordering artifacts of a particular type, such as pots, in an apparent developmental sequence from earlier to later.

Settlement pattern. The pattern of human distribution in a particular region.

Sexual dimorphism. Contrasts in size and strength between males and females.

Shovel-shaped incisors. Incisor teeth with curving-in sides, often found among Mongoloids.

Sickle-cell anemia, or **sicklemia.** A form of anemia caused by inheritance of the sickling gene.

Simian shelf. A bar of bone that binds together the lower jawbones of apes.

Slash-and-burn horticulture. See **Swidden cultivation.**

Social anthropology. A branch of anthropology concerned with analyzing networks of social relations.

Spear-thrower. A grooved board used for propelling a spear; an invention that appeared in the Upper Paleolithic period in the Old World.

Species. An interbreeding population of organisms reproductively isolated from other such groups.

Steatopygia. Englargement of buttocks with fat deposits, sometimes found among Bushman women in South Africa.

Stela. Sculptured stone slab or column, such as those found in Maya areas.

Stereoscopic vision. Depth perception made possible by having both eyes on the frontal plane with an overlapping field of vision.

Stratigraphy. A) Series of layers or strata in an archeological site. B) Interpretation of the strata in an archeological site.

Superposition, law of. In geology, the lower strata of earth are generally older than those above them.

Suture. Lines of contact where the edges of bones of the skull come together and gradually fuse.

Swidden cultivation, or **slash-and-burn horticulture.** A method of food production that involves clearing a patch of land by burning, planting crops, and tending them until the fertility of the soil begins to be exhausted; the land is then allowed to lie fallow.

T

Taurodontism. Enlargement of the pulp cavities in molar and premolar teeth.

Taxonomy. Classification of organisms in biology and physical anthropology.

Temper. Material such as plant fiber, sand, or grit which is added to clay to keep pottery from cracking when fired.

Terrestrial. Ground-dwelling.

Thalassemia. A form of anemia caused by hereditary genetic factors.

Thermoluminescence. A method of chronometric dating based on the measurement of radiation in ceramic ware.

Throwing-board. See **Spear-thrower.**

Trans-Pacific diffusion. The notion that some American Indian culture patterns, including some art motifs, reached the New World by diffusion across the Pacific Ocean in pre-Columbian times.

Tree-ring dating. See **Dendrochronology.**

Treponematosis. A widespread disease having different manifestations in different regions, including yaws and syphilis.

Tuff. Petrified volcanic ash; rock composed of volcanic detritus.

U

Uniformitarianism. The doctrine that the same natural agencies that help shape the earth today, such as wind, water, heating, cooling, erosion, etc., have always done so in the past.

V

Varve analysis. Analysis for dating purposes of the bands of clay deposited annually in glacial lakes by melting of ice sheets.

Vertebrates. Bilaterally symmetrical animals with segmented backbones.

Villafranchian. Referring to a group of mammals, including elephants, horses, and cattle, that were present at the beginning of the Pleistocene epoch; the term is also applied to the early Pleistocene.

Y

Y-5 pattern. See **Dryopithecus pattern.**

Z

Ziggurat. A large pyramidal mound in Bronze Age Mesopotamia having a shrine at the top.

References cited

Adams, Richard E. W.
  1977 Prehistoric Mesoamerica. Boston: Little, Brown.
Adams, Richard E. W., ed.
  1977 The Origins of Maya Civilization. Albuquerque: University of New Mexico Press.
Adams, Robert McCormick
  1966 The Evolution of Urban Society: Early Mesopotamia and Prehispanic Mexico. Chicago: Aldine.
Aitken, Martin J.
  1974 Physics and Archaeology. Oxford: Clarendon Press.
Andrews, Peter, and Alan Walker
  1976 The Primate and Other Fauna from Fort Ternan, Kenya. In Isaac and McCown 1976, pp. 279–304.
Armelagos, George J., and Alan McArdle
  1975 Population, Disease, and Evolution. In Population Studies in Archaeology and Biological Anthropology: A Symposium. Alan C. Swedlund, ed. Memoir 30, American Antiquity. Pp. 1–10.
Baker, Paul T.
  1969 Human Adaptation to High Altitude. Science 163:1149–56.
Bankes, George
  1977 Peru Before Pizarro. Oxford: Phaidon.
Barzun, Jacques
  1937 Race: A Study in Modern Superstition. New York: Harcourt Brace Jovanovich.
Bass, George F.
  1963 Underwater Archaeology: Key to History's Warehouse. National Geographic 124:138–56.

  1966 Archaeology Under Water. New York: Praeger Publishers.
Beals, Ralph L., and Harry Hoijer
  1965 An Introduction to Anthropology. Third ed. New York: Macmillan.
Bean, Robert Bennett
  1906 Some Racial Peculiarities of the Negro Brain. American Journal of Anatomy 5:353–432.
Bibby, Geoffrey
  1956 The Testimony of the Spade. New York: Alfred A. Knopf.
Binford, Lewis R.
  1968 Post-Pleistocene Adaptations. In New Perspectives in Archaeology. Sally R. Binford and Lewis R. Binford, eds. Pp. 313–41. Chicago: Aldine.
Binford, Lewis R., and Sally R. Binford
  1966 A Preliminary Analysis of Functional Variability in the Mousterian of Levallois Facies. American Anthropologist, Special Publication 68(2):238–95.
Birdsell, J. B.
  1972 Human Evolution: An Introduction to the New Physical Anthropology. Chicago: Rand McNally.
Boas, Franz
  1938 The Mind of Primitive Man. Rev. ed. New York: Macmillan.
Bordes, François
  1961 Mousterian Cultures in France. Science 134:803–10.
  1968 The Old Stone Age. J. E. Anderson, trans. New York: McGraw-Hill.

Borhegyi, Stephan de and Suzanne de Borhegyi
1963 The Rubber Ball Game of Ancient America. Lore 13:44–53.

Brace, C. Loring
1962a Refocusing on the Neanderthal Problem. American Anthropologist 64:729–41.
1962b Cultural Factors in the Evolution of the Human Dentition. *In* Culture and the Evolution of Man. M. F. Ashley Montagu, ed. Pp. 343–54. New York: Oxford University Press.
1964 A Nonracial Approach Towards the Understanding of Human Diversity. *In* Montagu 1964, pp. 103–52.
1973 Sexual Dimorphism in Human Evolution. Yearbook of Physical Anthropology, 1972. 16:31–49.
1979 Biological Parameters and Pleistocene Hominid Life-Ways. *In* Primate Ecology and Human Origins: Ecological Influences on Social Organization. Irwin S. Bernstein and Euclid O. Smith, eds. Pp. 263–89. New York: Garland Press.

Brace, C. Loring, and Frank B. Livingstone
1973 On Creeping Jensenism. *In* Man in Evolutionary Perspective. C. L. Brace and James Metress, eds. Pp. 426–37. New York: John Wiley & Sons.

Brace, C. Loring, and Ashley Montagu
1977 An Introduction to Biological Anthropology. New York: Macmillan.

Brace, C. Loring, Harry Nelson, Noel Korn, and Mary L. Brace
1977 Atlas of Fossil Man. New York: Holt, Rinehart & Winston.

Braidwood, Robert J.
1975 Prehistoric Men. Eighth ed. Glenview, Ill.: Scott, Foresman.

Braidwood, Robert J., and Gordon R. Willey
1962 Courses Toward Urban Life: Archaeological Considerations of Some Cultural Alternates. Chicago: Aldine.

Brose, David S., and Milford H. Wolpoff
1971 Early Upper Paleolithic Man and Late Middle Paleolithic Tools. American Anthropologist 73:1156–94.

Brothwell, Don, and Eric Higgs
1963 Science in Archaeology: A Comprehensive Survey of Progress and Research. New York: Basic Books.

Bryant, Vaughn M., Jr., and Glenna Williams-Dean
1975 The Coprolites of Man. Scientific American 232:100–109.

Buettner-Janusch, John
1966 Origins of Man: Physical Anthropology. New York: John Wiley & Sons.

Burrow, T.
1969 Dravidian and the Decipherment of the Indus Script. Antiquity 43:274–78.

Butzer, Karl W.
1964 Environment and Archaeology: An Introduction to Pleistocene Geography. Chicago: Aldine.

Campbell, Bernard G.
1974 Human Evolution: An Introduction to Man's Adaptations. Second ed. Chicago: Aldine.

Carneiro, Robert L.
1970 A Theory of the Origin of the State. Science 169:733–38.

Carrighar, Sally
1968 War is not in Our Genes. *In* Man and Aggression. M. F. Ashley Montagu, ed. Pp. 37–50. London: Oxford University Press.

Cavalli-Sforza, Luigi L.
1975 "Genetic Drift" in an Italian Population. *In* Biological Anthropology, Solomon H. Katz, ed. Pp. 208–15. San Francisco: W. H. Freeman.

Chang, Kwang-chih
1967 Rethinking Archaeology. New York: Random House.
1968 The Archaeology of Ancient China. Rev. ed. New Haven, Conn.: Yale University Press.
1970 The Beginning of Agriculture in the Far East. Antiquity 44:178–85.

Chard, Chester S.
1969 Man in Prehistory. New York: McGraw-Hill.

Chi, Li
1957 The Beginnings of Chinese Civilization: Three Lectures Illustrated with Finds at Anyang. Seattle: University of Washington Press.

Childe, V. Gordon
1953 Man Makes Himself. New York: Mentor Books.

Clark, Grahame
1963 Hunter-Fishers of Yorkshire. *In* The World of the Past. Jacquetta Hawkes, ed. Vol. I. Pp. 230–43. New York: Alfred A. Knopf.
1969 World Prehistory: A New Outline. Cambridge, England: The University Press.

Clark, J. Desmond
1960 Human Ecology during Pleistocene and Later Times in Africa South of the Sahara. Current Anthropology I:307–21.
1971 A Re-examination of the Evidence for Agricultural Origins in the Nile Valley. Proceedings of the Prehistoric Society 37:34–79.

Clark, J. G. D.
1971 Excavations at Star Carr. Cambridge, England: Cambridge University Press.

Clausen, C. J., A. D. Cohen, Cesare Emiliani, J. A. Holman, and J. J. Stipp
1979 Little Salt Spring, Florida: A Unique Underwater Site. Science, Feb. 16, vol. 203, no. 4381:609–14.

Clausen, Gerard, and John Chadwick
1969 The Indus Script Deciphered? Antiquity 43:200–207.

Coe, Michael D.
1962 Mexico. New York: Praeger Publishers.
1968 America's First Civilization. New York: American Heritage Publishing Co.
1977 Olmec and Maya: A Study in Relationships. *In* Adams ed. 1977, pp. 183–95.
1980 The Maya, rev. ed. London: Thames and Hudson.

Coe, Michael D., and Richard A. Diehl
1980a The Land of the Olmec, Vol. 1: The Archaeology of San Lorenzo. Austin: University of Texas Press.
1980b The Land of the Olmec, Vol. 2: The People of the River. Austin: University of Texas Press.

Cohen, Mark Nathan
1977 The Food Crisis in Prehistory. Overpopulation and the Origins of Agriculture. New Haven, Conn.: Yale University Press.

Comas, Juan
1961 Scientific Racism Again? Current Anthropology 2:303–40.

Coon, Carleton S.
1954 Climate and Race. *In* Climatic Change. Harlow Shapley, ed. Cambridge, Mass.: Harvard University Press.
1962 The Origin of Races. New York: Alfred A. Knopf.

Coon, Carleton S., Stanley M. Garn, and Joseph B. Birdsell
1950 Races: A Study of the Problem of Race Formation in Man. Springfield, Ill.: Charles C Thomas, Publisher.

Covarrubias, Miguel
1954 The Eagle, the Jaguar, and the Serpent: Indian Art of the Americas: North America, Alaska, Canada, and the United States. New York: Alfred A. Knopf.

Crawford, O. G. S.
1928 Archaeology from the Air. *In* Wessex from the Air. O. G. S. Crawford and Alexander Keiller. Oxford: The Clarendon Press.

Crook, John H., and J. Steven Gartlan
1966 On the Evolution of Primate Societies. Nature 210:1200–1203.

Crosby, Jr., Alfred W.
1972 The Columbian Exchange. Biological and Cultural Consequences of 1492. Westport, Conn.: Greenwood Publishing.

Dales, George F.
1973 Archaeological and Radiocarbon Chronologies for Protohistoric South Asia. *In* South Asian Archaeology, Norman Hammond, ed. Park Ridge, N.Y.: Noyes Press.

Daniel, Glyn
1980 Megalithic Monuments. Scientific American 243:78–91.

Darwin, Charles
1859 The Origin of Species by Means of Natural Selection or The Preservation of Favored Races in the Struggle for Life. New York: Modern Library.

Davidson, Basil
1959 The Lost Cities of Africa. Boston: Little, Brown.

Deetz, James
1967 Invitation to Archaeology. New York: Natural History Press

Deevey, E. S., Don S. Rice, Prudence M. Rice et al.
1979 Maya Urbanism: Impact on a Tropical Karst Environment. Science. Oct. 19, vol. 206 (4416):298–306.

Dennell, Robin W.
1978 Archaeobotany and Early Farming in Europe. Archaeology 31:8–13.

Díaz, Bernal
1956 The Bernal Díaz Chronicles. Translated and edited by Albert Idell. New York: Doubleday-Dolphin Books.

Dubos, René
1965 Man Adapting. New Haven, Conn.: Yale University Press.

Dumond, D. E.
1965 Population Growth and Cultural Change. Southwestern Journal of Anthropology 21:302–24.

Eckhardt, Robert B.
1975 *Gigantopithecus* as a Hominid. *In* Tuttle 1975:105–29.
1979 The Study of Human Evolution. New York: McGraw-Hill.

Edgerton, Robert B.
1971 The Individual in Cultural Adaptation: A Study of Four East African Peoples. Berkeley: University of California Press.

Eisenberg, J. F., N. A. Muckenhirn, and R. Rudran
1972 The Relation Between Ecology and Social Structure in Primates. Science 176:863–74.

Ekholm, Gordon F.
1953 A Possible Focus of Asiatic Influence in the Late Classic Cultures of Mesoamerica. *In* Asia and North America: Transpacific Contacts. Marian W. Smith, ed. Pp. 72–89. Memoirs of the Society for American Archaeology No. 9.
1964 Transpacific Contacts. *In* Prehistoric Man in the New World. Jesse D. Jennings and Edward Norbeck, eds. Pp. 489–510. Chicago: University of Chicago Press.

Ellefson, John O.
1968 Personality and the Biological Nature of Man. *In* The Study of Personality: An Interdisciplinary Approach. Edward Norbeck, Douglass Price-Williams, and William McCord, eds. Pp. 137–49. New York: Holt, Rinehart, & Winston.

Ellegård, Alvar
1981 Stone Age Science in Britain? Current Anthropology 22:99–125.

Estrada, Emilio, and Betty J. Meggers
1961 A Complex of Traits of Probable Transpacific Origin on the Coast of Ecuador. American Anthropologist 23:913–39.

Falk, Dean
1975 Comparative Anatomy of the Larynx in Man and the Chimpanzee: Implications for Language in Neanderthals. American Journal of Physical Anthropology 43:123–32.

Ferndon, Edwin N.
1968 Polynesian Origins. In Peoples and Cultures of the Pacific: An Anthropological Reader. Andrew P. Vayda, ed. Pp. 95–111. New York: Natural History Press.

Flannery, Kent V.
1965 The Ecology of Early Food Production in Mesopotamia. Science 147:1247–56.
1969 Origins and Ecological Effects of Early Domestication in Iran and the Near East. In The Domestication and Exploitation of Plants and Animals. Peter J. Ucko and G. W. Dimbleby, eds. Pp. 73–100. Chicago: Aldine Publishing.

Fleming, Stuart
1976 Dating in Archaeology. A Guide to Scientific Techniques. London: J. M. Dents & Sons.

Ford, Clellan S., and Frank A. Beach
1951 Patterns of Sexual Behavior. New York: Harper & Row.

Ford, James A.
1969 A Comparison of Formative Cultures in the Americas: Diffusion or the Psychic Unity of Man. Smithsonian Contributions to Anthropology, Vol. 2. Washington D.C.: Smithsonian Institution Press.

Foster, George M.
1965 Peasant Society and the Image of Limited Good. American Anthropologist 67:293–315.
1967 Introduction: What is a Peasant? In Peasant Society: A Reader. Jack M. Potter, May N. Diaz, and George M. Foster, eds. Pp. 2–14. Boston: Little, Brown.

Fouts, R. S.
1974 Language: Origins, Definitions, and Chimpanzees. Journal of Human Evolution 3:475–82.

Fox, Robin
1968 Chinese Have Bigger Brains than Whites—Are They Superior? New York Times Magazine, June 20, pp. 23–30.

Frankfort, Henri
1956 The Birth of Civilization in the Near East. New York: Doubleday-Anchor Books.

Frayer, D. W.
1973 Gigantopithecus and its Relationship to Australopithecus. American Journal of Physical Anthropology 39 (3):413–26.

Fried, Morton H.
1960 On the Evolution of Social Stratification and the State. In Culture in History. Essays in Honor of Paul Radin, Stanley Diamond, ed. Pp. 713–31. New York: Columbia University Press.

Friedmann, Theodore
1971 Prenatal Diagnosis of Genetic Disease. Scientific American 255:34–42.

Furst, Peter J.
1976 Hallucinogens and Culture. San Francisco: Chandler & Sharp.

Gardner, R. Allen, and Beatrice T. Gardner
1969 Teaching Sign Language to a Chimpanzee. Science 165:644–72.
1975 Early Signs of Language in Child and Chimpanzee. Science 187:752–53.

Garn, Stanley M.
1961 Human Races. Springfield, Ill.: Charles C Thomas, Publisher.

Garn, Stanley M., and Carleton S. Coon
1955 On the Number of Races of Mankind. American Anthropologist 57:996–1001.

Geschwind, Norman
1972 Language and the Brain. Scientific American 226:76–83.

Giles, Eugene
1973 Culture and Genetics. In Human Evolution: Readings in Physical Anthropology. Third ed. Noel Korn, ed. Pp. 234–47. New York: Holt, Rinehart & Winston.

Glass, Bentley
1955 On the Unlikelihood of Significant Admixture of Genes from the North American Indians in the Present Composition of Negroes of the United States. American Journal of Human Genetics 7:368–85.

Glass, Bentley, and C. C. Li
1953 The Dynamics of Racial Intermixture—An Analysis Based on the American Negro. American Journal of Human Genetics 5:1–20.

Goodall, Jane (see also Van Lawick-Goodall, Jane)
1971 In the Shadow of Man. Boston: Houghton Mifflin.
1978 Chimp Killings: Is it the 'Man' in Them? Science News, April, 113:276.
1979 Life and Death at Gombe. National Geographic: 592–621.

Griffin, John Howard
1960 Black Like Me. Boston: Houghton Mifflin.

Harris, Marvin
1977 Cannibals and Kings. The Origins of Cultures. New York: Random House.

Harrison, Richard J., and William Montagna
1969 Man. New York: Appleton-Century-Crofts.

Hawkes, Jacquetta, ed.
1963 The World of the Past. 2 vols. New York: Alfred A. Knopf.

Hawkins, Gerald S., in collaboration with John B. White
1965 Stonehenge Decoded. New York: Doubleday.

Hay, R. L.
1980 The KBS Tuff Controversy. Nature, vol. 284, April 3:401.

Hayes, Cathy
1951 The Ape in Our House. New York: Harper & Row.

Herre, Wolf
1963 The Science and History of Domesticated Animals. *In* Brothwell and Higgs 1963, pp. 235–49.

Hewes, Gordon
1973 Primate Communication and the Gestural Origin of Language. Current Anthropology, 14:5–24.

Hock, Raymond J.
1970 The Physiology of High Altitude. Scientific American 222:52–58.

Hockett, Charles F., and Robert Ascher
1964 The Human Revolution. Current Anthropology 5:135–47.

Hole, Frank, Kent V. Flannery, and A. Neely
1969 Prehistory and Human Ecology of the Deh Luran Plain. Ann Arbor: University of Michigan, Museum of Anthropology, Memoirs No. 1.

Hole, Frank, and Robert F. Heizer
1977 Prehistoric Archaeology. A Brief Introduction. New York: Holt, Rinehart & Winston.

Holloway, Ralph L.
1974 The Casts of Fossil Human Brains. Scientific American 231:106–15.

Hooton, Earnest Albert
1946 Up From the Ape. New York: Macmillan.

Hopkins, David M.
1979 Landscape and Climate of Beringia During Late Pleistocene and Holocene Time. *In* The First Americans. William S. Laughlin and Albert B. Harper, eds. Pp. 15–41. Stuttgart: Fischer.

Howell, F. Clark, and the Editors of Life
1965 Early Man. New York: Life Nature Series.

Howells, William
1973 Evolution of the Genus Homo. Reading, Mass.: Addison-Wesley Publishing.

Hsü, Immanuel C. Y.
1975 The Rise of Modern China, 2nd edition. New York: Oxford University Press.

Huxley, Julian
1957 Evolution in Action. New York: Mentor Books.

Isaac, Glynn Ll., and Elizabeth R. McCown, eds.
1976 Human Origins: Louis Leakey and the East African Evidence. Menlo Park, Calif.: W. A. Benjamin, Inc.

Jacobson, Jerome
1979 Recent Developments in South Asian Prehistory and Protohistory. *In* Annual Review of Anthropology, Vol. 8. Bernard J. Siegel, Alan R. Beals, and Stephen A. Tyler, eds. Pp. 467–502. Palo Alto, Calif.: Annual Reviews, Inc.

Janus, Christopher G., with William Brashler
1975 The Search for Peking Man. New York: Macmillan.

Jarrige, Jean-François, and Richard H. Meadow
1980 The Antecedents of Civilization in the Indus Valley. Scientific American 243 (2):122–37.

Jay, Phyllis
1963 The Indian Langur Monkey *(Presbytis entellus)*. *In* Primate Social Behavior: An Enduring Problem. Selected Readings. Charles H. Southwick, ed. Pp. 113–23. Princeton N.J.: Van Nostrand Reinhold.

Jensen, Arthur R.
1969 How Much Can We Boost I.Q. and Scholastic Achievement? Harvard Educational Review 39:1–123.
1980 Bias in Mental Testing. New York: Free Press.

Jett, Stephen C.
1978 Pre-Columbian Transoceanic Contacts. *In* Ancient Native Americans. Jesse D. Jennings, ed. Pp. 593–650. San Francisco: W. H. Freeman.

Johanson, Donald C., Tim D. White, and Yves Coppens
1978 A New Species of the Genus *Australopithecus* (Primates: Hominidae) from the Pliocene of Eastern Africa. Kirtlandia, No. 28:1–14.

Johnson, Steven C.
1981 Bonobos: Generalized Hominid Prototypes or Specialized Insular Dwarfs? Current Anthropology 22:363–75.

Jolly, Clifford J.
1970 The Seed-Eaters: A New Model of Hominid Differentiation Based on a Baboon Analogy. Man 5:5–26.

Jolly, Clifford J., ed.
1978 Early Hominids of Africa. London: Gerald Duckworth & Co.

Jordan, Winthrop D.
1968 White Over Black: American Attitudes Toward the Negro, 1550–1812. Chapel Hill: University of North Carolina Press.

Kehoe, Thomas F., and Alice B. Kehoe
1960 Observations on the Butchering Techniques of a Prehistoric Bison Kill in Montana. American Antiquity 25:420–23.

Kellogg, W. N., and L. A. Kellogg
1933 The Ape and the Child: A Study of Environmental Influence upon Early Behavior. New York: McGraw-Hill.

Klein, Richard G.
1973 Geological Antiquity of Rhodesian Man. Nature 244:311–12.
1974 Ice-Age Hunters of the Ukraine. Scientific American 230:96–105.

Klineberg, Otto
1935 Race Differences. New York: Harper & Row.

Kortlandt, Adriaan
1962 Chimpanzees in the Wild. Scientific American 206:128–38.

Kramer, Samuel Noah
1959 History Begins at Sumer. New York: Doubleday-Anchor Books.
1963 The Sumerians: Their History, Culture, and Character. Chicago: University of Chicago Press.

Krantz, Grover S.
1975 The Double Descent of Man. In Tuttle 1975:131–52.

Kretschmer, Norman
1972 Lactose and Lactase. Scientific American 227:70–78.

Kroeber, A. L.
1948 Anthropology. New York: Harcourt Brace Jovanovich.

Krogman, Wilton Marion
1962 The Human Skeleton in Forensic Medicine. Springfield, Ill.: Charles C Thomas, Publisher.

Kummer, Hans
1971 Primate Societies: Group Techniques of Ecological Adaptation. Chicago: Aldine and Atherton.

Lack, David
1947 Darwin's Finches. Cambridge, England: University Press.

Lamberg-Karlovsky, C. C., and Martha Lamberg-Karlovsky
1971 An Early City in Iran. Scientific American 224:102–11.

Landa, Diego de
1941 Relación de las Cosas de Yucatán. Alfred M. Tozzer, ed. and trans. Papers of the Peabody Museum of Archaeology and Ethnology. Cambridge: Harvard University, Vol. 18.

Lanning, Edward P.
1967 Peru Before the Incas. Englewood Cliffs, N.J.: Prentice-Hall.

Laska-Mierzejewska, Teresa
1970 Effects of Ecological and Socio-economic Factors on the Age at Menarche, Body Height and Weight of Rural Girls in Poland. Human Biology 42:284–92.

Laughlin, William S.
1968 Hunting: Its Evolutionary Importance. In Lee and DeVore 1968, pp. 304–20.

Leakey, Mary D.
1979 Footprints in the Ashes of Time. National Geographic 155 (4): 446–57.

Leakey, Richard E.
1973 Skull 1470. National Geographic 143:819–29.

Leakey, Richard E., and Alan C. Walker
1976 Australopithecus, Homo erectus, and the Single Species Hypothesis. Nature 261:572–74.

Lee, Richard B. and Irven DeVore, eds.
1968 Man the Hunter. Chicago: Aldine.

LeMay, Marjorie
1975 The Language Capability of Neanderthal Man. American Journal of Physical Anthropology 42:9–14.

Leonard, Jonathan Norton
1967 Ancient America. New York: Time Inc.

Leonard, Jonathan Norton and the Editors of Time-Life Books
1973 The First Farmers. New York: Time-Life Books.

León-Portilla, Miguel
1963 Aztec Thought and Culture. A Study of the Ancient Nahuatl Mind. Norman: University of Oklahoma Press.

Leroi-Gourhan, André
1967 Treasures of Prehistoric Art. New York: Harry N. Abrams.

Lewis, Thomas M. N., and Madeline Kneberg
1958 Tribes that Slumber: Indian Times in the Tennessee Region. Knoxville: University of Tennessee Press.

Lieberman, Philip, Edmund S. Crelin, and Dennis H. Klatt
1972 Phonetic Ability and Related Anatomy of the Newborn and Adult Human Neanderthal and the Chimpanzee. American Anthropologist 74:287–307.

Linden, Eugene
1974 Apes, Men, and Language. New York: Saturday Review Press/E. P. Dutton & Co.

Livingstone, Frank B.
1958 Anthropological Implications of Sickle Cell Gene Distribution in West Africa. American Anthropologist 60:533–62.
1964 On the Nonexistence of Human Races. In Montagu 1964, pp. 46–60.

Loomis, W. Farnsworth
1973 Skin Pigment Regulation of Vitamin-D Biosynthesis in Man. In Human Evolution: Readings in Physical Anthropology. Third ed. Noel Korn, ed. New York: Holt, Rinehart & Winston.

Lovejoy, C. Owen, K. G. Heiple, and A. H. Burstein
1973 The Gait of Australopithecus. American Journal of Physical Anthropology 38:757–79.

MacNeish, Richard S.
1976 Early Man in the New World. American Scientist 64:316–27.

Mall, Franklin P.
    1909 On the Anatomical Characters of the Human
    Brain Said to Vary According to Race and Sex, with
    Special Reference to the Frontal Lobe. American Jour-
    nal of Anatomy 9:1–32.
Mann, Alan E.
    1972 Hominid and Cultural Origins. Man 7:379–86.
Marshack, Alexander
    1972 The Roots of Civilization. New York: McGraw-
    Hill.
Mason, J. Alden
    1957 The Ancient Civilizations of Peru. Harmonds-
    worth: Penguin Books.
Matheny, R. T.
    1976 Maya Lowland Hydraulic Systems. Science
    193:639–46.
McCracken, Robert D.
    1971 Lactase Deficiency: An Example of Dietary Evolu-
    tion. Current Anthropology 12:479–517.
McHale, John
    1969 The Future of the Future. New York: George Bra-
    ziller.
McHenry, Henry M., and Robert S. Corrucini
    1980 Late Tertiary Hominids and Human Origins. Na-
    ture 285:397–98.
McKinley, Kelton R.
    1971 Survivorship in Gracile and Robust Australopithe-
    cines: A Demographic Comparison and a Proposed
    Birth Model. American Journal of Physical Anthropol-
    ogy 34:417–26.
Meggers, Betty J.
    1964 North and South American Cultural Connections
    and Convergences. In Prehistoric Man in the New
    World. Jesse D. Jennings and Edward Norbeck, eds.
    Pp. 511–16. Chicago: University of Chicago Press.
Mellaart, James
    1967 Çatal Hüyük: A Neolithic Town in Anatolia. New
    York: McGraw-Hill.
Miller, Dorothy A.
    1980 Evolution of Primate Chromosomes. Science.
    4322:1116–24.
Mitchell, William P.
    1973 The Hydraulic Hypothesis: A Reappraisal. Current
    Anthropology 14:532–53.
Montagu, Ashley
    1963 Race, Science, and Humanity. Princeton, N.J.:
    Van Nostrand Reinhold.
    1964 Ed. The Concept of Race. London: Free Press,
    Collier-Macmillan, Ltd.
Morley, Sylvanus Griswold
    1956 The Ancient Maya. Third ed. Rev. by George
    W. Brainerd. Stanford, Calif.: Stanford University
    Press.

Morris, Desmond
    1967 The Naked Ape. New York: McGraw-Hill.
Neel, J. V.
    1962 Diabetes Mellitus: A 'Thrifty' Genotype Rendered
    Detrimental by 'Progress'? American Journal of Hu-
    man Genetics 14:353–62.
Nordenskiöld, Erland
    1930 Modifications in Indian Customs Through Inven-
    tions and Loans. Comparative Ethnological Studies
    No. 8.
Oakley, Kenneth P.
    1964a Man the Tool-Maker. Chicago: University of Chi-
    cago Press, Phoenix Books.
    1964b Frameworks for Dating Fossil Man. Chicago: Al-
    dine.
Oxnard, Charles E.
    1975 Uniqueness and Diversity in Human Evolution:
    Morphometric Studies of Australopithecines. Chi-
    cago: University of Chicago Press.
Patrusky, Ben
    1979 Split Genes. More Questions than Answers. Mo-
    saic 10 (5):38–54.
Patterson, Thomas C.
    1973 America's Past: A New World Archaeology. Glen-
    view, Ill.: Scott Foresman.
Pehrson, Robert N.
    1966 The Social Organization of the Marri Baluch. New
    York: Viking Fund Publications in Anthropology No.
    43.
Pfeiffer, John E.
    1969 The Emergence of Man. New York: Harper &
    Row.
Pilbeam, David
    1972 The Ascent of Man: An Introduction to Human
    Evolution. New York: Macmillan.
Polanyi, Karl
    1957a The Great Transformation. Boston: Beacon Press.
    1957b Marketless Trading in Hammurabi's Time. In
    Trade and Market in the Early Empires: Economies
    in History and Theory. Karl Polanyi, Conrad M. Ar-
    ensberg, and Harry W. Pearson, eds. Pp. 12–26. New
    York: Free Press.
Polgar, Steven
    1964 Evolution and the Ills of Mankind. In Horizons
    of Anthropology. Sol Tax, ed. Pp. 200–211. Chicago:
    Aldine.
Premack, Ann James, and David Premack
    1972 Teaching Language to an Ape. Scientific American
    22:92–99.
Protsch, Reiner, and Rainer Berger
    1973 Earliest Radiocarbon Dates for Domesticated Ani-
    mals. Science 179:235–39.

Redfield, Robert
1957 The Primitive World and Its Transformations. Ithaca: Cornell University Press.

Renfrew, Colin
1973 Before Civilization: The Radiocarbon Revolution and Prehistoric Europe. New York: Alfred A. Knopf.

Revere, Robert B.
1957 "No Man's Coast": Ports of Trade in the Eastern Mediterranean. In Trade and Market in the Early Empires: Economies in History and Theory. Karl Polanyi, Conrad Arensberg, and Harry W. Pearson, eds. Pp. 38–63. New York: Free Press.

Riesenfeld, A.
1973 The Effects of Extreme Temperatures and Starvation on the Body Proportions of the Rat. American Journal of Physical Anthropology 39:426–60.

Robinson, John T.
1962 The Australopithecines and Their Bearing on the Origin of Man and of Stone Tool-Making. In Ideas on Human Evolution: Selected Essays, 1949–1961. William Howells, ed. Pp. 279–94. Cambridge, Mass.: Harvard University Press.
1963 Adaptive Radiation in the Australopithecines and the Origin of Man. In African Ecology and Human Evolution. F. Clark Howell and François Bourlière, eds. Pp. 385–416. Viking Fund Publications in Anthropology No. 36. Chicago: Aldine.
1972 Early Hominid Posture and Locomotion. Chicago: University of Chicago Press.

Rosenfeld, Albert
1975 The Second Genesis: The Coming Control of Life. New York: Random House, Vintage Books.

Rovere, Richard
1965 Letter from Washington. The New Yorker 41 (September 11):116–30.

Rowe, John H.
1946 Inca Culture at the Time of the Conquest. In Handbook of South American Indians, Bulletin No. 143. Julian H. Steward, ed. Pp. 183–330. Washington, D.C.: Smithsonian Institution, Bureau of American Ethnology.
1967 Urban Settlements in Ancient Peru. In Peruvian Archaeology. Selected Readings. John H. Rowe and Dorothy Menzel, eds. Pp. 293–312. Palo Alto, Calif.: Peek Publications.

Sanders, William T., and Barbara J. Price
1968 Mesoamerica: The Evolution of a Civilization. New York: Random House.

Sarich, Vincent
1971 A Molecular Approach to the Question of Human Origins. In Background for Man: Readings in Physical Anthropology. Phyllis Dolhinow and Vincent Sarich, eds. Pp. 60–81. Boston: Little, Brown.

Savage-Rumbaugh, E. Sue, Duane M. Rumbaugh, and Sally Boysen
1978 Symbolic Communication Between two Chimpanzees (Pan troglodytes). Science 201:641–44.

Schaedel, Richard P.
1978 Early State of the Incas. In The Early State. Henri J. M. Claessen and Peter Skalník, eds. Pp. 289–320. The Hague: Mouton.

Schaller, George
1963 The Mountain Gorilla: Ecology and Behavior. Chicago: University of Chicago Press.

Sebeok, Thomas A., and Dorothy Jean Umiker-Sebeok, eds.
1980 Speaking of Apes: A Critical Anthology of Two-Way Communication with Man. New York: Plenum Press.

Service, Elman R.
1975 Origins of the State and Civilization. The Process of Cultural Evolution. New York: W. W. Norton.

Shapiro, Harry L.
1974 Peking Man. New York: Simon & Schuster.

Sharp, Andrew
1957 Ancient Voyages in the Pacific. Harmondsworth: Penguin Books.

Siegel, Michael I., William J. Doyle, and Catherine Kelley
1977 Heat Stress, Fluctuating Asymmetry, and Prenatal Selection in the Laboratory Rat. American Journal of Physical Anthropology 46:121–26.

Siemens, A. H., and D. E. Puleston
1972 Ridged Fields and Associated Features in Southern Campeche: New Perspectives on the Lowland Maya. American Antiquity 34:228–39.

Simmons, Katharine
1942 Cranial Capacities of Both Plastic and Water Techniques with Cranial Linear Measurements of the Reserve Collection. Human Biology 14:473–98.

Simonds, Paul E.
1974 The Social Primates. New York: Harper & Row.

Simons, Elwyn L.
1978 Diversity among the Early Hominids. A Vertebrate Paleontologist's Viewpoint. In Jolly 1978:543–66.

Simpson, George Gaylord
1967 The Meaning of Evolution. New Haven, Conn.: Yale University Press.

Soustelle, Jacques
1970 The Daily Life of the Aztecs on the Eve of the Spanish Conquest. Translated from the French by Patrick O'Brian. Stanford, Calif.: Stanford University Press.

Stern, Theodore
1948 The Rubber Ball Game of the Americas. Monographs of the American Ethnological Society, No. 17. New York: J. J. Augustin.

Steward, Julian H.
1955a Theory of Culture Change: The Methodology

of Multilinear Evolution. Urbana: University of Illinois Press.

1955b Development of Complex Societies: Cultural Causality and Law: A Trial Formulation of the Development of Early Civilizations. *In* Steward 1955a, pp. 178–209.

Steward, Julian H., and Louis C. Faron
1959 Native Peoples of South America. New York: McGraw-Hill.

Steward, Julian H. et al.
1955 Irrigation Civilizations: A Comparative Study. A Symposium of Method and Result in Cross-Cultural Regularities. Washington D.C.: Pan American Union.

Straus, William L., Jr.
1962 The Riddle of Man's Ancestry. *In* Ideas on Human Evolution: Selected Essays, 1949–1961. William Howells, ed. Pp. 69–104. Cambridge, Mass.: Harvard University Press.

Stuckert, Robert P.
1976 Race Mixture: The Black Ancestry of White Americans. *In* Physical Anthropology and Archaeology: Introductory Readings. Second ed. Peter B. Hammond, ed. Pp. 135–39. New York: Macmillan.

Suggs, Robert C.
1960 The Island Civilizations of Polynesia. New York: Mentor Books.

Teleki, Geza
1975 The Omnivorous Chimpanzee. *In* Biological Anthropology. Solomon H. Katz, ed. Pp. 91–102. San Francisco: W. H. Freeman.

Terrace, Herbert S.
1979 Nim: A Chimpanzee who Learned Sign Language. New York: Alfred A. Knopf.

Thom, Alexander
1971 Megalithic Lunar Observatories. Oxford: Clarendon Press.

Thomas, David Hurst
1973 An Empirical Test for Steward's Model of Great Basin Shoshone Subsistence and Settlement Patterns. American Antiquity 38:156–76.

Tobias, Phillip V.
1973 Implications of the New Age Estimates of the Early South African Hominids. Nature 246:79–83.

Treistman, Judith M.
1972 The Prehistory of China: An Archaeological Exploration. New York: Natural History Press.

Turner, B. L.
1974 Prehistoric Intensive Agriculture in the Maya Lowlands. Science 185:118–24.

Turner, B. L., and William C. Johnson
1979 A Maya Dam in the Copan Valley, Honduras. American Antiquity 44:299–305.

Tuttle, Russell H., ed.
1975 Paleoanthropology. Morphology and Paleology. The Hague: Mouton.

Ucko, Peter J., and Andree Rosenfeld
1967 Paleolithic Cave Art. New York: McGraw-Hill.

Vaillant, George C.
1956 The Aztecs of Mexico: Origin, Rise and Fall of the Aztec Nation. Baltimore: Penguin Books.

Van Lawick-Goodall, Jane (*See also* Goodall, Jane)
1971 In the Shadow of Man. Boston: Houghton Mifflin.

Vint, F. W.
1934 The Brain of the Kenya Native. Journal of Anatomy 68:216–23.

Vita-Finzi, C. and Eric S. Higgs
1970 Prehistoric Economy in the Mt. Carmel Area of Palestine: Site Catchment Analysis. Proceedings of the Prehistoric Society 36:1–37.

Von Hagen, Victor W.
1957 Realm of the Incas. New York: Mentor Books.

Washburn, Sherwood L.
1971 The Study of Human Evolution. *In* Background for Man: Readings in Physical Anthropology. Phyllis Dolhinow and Vincent Sarich, eds. Pp. 82–121. Boston: Little, Brown.

Washburn, Sherwood L., and David A. Hamburg
1965 The Study of Primate Behavior. *In* Primate Behavior: Field Studies of Monkeys and Apes. Irven L. De Vore, ed. Pp. 1–13. New York: Holt, Rinehart & Winston.

Washburn, Sherwood L., and Ruth Moore
1974 Ape Into Man: A Study of Human Evolution. Boston: Little, Brown.

Webb, Malcolm C.
1975 The Flag Follows Trade: An Essay on the Necessary Interaction of Military and Commercial Factors in State Formation. *In* Ancient Civilization and Trade. Jeremy A. Sabloff and C. C. Lamberg-Karlovsky, eds. Pp. 155–209. Albuquerque: University of New Mexico Press.

Wells, Philip V.
1966 Late Pleistocene Vegetation and Degree of Pluvial Climatic Change in the Chihuahuan Desert. Science 153:970–74.

1970 Postglacial Vegetational History of the Great Plains. Science 167:1574–81.

Wells, Philip V., and Clive D. Jorgensen
1964 Pleistocene Wood Rat Middens and Climatic Change in Mohave Desert: A Record of Juniper Woodlands. Science 143:1171–73.

Wheat, Joe Ben
1972 The Olsen-Chubbuck Site: A Paleo-Indian Bison Kill. Memoirs of the Society for American Archaeology 26.

White, Leslie A.
1959 The Evolution of Culture: The Development of Civilization to the Fall of Rome. New York: McGraw-Hill.

Wilber, Charles C.
1960 Physiological Regulations and the Origins of Human Types. *In* Readings on Race. Stanley M. Garn, ed. Pp. 107–15. Springfield, Ill.: Charles C Thomas, Publisher.

Willey, Gordon R.
1971 An Introduction to American Archaeology. Volume Two. South America. Englewood Cliffs, N.J.: Prentice-Hall.

Wilson, John A.
1951 The Culture of Ancient Egypt. Chicago: University of Chicago Press.

Wittfogel, Karl A.
1957 Oriental Despotism: A Comparative Study of Total Power. New Haven, Conn.: Yale University Press.

Wolberg, Donald L.
1970 The Hypothesized Osteodontokeratic Culture of the Australopithecines: A Look at the Evidence and Opinions. Current Anthropology 11:23–37.

Wolf, Eric R.
1966 Peasants. Englewood Cliffs, N.J.: Prentice-Hall.

Wolpoff, Milford H.
1971a Vértesszöllös and the Presapiens Theory. American Journal of Physical Anthropology 35:209–15.
1971b Competitive Exclusion Among Lower Pleistocene Hominids: The Single Species Hypothesis. Man 6:601–14.
1973 Posterior Tooth Size, Body Size, and Diet in South African Gracile Australopithecines. American Journal of Physical Anthropology 39:375–91.

Woolley, Leonard
1953 A Forgotten Kingdom. Baltimore: Penguin Books.
1965 The Beginnings of Civilization: History of Mankind, Cultural and Scientific Development. Vol. I. Part 2. New York: Mentor Books.

Zihlman, Adrienne L., John E. Cronin, Douglas L. Cranmer, and Vincent M. Sarich
1978 Pygmy Chimpanzee as a Possible Prototype for the Common Ancestor of Humans, Chimpanzees and Gorillas. Nature 275:744–46.

Illustrations

Part four

Index

This book has been set CAP, in 10 and 9 point Avanta, leaded two points. Part numbers and titles are 24 point Roma. Chapter numbers are 16 and 32 point Roma and chapter titles are 18 point Roma Semibold. The size of the overall type page is 36 by 47½ picas.